Conception, Pregnancy and Birth

CONCEPTION, PREGNANCY AND BIRTH

Dr. Miriam Stoppard

DK

DORLING KINDERSLEY
London • New York • Stuttgart

For my girlfriends

A DORLING KINDERSLEY BOOK

Created and Produced by
CARROLL & BROWN LIMITED
5 Lonsdale Road
London NW6 6RA

Editorial Director Amy Carroll
Project Editor Claire Burdett
Editor Ian Wood
Assistant Editor Patricia Shine

Design Director Denise Brown
Art Editor Tracy Timson
Designer James Arnold

Production Consultant Lorraine Baird
Production Editor Wendy Rogers

First American edition, 1993
2 4 6 8 10 9 7 5 3 1

Published in the United States by Dorling Kindersley, Inc.,
232 Madison Avenue, New York, New York 10016

Published in Great Britain by Dorling Kindersley Limited.
Distributed by Houghton Mifflin Company, Boston.

Library of Congress Cataloging-in-Publication Data
Stoppard, Miriam.
  Conception, pregnancy, and birth
  by Miriam Stoppard. – 1st Amer. ed.
    p.   cm.
  Includes index.
  ISBN 1-56458-182-9
  1. Pregnancy – Popular works
  2. Childbirth – Popular works I. Title
RG525.S7523   1993   92 – 34181 618.2 – dc20

Reproduced by Colourscan, Singapore
Printed and bound in Great Britain by Butler and Tanner

PREFACE

I have tried to do several new things with this book on pregnancy and birth, the most important of which is to write it from the baby's point of view. To most pregnant women, including me when I was pregnant, carrying a baby to term is largely a mysterious process. Despite all the books on the subject, all the prenatal classes that inform and educate, all the office visits to check and monitor, pregnancy remains for the most part a journey into the unknown. The one unifying factor in it all is that we have a baby growing inside of us, whose development progresses reassuringly to delivery and birth through well-established and reliable stages.

Focusing on your developing baby pays off from the first moment. Much of what doctors encourage women to do has little real significance until we consider it in the light of the unborn child. For instance, all pregnancy books exhort pregnant women to eat a diet rich in iron-containing foods. Well, yes, seems logical enough, we'll include a few greens now and then. But reconsider. Your developing baby is using up the iron in its blood (taken from the iron in your blood) so fast that theoretically your baby is always iron-deficient. Now will you eat those greens? You bet. Suddenly it all makes sense. Everything you do, feel, and think affects your growing baby in some way, so throughout the book I've tried to keep you tuned in to all the important things you can do for your baby, and how your baby will respond to them. Pregnancy takes on a new and exciting significance as you form a relationship with your unborn child.

By any criteria, this book is big, and its bigness provides space to discuss many matters which smaller books must neglect, subjects which interest and worry prospective parents who have difficulty finding information and guidance elsewhere. In this book you will find wide-ranging discussions on genetic disorders and genetic counseling, *in vitro* fertilization, fetal surgery, and birth choices – not just detailed from the point of view of facts, but encompassing your questions, anxieties, and your dilemmas, including ethical and moral ones.

By rights, having a baby ought to give you a feeling of fulfillment. As a doctor who goes in to bat for the patient, a basic premise of the book is that it will help you to negotiate pregnancy with common sense, calmness, and confidence, so that you end up enjoying yourself, getting the birth you want, and looking back on your experience as happy and enriching.

CONTENTS

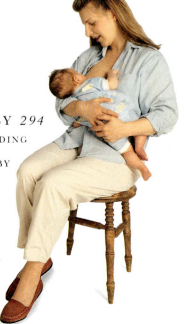

INTRODUCTION

PREPARING FOR PREGNANCY

As we find out more and more about ova and sperm and what makes them healthy, it seems sensible to prepare for pregnancy by changing to a more healthy lifestyle. Giving up smoking and alcohol at least three months prior to conception is a good idea for everyone. A healthy and fit body is the best possible place to implant and carry a fetus to term. Not everything, of course, is straightforward – genes and chromosomes may be imperfect and fertilization may be difficult – but many of these problems have now been identified and some of them can be successfully treated.

YOUR DEVELOPING BABY

There is very little as exciting as the month-by-month development of your baby. No other organism in the world grows with such complexity as the human baby, and understanding the development of the fetus will help you to establish a relationship with your growing baby. For convenience, the sequence of developmental stages can be roughly divided into three phases: the first, second, and third trimesters. These are so divided because certain physiological changes occur in mother and baby during each of the three stages.

In the first trimester your baby's organs form, in the second these organs become complex, and in the third they grow in size. For you, the first trimester is when your body becomes primed for pregnancy: the breasts grow, your internal organs adapt, and the muscles and ligaments start to slacken in preparation for labor. High levels of pregnancy hormones bring on pregnancy sickness, the desire to go to the bathroom more often, and tenderness of the breasts. During the second trimester the body goes into a phase of consolidation. The third trimester sees your body preparing for delivery and making sure that your baby is growing healthfully.

THE BIRTH OF YOUR CHOICE

Labor and birth should be managed in the way you choose. There are many decisions for you to make and you should be aware of all your options. In theory, it's possible to have exactly the kind of birth you want, but this involves extensive reading, soul-searching, and discussion with your partner. You'll also have to talk things over with your medical attendants so that any difficulties that might arise later on can be dealt with. Home birth is becoming more widely accepted and is something to which you should give serious consideration.

Alternatively, you can choose a doctor or midwife and a hospital that provide the facilities, the atmosphere, and the cooperative approach that you prefer. It is extremely useful to make a birth plan outlining the kind of birth you want. By discussing your plans with your attendants, you can usually achieve your aims. It's up to women and their partners to take a more assertive role in the way the delivery and birth of their baby will be handled. Having access to information is crucial, but practical and moral support from a partner is just as important. If both parents attend childbirth classes, they will become better informed and, vitally, more mutually supportive.

FOOD IN PREGNANCY

While there is no special diet in pregnancy, every mother would wish to ensure a healthy environment in which her baby can develop. This requires that you keep yourself as well nourished as possible. Eating healthfully in pregnancy is mainly a question of eating a wide variety of those foods that are rich in essential nutrients. Emphasize fresh fruit and vegetables, whole grains, and raw food in your diet. Ensure that you have a healthy intake of protein by eating fish, poultry, and low-fat dairy products, with red meat and eggs now and then. Fish is also a good source of vitamin B_{12} and vitamin A, which is also found in green and yellow vegetables. And if you bear in mind that your baby uses up iron so fast that it needs fresh supplies every day, you will remember to eat plenty of iron-rich foods, such as kidneys, apricots, red meat, and fish.

A FIT PREGNANCY

During pregnancy, labor, and birth, certain demands are placed on your body. It is therefore essential that you do special exercises that strengthen but do not strain or injure. Regular exercise will keep you mentally, as well as physically, in good shape because exercise causes the body to release tranquilizing chemicals, helping you to relax, and soothing away tension and anxiety. The fast circulation of the blood during exercise means that your body and your baby are well oxygenated. It is probable that labor will to be easier and more comfortable if your muscles are toned, and many of the exercises taught in prenatal classes, combined with relaxation and breathing techniques, will help enable you to be more in touch with what is happening to you during labor and delivery. Learn to conserve energy, sleep as much as you can, and rest whenever possible.

YOUR PRENATAL CARE

Good prenatal care is usually rewarded with healthy mothers and babies. Routine tests are performed at every visit to the doctor or midwife's office. These tests are designed to spot any problems which may arise, to avoid them where possible, and to enable any necessary treatment to be performed promptly. Frequently, special tests such as sonograms and amniocentesis are carried out for mothers and babies with special needs. The social and personal aspects of prenatal care are as important as the medical ones. Reassurance gained by talking to other mothers, doctors, nurses, and midwives will help make you feel confident about labor and birth. The office of your doctor or midwife provides an opportunity to ask questions, to explore the different circumstances in which you can have your baby, and to plan ahead for the kind of birth you want.

CARING FOR YOUR UNBORN BABY

By being observant and aware, you can be in touch with your unborn baby throughout pregnancy. The first time that your baby communicates with you is the moment you feel fetal movements. Respond by talking to your unborn child. Babies have very sensitive hearing and at birth can recognize both their mother's and father's voices from simply having heard them as they were growing and developing in the uterus. It's not silly to talk and sing to your child, nor to massage it gently through your abdominal wall. Not all babies develop normally, but modern techniques are so advanced that we can even care for the developing fetus while still *in utero*. Advanced surgery can be undertaken while the baby is still inside you so that he has every chance of being born normal and healthy.

Not all babies enjoy the perfect conditions for development but, even so, diabetic mothers and mothers with Rhesus incompatibility, for example, can, with careful monitoring and treatment, progress through pregnancy to a healthy and successful outcome.

COMMON COMPLAINTS

Very few women go through pregnancy without suffering minor complaints. For the most part, these are uncomfortable rather than serious. There is a group of complaints that go hand-in-hand with being pregnant. Being prepared for them is half the battle in dealing with them, particularly if you are aware of the treatments that are available. Most are easily dealt with and, for the most part, disappear within a specific length of time leaving no long-term effects.

MEDICAL EMERGENCIES

The risk of medical emergencies tends to be concentrated in the first and third trimesters of pregnancy. Nearly all of the classic emergencies are accompanied by classic symptoms, and should you experience any of them, you must call your doctor immediately. These symptoms would include severe abdominal pain, vaginal bleeding, a fever in excess of 100°F (37.8°C), severe nausea or vomiting, unremitting headache, blurred vision, swelling of the ankles, fingers, or face, absence of fetal movement for more than 24 hours, and rupture of the membranes. In the first trimester most emergencies are associated with loss of the fetus due to hemorrhage or miscarriage, or to the blastocyst being wrongly implanted, as in an ectopic pregnancy. Later on, an emergency might be precipitated by very high blood pressure leading to preeclampsia, by recurrent late abortion, by Rhesus incompatibility, or by abnormalities of the placenta, such as placenta previa. Nonetheless, the majority of babies are delivered safely.

A SENSUAL PREGNANCY

For most women certain parts of the body, such as the breasts, nipples, and genital area, become more sensitive in pregnancy than they have ever been. The sexual organs become more capable of arousal during pregnancy. This increased sensuality is due to very high levels of pregnancy hormones and means that a woman has the potential to enjoy to the fullest all aspects of sex, including erotic massage, caressing, and other forms of intimacy, as well as sexual intercourse itself. Your partner is likely to find your pregnant body extremely attractive and erotic. Sexual intercourse can be better than ever, with more heightened sensations, earlier arousal, and more intense orgasms. Some women may experience orgasm for the first time, while others may find they are now able to attain multiple orgasms. As your abdomen swells, you may find some positions uncomfortable. Sexual problems can develop, or become emphasized, during pregnancy, although the majority can be resolved with open communication. The realization that there is a great deal more to sensuality than penetrative sex will also help you both resolve any problems, as well as enable you to achieve greater intimacy.

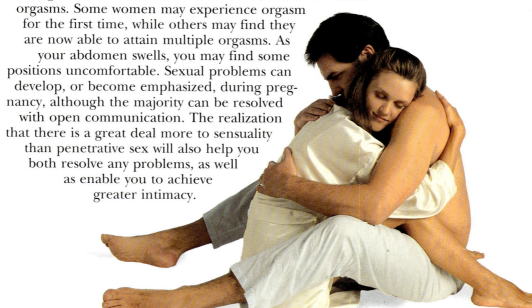

GETTING READY FOR YOUR BABY

From the 36th week, nesting begins in earnest. You may have stopped working and you'll also be slowing down on your social and domestic routine. There is much to do in terms of preparing the baby's room, choosing nursery equipment, buying the essential baby clothing, finalizing your baby's names, figuring out how long you're going to take off from work, and deciding what kind of care you will seek for your child and for your other children. Opting to have your baby at home means that you must prepare a room for the birth and have all your equipment carefully chosen and organized. Getting ready to go into the hospital is worthy of some time and thought; draw up checklists, go to the hospital and make yourselves familiar with admitting procedures so that you feel in control and free of anxiety.

MANAGING YOUR LABOR

Labor is the culmination of your pregnancy and it can be divided into well defined stages. Pre-labor is a stage before labor when you experience dull backache, your membranes rupture, and you may pass a "show." The first stage of labor is entirely taken up with dilation of the cervix to a size which will allow your baby to exit from the uterine cavity into the birth canal. This stage is usually straightforward, particularly if you remain mobile and, by maintaining an upright position, use the force of gravity to help the cervix to dilate. Help and support from your partner can be invaluable in enabling you to experience a smooth, quick, comfortable labor. Very few labors are pain-free, but there are many methods and types of pain relief from which to choose.

YOUR BABY IS BORN

The second stage of labor rarely lasts longer than two hours. The average is around an hour and, if you've had previous babies, it may take as little as 15 to 20 minutes. During the second stage you are overcome by the instinctive urge to bear down – the desire to push the baby out caused by the pressure of the baby's head on the pelvic floor and rectum. The delivery of the placenta in the third stage is caused by the uterus contracting down into a tight, hard ball. After delivery, your baby is quietly checked, then returned to you and your partner so you can get to know one another.

GETTING TO KNOW YOUR NEWBORN BABY

Establishing a relationship with your baby begins the second she is born, and you and your partner should be left in private with a minimum of interruption. Parents who bond closely with their children are more constructive, more sympathetic parents. The importance of paternal bonding cannot be over-emphasized and your partner should be given the opportunity to hold his baby immediately after her birth. The first few days will be harder than you think; even feeding can take longer than you expect, as can your baby's daily care. A routine is not always easy to set up, but the guiding rule is that you should take your lead from the baby. Parents of special-care babies who need to be nursed in hospital intensive care units, have no need to worry about being unable to bond with their babies. As long as parents, under the guidance of the nursing staff, become intimately involved in the day-to-day care of their baby, they should not suffer any disadvantages.

ADJUSTING TO PARENTHOOD

Getting to know your newborn baby is a thrilling experience, but don't be surprised if you feel a slight let-down at times. There are many adjustments to make and few of them are easy. Somehow you have to coax your baby to fit in with your established family routine, maintain the loving relationship with your partner, and attend to your baby's needs and constant demands for attention. Many women get bouts of sadness, and not just the "baby blues" that are so common in the first week after delivery. Much more serious is postpartum depression, which needs immediate attention from your doctor. The responsibilities of parenthood may weigh heavily upon you, but watching your baby grow and develop should bring more than enough joy to counteract the negative feelings that may occasionally creep in. Having time just for yourself will enable you to re-charge your batteries, while time alone with your partner will help you keep your relationship alive.

1

PREPARING
for pregnancy

As we find out more and more about ova and sperm and what makes them healthy, common sense tells us to prepare for pregnancy by following a healthy lifestyle. Not everything, of course, is always straightforward, but many of the problems surrounding conception have been identified and some can be treated.

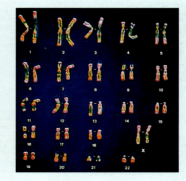

FIT FOR PARENTHOOD

A successful pregnancy and labor, and the birth of a healthy baby, are the responsibilities of both parents to an equal degree. A baby's health depends to a large extent on the health of her parents at the moment of conception, and her well-being can be put in jeopardy not only by long-standing medical conditions or familial genetic defects, but also by her parents' lifestyle before conception. Many couples do not plan for pregnancy with the same care as other important life events, yet it is one of the most important things parents can do. Starting a family is a time of reassessment because becoming a parent will fundamentally change your life.

LIFESTYLE CONSIDERATIONS

Many things that we take for granted – who we are and what we do – will affect or be affected by a baby.

Time Most people's lives are extremely busy, and many new parents assume that a new baby will somehow fit in. They don't. Babies and children need time, and mothers and fathers will always have less time than they did before – for themselves, for each other, and for other people.

Costs The average experience is that you will spend 15–25 percent of your income, regardless of how much you earn or the size of your family, on child-related expenses such as clothing and equipment. But there are also hidden costs, such as heating, transportation, and what you may give up for your children – meals out, vacations, and, perhaps, some of your ambitions.

Relationships It is not only your relationship with your partner that changes when you have a baby. Your relationship with your parents will alter, and you may find that you grow away from your childless friends and seek new friendships with other parents who are going through the same experiences as you.

Smoking This is one of the most damaging factors to the health of your unborn baby and the major cause of avoidable health problems. The associated risks include miscarriage and stillbirth, damage to the placenta, a low-birthweight baby who fails to thrive, and an increased chance of fetal abnormalities. Smoking is also one of the factors that can lead to a low sperm count, and a man who continues to smoke while his partner is pregnant can risk

Prepared parents
Happy, healthy parents make happy, healthy children, so make sure you are physically and emotionally fit for a baby.

damaging the health of his unborn baby via passive smoking. Smoking also can have long-term effects – children of heavy smokers tested at five, seven, and eleven years have been found to suffer from impaired growth and learning difficulties.

Alcohol This is a drug that may damage the sperm and ovum before conception, as well as the developing embryo. The main risks to the unborn baby are mental retardation, retarded growth, and damage to the brain and nervous system – well documented as fetal alcohol syndrome. Alcohol can also cause stillbirth.

Research suggests that the effect of alcohol is variable: some heavy drinkers seem to get away with it, while some women who drink only a small amount don't. The only certainty is that there will be no effect if alcohol is avoided. Women tend to have a lower tolerance than men and have a higher proportion of fat to water in the body, so alcohol can become highly concentrated in the blood that nourishes your developing baby.

Drugs Over-the-counter medicines should only be taken when necessary, and social drugs definitely should be cut out long before you conceive. Marijuana interferes with the normal production of male sperm, and the effects take three to nine months to wear off. Hard drugs such as cocaine, heroin, and morphine can damage the chromosomes in the sperm and ovum, leading to abnormalities.

When syringes are shared, there is a high risk of acquired immunodeficiency syndrome (AIDS), which affects the baby before and after birth. So far no human immunodeficiency virus (HIV)-positive baby has survived beyond the first few years of life.

Diet and exercise Both are vital to your health and the health of your baby. You should have a balanced diet that is low in fat content, particularly animal fat, with high intakes of raw fruit and vegetables (see p.112). Good eating habits must be coupled with moderate forms of exercise (see p.126). During pregnancy, all the ligaments and cartilages slacken up so that the pelvis can expand more easily. This can put some strain on your muscles and joints, and so the more fit you are, the better you will cope.

Age Many women are delaying pregnancy until their 30s, and even early 40s, and this is usually no more hazardous than being in your 20s as long as you are fit and healthy. Whatever your age, you are likely to have a normal pregnancy and birth, although some problems such as infertility and chromosomal defects, for example, Down's syndrome (see p.20), do become more frequent with the increasing age of both parents. Tests for chromosomal abnormalities are always offered to older women.

Hazards Be aware of your environment, both in and out of the home, and avoid anything that is potentially hazardous. What we eat, where we work, the places we travel to, and sometimes even the people we meet may be risky for a pregnant woman (see p.150).

STOPPING CONTRACEPTION

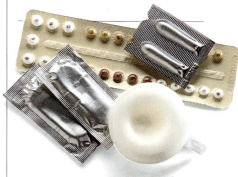

Barrier methods, such as the diaphragm and condom (sheath), can be dispensed with immediately. However, if you are on the pill or are using an IUD, a bit more forethought is required.

The pill *It is advisable to stop taking the pill a month or more before trying to conceive, so that you have at least one normal menstrual period before becoming pregnant. However, there is some evidence to suggest that women are more fertile immediately after stopping the pill, so this could be the ideal time to try, if you have previously suffered from low fertility or had a miscarriage.*

If you think you are pregnant while you are still taking the pill, consult your doctor immediately. Some forms of the pill contain a high dose of synthetic progesterone (called progestogen) that may interfere with development in the first weeks of life.

The intrauterine device *The IUD probably works by irritating the lining of the uterus, so that the fertilized egg cannot implant. A very small number of women do get pregnant with the IUD. The IUD is usually left in place as the risk of miscarriage is higher if removal is attempted. It is usually delivered with the placenta after the baby is born.*

TESTING YOUR URINE

If sugar is found in your urine, it may mean you have diabetes or, more likely, simply that some sugar has leaked through your kidneys, whose threshold to sugar is lowered by your pregnant state. More tests will be necessary to make sure.

Testing urine
A chemically impregnated strip is dipped into a sample of your urine. The color it turns indicates whether sugar is present when it is compared with a chart to give the glucose level.

HEALTH CONSIDERATIONS

If you're a woman with a chronic long-term condition, such as diabetes mellitus, heart disease, or epilepsy, you should not be discouraged about having children. However, you must talk things over with your doctor before you become pregnant. This will help both you and your doctor manage the pregnancy effectively.

Asthma The most common respiratory problem in mothers-to-be, this is usually controlled by inhalation of bronchodilator drugs and inhaled steroids. There seems to be little risk to the growing fetus from the medication, although yeast infection (see p.194), a condition that is often aggravated by pregnancy, can be a side effect for the mother, and sometimes labor may be brought on prematurely. If you are asthmatic, you should take care of your lifestyle throughout pregnancy as stress and tension, as well as dust, pollen, and pollution, can cause breathlessness, which may increase the chances of a miscarriage.

Epilepsy From the momentary loss of consciousness to grand mal seizures, epilepsy affects one in every 200 people. Research has found that pregnancy has a variable effect on the frequency and intensity of seizures, with 50 percent of epileptic mothers unaffected, 40 percent slightly improved, and 10 percent worse.

During pregnancy, drug treatment will be continued, but you will need to be seen frequently by a neurologist who can adjust your dosage. During labor, drugs may not be absorbed and medication should be carefully supervised to prevent fits from recurring. With phenytoin, folic acid is not absorbed, and there is a risk of fetal malformations, although most pregnant women can be changed over to sodium valproate, which does not carry the same hazards. If phenytoin is prescribed, folic acid supplements are always given to prevent damage to the fetus. If you suffer from epilepsy, discuss your situation with your doctor well before you hope to conceive.

Diabetes mellitus When the pancreas is producing insufficient insulin to cope with glucose (sugar) levels in the body, diabetes results. Pregnancy hormones have an anti-insulin effect, which increases the severity of established diabetes, and can also lead to the development of gestational diabetes in those with an underlying tendency (see p.205). The urine of all mothers-to-be is routinely screened for sugar and ketones (the usual indicator of diabetes), and any woman with a family background of diabetes should have a urine test before attempting to conceive and have her urine monitored throughout pregnancy.

It is important that pregnant, insulin-dependent diabetics monitor their blood-sugar levels extremely closely, since diabetes can lead to very large babies and fetal abnormalities such as heart and respiratory problems, as well as maternal complications ranging from chronic yeast infections to preeclampsia (see p.204). However, with strict control, every diabetic mother has an excellent chance of having a healthy baby with minimal side effects.

Heart disease Women with a diagnosed disease will be given specialized advice according to its nature. However, as a general rule, it is advisable to avoid over-activity – try to rest each afternoon for at least two hours, and spend ten hours in bed at night.

Most women with heart disease have easy spontaneous labors. During labor the additional strain on the heart is intermittent and, in total, is less than that imposed upon the heart in the third trimester. There is usually no reason to anticipate premature induction of labor or Caesarean section.

Kidney disease This does not necessarily preclude having children, but a pregnant woman with kidney disease must be carefully monitored. As long as the kidneys remove waste effectively, pregnancy will be allowed to continue, but if there is poor fetal growth, early induction of labor will be recommended. (Renal dialysis does pose a risk, as the mother's kidneys are unlikely to be able to cope with the additional waste from the fetus.)

Sexually transmitted disease Herpes presents the highest risk of infection to your baby if you have a primary infection in the last quarter of pregnancy and you are symptomatic at the time of your baby's birth. Herpes simplex II virus infection may lead to growth retardation in your baby, and about half of infants born under these conditions will acquire some form of herpetic infection after birth, possibly involving the eyes, mouth, and skin.

However, if you have no symptoms, and are not shedding the virus from your cervix or vagina, the risk that your baby will become infected is less than one per thousand.

If you have a history of genital herpes, you can expect a normal vaginal delivery unless a recurrence or a urinary infection occurs during pregnancy. If herpes ulcers are present or a cervical culture shows an active infection just before labor commences, you will probably need a Caesarean section to reduce the risk of your baby catching herpes as he descends the birth canal.

If genital herpes occurs or recurs in pregnancy after the 34th week, your doctor will test for the presence of the virus and will probably perform a Caesarean section.

AIDS Infected women who become pregnant have a very high risk of transmitting the virus to their babies (either *in utero* or by breastfeeding). The infected babies will then become antibody-positive (positive HIV tested) and will acquire AIDS. Having the HIV infection has no adverse effect on pregnancy as far as you are concerned, nor has the pregnancy any adverse effect on the progress of the HIV infection. But as the HIV virus infects the amniotic fluid as well as your blood and other bodily fluids, your delivery will be accompanied by full infectious precautions.

Because of all the problems involved with HIV infection, you will be given the opportunity to choose to have an abortion rather than giving birth to a baby that has a high chance of having the HIV infection and dying very early.

GERMAN MEASLES

Before conceiving, check with your doctor to see if you have antibodies to the German measles (rubella) virus.

Don't assume you are immune to the disease if you have been vaccinated in the past – the antibodies lose their efficiency after a period of time, so check. If you are not immune, you should be vaccinated. After a successful vaccination, you should wait at least 3 months before you try to conceive, as the vaccine is live.

If you come into contact with someone who has, or is suspected of having, German measles, tell your doctor immediately, and a blood sample will be taken and sent to a laboratory for antibody testing.

Depending on the result, the test may be repeated in 10 days. Should this test result in a suggestion that you have German measles, you and your partner will have to face the decision of whether to abort the pregnancy at this point. Some doctors may recommend the administration of antibodies in the form of gamma globulin to help avoid fetal damage.

TAKE CARE

German measles (rubella), particularly if caught in the first 3 months of pregnancy, can cause malformations in your baby. These may include deafness, blindness, and heart disease.

DOWN'S SYNDROME

This chromosomal disorder (see column, right) occurs when the fertilized egg has 47 chromosomes instead of the usual 46.

In most cases, the egg itself is defective, being formed with the extra chromosome, or the sperm may be similarly affected. This type of Down's syndrome is known as trisomy. Less commonly, one parent may have a chromosomal abnormality that results in his or her child inheriting extra chromosomal material. This is known as translocation. Down's syndrome may be diagnosed by amniocentesis or chorionic villus sampling (see p.164). Maternal blood alphafetoprotein levels (see p.159) are generally lower if a mother has a fetus with Down's syndrome.

The risk of having a Down's syndrome baby increases in women over age 35 (see p.165) but can also be caused by an older father. Genetic counseling should be sought if either parent is over 35.

Down's syndrome child
One baby in every 1,000 will be born with this disorder. Down's syndrome is either the result of trisomy, which is random, or of translocation, which is inherited. It is therefore vital to determine the cause of any family history of Down's syndrome.

GENETIC CONSIDERATIONS

Within the nucleus of each cell are genes and chromosomes that contain DNA, which determines the growth and functioning of the body (see also p.22). Genetic disorders occur when genes and chromosomes are abnormal. There are three reasons why genetic diseases can occur: a single gene may be defective, there may be a fault in the number or shape of chromosomes, or several genes may be faulty. There may also be complicating environmental factors. A single gene that is defective and results in a genetic disorder can be either dominant or recessive, a mutation, or attached to the X chromosome (see below). Abnormal chromosomes that result in genetic disorders are usually new mutations, although they can sometimes be inherited (see column, left).

Where more than one gene or environmental factor is involved in producing a disorder, there is as yet no straightforward method of determining why it has happened.

If either partner has a history of a genetic disease or condition in the extended family, counseling (see p.24) should be sought. The number of reliable tests for genetic diseases that can be performed is increasing yearly, although they cannot predict the severity of the condition. The ultimate decision about whether to attempt to conceive, to go ahead with an existing pregnancy, or to request a termination will always rest with you, the parents. Bear in mind, however, that although a handicapped child will need special care, many such children are both affectionate and responsive and can lead happy, fulfilled lives.

DOMINANT GENETIC DISEASES

Fatal diseases caused by dominant genes are rare because affected individuals normally die before they can pass on the genes. However, some conditions, such as familial hypercholesterolemia (see below), present a significant, but manageable, risk to health.

Familial hypercholesterolemia FH is the most common dominant genetic disease. In it the blood cholesterol levels are so high that there is a risk of heart attacks and other complications caused by the narrowing of the arteries. The condition affects one in 500 people and can be detected at birth by a test in which a sample of the baby's blood is taken.

RECESSIVE GENETIC DISEASES

A defective recessive gene is usually masked by a normal dominant one. However, if both parents carry a defective recessive gene, each of their children has a one in four chance of inheriting both recessive genes (and therefore one of several disorders) or neither, and a two in four chance of being a carrier. Thus there are always more people who are carriers rather than sufferers.

Cystic fibrosis CF is the most common recessive gene disorder. One in 20 of the Caucasian population carries the CF gene, and one in 2,000 Caucasian babies born is affected by the disease. In other groups, the incidence is about one in 90,000. This disease mainly affects the lungs and the digestive system. The mucus within the lungs becomes thick and sticky, and accumulates, causing chest infections. The mucus also blocks the ducts of various organs, particularly the pancreas, thus preventing the normal flow of its digestive enzymes. If not treated promptly, CF results in malnutrition. Rapid and accurate carrier testing involving analysis of blood or mouth cells is possible. More than 60 percent of sufferers survive into adulthood, although few are in good health.

Sickle cell anemia This is the most common genetic disease among black people (one in 400). It is so called because the red cells are sickle shaped from defective hemoglobin; this causes the red cells to break down and the small blood vessels to clog, which may result in a stroke. It is usually diagnosed by a blood test. Sufferers are susceptible to meningitis and other serious infections but can, with care, live a productive life despite some ill health.

Thalassemia This disease is most common among Asians, blacks, and people of Mediterranean descent. It produces anemia and chronic ill health, and blood transfusions may sometimes be necessary. A blood test will reveal the disease. Other blood tests will indicate whether the hemoglobin level is reduced. Not all cases are severe, and some sufferers may survive for many years.

Tay–Sachs disease Common among Ashkenazie Jews but appearing in other groups, this fatal condition results in deterioration of the brain caused by a deficiency in enzymes. Few victims live beyond three years, and no adequate treatment is known. Tay–Sachs is diagnosed by testing blood for enzyme deficiency.

GENDER-LINKED DISEASES

These are conditions caused by defects on the X chromosome. If a second normal X chromosome is present, as in a healthy female, the defect won't show because it is masked. Women therefore carry the disease. If, however, a Y chromosome is present, as in a male, the disease will express itself as a Y chromosome because it can't mask an X chromosome. Therefore, males are affected.

Hemophilia This happens when the crucial clotting factor VIII is missing and results in profuse bleeding from any injury, external or internal. Effective treatment with factor VIII derived from normal blood is now available to hemophiliacs, and they can lead relatively normal lives. Diagnosis can be made from a sample of fetal blood at 18–20 weeks of pregnancy.

Duchenne muscular dystrophy This is the most common type and affects only boys (one per 5,000). Between the ages of four to ten, a boy with Duchenne muscular dystrophy will lose his ability to walk, and is usually confined to a wheelchair during his comparatively short life. The condition can be detected before birth.

CHROMOSOMAL DISORDERS

These are usually due to some fault in the process of the chromosome division in the formation of the egg or sperm, or during the initial divisions of the fertilized ovum. More rarely, one parent has an abnormal arrangement of chromosomes.

The severity and type of abnormality depend on whether one or both of the sex chromosomes, or one of the other 44 chromosomes (autosomes), are affected. The latter are slightly less common than sex chromosomal abnormalities but tend to produce more serious and widespread effects. An extra autosome means that one of the 22 pairs of autosomes occurs in triplicate, which is known as a trisomy (see p.180). The most common trisomy is Down's syndrome (see column, left).

Trisomy is when a part of a chromosome is missing, or an extra bit is present and joined to another chromosome. Trisomy can cause mental and physical defects.

Occasionally, however, the problem can be caused by translocation. This is where there is a normal complement of chromosomal material, but they are not arranged correctly (part of a chromosome is joined to another). The parent carrier is normal, but his or her child may suffer from an abnormality if the child inherits the extra chromosomal material.

Abnormalities of the sex chromosomes result in defects in the sexual development, infertility, and occasionally mental retardation. Boys suffer from Klinefelter's syndrome, girls from Turner's.

Abnormalities can be diagnosed by chromosome analysis, one of the techniques used in genetic counseling (see p.24).

INHERITING GENES

WHAT IS A GENE?

A gene is a minute unit of DNA (deoxyribonucleic acid) carried on a chromosome, which also consists of DNA. In the nucleus of every cell of the body, about 50,000 unique genes are divided among 23 pairs of chromosomes.

Half of a baby's genes come from his mother, via the ovum, and half come from his father, via the sperm.

Each ovum and sperm contains a different "mix" of the parents' genes, so each child inherits a different and unique selection of genetic information from that inherited by his siblings.

Most of our individual mix of genes blends together, but some genes are dominant over their counterparts. In those cases, the dominant gene, say for brown eye color, will prevail over a recessive, such as the gene for blue eyes.

THE "BLUEPRINT" OF THE BODY

Genes influence and direct the development and functioning of all the organs and body systems. They determine the pattern for growth, survival, reproduction, and possibly aging and death for each individual. Because all cells (except for egg and sperm cells) derive from the single fertilized egg, the same genetic material is duplicated in every cell in your body. However, not all the genes contained within a cell are active; it is the site and function of the cell that determines which genes are active. For example, different sets of genes are active in bone cells and blood cells.

Except for identical twins, individuals differ greatly in the composition of their genes, and it is their genes that entirely account for any variation in height, hair and eye color, body shape, and gender, for example. An individual's genetic inheritance will also determine his or her susceptibility to certain diseases and disorders, for example, breast cancer.

Genes are held in pairs along a chromosome (see below), and each gene is either dominant or recessive. A recognizable effect is the result of the dominant gene or genes in each individual pair; the effect of recessive genes will be noticeable only when there are two recessive genes.

Chromosomes Twenty-three pairs of these thread-like structures are found in the nucleus of every cell, except for egg and sperm cells. These cells contain only 22 chromosomes plus an X or Y chromosome. Each chromosome contains thousands of genes arranged in single file along its length. Chromosomes are made up of two chains of DNA, which are arranged together to form a ladderlike structure, the sides of which are sugar-phosphate molecules. This spirals around upon itself and is known as a double helix. DNA has four bases – adenine, cytosine, guanine, and thymine which are arranged in different combinations according to the functions of the genes on the different parts of the chromosome. Each combination provides coded instructions that regulate the various activities of the body.

The genetic mix
Your baby will be a unique combination of his parents' genes.

CHROMOSOMES, GENES, AND DNA

Chromosomes

There are 23 pairs (22 general pairs plus the gender chromosomes – see left) of these threadlike structures in the nucleus of every body cell – except the egg and sperm, which carry only half this amount. They contain the information that controls the body's growth and functioning.

The double helix

The 2 chains of DNA, which make up each of the 46 chromosomes, are arranged to make a spiraling ladder.

Chromosome

Sugar-phosphate molecules form the sides of the DNA ladder

Each of the 4 DNA bases – adenine, cytosine, guanine, and thymine – is represented here by a different color

Gene

DNA replication

When a new cell is about to be formed, the DNA in each of the chromosomes "unzips" along the center of the rungs of the ladder, and each half of DNA then duplicates itself. The new chains thus created are genetically identical to the original chromosomes.

MUTANT GENES

Sometimes when a cell divides and duplicates its genetic material, the copying process is not perfect, and a fault occurs. This leads to a small change, or mutation, in the structure of the genetic material.

Carrying a mutant gene normally has a neutral, or harmless, effect – most, if not all, of us have a mutant gene as part of our genetic makeup. Occasionally, however, it can have a disadvantageous effect and, more rarely, a beneficial one.

The effects of a mutant gene depend largely on whether it is carried within the fused ovum and the sperm, or whether it is a fault in the later copying process of the cells (somatic or body cells).

A mutation in the ovum or sperm will reproduce itself in all the body's cells, resulting in genetic diseases such as cystic fibrosis (see p.20). A mutated somatic cell, at worst, will multiply to form a group of abnormal cells in a specific area. These may have only a minor local effect, or they may cause deformity or disease. This type of mutation is usually triggered by outside influences, such as radiation or exposure to carcinogens.

Genetic counseling

Genetic counseling is aimed at determining the risk you run of passing on an inheritable disease to your child. The second goal is to help you decide whether or not to go ahead and conceive, in the light of that assessment. You may be concerned because you have a blood relative (including, perhaps, a previous child) who has suffered from an inheritable disorder.

How genetic counseling works

When you are referred for genetic counseling, the counselor will ask both of you about your health, and discuss your family background. Virtually every case dealt with by a genetic counselor is unique. The advice depends on a precise diagnosis of the disease (what it is and why it occurred), and on the creation of a comprehensive family tree, which details all blood relationships and any diseases suffered. Birth or death certificates may be used, if necessary, and it is important that you take along as much information as you can. Be prepared for the whole process to take some time as it can be a long and involved process of investigation. Genetic counselors are trained in genetics and psychology: they will assess the degree of risk and help you make an informed decision. If there is a small risk, you may decide to go ahead and try for a baby. If, however, the risks are very great, you may prefer not to take that chance.

For many genetic disorders, such as sickle cell anemia or Tay–Sachs (see p.21), it is possible to establish whether the parents are carriers. This can be done by seeing the disease itself, such as sickle-shaped cells on a blood sample; by looking for the product of the disease, such as the proteins that are present in Tay–Sachs; or by flagging a gene or chromosome. Flagging is a sophisticated technique that is used to find out if a fragment of DNA will attach itself to the patient's chromosome. If it does, the gene, and therefore the disease, is present; if not, it is absent. However, in most diseases, more than one gene is involved, so it can be difficult to check all the elements. This is true of cystic fibrosis, for example, although at present the diagnosis can be more than 90 percent certain.

In some cases, such as Huntington's chorea, the responsible part of a chromosome has been identified, but it has not been narrowed to the specific gene. In this situation, geneticists use a "town plan" as an example. They would say that they know which part of the town contains the problem, they just do not know which house.

Can you Benefit?

It is important to seek expert advice if you fall into any of the following groups:

• *If a previous child was born with a genetic disorder such as cystic fibrosis, or a chromosomal disorder such as Down's syndrome*

• *If a previous child was born with a congenital defect, for example, a clubfoot (see p.181)*

• *If there is a family history of mental handicap, or abnormal development*

• *If there is a blood relationship between you and your partner*

• *If you have a history of repeated miscarriages (see pp.200 & 206)*

• *If either parent is over 35*

Seeing a counselor
If you think you can benefit, visit a genetic counselor before you try to conceive.

Consequently, it is possible for a counselor to predict that a person is likely to develop Huntington's chorea, but no more than that. If a couple has already had an affected child, the counselor will first rule out a cause that is not inherited, for example German measles (see p.19). Possible causes such as exposure to radiation, drugs, or injury will also be considered. The counselor will examine the child and will arrange for genetic testing to be done on blood or cells washed from the mouth with water.

Sometimes it can be difficult for the genetic counselor to pinpoint the exact cause, but he or she will give you as thorough a diagnosis as possible, and your chances of having another affected child will be outlined. If there is no evidence of an inheritable disease, you will be reassured completely.

THE IMPORTANCE OF YOUR FAMILY HISTORY

James's mother and some other female relatives are carriers of hemophilia. They do not suffer from the disease themselves, but pass on the gene to some of their sons, who develop hemophilia, and to some of their daughters, who become carriers.

Great-uncle
(died in childhood)

Cousin

James

Family tree
By examining the medical history of your family network, a counselor will be able to detect the pattern of a disease over several generations. For example, James, a 6-year-old boy, had painful, swollen joints. During a conversation with James's parents, the doctor learned that a cousin and probably a great-uncle suffered from the genetic bleeding disorder hemophilia (see family tree). This information pointed almost immediately to the probable diagnosis – James, too, had hemophilia. The pain and the swelling was caused by the blood that was leaking into his joints.

Males with hemophilia

Unaffected males

Probable female carriers of hemophilia gene

Possible female carriers of hemophilia gene

YOUR HORMONES

The ovarian cycle is mostly controlled by the hormones estrogen, progesterone, follicle-stimulating hormone (FSH), and luteinizing hormone (LH).

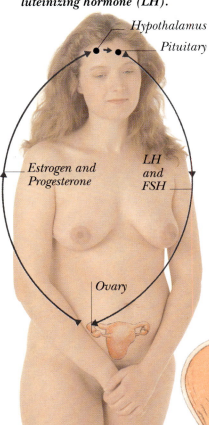

Hypothalamus

Pituitary

Estrogen and Progesterone

LH and FSH

Ovary

Hormonal control
Ovarian follicle development is triggered by FSH from the pituitary gland. The follicles produce estrogen, which causes the pituitary to release a burst of LH that cuts FSH production. The LH triggers the release of the egg from the most mature follicle, and the corpus luteum, which forms when the egg has been released, then produces progesterone.

CONCEIVING A BABY

The miracle of birth begins when a sperm from the father fuses with an egg from the mother to form a single cell with its own unique genetic blueprint. This single cell then divides and redivides, until eventually a new human being is created. The vast majority of normally fertile couples achieve a pregnancy within the first two years of trying.

A woman's entire stock of ova, or eggs, are formed in her two ovaries before her birth. By the fifth month of pregnancy, a baby girl's ovaries contain around seven million eggs. Many of these eggs will die before she is born, leaving her with approximately two million eggs at birth. This process of degeneration continues until puberty, by which time between 200,000 and 500,000 eggs survive. Of these, only 400-500 mature and are released by the ovaries during a woman's fertile years – roughly one per lunar month. The ovaries are located in the pelvis, close to the trumpetlike endings (fimbriae) of the Fallopian tubes. The germ cells that ultimately

THE FEMALE REPRODUCTIVE TRACT

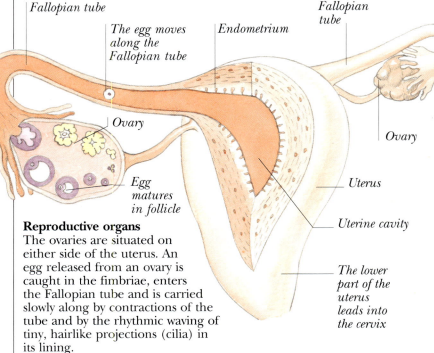

Fallopian tube

The egg moves along the Fallopian tube

Endometrium

Fallopian tube

Ovary

Egg matures in follicle

Ovary

Uterus

Uterine cavity

The lower part of the uterus leads into the cervix

Reproductive organs
The ovaries are situated on either side of the uterus. An egg released from an ovary is caught in the fimbriae, enters the Fallopian tube and is carried slowly along by contractions of the tube and by the rhythmic waving of tiny, hairlike projections (cilia) in its lining.

develop into a woman's ova are formed in the yolk sac that sustains the embryo in the first weeks of life. If the embryo is male, these cells are reabsorbed as the placenta develops. When the embryo is female, however, about 100 germ cells actually move from the yolk sac, along the umbilical tissue, and into the minute female embryo. They migrate to the tissues that will later develop into the ovaries, and there they begin to multiply.

THE OVARIAN CYCLE

During a woman's reproductive life, her ovaries release ova in cycles. Each of these ovarian cycles lasts about 28 days (from 21 to 35 is considered normal), and the development and release of an ovum ready for fertilization by a sperm is called ovulation. Ovaries ovulate alternately. In the first half of each ovarian cycle, about 20 ova begin to ripen and occupy fluid-filled sacs (follicles). One of these follicles, outgrowing the others, matures and ruptures, thus releasing its ovum. This happens on or around 14 days before the end of the cycle, regardless of the total length of the cycle. The other follicles that had started to ripen then shrivel up and their eggs die. The ruptured follicle becomes a yellow-colored structure, called the corpus luteum, which grows for some days and produces the hormone progesterone, essential for the development of an embryo. In the absence of pregnancy, however, it withers away, and a new cycle begins when the lining of the uterus is shed at the beginning of the woman's next period.

FERTILITY FACTS

Fertility varies from person to person and at different stages of our lives. The following facts are true for most people.

• *The fertility of both men and women reaches its peak at about the age of 24*

• *Among couples having intercourse without contraception, 25% of the women will conceive within the first month, 60% within 6 months, 75% within 9 months, 80% within a year, and 90% within 18 months*

• *After ovulation, an egg can only be fertilized for approximately 12–24 hours*

THE MONTHLY CYCLE

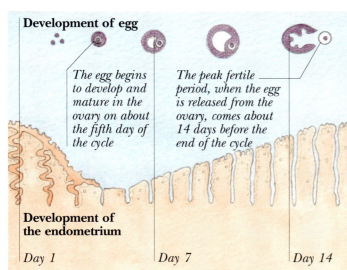

Development of egg

The egg begins to develop and mature in the ovary on about the fifth day of the cycle

The peak fertile period, when the egg is released from the ovary, comes about 14 days before the end of the cycle

Development of the endometrium

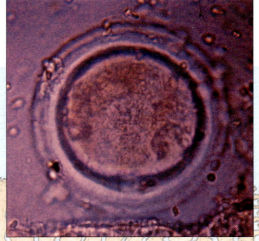

The mature egg
After leaving the ovary, the egg is drawn into the Fallopian tube, where it awaits fertilization by a sperm.

Day 1   Day 7   Day 14   Day 21   Day 28

The cycle begins
Menstruation, the shedding of the endometrium, heralds the start of the ovarian cycle. Under the influence of estrogen, the endometrium is then rebuilt.

Fertile period
After ovulation, under the influence of estrogen and progesterone, the endometrium becomes thicker and spongy, to receive a fertilized egg.

The cycle ends
If the egg is not fertilized, the corpus luteum dies and, because estrogen and progesterone levels fall, the endometrium is shed.

SPERM PRODUCTION

The process of sperm production within a man's testes is known as spermatogenesis. Sperm production is continuous and the whole process, from the initial generation of a sperm to its maturation and ejaculation, takes about 7 weeks.

Sperm
Each sperm has a head, containing its genetic material, and a long, thin tail for propulsion. A complex network of microscopically tiny tubes within the testes produces spermatids, the forerunners of sperm.

The testes
A cross-sectional view of a testis shows the network of minute tubes that contain the spermatogonia, the cells from which spermatids are created. These tubes connect with about 8 larger tubes, the efferent ducts, that convey the developing sperm into the epididymis, where they mature and grow their tails. The testes also produce hormones, the most important being the male sex hormone testosterone. Testosterone is the most powerful of the androgens, the hormones responsible for male secondary sexual characteristics such as facial hair and deepening of the voice and male and female sex drives.

THE ROLE OF A MAN

Sperm, a man's contribution to the conception of his child, are formed in his testes (testicles). Sperm formation begins at puberty under the influence of testosterone from the testes, and luteinizing hormone (LH) and follicle stimulating hormone (FSH), which are produced by the pituitary gland and act on the testes in exactly the same way that they do on the ovaries. Production continues throughout a man's fertile life and, although the numbers and quality of sperm produced diminish from the age of 40, men in their nineties have been known to father children. Sperm production speeds up at times of sexual activity, but if ejaculation is extremely frequent, sperm numbers decrease, lowering a man's fertility.

The mature sperm Each individual sperm is tadpole shaped and, because it is only about a twentieth of a millimeter long, it cannot be seen by the naked eye. It has a head that is dark in color owing to the concentration of genetic material within it, and a strong, lashing tail, five to six times longer than the head, with which it "swims." The tail is attached to the head by a short middle section or body. This section contains special cell components called mitochondria, which are its energy-producing apparatus.

The newly formed sperm pass into the epididymis at the rear of each testis, where they mature. From the epididymis, matured sperm travel up a tube, the vas deferens, to a small, saclike structure called the seminal vesicle.

When a man ejaculates, the sperm is mixed with fluid produced by the seminal vesicle and this, together with fluids secreted by the prostate and other glands, makes up the seminal fluid (semen) that is discharged from the penis via the urethra.

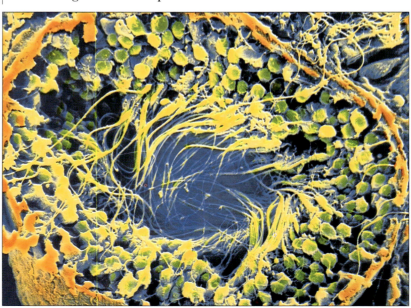

THE MALE REPRODUCTIVE TRACT

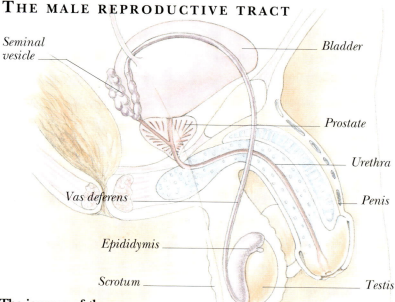

Seminal
vesicle

Bladder

Prostate

Urethra

Vas deferens

Penis

Epididymis

Scrotum

Testis

The journey of the sperm
The sperm leave the epididymis via a tube called the vas deferens. Each vas deferens, about ¹/₆ in (4 mm) in diameter, runs up the spermatic cord, from which the testis is suspended. From there, it loops up around the bladder, down past the seminal vesicle, and into the prostate gland. From the seminal vesicle onward, the vas deferens is known as the ejaculatory duct; at the prostate it joins the urethra, the hollow tube within the penis through which the semen is ejaculated.

EJACULATION

The average amount of seminal fluid ejaculated is three and a half milliliters (about two-thirds of a teaspoonful), the normal range being from two to six milliliters. Each milliliter of ejaculate contains 60–150 million sperm, and of these, nearly a quarter will be abnormal and only about three-quarters will be motile (capable of sustaining independent movement).

Reaching the egg Although sperm are capable of moving two to three millimeters per minute, their actual speed varies with the acidity of their environment – the higher the acidity, the slower their movement. The vaginal secretions are slightly acidic, and so sperm that have been ejaculated into the vagina probably move quite slowly until they reach the more friendly alkaline environment of the uterine cavity. After withstanding the hostile (acidic) vaginal conditions they then face a much longer and more dangerous journey before they reach the egg way down a Fallopian tube. Of a total sperm count of 300 million sperm per ejaculation, only a few hundred will actually reach the egg. A large quantity of the remainder may trickle out of the vagina, or be destroyed by vaginal acidity. Other sperm may be swallowed up by cleansing cells within the uterus, enter the wrong Fallopian tube, or enter the correct tube but miss the egg altogether.

YOUR BABY'S SEX

The gender of a child is determined by whether the fertilizing sperm is an X sperm (female) or a Y sperm (male), as the woman's ovum is always female, X.

The X and the Y sperm have different properties, the X sperm (female) being larger, slower, and longer-lived than the Y sperm (male). The X sperm also appears to be favored by the slightly acidic conditions in the vagina.

Bearing in mind that there is very little scientific evidence to support them, the following ideas may be of interest if you are trying to choose the gender of your baby.

When *For a female baby, make love up to 2 or 3 days before ovulation, as only female sperm survive this long; for a male baby, make love on the day of, or just after, ovulation, as the faster male sperm will reach the ovum before the female sperm.*

Frequency *For a female baby, make love fairly frequently, as this lowers the proportion of male sperm in the semen; for a male baby, make love infrequently, as this increases the proportion of male sperm.*

PENETRATION

This sequence of pictures, taken with an electron microscope, shows fertilization taking place – a sperm penetrating the tough outer membrane of an egg and then entering the egg itself.

Membrane penetration
The sperm penetrates the membrane by releasing enzymes that create a hole in it.

Oocyte penetration
The sperm prepares to penetrate the oocyte, the innermost part of the egg.

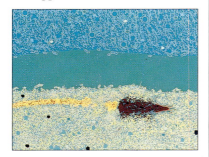

Chromosome transfer
The sperm sheds its body and tail before joining its chromosomes to those of the egg.

FERTILIZATION

Fertilization occurs when a sperm meets and penetrates an ovum. All human cells contain 46 chromosomes, threadlike structures that carry their genetic information.

The exception to the rule are sperm and ova, which have only 23 chromosomes, so that when they meet, the single fertilized cell that results has the full 46 chromosomes. The new cell (zygote) splits first into two identical cells, each with 46 chromosomes, and continues to divide slowly as it travels down the Fallopian tube, until it reaches the uterus. It is now called a blastocyst or blastula, and is a hollow clump of about 100 cells.

CONCEPTION

Egg meets sperm
The egg is released from its follicle. It travels one-third of the way along the Fallopian tube, where it is fertilized.

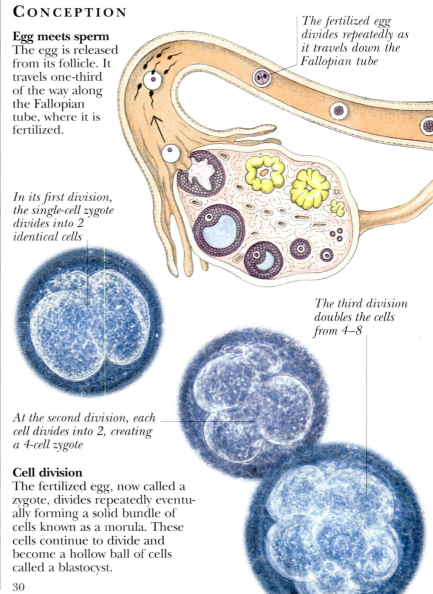

The fertilized egg divides repeatedly as it travels down the Fallopian tube

In its first division, the single-cell zygote divides into 2 identical cells

The third division doubles the cells from 4–8

At the second division, each cell divides into 2, creating a 4-cell zygote

Cell division
The fertilized egg, now called a zygote, divides repeatedly eventually forming a solid bundle of cells known as a morula. These cells continue to divide and become a hollow ball of cells called a blastocyst.

Implantation A week after fertilization the blastocyst secretes a hormone that helps it to burrow its way into the endometrium. Implantation is usually in the upper one-third of the uterus. The pregnancy is now established, and the placenta will start to form.

Twins When a woman produces more than one egg at a time, non-identical twins may develop from two separate eggs, fertilized by two separate sperm. Each has its own placenta within the uterus. Identical twins come from a single egg, fertilized by a single sperm. This egg divides into two, and each develops independently into a genetically identical twin sharing a single placenta. Other multiple pregnancies, such as triplets, originate in the same ways as twins; similarly, the siblings may be identical or fraternal.

BOY OR GIRL?

Of the 46 chromosomes that carry the complete human genetic blueprint, the sex of a child is determined by just 2, known as the X and the Y.

The sex chromosomes *A woman's eggs each contain a single X chromosome, while a man's individual sperm have either an X or a Y chromosome. If an egg is fertilized by an X chromosome sperm, the baby that is created will be a girl (XX). If the sperm has a Y chromosome, the resulting child will be a boy (XY).*

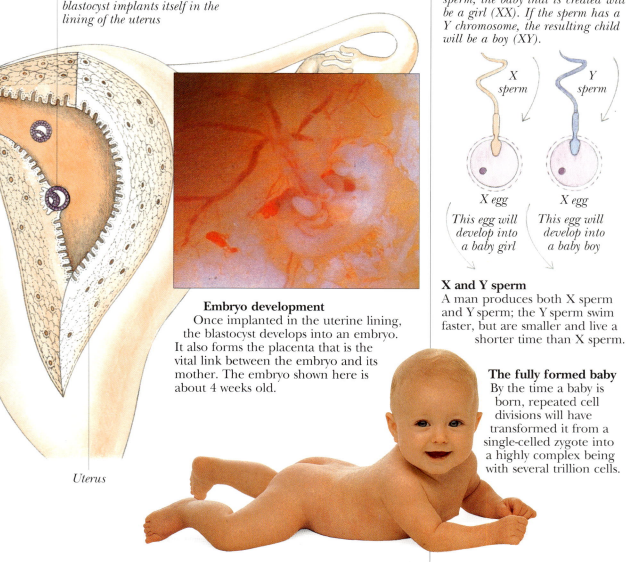

7 days after fertilization, the blastocyst implants itself in the lining of the uterus

X sperm

Y sperm

X egg

X egg

This egg will develop into a baby girl

This egg will develop into a baby boy

X and Y sperm
A man produces both X sperm and Y sperm; the Y sperm swim faster, but are smaller and live a shorter time than X sperm.

Uterus

Embryo development
Once implanted in the uterine lining, the blastocyst develops into an embryo. It also forms the placenta that is the vital link between the embryo and its mother. The embryo shown here is about 4 weeks old.

The fully formed baby
By the time a baby is born, repeated cell divisions will have transformed it from a single-celled zygote into a highly complex being with several trillion cells.

NAME *Penny Stone*

AGE *42 years*

PAST MEDICAL HISTORY *Gallbladder operation at the age of 35*

FAMILY HISTORY *Mother had 8 children, the last born at age 47*

OBSTETRIC HISTORY *No previous pregnancies*

Penny and her husband, Ken, had put off having children because both of them wished to pursue their careers. Penny is a senior manager in a bank. Both Penny and her husband became fearful that her fertile years were running out; they had been actively trying to have a baby for a year without success.
At Christmas they went on a ski trip, away from the daily routine of work and chores. Penny returned home relaxed, fit, and energetic, to find a few weeks later that she was pregnant.

THE OLDER MOTHER

There are many reasons that can lead to having a baby after the age of 35 – career development, late marriage, remarriage, or difficulties in conceiving. There is an increasing number of older mothers like Penny; the biggest rise in the birth rate recently has been in the 35 to 40-plus age group.

IS AGE A FACTOR?

Most doctors agree that the optimum age to have a baby is between 20 and 35, as there are certain chromosomal risks (see p.20) that increase when a woman over 35 is having a baby. I told Penny that 20 to 35 are not magic numbers between which problems do not arise, nor are they a rigid rule. Statistics can be misleading. In reality, the experience of a pregnant woman aged 36 and those of a woman aged 34 rarely differ. As long as the older mother-to-be and her caregivers are aware of possible complications, problems can be successfully averted or dealt with.

Penny feels that in terms of her lifestyle, now is the right time for her to have a child. She loves her job and has made a success of her career, but she's not intending to go back to work for several years after the birth of her child. Having waited so long to be a mother, she's now going to enjoy it.

Statistics on the age of parents show that the odds are greatly in favor of Penny having a successful pregnancy. In studies conducted on pregnancies in older women, the general conclusion is that the health of the mother is a far more important factor than her age. Penny takes great care of herself. She works out in a gym four times a week and pays attention to her diet. Both she and her husband eat a good, well-balanced, and healthy diet with lots of fresh fruit and vegetables. Given that Penny is so fit and healthy, I reassured her immediately that the chances of her having a perfectly normal baby and a normal delivery were excellent.

PENNY'S SPECIAL NEEDS

Because of her age, Penny is known medically as an "elderly primagravida" and will have special care throughout her pregnancy. She will need to have more prenatal visits than a younger mother. As with all pregnant women, her blood pressure will be checked at each visit, as any increase would be particularly significant in a woman over 40, and her urine will be tested regularly to detect any early warning signs of preeclampsia. For the same reason, she will be asked to note any swelling of her feet, hands, or face. It's likely that she will be advised to rest for a minimum of half an hour every day, increasing this to an hour in the second trimester, and adding an afternoon nap in the third.

Amniocentesis Most women over the age of 35 are concerned to see whether their babies have any abnormalities, and most doctors advise that an amniocentesis be done at about 14 weeks. This procedure involves taking a sample of the fluid surrounding the baby in the uterus; skin cells shed by the baby will be found in the fluid and these are studied to provide chromosomal information.

In the first place, you can find out if any gender-linked disorders might have been inherited (see p.21), as one result of the test is to determine the sex of the baby. Penny's husband is color-blind, which is a gender-linked minor defect, so she is interested in finding out whether the baby is a boy. Many more boys (1 in 12) than girls (1 in 250) are color-blind.

Just as importantly, certain chromosomal abnormalities, such as Down's syndrome, increase with age, and amniocentesis is used routinely to detect Down's. The test can also reveal other defects, including spina bifida, which may have been signaled by Penny's increased levels of alpha-fetoprotein (see p.159).

Hospital care Penny wants to have her baby in the hospital, as she is concerned that absolutely nothing should go wrong. I suggested that she find a group practice of doctors and midwives who favor natural birth. The practice should be affiliated with a large, well-respected hospital. On her prenatal visits she will get to know the team, one of whom will be present at the birth of her baby. The more secure, happy, and relaxed Penny is about her pregnancy, the easier she is likely to find the birth.

However, obstetricians are very sensitive to the possibility that the placenta will fail to function (placental insufficiency) just before term in a woman who is over 35. Penny's doctor therefore raised the possibility of artificially inducing her labor, although he said that she wouldn't automatically be induced because of her age alone. Penny stated her preference for spontaneous labor but agreed to have medical intervention at the first sign of fetal distress.

Exercise Penny is very eager to continue exercising during pregnancy. I told her there is no problem in her doing so, provided she follows the basic ground rules that apply to all pregnant women – exercise regularly, not sporadically; don't overdo it, and don't ask your body to cope with a new sport. In addition, do not jog as it is very hard on the breasts and jarring to the back; avoid backpacking and other weight-bearing sports and, in later pregnancy, do not ski or ride horses (see also p.126). Usually a woman can regain any lost energy by lying down for half an hour, but it can take a pregnant woman several hours to recover from exhaustion, and it doesn't matter whether it's from exercise or house cleaning. Therefore, I also advised Penny that she should not neglect her rest periods.

PENNY'S BABY

Having mature parents will be beneficial for the baby.

- *His parents are in a stable and well-established relationship*

- *His home environment is emotionally and financially secure*

- *His mother has fulfilled her ambitions and will not see him as a hindrance to her career*

- *As he is wanted so much, Penny's baby will have a deep sense of security*

- *His father is eager to be involved in parenting*

- *Both Penny and Ken feel relaxed and confident about the prospect of parenthood*

WANTING CHILDREN

The reasons people have for wanting children are many and varied, and can range from the completely straightforward to the extremely complex.

"I want something of me to live on in my children"

"It will be proof of the love between me and my partner"

"Our children will be continuing the family line"

"Children will create bonds between my partner's family and mine"

"I want someone of my own blood because I am adopted"

"I think my partner and I would make good parents"

"I want to discover an individual who is a unique combination of my partner and me"

"By looking after and influencing my children, I will have an input into the next generation"

"Having children is a major life experience – a rite of passage, a symbol of adulthood"

"I want someone to love and someone who will love me"

"I want to create a happy childhood for my children"

"I don't want to be alone in my old age – I want to be surrounded by children and grandchildren"

"A child will give me a purpose in life – someone to work for"

PROBLEMS IN CONCEIVING

It is not a simple matter for a couple to find out if they are truly infertile. Infertility means different things to different people, and it certainly means something different to doctors and to couples. Most couples who think they are infertile are only subfertile and with help can conceive successfully.

WHAT IS INFERTILITY?

To most people infertility means the inability to have children, but it's more complex than that. A couple may have no difficulty in conceiving their first child but find they cannot have a second; they are suffering from secondary infertility. Another couple, who have had children by their previous partners, may now find that they cannot conceive together.

This is known as subfertility and happens because the fertility of a couple is the sum of their fertilities. If both partners' fertilities are marginal, conception may not occur, but if one partner's fertility is strong, it may still be possible for the couple to conceive.

There are now many ways in which a couple can be helped to conceive a child. However, the emotional costs can be exceedingly high – and not just for you, your partner, and other family members, including the child or children you may conceive, but also for those people (donors, surrogates) who may help you.

THE STRESS OF INFERTILITY

Finding out that you are infertile or even subfertile can be a blow that raises strong emotions such as depression, anger, resentment, and guilt. Some infertile people even report that they have dreams and thoughts of self-mutilation, because of the anger they feel toward their bodies, particularly their reproductive organs. In addition, a sense of isolation can be crushing (even though one in six couples consults their doctor because they are worried about not having conceived), and the stresses placed on you as a couple can be intolerable and, for some, ultimately destructive.

THE DESIRE FOR CHILDREN

Being able to make a choice about whether or not to have children is a relatively new phenomenon because contraception became reliable only during the last 30 years. Yet despite being able to choose not to have children, the desire for children remains inextricably linked to sexuality for the vast majority of people. There are many different reasons for wanting children, not least because the ability to reproduce tends to be fundamental to most people's self-image even if they are not consciously aware of it.

Having children is a major "rite of passage" and is probably the most significant life experience you will ever go through. It is exciting, frightening, and rewarding and, more than any other event, it signifies adulthood – you are no longer just your parents' child, you are also a parent.

Ethical considerations Like all major life decisions, becoming a parent involves a number of ethical decisions – particularly if your child is born as a result of assisted conception. A number of issues are raised by these processes that may not be anticipated until treatment is started (see also column, right), or until conception, or even until the child becomes an adult.

For example, having gone through complicated procedures to create life, how would you cope if the fetus was found to have abnormalities? Or if all the embryos "took," thus creating a multiple pregnancy, would you consider fetal reduction – when one or more multiple fetuses are injected with a drug to make them abort? This gives the remaining embryos a better chance of surviving, but there is also a risk that all will abort. Would you choose to give all of them a chance to survive, however slim?

Using donated sperm, eggs, or embryos can lead to a number of problems, such as matching the donor to the couple – whether by general characteristics or something more crucial, such as race (there are few Asian donors in the Western world). Although the child is nearly always registered as the couple's own, its origins may never be discussed, which means that secrecy can begin at birth. If there may be inheritance problems, see a lawyer beforehand.

When does life begin? Can an embryo be judged to be a unique human being or as merely having that potential – much like an acorn has the potential to become an oak tree? How you view this will undoubtedly have a bearing on what you would prefer to do with any "surplus" sperm, eggs, or embryos – always assuming that you have a choice.

Perhaps you would like to donate them to another infertile couple, or you may be happy for them to be used to further genetic research. If you do donate them, will you feel happy that there is a full or half-sibling to your child somewhere else in the world? There are no easy answers. Each of us must do what suits us best. A good fertility clinic will offer counseling to help you reach the best decision for everyone concerned.

ARE YOU INFERTILE?

Before you as a couple can be confirmed infertile and referred to a fertility clinic, your doctor will talk to you about your health and your sex life. He or she will want to know your age; how long you have been trying for a baby with your partner; whether you have had a child with a previous partner; whether either of you smokes, drinks, or takes drugs; whether you have been on any regular medication or had any serious illnesses or operations; how often, and when, you make love; and what the woman's periods are like.

ISSUES TO CONSIDER

There are a number of issues to resolve as a couple before you attempt to conceive using any infertility treatments.

• *If you were to have a child using donor sperm or eggs, or both, would the fact that the child wasn't "yours" prevent you from loving her as your own?*

• *Would you feel jealous if a donor conceived a child with your partner when you couldn't?*

• *Would you tell your child about how she was conceived, or would you try to keep it a secret?*

• *Would you tell friends and family, or would you attempt to keep your fertility treatment a complete secret?*

• *If you intend to keep it a secret, can you be sure that the truth won't come out, perhaps destructively, at a time of crisis?*

• *If your child was conceived using donor eggs or sperm, or both, how would you cope if she wanted to trace her genetic history in later life? What if she couldn't because records were destroyed – as they often are?*

• *How long would you persist with infertility treatment?*

• *What would you do with frozen sperm, eggs, or embryos that you do not want to use? What if you weren't given a choice?*

• *Could you cope with a multiple pregnancy? What if one, some, or all of the babies died?*

• *Having committed so much time and money to having a baby, how easy will you find it to let her go once she grows up?*

ENVIRONMENTAL FACTORS

The effect of pollutants in our lives and surroundings on male fertility has only recently begun to be appreciated.

Polychlorinated biphenyls (PCBs)
Research suggests that chemical pollutants, such as these non-degradable compounds, may be responsible for the overall fall in male fertility in the West. PCBs were used extensively in the plastics industry and as electrical insulators throughout the '50s and '60s, but they were banned in the late '70s because they were so hazardous to health.

However, they have remained in the environment and have entered the food chain. PCBs are stored in fat cells and have a mild estrogenlike effect that may interfere with sperm production.

Smoking, alcohol, and stress
These can affect the quality and quantity of the sperm that a man produces. If a man tends to underproduce sperm normally, he may suffer a catastrophic drop in his sperm count if he smokes or drinks heavily.

A man also should avoid drinking too much coffee because caffeine seems to cause defects in sperm (and in ova). Stress is also thought to be a cause of male infertility, and its effects are exacerbated if it also leads the sufferer to excessive smoking, drinking, or coffee consumption.

Drugs *"Social drugs" such as marijuana and cocaine dramatically reduce sperm numbers and motility, and with their use the percentage of defective sperm soars. Medicinal drugs such as antidepressants and antimalarials may also have an adverse effect.*

MALE INFERTILITY

Taken overall, male fertility in the Western world has declined in the last 50 years, and many scientists suspect that this may be due to common environmental factors (see column, left). However, fertility clinics are now beginning to offer andrology services, which deal with male problems and diseases, as well as gynecology services, which deal with female problems and diseases, so there is more chance than ever before that men who are subfertile or infertile can be helped to achieve natural fatherhood.

Male and female infertility can be a touchy subject, and for men it still appears to be linked with virility. This is a shame because the two are not linked at all. A man's sperm may be incapable of fertilizing an egg, yet he may be an excellent lover. By contrast, a man who is unable to make love to a woman may have perfectly viable, fertile sperm.

PROBLEMS WITH SPERM

Sperm are extremely vulnerable cells. They take seven weeks to form and can be affected by outside influences at any point in their development. Because of this, it is entirely possible for a man to give sperm samples on separate occasions that differ widely both in quality and in quantity.

Testicular failure This is a very rare condition that results in semen that contains no sperm. The cause is usually difficult to establish but may be due to a chromosomal problem such as Klinefelter's syndrome (when the man has two or more X chromosomes rather than one); testes that did not descend properly after birth; a blow to the testes, such as a sports injury; or mumps during adulthood. Complete testicular failure, like complete ovarian failure, tends to be untreatable. It does not, however, always affect both testes.

Low sperm counts These in themselves do not equal infertility. Many men with low sperm counts do father children, although it tends to take longer than normal to achieve conception. Unfortunately, however, when there are few sperm, the majority tend to be abnormal or have poor motility.

Low sperm counts and sperm abnormalities may be due to hormonal problems, anatomical problems, immunological problems, or environmental factors.

HORMONAL PROBLEMS

Adequate production of testes-stimulating hormones by the pituitary gland, including luteinizing hormone (LH) and follicle-stimulating hormone (FSH) is essential for healthy sperm creation. If a man's pituitary gland is not releasing enough FSH and LH, his ability to produce sperm will be impaired. Incorrect functioning of his thyroid and adrenal glands (which also produce hormones) will also affect his sperm production.

ANATOMICAL PROBLEMS

Some of these problems can be present at birth and may remain undiagnosed; others can be caused at a later time by injury, infection, or disease.

Abnormal conditions of the testes A hydrocele (an excess of normal lubricating fluid around the testes) or a varicocele (when the veins of the scrotum and testes become enlarged) may be present. These conditions appear to raise the temperature of the testes, inhibiting sperm production.

Retrograde ejaculation About one percent of men find that they do not ejaculate at the time of orgasm. This is because of retrograde ejaculation (a "dry run"), when the semen is ejaculated backward into the bladder instead of forward along the urethra.

Blockage of the vas deferens A blockage of either or both of the tubes that connect the testicles to the seminal vesicles may exist from birth or be the result of an infection, such as gonorrhea.

IMMUNOLOGICAL PROBLEMS

In some cases of male infertility, the man is producing antibodies that attack his own sperm. These antibodies are produced by his immune system, which for some reason interprets the sperm as foreign. This may be the result of an injury or infection and is detectable by the presence of white blood cells in semen.

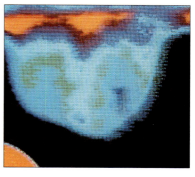

Healthy testes
This thermal photograph shows how healthy testes (blue) are at a lower temperature than the body (orange, top of picture).

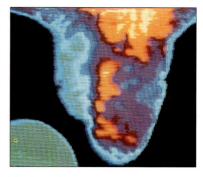

Varicocele
The orange patches on the nearer testis are a varicocele; the orange color indicates a raised temperature, which can inhibit sperm production.

CAUSES OF MALE INFERTILITY

In about 30% of infertile couples, the problem lies with the man. A similar percentage is due to the woman, and the remainder is due to shared problems. Male problems include the complete inability of the testes to produce sperm (fortunately very rare); an abnormality such as a hydrocele or a varicocele, which will inhibit sperm production; and impotence, premature ejaculation, or inability to sustain an erection.

In addition, a valve at the base of the bladder should close during ejaculation, but if it fails to do so the semen will be ejaculated back into the bladder instead of out through the urethra. This retrograde ejaculation occurs most commonly in diabetic men who have had surgery to the urethra and in men with spinal cord injury.

The valve at the base of the bladder may fail to close

Obstruction of the vas deferens may impede sperm mobility

Man may be unable to ejaculate sperm into partner's vagina

Sperm production may be nonexistent or may be inhibited

INVESTIGATING MALE INFERTILITY

There are a number of investigations that look at what happens when healthy sperm come into contact with the cervical mucus, which they must swim through in order to reach and fertilize an ovulated egg. These investigations are carried out after preliminary tests have established that your sperm is healthy: good semen has a volume of two milliliters or more and a count of more than 30 million sperm per milliliter, of which at least 60 percent should be motile. There should be an abnormality rate of less than 30 percent and no white cells or bacteria present.

SPERM ASSESSMENT

Your doctor will arrange for preliminary tests on your semen before making more detailed investigations of your fertility. The semen samples are examined by a trained technician, using a microscope and a computer-assisted semen motility analyzer. The results predict how fertile you are likely to be.

POST-COITAL TEST

Known as a PCT, this assesses what happens once your sperm are inside your partner's vagina. For the PCT your partner should visit the doctor or clinic as close as possible to the estimated time of her ovulation. It is at this time of the menstrual cycle that the cervical mucus is particularly receptive to sperm. The mucus, which at other times is quite thick, is then profuse, clear, very stretchable, and similar in appearance to saliva. Sperm penetrate it easily.

Ideally you should have intercourse several hours (6–12 hours is best) beforehand. For some couples, however, the clinical background to the test can make intercourse impossible and some men may fail to have an erection or be unable to ejaculate. Tension is quite normal, and the medical staff will be very understanding.

The sperm count
This basic determinant of male fertility is ascertained by 2 semen analyses, which also investigate any sperm abnormalities. Each milliliter of semen should contain at least 30 million sperm, the majority of which should be normal. The picture on the left is of a good sperm sample. If there are fewer than 20 million sperm discernible and there is a high proportion of abnormal sperm, the semen is described as being poor. The sperm sample shown in the picture on the right is an example of poor semen.

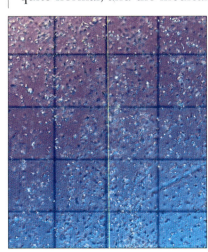

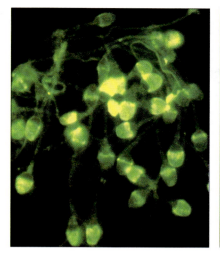
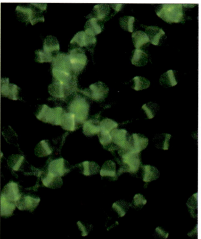

Sperm acrosome test
The head of a normal sperm is surrounded by a cap, the acrosome, containing enzymes that enable the sperm to break through the outer membrane of the egg. If sperm lack this acrosomal cap, they are incapable of fertilizing an egg. Sperm are tested by using chemicals that fluoresce (glow) when they react with the acrosome. These pictures show defective sperm (on the left) and normal sperm.

When your partner goes to the clinic she will be asked what time she had intercourse, and then she will have an internal examination. A sample of cervical mucus will be removed, assessed for stretchability, and then examined under a microscope for sperm. Sperm motility is graded from zero to four. A good PCT implies that the sperm count is satisfactory, the sperm are sufficiently motile, and the cervical mucus is not hostile.

A negative test This may be because of incorrect timing; a cycle in which ovulation has not occurred; the mucus being thick and gluelike rather than clear and flowing; antibodies that attack sperm being present in either the cervical mucus, or in the seminal fluid carrying the sperm; failure to ejaculate the sperm into the vagina; the sperm being destroyed by the use of a spermicide in a lubricant or washed away because your partner wanted to make herself clean for the clinic. It could also be that you just happened to produce poor-quality semen that time, resulting in a low or zero sperm count. If a PCT is negative, it is repeated. Only when the second test also proves negative are additional tests performed.

SPERM TESTS

Sperm tests are performed to assess whether your sperm are capable of swimming to and penetrating your partner's egg. In the sperm invasion test, the interaction between your sperm and your partner's cervical mucus is examined under a microscope. If sperm are unable to cross into the mucus or cannot move through it properly, a negative PCT could result, but the finding does not itself indicate whether the problem lies with the sperm or the mucus. The crossover sperm invasion test is performed to answer that question. This uses exactly the same procedure as the sperm invasion test, but first, your sperm and normal mucus from a donor female will be used, and second, normal sperm from a donor male will be combined with your partner's mucus. These may reveal the problem but, if not, further tests such as the acrosome test (see above) and the egg penetration test (see box) may be necessary.

EGG PENETRATION TEST

The potential of the sperm to fertilize an egg can be tested even more accurately with the egg penetration test than by the acrosome test (see above).

The egg penetration test involves introducing the sperm to transfer oocytes (hamster eggs) and measuring how well the sperm penetrate, and fuse with, them.

The use of transfer oocytes means that your partner does not have to go through stressful IVF treatment (see pp.46 & 48), collecting her eggs for testing. There is no danger of an embryo resulting from the fusion of sperm and transfer oocytes.

FIBROIDS AND INFERTILITY

Fibroids are benign endometrial muscle tumors that can form anywhere within the uterus. They can sometimes be a cause of infertility, but rarely.

These tumors consist of bundles of muscle and range in size from a pea to a grapefruit. They can cause the uterus to become mis-shapen and may compress one or both of the Fallopian tubes.

If they are very near the surface of the uterine lining, they can interfere with normal implanta-tion, and if they occur near the junction of the uterus and the Fallopian tubes, they may prevent the blastocyst from reaching the uterus. Fibroids may also interfere with muscle contractions during labor, although this depends mainly on where they are in the uterus and their size.

Fibroids are very common but often symptomless, and affect about 1 in 5 women over the age of 30. They appear most frequently in women over the age of 35 and if they are causing problems they can be removed by surgery. The operation (called a myomectomy) is simple and straightforward and leaves the uterus and ovaries intact.

FEMALE INFERTILITY

The inability of some women to conceive has been rigorously investigated over the past 30 years, and great advances in diagnos-ing and treating infertility have been made. The causes of female subfertility tend to fall into four main areas. All these can now be treated, but with varying degrees of success.

FAILURE TO OVULATE

The inability to release an egg is the most common cause of female infertility and this accounts for about a third of all infertile women. Anovulation is usually due to hormonal problems. Occasionally, however, the ovaries are damaged or, rarely, have run out of eggs.

Hormonal problems We have already seen in the normal ovarian cycle (see p. 26) that hormones from the pituitary gland and ovary are responsible for the growth and maintenance of the ovum. However, in many cases of infertility, too little of one or too much of the other hormone may be present. For example, at mid-cycle the hypothalamus should stimulate the pituitary gland to release a massive amount of FSH and LH to bring about ovulation, but in 20 percent of cases it fails to do so. Therefore there is some FSH and LH but not enough for ovulation. Alternatively, the pituitary gland may be damaged or malfunctioning, and either produce none or too much FSH and LH. Or as a result of excessive LH stimulation and a relative deficiency of FSH, the ovaries may become polycystic and no longer capable of producing mature ova.

Problems due to incorrect amounts of hormones are normally treated by fertility drugs that include Clomiphene, human chorionic gonadotrophin (hCG), and human menopausal gonadotrophin (hMG), in addition to the female and pituitary hormones them-selves. For 90 percent of women whose problems are hormonal modern drug therapy can result in regular ovulation but, for reasons unknown, only about 65 percent of these women will achieve a pregnancy.

Ovarian problems Scarring due to surgery on cysts, infection, or as a side effect of radiation treatment can damage the ovary. A woman's supply of eggs may become exhausted. This can be due to the menopause or its premature onset, surgical damage, or radiation therapy. In such cases, *in vitro* fertilization (see pp.46 & 48), sometimes using donated eggs, is the only option.

HORMONAL IMBALANCE

Hormones may interfere with conception in other ways than influencing ovulation. For example, progesterone is necessary for a fertilized egg's survival. If too little is produced or it is produced for too short a time, the egg may not survive. Known as an inadequate luteal phase, this may be treated successfully with drugs as described under above **Failure to ovulate**.

STRUCTURAL PROBLEMS

Healthy Fallopian tubes are a requirement for a pregnancy to occur naturally. They are the pathways that permit the ascending sperm to reach the egg and then allow the developing embryo to reach the uterus for implantation. A previous ectopic pregnancy, pelvic inflammation, previous surgical procedures, or infection of any kind (including sexually transmitted disease) may cause a blockage in the tubes or damage, such as scarring, that will prevent you from conceiving naturally.

Problems with the uterus account for at least 10 percent of infertility cases. The uterus may be congenitally abnormal; contain adhesions (bands of scars), polyps, or fibroids (see column, left); or be subject to endometriosis. In endometriosis, tissue normally found in the uterine lining grows on adjacent surfaces, including the Fallopian tubes, the ovaries, and the inside of the abdomen. This can lead to scarring and the formation of adhesions. Various treatments are available to correct many of the above conditions.

In order to reach an egg to fertilize it, sperm must swim through a large quantity of mucus secreted by the cervix. If there is too little mucus, or if it is so thick that the sperm cannot penetrate it, or if it contains antibodies that attack the sperm directly, the sperm will never reach the egg, and fertilization cannot occur. No single proven treatment has emerged as yet, but artificial insemination may be one option that is considered.

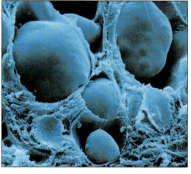

Developing eggs
This picture of a normal ovary, viewed through an electron microscope, shows eggs developing in their follicles. An abnormality of an ovary, such as a tumor, can prevent it from producing and releasing eggs.

CAUSES OF FEMALE INFERTILITY

Either or both of the Fallopian tubes may be blocked, damaged, or missing, preventing sperm and egg from meeting

The ovaries may fail to produce mature eggs or be unable to release them because of an abnormality, scarring, or adhesions

Tubal blockage
This picture shows the fimbriae of a Fallopian tube. These delicate, fingerlike projections intercept eggs released by the nearby ovary and waft them into the tube to await fertilization. If the tube is blocked, sperm will be unable to ascend it, meet, and fertilize the egg.

Infertility can arise if the mucus remains thick and sperm are unable to swim through it, or if it contains antibodies that attack sperm

The uterus may contain fibroids, and its lining may be affected by endometriosis

CHECKING YOUR OVULATION

The first step in investigating your infertility is to determine whether or not you are ovulating. If these simple tests show that you are, then your doctor will refer you for further investigation.

The BBT chart *Your doctor will show you how to compile a basal body temperature (BBT) chart covering a period of 3 months.*

This will show whether or not your body temperature rises at the time of ovulation and stays raised for the rest of the month. If it does, it generally indicates that you are ovulating at regular intervals.

Progesterone blood test *Determining the level of progesterone in the blood gives circumstantial evidence that ovulation has taken place. Following ovulation, the normal level of progesterone is 10ng (10 thousand millionths of a gram) per liter. If, around the middle of your menstrual cycle, your blood level contains this amount of progesterone, it is assumed that you are ovulating normally.*

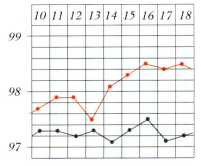

Normal and abnormal cycles
This chart shows (top – day by day; side – °F) the typical temperatures of a normal cycle (red line) and those that might occur when ovulation fails (gray line).

INVESTIGATING FEMALE INFERTILITY

When preliminary tests indicate that you are probably ovulating, fertility specialists employ a range of more advanced tests to help them discover why you have been unable to conceive. These tests investigate the condition and functioning of your hormones, ovaries, uterus, and Fallopian tubes.

HORMONE AND OVULATION TESTS

Measuring the levels of hormones in your blood or urine every day for an entire menstrual cycle can give useful information. It gives information on the interaction between your ovaries, brain, pituitary, and hypothalamus, and can help pinpoint an imbalance in your hormones if there is a problem with ovulation. Normally, your estrogen, luteinizing hormone (LH), and progesterone levels are measured and compared with those of women known to be ovulating normally. Other hormones that can be measured if there are ovulatory problems are follicle-stimulating hormone (FSH), testosterone, and prolactin.

Ultrasound scanning One of the most useful tests is ovarian ultrasound scanning (ultrasonography), with which your fertility specialist can check the development of your ovarian follicles and confirm whether ovulation is occurring. This tracking of the follicle can also be of great value when a particular treatment, such as artificial insemination, is being carried out, because it pinpoints ovulation with great accuracy (see also p.48). Accurate assessment of follicular growth is also essential for complex assisted conception techniques such as *in vitro* fertilization (see pp.46 & 48).

Endometrial biopsy The endometrium (the inner lining of the uterus) undergoes cyclical changes under the influence of the hormones estrogen and progesterone. There is a clear increase of endometrial thickening and growth in the second half of the cycle, after ovulation, and this is due to the increase in progesterone production. If progesterone output is inadequate, development of the endometrium may not be sufficiently advanced to allow implantation to take place. The biopsy, in which a tiny sample of your endometrium is examined under a microscope, is carried out in the second half of the menstrual cycle so that any changes due to progesterone will be visible.

TUBAL PATENCY TESTS

The Fallopian tubes are extremely delicate structures, less than four millimeters in diameter at their narrowest, and they are easily damaged. About 50 percent of all women who seek infertility treatment or care are found to have a Fallopian tube problem. A number of tests exists that can demonstrate their health.

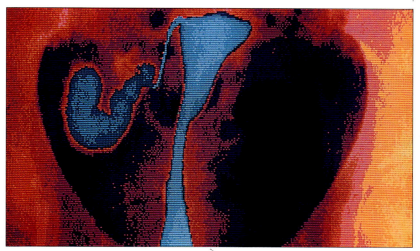

Uterus and tube X-rays

A hysterosalpingogram (HSG) is an X-ray taken of your uterus and tubes while they are filled with a dye that shows up on X-ray. The dye is slowly injected through your cervix into your uterus, and then observed on an X-ray screen. In this HSG, the dye shows up as light blue and the uterus is the upper triangular area. The dye has not entered the right-hand tube, which shows that it is blocked near the uterus; the left-hand tube is blocked farther away from the uterus and is somewhat swollen.

Laparoscopy This is the most important and informative test (see below). In addition to determining whether your tubes are damaged or blocked, the other internal organs may be viewed for evidence of endometriosis, adhesions, fibroids, or malformations.

Hysterosalpingography This may give further unique information about the Fallopian tubes (see picture above). It reveals whether there is any scar tissue in the area where the tubes join the uterus or in the lining of the tubes. It can also pinpoint any uterine polyps.

USING A LAPAROSCOPE

The surgeon uses a laparoscope – a thin viewing tube inserted through a tiny incision in the patient's abdomen

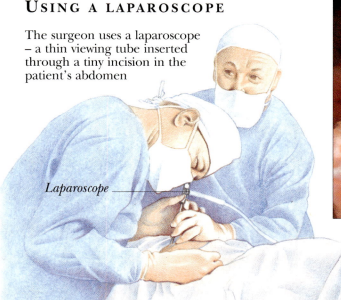

Laparoscope

The patient is given a general anesthetic so that she is asleep for the 10–40 minutes the laparoscopy takes

Healthy ovary (above)

Laparoscopy can show that things are healthy as well as revealing any problems. This picture, taken via a laparoscope, shows a healthy ovary with a mature follicle that will soon burst to release the egg.

SELECTING A SPERM DONOR

A major area of concern for a couple seeking donor insemination is how a clinic selects and screens its donors, matches donors to their partners, and maintains confidentiality.

Donors are often students recruited from medical schools and universities. Hospitals and clinics that provide donor insemination take great care to ensure that all potential donors are in good physical and mental health and have no known inheritable disorder in their family.

Before insemination, you will probably want to be assured that the donor's physical characteristics are similar to those of your partner, and clinics can usually satisfy you on points that may cause you concern, such as hair and eye coloring, height, complexion, body build, and blood group. Donors may also be of a particular ethnic or religious group.

All information about the donor is strictly confidential; usually, records are destroyed to preserve the donor's anonymity.

ASSISTED CONCEPTION

Assisted conception – by sperm or egg donation or by in vitro *fertilization – has helped many childless couples become parents. However, the emotional costs can be high, and it is essential that all the issues involved be discussed thoroughly. Counseling for couples considering assisted conception is provided by fertility clinics and hospitals.*

SPERM DONATION

The most straightforward method of assisted conception is the artificial insemination of a woman with her partner's sperm, a technique known as AIP (artificial insemination by partner). Artificial insemination with sperm from a donor other than your partner is also possible. This used to be known as artificial insemination by donor, or AID, but it is now referred to as donor insemination (DI), so that it will not be confused with AIDS.

Artificial insemination by partner Your partner's sperm is placed against your cervix, using a cap just like a diaphragm. It can also be introduced into your cervical canal or uterus using a syringe. Before you are inseminated you should use basal body temperature (BBT) charts or a luteinizing hormone (LH) predictor kit to ensure that you are ovulating. A sonogram just before ovulation can detect follicle growth.

Artificial insemination with sperm from a partner is not suitable for everyone. If a man has a very low sperm count, he and his partner may be wasting time and subjecting themselves to unnecessary anguish by attempting AIP (sometimes called AIH – artificial insemination by husband). But for men whose problem is depositing the sperm within the vagina, this method is perfect.

Donor insemination This can be considered in cases where men are sterile or have subfertile (very low) sperm counts that do not respond to treatment; where there is a major blood group incompatibility between the couple (for example, where a Rhesus-negative woman has developed antibodies to the Rhesus-positive blood group of her partner); when a man is known to be a carrier of a very damaging hereditary abnormality; or when a mature, stable single woman wants a child but not a partner.

Donor insemination (DI) can seem to be the ideal solution for many couples, but there are a number of points that should be carefully considered. First and foremost are the feelings of your partner. It is not uncommon for men to feel inadequate or jealous of donors who impregnate their partners when they could not.

This can rebound on your life together, and on the child after it is born. In addition, some women are repelled by the circumstances in which they conceive or by the fact that a different man's sperm is used at each visit. Others worry about what sort of man the donor was, or idealize him as a "perfect man," or wonder if their child will meet, and perhaps marry, a half-sibling.

Using sperm from a donor that you know, or are related to by marriage, can relieve some of these problems but can magnify others. It can also raise its own problems, such as what happens if the father wants visiting rights.

It is still usual for doctors to advise secrecy (records are normally destroyed to ensure the anonymity of the donor), but this can be a heavy burden for a couple to carry. DI could also become very damaging to the child, especially if other people know and let it slip, or if it comes out at a time of crisis, such as divorce. As this method of conception (about which most couples feel hesitant) is exceedingly stressful, good counseling is essential.

You can insist that there is no mention of this aspect of your infertility treatment in your maternity records, and your joint names can be given on the birth certificate.

EGG DONATION

In cases in which a woman is unable to produce an egg, a donor's may be used during *in vitro* fertilization (IVF). Egg donation has the advantage that both of you are involved: your partner fertilizes the egg, and you will carry and give birth to the baby. However, it is more complicated than sperm donation. It relies on hormonal drugs and egg collection techniques (see p.48). Consequently, donor eggs are hard to come by, the main sources being anonymous donors, IVF patients who sometimes donate extra eggs, and relatives. Problems may arise from these sources: the eggs donated by IVF mothers have an increased risk of chromosomal disorders because IVF patients tend to be older than average, and donated eggs from relatives or friends may lead to family tensions. As with sperm donations, records of donors are often destroyed, and this secrecy may adversely affect your child later in life.

If you are not producing eggs, you will probably not be menstruating, and this means that the lining of your uterus (endometrium) will be thin and incapable of nourishing a developing embryo. Consequently, you will be given drugs to stimulate it to thicken so that the blastocyst can implant.

EMBRYO DONATION

Embryo donation occurs occasionally when, after successful IVF, couples have no further need for unused embryos that have been frozen and stored, and donate them to childless couples. This has been the focus of much debate, and raises many sensitive issues such as the donor parents' feelings if their own child, or children, die, and the chances of the siblings meeting and perhaps having children together. However, it does mean that it is an "adopted" child for both of you.

STORING AND TESTING THE SEMEN

Fresh semen is usually used for AIP, but frozen semen is used for donor insemination. Because the donated semen is frozen and stored, the clinic has time to test both it and the donor for infections.

Donated semen is put into a sterile vial and frozen by immersion in liquid nitrogen. The frozen semen is stored for a period of months, during which time tests are carried out on the donor to ensure that he is free of any infection, such as hepatitis B or HIV, that could be transmitted via his semen.

When it has been established that the donor was free of infection at the time of donation, the semen itself is tested to ensure that it contains no harmful microorganisms, such as bacteria, and if these tests prove negative the semen can then be used for insemination.

Up to 50% of the sperm in the semen are unlikely to survive the freezing and thawing, although this fall in sperm numbers is partly offset by the fact that it is the healthiest, most robust sperm that will survive the process.

Donor insemination is carried out under exactly the same conditions as artificial insemination with sperm from a partner.

SURROGATE MOTHERS

Surrogate motherhood – where a woman bears a child on behalf of another – is physically straightforward but fraught with potential emotional, legal, and moral difficulties.

Full surrogacy The simplest form of surrogacy, known as full surrogacy, is where a surrogate conceives and carries the child of an infertile woman's partner. Insemination may be indirect (the surrogate is artificially inseminated with the man's sperm) or direct (the man has sexual intercourse with the surrogate).

Partial surrogacy In this arrangement, an egg from the woman who is unable to conceive is fertilized with her partner's sperm and then implanted into the surrogate mother's uterus.

Surrogacy problems In theory, after the child is born, it is handed over to the couple who "commissioned" it. They then legally adopt it, and the surrogate mother subsequently has little or no involvement or contact with it. The surrogate may, however, find it very hard to part with the child, especially if she is its genetic mother. In some well-publicized cases, couples have had to take lengthy and costly legal action in order to get custody.

Other problems can arise if the child is born handicapped or if the surrogate wants to maintain a close relationship with her child and is not allowed to do so. There is also the possibility that one or both of the commissioning parents may find it hard to accept the child fully and lovingly.

IN VITRO FERTILIZATION

Since the first test-tube baby was born, in 1978, several thousand babies have been born by *in vitro* fertilization (IVF) to couples who would have otherwise remained childless. *In vitro* means "in glass" or "in the laboratory," hence the term "test-tube babies."

In IVF, fertilization occurs in a shallow glass or porcelain dish. The method is very complex but, at its very simplest, involves the removal of eggs from the ovaries, fertilization with sperm in the laboratory, and transferral of the early embryos into the uterus. IVF has rather a glamorous image but the success rate (see **Outlook**) is not always what the media would suggest; for many couples, however, it is their only hope of pregnancy.

Sperm viability Before IVF is carried out, the sperm viability is assessed by a "swim-up" test. This involves mixing the semen with a prepared culture medium, spinning it in a centrifuge machine, and then incubating it.

The most motile sperm swim up to the top and the ratio of motile sperm to immotile sperm is then assessed. The sperm count must be higher than 20 million per milliliter, at least 40 percent of the sperm must be actively moving after two hours, and some sperm should remain active for 24 hours. If the sperm are viable, IVF can proceed to the next stage; if not the couple must then decide if they wish to continue with IVF using donor sperm.

Egg retrieval Ovulation is stimulated under various drug regimens. When the leading follicle reaches maturity (17 millimeters in diameter) around the tenth day, as viewed by ultrasonic examination, the woman is given the hormone human chorionic gonadotrophin (hCG), timed for 33–36 hours before the planned time of egg retrieval.

Most egg retrievals are done in the early morning – otherwise, the hCG injection would have to be given inconveniently late at night or even in the early hours of the morning. (The process of egg retrieval is illustrated on page 48.) The extracted eggs are then incubated in a culture medium that maintains their growth for 2 to 24 hours, depending on their maturity.

Once the eggs are fully mature, they are isolated in a bubble of culture medium, and 100,000–200,000 sperm provided by your partner are added to each egg. Your partner is usually expected to provide fresh semen. This often means masturbating in the hospital. Frozen sperm can be used but they tend to be less viable than fresh sperm. Up to eight bubbles of culture medium containing eggs and sperm are placed in a Petri dish and kept for 12–15 hours, the time taken to achieve fertilization.

Embryo transfer After two or three days in the incubator, three of the best embryos are transferred into your uterus. Before this, you will be invited to view the embryos under the microscope, and you will probably see that your eggs have reached the four-cell stage. The embryo transfer itself is a painless procedure, taking only a few minutes. You may be given a mild sedative to relax you and then a fine tube is inserted into your cervix and the embryos are gently injected into your uterine cavity. (By law, no more than three can be injected at any one time).

Follow-up After the embryo transfer and a short rest, you can return home to lead a normal, but not too vigorous, life. One week after the day of egg retrieval, a blood sample is taken so that your progesterone level can be measured. In some clinics you will be given additional hormone support in the form of further hCG injections, or progesterone as injections or vaginal suppositories.

If you have not had a period by 16 days after retrieval, a blood test is performed to detect the pregnancy hormone beta-hCG. Finding the hormone present means that at least one of the embryos has successfully implanted. The actual number of implanted embryos can be ascertained as early as 35 days after implantation by using ultrasound.

Outlook Up to the age of 34, according to a recent study, IVF treatment is almost as successful as normal methods of conception in fertile couples. The study concluded that 55 percent of women can expect to become pregnant, and 45 percent will have a live birth within five cycles of treatment. However, the success rate declines greatly after this age, and the chances of producing a baby are 30 percent for women between 35 and 39, and less than 15 percent for women aged 40 and over.

IVF is, without a doubt, the most emotionally demanding of all the infertility methods that you might undertake. Most infertility specialists will put patients through a thorough course of testing and observation – lasting up to a year – and explore other options before embarking on *in vitro* fertilization. This waiting period can seem like a long time if you have postponed having a family until your mid-thirties but, since other routes are less grueling, it is advisable to follow your specialist's advice.

In addition, because undergoing IVF treatment is so very stressful and can invade your sex life to a much greater extent than the majority of fertility doctors will admit, most clinics are only prepared to treat heterosexual couples who have a stable, long-term, and preferably married relationship.

GAMETE INTRAFALLOPIAN TRANSFER

The technique of GIFT (transferring sperm and egg into a Fallopian tube) is exactly as described for IVF except that the sperm and the eggs are transferred together into the open end of a Fallopian tube, thereby allowing fertilization to occur naturally. The resulting embryo can then arrive in the uterus at the correct point in the cycle, allowing implantation to occur. The essential requirement is that at least one of your Fallopian tubes is 100 percent healthy and clear, and the drawback is that you have no idea whether fertilization has occurred, let alone implantation. The follow-up treatment is identical to that of IVF.

ALTERNATIVE TECHNIQUES

Some fertility specialists use a number of other techniques to bring about pregnancy. Some are variations of IVF, others are less invasive. All are experimental.

ZIFT *Zygote intrafallopian transfer is a variant of GIFT, itself a type of IVF. In GIFT, fertilization takes place in the Fallopian tube; in ZIFT, the egg is transferred to the tube after it has been fertilized but before it begins to divide.*

TEST *Tubal embryo stage transfer is a version of IVF in which the embryos are transferred to the Fallopian tubes rather than the uterine cavity.*

POST *In peritoneal ovum and sperm transfer, sperm from the male partner is drawn into a syringe. Next, the syringe is inserted through the woman's abdomen, and her ovulated eggs are drawn into it to mingle with the sperm. Then the mingled eggs and sperm are injected into the abdomen near the ends of the Fallopian tubes, so that they can enter the tubes and fertilization can occur.*

DIPI *Direct intraperitoneal insemination is a simplified version of POST. Washed sperm are injected through the rear of the woman's vagina into a space near the open end of a Fallopian tube, where they can intercept her eggs when they leave the ovary.*

IVF TECHNIQUES

Producing a test-tube baby depends on the successful harvesting of the mother's eggs, fertilization by a single healthy sperm, the implantation of at least one embryo into your uterus, and the delivery of a viable baby.

ENSURING A GOOD EGG SUPPLY

In order to maximize the chances of a successful pregnancy through IVF, more than one egg is removed for fertilization. Normally only one egg is shed during each ovarian cycle, and so one of the first steps in the IVF treatment cycle (which begins a few days after the end of your period) is the stimulation of your ovaries to make them

RETRIEVING THE MATURE EGGS

Using ultrasound to give a clear picture of the reproductive tract, a gynecologist delicately guides a thin, hollow probe through the vagina and uterus and along a Fallopian tube toward the ripened eggs. These eggs are then drawn into the probe by gentle suction.

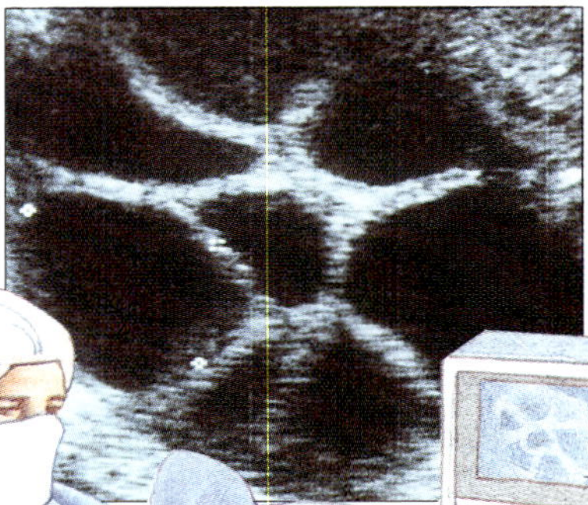

Monitoring your follicles
The medical team clearly views the swollen follicles on an ultrasound screen as they retrieve the ripe eggs. Using ultrasound to guide the probe is more straightforward and convenient than using laparoscopy.

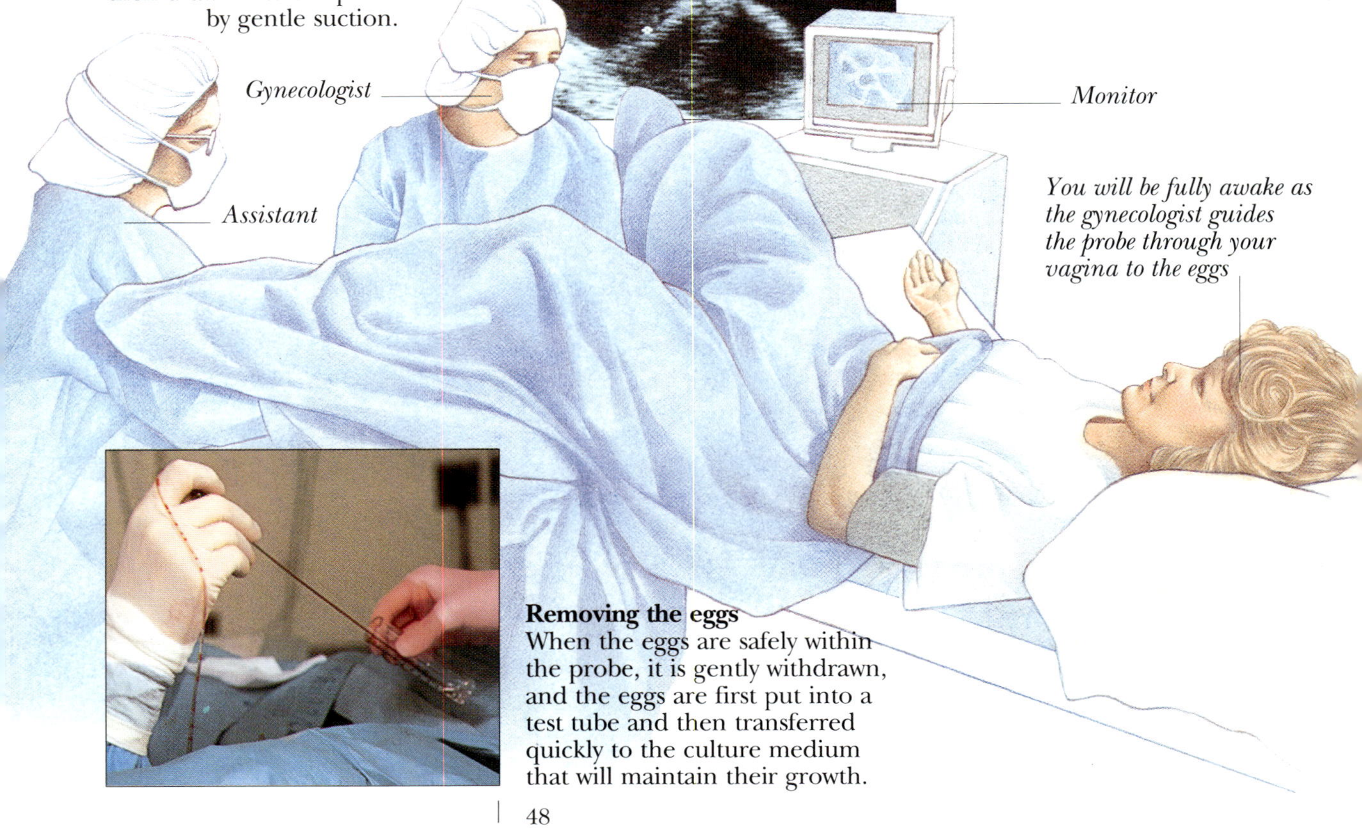

Gynecologist

Monitor

Assistant

You will be fully awake as the gynecologist guides the probe through your vagina to the eggs

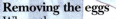

Removing the eggs
When the eggs are safely within the probe, it is gently withdrawn, and the eggs are first put into a test tube and then transferred quickly to the culture medium that will maintain their growth.

more productive. This is done by giving you ovary-stimulating drugs, such as clomiphene or hMG, so that your ovaries produce a number of mature eggs simultaneously. Over the next week or so you will make daily visits to the clinic so that the development of the eggs can be monitored. As the eggs mature, the follicles containing them swell and produce increasing amounts of estrogen. A series of blood tests will detect this increase in estrogen and the growth of the follicles can be measured by daily sonograms.

COLLECTING THE EGGS

When your ovulation is due, you go to the clinic to have your matured eggs collected – using either ultrasound or laparoscopic guidance – and then fertilized with your partner's sperm.

Ultrasound guidance The use of ultrasound for guiding the egg retrieval probe is a simpler procedure than using a laparoscope. It is carried out under light or local anesthesia and you only need to spend a few hours at the clinic instead of having to stay overnight, as you do with laparoscopy.

Laparoscopy In this method, the doctor uses a laparoscope – a small, thin telescope – to view your ovaries and guide the fine, hollow probe that collects the ripened eggs. You are given a general anesthetic, and carbon dioxide gas is injected into your abdominal cavity. This separates the organs within it so that they can be seen more easily. Then the laparoscope is inserted through a small incision made in your navel, and your eggs are carefully collected with the probe.

IVF BABIES

The first successful in vitro fertilization occurred in 1978. During the past 15 years, several thousand test-tube babies have been born.

A healthy baby
Test-tube babies are no different from babies that have been conceived normally.

CONFIRMING CONCEPTION

About 18 hours after they have been mixed with your partner's semen, the eggs are inspected under a microscope to find out whether any of them have been fertilized. It is very uncommon for all of the eggs to be fertilized and to subsequently develop into embryos, although for 2 or 3 to be fertilized is quite normal. If any of the eggs have been fertilized, they are kept in the incubator for another 48 hours or more, when they will normally have divided into about 2–4 cells, although growth may be more advanced. Then, provided that they show no signs of abnormality, a maximum of 3 are normally transferred to your uterus. In the picture on the right, a single sperm can be seen approaching an egg.

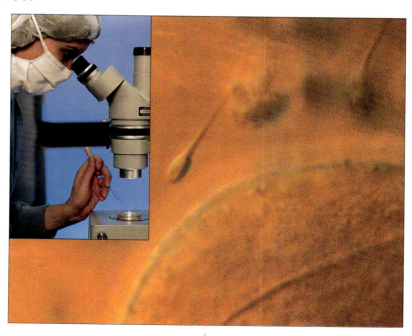

Discovering a new life
Finding out you are pregnant is often one of the most special moments in your life.

PREGNANT!

Many women "know" when they conceive. This special intuitive feeling is probably due to the very early outpouring of female hormones, initially prolonged high levels of progesterone (which a woman does not experience unless she is pregnant), followed by the production of human chorionic gonadotrophin (hCG) by the fetal tissues as soon as the embryo achieves implantation, about seven days after fertilization.

SUSPECTING THAT YOU ARE PREGNANT

There are certain classic signs that can make you suspect that you are pregnant before seeking confirmation.

Amenorrhea Within two weeks of fertilization, a woman will usually miss a period. Although pregnancy is the most common cause of amenorrhea, it is not the only one, so a missed period should not be taken as an absolute sign of pregnancy. Several other factors such as jet lag, severe illness, surgery, shock, bereavement, or great stress also can cause amenorrhea. Periods, however, do not always stop in pregnancy: some women have been known to have light periods up to the sixth month and, occasionally, all the way through their pregnancies.

Frequency of urination As soon as progesterone levels rise and the embryo starts to secrete hCG, the blood supply to the pelvic area increases, leading to pelvic congestion. This communicates itself to the bladder, which itself becomes irritable and tries to expel even the smallest quantity of urine. Most women therefore experience the desire to pass urine (micturition) more frequently than usual, although it may be in only very small quantities. This can happen as early as one week after conception.

Tiredness Fatigue is partly due to very high levels of progesterone, which has a sedative effect. During early pregnancy, your metabolism speeds up in order to support your developing embryo and your vital organs, which have to cope with an enormously increased amount of work. This can lead to fatigue, that is sometimes so overwhelming that you may *have* to sleep.

Odd tastes and cravings The saliva often reflects the chemical content of the blood and, with rising hormone levels, the taste within your mouth can change, often being described as metallic. This can also make the taste of certain foods different from normal, with some that you may usually enjoy (coffee is a common example) even becoming intolerable. There is no real scientific

50

explanation for cravings, which can sometimes be for very odd things, such as coal, but they are thought to be the body's response to deficiency in certain minerals and trace elements. Try to control or distract cravings for inedible substances and high-calorie foods that are low in nutritional value. Otherwise feel free to indulge yourself within reason.

Morning sickness Most common in the morning, morning sickness can come on at any time of day, especially when you do not eat often enough and your blood sugar is allowed to drop.

Smell Pregnancy often heightens your sense of smell, and you may find that common odors such as cooking smells make you nauseous. Perfume can also have this effect, and you may notice that the way your perfume smells also changes, owing to alterations in your skin's chemistry.

Breast changes Even at the start of pregnancy, breast changes may be quite obvious: your breasts can become quite lumpy and sore to the touch; the nipple area may become tender and sensitive, and will deepen in color; and veins can become enlarged over the surface of the breasts.

CONFIRMING PREGNANCY

Once you suspect that you are pregnant, you should seek confirmation as soon as possible. There are a variety of tests available that can be performed at different intervals after conception. Some are more accurate than others.

Blood test This test has to be performed by your doctor; it is becoming more widely available. It can accurately detect the pregnancy hormone hCG (human chorionic gonadotrophin) in the blood as early as two weeks after conception – about the time your next period is due.

Urine tests The hormone hCG can also be detected in your urine. Urine tests can be conducted at home, in a hospital, at your doctor's office, or at a family planning clinic. They are more than 90 percent reliable and can be performed as soon as two weeks after conception, although you will get the most reliable result if you wait four weeks longer (see also p.52).

Internal examination This is very reliable and can be performed by your doctor once the signs are obvious, which is usually four weeks or more after conception.

Pregnancy hormones soften the consistency of your cervix and uterus, and cause more blood to be directed to your pelvis (see **Frequency of urination**), which gives the color of your vagina and cervix a purplish tinge. Your uterus will also be slightly enlarged. An internal examination may possibly be mildly uncomfortable but it should not be painful.

TELLING THE WORLD

You will obviously tell your partner, and possibly your immediate family, as soon as you know yourself.

Obstetrician *Your pregnancy may be confirmed by your obstetrician, so he or she will obviously know immediately. If not, you should get in contact as soon as you can to discuss birth options and prenatal care.*

Employer *You should consider telling your employer when the pregnancy is well established, at about 3 months.*

Friends and acquaintances *Many women delay telling friends and acquaintances that they are pregnant until after the first trimester. Although this is understandable, it is probably unnecessary once your pregnancy has been confirmed.*

Do you have The correct Result?

A number of factors can affect whether your pregnancy test results are accurate.

• *In older women, hormonal changes caused by approaching menopause can give false-positive or false-negative results*

• *Improperly collected or stored urine can lead to errors*

• *If the test is performed too early, the concentration of hCG will be too low to detect. It is important to know when your period was due. Irregular or infrequent periods can affect an accurate indication of pregnancy*

• *Antidepressant or fertility drugs containing hCG or hMG can change the results. Contraceptive pills, antibiotics, and analgesics should not have any effect*

• *If the equipment used for the test is too hot, the result may be false. Urine must be room temperature at the time of the test*

HOME TESTING

Finding out whether you are pregnant in the privacy of your own home may help ease any nervous feelings, and you can be sure of complete confidentiality. There are a variety of pregnancy testing kits available from pharmacies. These are simple to use and offer immediate results with an accuracy of over 90 percent.

How the tests work All the urine tests check for the presence of hCG (human chorionic gonadotrophin), the hormone manufactured by the blastocyst. Two of the main types, the ring and the color tests, involve mixing the chemical solution provided with a sample of your urine. The chemicals react according to the amount of hCG in the urine. The reaction is shown by a color change in the tube or window strip, or coagulation is prevented, thereby causing the appearance of a dark ring in the tube. A third test can be performed by simply placing the absorbent part of the test in contact with the urine. From two weeks after conception, hCG may be detected in urine. Most kits advise using the test between one and four days after the first day of your missed period. However, if you do perform the test then, repeat it two weeks later when the hCG is more concentrated and the result will be more reliable. Most kits provide two tests for the purpose of confirmation.

Necessary precautions Make sure your sample of urine is the first passed that morning (it will have a higher concentration of hCG) and that it is collected in a clean, soap-free container. Do not have any liquids before the test as this will dilute the sample. Follow the kit's instructions very carefully, and do not use the test if it has been damaged in any way or is past its use-by date. If you cannot perform the test immediately, store the specimen in the refrigerator, but don't keep it for more than 12 hours.

Unexpected result There is the possibility that a test will show a positive result that becomes negative when repeated, and your period may start a few days later. Don't worry. Half of all conceptions do not become established pregnancies, as the fertilized egg fails to implant in the lining of the uterus and there is a natural termination. The test may have been positive because it was done before the loss of the fertilized egg. To avoid this error, do the test around the time of your first missed period. If there is a weak but positive result, repeat the test a few days later with a fresh sample.

EXPECTED ARRIVAL DATE

Once you have confirmed that you are pregnant, your next question almost certainly will be, "When will my baby be born?"

About 266 days or 38 weeks pass between conception and birth. This is the same as 40 weeks from the start of your last menstrual period (LMP) because ovulation, and therefore conception, is normally two weeks after the start of your LMP (see chart, right). You can work out the approximate date of your baby's arrival with calculations using the first day of your LMP. The estimated date of your baby's delivery (EDD) is therefore at 280 days (40 weeks) from the first day of your last period. The accuracy of this date is dependent on a regular 28-day cycle. If you have a shorter or longer menstrual cycle, your delivery date will probably be earlier or later. If you conceived immediately after coming off the pill it may be difficult for your caregivers to give you a firm date and they will probably have to be guided by your baby's development.

Physicians use the EDD when monitoring the baby's development to ensure that there are no problems with the expected rate of growth. Unnecessary intervention can occur if too much emphasis is put on this date and doctors may decide to induce labor if they believe your baby is overdue. However, risks to you and your baby do not rise much until after 42 weeks, and most doctors are prepared to let the pregnancy continue, without inducing, if tests show the baby is not at risk (see p.170).

HOW THE EDD CHART WORKS

Find the first day of your last period on the chart by looking for the month in bold type on the left-hand side, and then looking along the line until you find the actual date of your LMP. Then look at the figure below it. This is your baby's estimated date of arrival.

YOUR BABY'S ARRIVAL

Don't be anxious if your baby does not show signs of arriving on the day you had planned. About 85% of babies born from normal pregnancies are delivered within a week before or after the date predicted.

The EDD is used to give you an approximate idea of when your baby will arrive. Be flexible – don't see it as the exact day that you will go into labor. A healthy pregnancy may last between 38 and 42 weeks.

YOUR ESTIMATED DATE OF DELIVERY

January	1	2	3	4	5	6	7	8	9	10	11	12	13	14	15	16	17	18	19	20	21	22	23	24	25	26	27	28	29	30	31
October	8	9	10	11	12	13	14	15	16	17	18	19	20	21	22	23	24	25	26	27	28	29	30	31	1	2	3	4	5	6	7
February	1	2	3	4	5	6	7	8	9	10	11	12	13	14	15	16	17	18	19	20	21	22	23	24	25	26	27	28			
November	8	9	10	11	12	13	14	15	16	17	18	19	20	21	22	23	24	25	26	27	28	29	30	1	2	3	4	5			
March	1	2	3	4	5	6	7	8	9	10	11	12	13	14	15	16	17	18	19	20	21	22	23	24	25	26	27	28	29	30	31
December	6	7	8	9	10	11	12	13	14	15	16	17	18	19	20	21	22	23	24	25	26	27	28	29	30	31	1	2	3	4	5
April	1	2	3	4	5	6	7	8	9	10	11	12	13	14	15	16	17	18	19	20	21	22	23	24	25	26	27	28	29	30	
January	6	7	8	9	10	11	12	13	14	15	16	17	18	19	20	21	22	23	24	25	26	27	28	29	30	31	1	2	3	4	
May	1	2	3	4	5	6	7	8	9	10	11	12	13	14	15	16	17	18	19	20	21	22	23	24	25	26	27	28	29	30	31
February	5	6	7	8	9	10	11	12	13	14	15	16	17	18	19	20	21	22	23	24	25	26	27	28	1	2	3	4	5	6	7
June	1	2	3	4	5	6	7	8	9	10	11	12	13	14	15	16	17	18	19	20	21	22	23	24	25	26	27	28	29	30	
March	8	9	10	11	12	13	14	15	16	17	18	19	20	21	22	23	24	25	26	27	28	29	30	31	1	2	3	4	5	6	
July	1	2	3	4	5	6	7	8	9	10	11	12	13	14	15	16	17	18	19	20	21	22	23	24	25	26	27	28	29	30	31
April	7	8	9	10	11	12	13	14	15	16	17	18	19	20	21	22	23	24	25	26	27	28	29	30	1	2	3	4	5	6	7
August	1	2	3	4	5	6	7	8	9	10	11	12	13	14	15	16	17	18	19	20	21	22	23	24	25	26	27	28	29	30	31
May	8	9	10	11	12	13	14	15	16	17	18	19	20	21	22	23	24	25	26	27	28	29	30	31	1	2	3	4	5	6	7
September	1	2	3	4	5	6	7	8	9	10	11	12	13	14	15	16	17	18	19	20	21	22	23	24	25	26	27	28	29	30	
June	8	9	10	11	12	13	14	15	16	17	18	19	20	21	22	23	24	25	26	27	28	29	30	1	2	3	4	5	6	7	
October	1	2	3	4	5	6	7	8	9	10	11	12	13	14	15	16	17	18	19	20	21	22	23	24	25	26	27	28	29	30	31
July	8	9	10	11	12	13	14	15	16	17	18	19	20	21	22	23	24	25	26	27	28	29	30	31	1	2	3	4	5	6	7
November	1	2	3	4	5	6	7	8	9	10	11	12	13	14	15	16	17	18	19	20	21	22	23	24	25	26	27	28	29	30	
August	8	9	10	11	12	13	14	15	16	17	18	19	20	21	22	23	24	25	26	27	28	29	30	31	1	2	3	4	5	6	
December	1	2	3	4	5	6	7	8	9	10	11	12	13	14	15	16	17	18	19	20	21	22	23	24	25	26	27	28	29	30	31
September	7	8	9	10	11	12	13	14	15	16	17	18	19	20	21	22	23	24	25	26	27	28	29	30	1	2	3	4	5	6	7

PATERNITY LEAVE

In the USA, there is no provision in law for paid paternity leave.

In practice, most fathers take some time off around the birth of a child, usually either unpaid leave or as part of their paid leave.

Trade unions and enlightened employers are gradually recognizing the importance of this time and are beginning to include paternity leave in their contracts.

In Scandinavian countries fathers receive pay while taking paternity leave which means that nearly all fathers take it, to the benefit of all concerned. The family group is strengthened and bonded.

YOUR RIGHTS

In an ideal world, every pregnant woman would be able to take time off both before and after the birth of her baby. The time before the birth would be spent resting, preparing, and daydreaming; the time after the birth would be spent adjusting to parenthood, getting back to prepregnancy shape, and enjoying the new baby. Sadly, in reality, working women seldom have the luxury of time.

BENEFITS FROM YOUR EMPLOYER

Benefits for new mothers (and fathers) are woefully lacking in the United States. As of this writing, the law mandates simply that companies with more than 15 employees must treat pregnancy like "any other" medical disability. Of course, pregnancy is not a disability, and this thinking encourages many employers and employees to view pregnant women as incapable, unwell, and even unstable. This, in turn, can create difficulties for women negotiating for maternity leave and benefits – employers often rationalize discrimination against pregnant women and new mothers.

However, there are bright spots for working women. Many employers exceed the minimum requirements of the law in this area. You are more likely to get good benefits and good treatment in a large company competing to attract and keep young talent. If you work for a small company, you are really at the mercy of management. A small company may be very paternalistic – or, perhaps more likely, it could be totally unsympathetic to your concerns.

It pays to have a plan of attack when approaching your employer to negotiate your leave and your return to work. Thoroughly research the maternity benefits, sick leave, insurance policies, and disability provisions that have been offered in the past, and decide what your ideal maternity leave would be. Then reconcile the two into a plan that you feel your employer may reasonably meet. You may not get everything you ask for but, on the other hand, it probably doesn't hurt to ask.

BENEFITS FROM THE GOVERNMENT

If you fall into a low-income category, you may be eligible to receive Women, Infants, and Children's (WIC) supplements, food stamps, welfare, Medicaid, and other government benefits. Many social services are available; unfortunately, pregnant women must be persistent in their investigation. For example, in New York City, the Human Resources Administration sponsors the Teen Age Services Act program, which helps poor mothers under the age of 18. Your phone book is an excellent place to start looking for help. Blue pages list government agencies; comb these listings, underline any entries that seem remotely related to maternity benefits, and call them and ask about the benefits you may be entitled to receive.

Maternity leave

To a great extent, you're dependent on your employer's policies. The Pregnancy Discrimination Act of 1978 requires companies with more than 15 employees to treat pregnancy as they would any medical disability. Many companies – especially large companies – offer better benefits than the law requires. Before revealing that you are pregnant, make quiet inquiries about the benefits other employees, especially those in comparable positions, have received. Your state's Department of Labor can help you determine your minimum leave. Again, your employer generally determines how much paid leave you will receive – but the better informed you are before broaching the subject, the better prepared you will be to negotiate.

Disability

Disability benefits are available to pregnant women in many states. Call your state disability office to determine what you are entitled to (they may be able to tell you what the standard pregnancy disability allowance is), and ask them to send you the correct forms; fill out your section and give the form to your doctor to complete and return. Most human resources personnel, as well as obstetric nurses and managers, will be quite conversant with disability procedures, so ask for help and information.

Medical Coverage

If you are employed and have medical benefits, it is advisable to look into pregnancy benefits before you get pregnant. If you are married, your husband's medical coverage may also play a part here. Make every effort to get covered before you get pregnant – otherwise the insurance company may not pay for your prenatal treatment and delivery costs.

Government Assistance

Government agencies have programs to help you get adequate medical treatment for you and your baby. Check with state and local health departments to find out what is available. The federal government operates clinics for women in many states, as well as immunization programs and well-baby clinics. The Women, Infants, and Children's Supplementary Food program (WIC) provides nutritious food, welfare, and Medicaid.

The 1993 Family Leave Act requires employers with more than 50 workers to allow up to 12 weeks of unpaid leave for family emergencies, including the birth of a child. Both fathers and mothers may take advantage of this benefit.

Some social service programs have been curtailed in recent years, but there has been renewed concern as the effects of these cutbacks start to appear as public-health problems. Social workers, pediatric and obstetric nurses, and doctors and midwives can be excellent sources of information about what's available in your area.

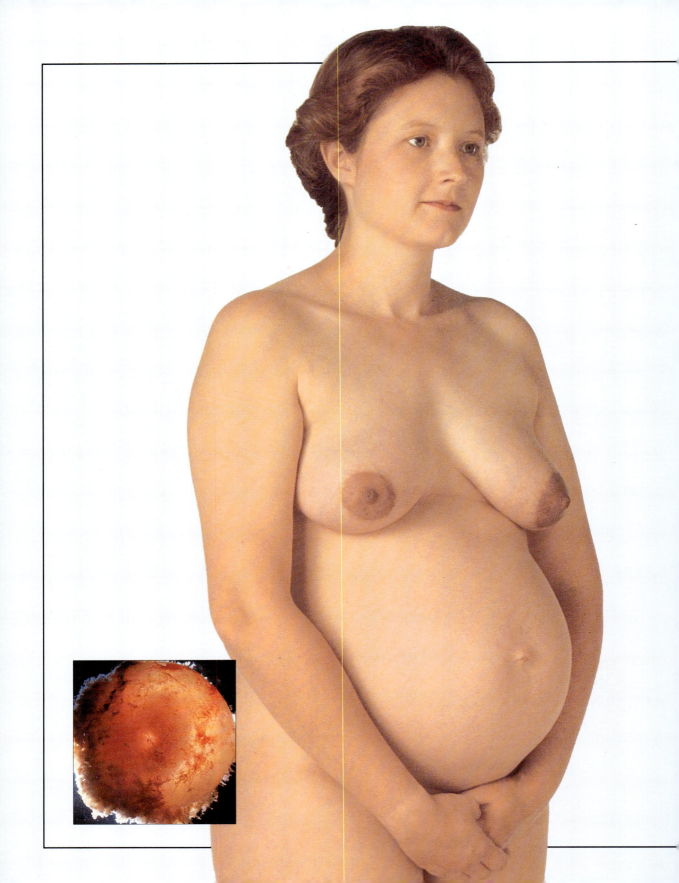

2

You and your

DEVELOPING

baby

The month-by-month development of your baby is truly exciting and dramatic. Understanding exactly how the fetus grows will help you establish a relationship with your child even before birth.

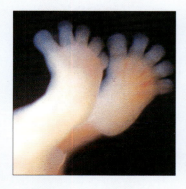

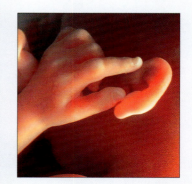

FIRST TRIMESTER

During pregnancy, the trimesters are the major milestones of the mother-to-be. Rather than representing three three-month periods, they are periods of uneven length and are defined by the physiology of fetal growth. However, by convention, the trimesters date from presumed conception (two weeks after your LMP), and the first trimester represents the first 12 weeks of your baby's fetal life. The second trimester ends at 28 weeks, and the third trimester encompasses the rest of your pregnancy.

During the first trimester, your body adjusts to pregnancy. At the beginning, you won't look pregnant, and you may not feel pregnant either, but the activities of your hormones will soon start to affect you in various ways. Your moods may change capriciously, your libido may decrease or increase, and you may find that your appetite changes and that you prefer simpler, blander food.

PHYSICAL CHANGES

Your pregnant body is having to work hard to accommodate the developing embryo and the placenta. Pregnancy induces a higher metabolic rate – between 10 percent and 25 percent higher than normal – which means that the body accelerates all of its functions. The work level of your heart rises steeply, almost to the maximum level that will be maintained throughout the rest of the pregnancy. Your heart rate rises too, and will continue to do so until the middle of the second trimester. Your breathing becomes more rapid as you now send more oxygen to the fetus and exhale more carbon dioxide.

Owing to the action of estrogen and progesterone, your breasts quickly become larger and heavier, and are usually tender to the touch from very early on. Fatty deposits are increased, and new milk ducts grow. The areola around the nipple becomes darker and develops little nodules called Montgomery's tubercles. Underneath the skin, you will notice a network of bluish lines appearing as blood supply to the breasts increases.

Your uterus enlarges even in early pregnancy, but it cannot be felt through the abdominal wall until the end of the first trimester, when it begins to rise above the pelvic brim. While it is still low in the pelvis, your uterus will increasingly press upon your bladder as it enlarges, so that you will almost certainly find that you need to urinate more often.

In addition, the muscle fibers of your uterus begin to thicken until it becomes very solid. However, you probably won't notice any increase in your waistline until the end of this trimester.

TAKING CARE OF YOURSELF

You have an increased need for carbohydrates and protein to supply your growing baby and the placenta, as well as your uterus and breasts, so it is imperative that you eat healthfully right from the beginning of your pregnancy. You will have an increased need for water and suitable beverages, so try to drink at least eight glasses of fluid a day. Make sure, too, that you are getting plenty of rest. Drugs, caffeine, alcohol, and smoking should be avoided throughout your entire pregnancy, but particularly at this time.

Clothes Make sure that your clothes are comfortable. While there is probably no need to invest in maternity clothes just yet, there's nothing worse than having to put up with your clothes feeling tight and uncomfortable, even if it's only for a few days, so do make sure that you keep one step ahead of your increasing size. However, you will almost certainly need a larger bra from early on, and this should be a properly fitted maternity bra (see **Maternity wear**, p.145).

YOUR PRENATAL CARE

Your doctor may be the one who confirms your pregnancy, or you may make an appointment with a prenatal clinic as soon as you have a positive test result. (If this is the case, you may not be seen immediately.) At the first visit, you will be asked about yourself and about your family's medical histories, and you will have a thorough physical examination, which will include urine and blood tests.

MAKING PLANS

Your doctor will be able to advise you as to the childbirth options that are open to you. You'll need to start thinking about the type of delivery you want and where you are most likely to get it. Books like this one can help you determine your choices in childbirth, as well as providing in-depth information on aspects of pregnancy, birth, and baby care. You will also want to talk to friends and relatives about their childbirth experiences.

Soon after pregnancy is confirmed, most women are unable to resist buying their unborn babies at least one small gift, such as a teddy bear, although many feel that to do more than this is to "tempt fate."

If you feel inclined to do so, this is the time to start keeping a journal, so that you will have a complete record of your pregnancy.

YOUR PREGNANCY

Finding out that you are pregnant, especially for the first time, is extremely exciting, and you will undoubtedly long for the physical signs that will confirm the pregnancy test.

• *Your breasts will grow larger, heavier, and more sensitive*

• *The pigmentation of your nipples and any moles and freckles will increase*

• *You may feel very tired*

• *You will probably experience nausea, especially first thing in the morning*

Your appetite in pregnancy
You may experience unusual food cravings, or you may avoid foods that you normally like.

SECOND TRIMESTER

YOUR WEIGHT GAIN

During the second 3 months, you will probably gain approximately 12lb.

Of this, only about 2lb will actually be your baby. The rest is made up of the baby's support system (such as the placenta and amniotic fluid), your enlarged uterus and breasts, and your increased blood and fluid volume. Maternal fat stores will usually account for approximately the same weight gain as your growing baby.

Now is the time when pregnancy is well established and many of the minor complaints associated with early pregnancy will have disappeared. It is, however, the time when certain tests may be done. Amniocentesis, for example, will be offered to women over 35, to those with a family history of congenital abnormalities, and to those who have suffered repeated miscarriages.

PHYSICAL CHANGES

You may notice that your nipples begin to secrete colostrum. Your waistline will disappear, and you will now "look" pregnant. Pigmentation may increase (see p.140). Your gums may become slightly spongy, probably owing to the action of pregnancy hormones. However, there is no evidence for increased dental decay during pregnancy and absolutely no evidence to suggest that there is any truth in the saying "a tooth lost for every child."

Digestion The entire musculature of your intestinal tract is relaxed, and this is the cause of many of the minor discomforts in pregnancy.

Esophageal reflux may cause heartburn because of the relaxation of the sphincter at the top of the stomach. Gastric secretion is also reduced, and therefore food remains in the stomach longer.

The relaxed intestinal muscle also leads to fewer bowel movements and, although this permits more complete absorption of the nutrients in foodstuffs, it can also often lead to constipation.

Your increasing size Once your uterus has grown above your pelvis, your waistline will begin to disappear, and you will need to wear larger and looser clothing (see p.144).

On the other hand, the second trimester is a classic time for women to be told that they look small for dates. If this happens to you, don't worry. How big you will look will depend on many factors, including your height and build; whether this is your first pregnancy or not, as the uterine muscle tends to get stretched after the first child; and the size of your baby. If your doctor is satisfied with the progress of pregnancy, you should be too.

TAKING CARE OF YOURSELF

This is the trimester in which you will gain the most weight overall (approximately 12lb) and it is essential that you continue to eat well (see p.112). Your posture may also change as the muscles of the abdominal wall become stretched in order to accommodate your enlarging uterus.
As your uterus enlarges it will produce an alteration in your center of gravity because you are carrying an increasing amount of weight in front. Leaning backward to try and counter this may result in backache (see also p.142).

Backache This usually happens because of the increased blood flow to your pelvis, which causes some softening and relaxation of the ligaments of the sacroiliac joints that join your pelvic bones to your spine at the back. In addition, the ligaments and the cartilage at the front of your pelvis also loosen, so the mobility of these joints is slightly increased.

To prevent backache, sit with your back straight and don't slouch, don't wear high-heeled shoes, and preferably sit on a hard chair or the floor. Always bend with a straight back or, if lifting, bend from the knees and lift from a crouching position. Avoid lifting if you possibly can (see also p.142).

YOUR PRENATAL CARE

Regular checks of your urine, weight, and blood pressure may be augmented by testing for chromosomal defects. From this time, too, your doctor will concentrate on measuring the adequate growth of your fetus. He or she will palpate your abdomen to feel the size and shape of the uterus and check for the height of the fundus (see p.160), and will listen for the baby's heartbeat.

During the fourth month you will probably have a sonogram, and it will give you a special thrill to see your baby for the first time. You will be able to hear the incredibly fast heartbeat (see column, p.161), and you may be able to see your baby moving.

PREPARING FOR BABY

Toward the end of this trimester, when you are still feeling good and full of energy, is the ideal time to prepare your baby's room (see p.222) and shop for the layette and baby equipment (see pp.224 & 226).

YOUR PREGNANCY

During the second trimester, you will begin to feel comfortable with being pregnant. You will enjoy the sensation of your baby moving within you, and will feel energetic and full of life.

- *Your libido will return or increase – it is not uncommon for women to experience orgasm or multiple orgasm for the first time*

- *Your abdomen will become rounded – you will lose your waistline and "look" pregnant*

- *Pigmentation will continue to increase and you may notice a darker line developing down the center of your abdomen – the* linea nigra *(see p.140)*

- *You may suffer from indigestion and rib pain*

Hormonal effects
As the placenta takes over the production of pregnancy hormones, your hormone levels should begin to balance out. This means that you will feel more serene and positive than you did in the first trimester. Your appearance will also benefit from thicker and shinier hair and a clear and glowing complexion.

THIRD TRIMESTER

You will probably feel anxious about labor and wish you could have the baby right away. This doesn't mean that there is anything wrong with your baby. The sense of urgency is due to metabolic changes in the brain. Subtle shifts have gone on in each trimester, bringing about the fatigue of the first, the elation and vigor of the second, and now the anxiety of the third.

YOUR WEIGHT GAIN

During the final months, you will probably gain approximately 10lb.

Of this, approximately 6–8lb will be accounted for by your baby. The rest is made up of the baby's support system (the placenta and amniotic fluid), your enlarged uterus and breasts, and your increased blood volume. Maternal fat stores will usually account for approximately the same weight gain as your baby.

PHYSICAL CHANGES

Your size is now increasing rapidly, and you are bound to feel tired. You may find that you are not sleeping as well as usual, and this will increase your need for rest (see opposite). As your ligaments stretch and loosen, walking even short distances may become increasingly uncomfortable. Once your baby has settled into your pelvis, you will find that breathlessness will diminish because the pressure on your diaphragm is relieved.

Breathing Because of the reduced movement of the diaphragm as the baby grows bigger in the abdomen, pregnant women breathe more deeply, taking more air in with each breath, which allows for more efficient consumption of oxygen. This raises the ventilation rate from the normal seven liters of air per minute to ten liters (three pints per minute to five pints), an increase of more than 40 percent. However, the oxygen requirements are increased by only 20 percent. This leads to overbreathing, which means that more carbon dioxide is exhaled per breath than normal. The low carbon dioxide in the blood gives rise to a shortness of breath, and this may be bothersome during this trimester. Relief should come when your baby engages in your pelvis (lightening). Meanwhile, sit in a semi-propped position and avoid overdoing things.

Possible problems Hypertension (high blood pressure – see p.161) may be a problem in later pregnancy. The major warning signs are swollen and puffy hands, wrists, ankles, feet, and face. Preeclampsia (see p.204) may interfere with the functioning of the placenta and prevent it from transporting nutrients to your baby efficiently. You may have to be hospitalized.

CARING FOR YOURSELF

As the third trimester continues, the extra weight you are carrying can result in more backache and cause you to feel continually tired. Sleep can become a problem as you get bigger, as very few positions in bed seem to be comfortable. Don't be tempted to take sleeping pills – they will make the baby sleepy, too. Take your time with everything during the last month, and make certain you get adequate rest; catnap whenever you can and set aside periods when you can relax – even if you don't sleep. As your desire for making love may diminish or be frustrated by your increasing size, you may find that massage can help you relax and unwind, particularly if your partner makes it sensual.

Continue to eat lots of fresh fruit and vegetables and drink at least eight glasses of fluid per day. You will probably pass urine more often and you may find that you are constipated at times.

YOUR PRENATAL CARE

You will be checked more frequently during this time. There are many tests that your doctor may use to judge the baby's health or well-being, such as ultrasound, fetal heart rate monitoring, and hormonal measurements, and your doctor will discuss at each stage what is being done and why. Unlike the special tests in the second trimester – amniocentesis, chorionic villus sampling, and cordocentesis (see pp.164 & 165) – none of the tests at this time are invasive of the uterus. Urine and blood pressure testing will be done frequently as will checks for possible swelling of your feet and hands. From the 36th week until the onset of labor you will be seen and checked at weekly intervals.

PREPARING FOR BABY

Toward the end of this trimester, you should have completed your baby's layette, sorted out the nursery, and purchased the essential equipment. You are likely to have stopped working some time before your due date and will be able to take life at your own pace. Labor may be increasingly on your mind, and some women do worry obsessively about it. Although no one can predict exactly what will happen during labor, as your experience will be unique, be reassured that the vast majority of births go without a hitch.

YOUR PREGNANCY

Practical matters such as attending childbirth classes and preparing your baby's clothes and room will vie with daydreaming and fantasizing about the new arrival.

- *You will probably be feeling easily tired, although you may find it hard to rest*

- *You will become increasingly aware of Braxton Hicks contractions (see p.250)*

- *You will have visited the hospital and become familiar with it and the staff. If you are having a home birth, you should have all the items you will need on hand*

You will be concerned about whether you can tell that you are in labor or not. Even for an experienced midwife or doctor, it is difficult to know when you are in established labor. Regularly occurring contractions and the appearance of the show are the classic signs.

Baby's clothes and accessories
Prior to the birth, you should have on hand a selection of baby clothes, diapers, and bedding.

MOTHER

At the end of the first month of pregnancy – 6 weeks after your last period and 4 weeks since conception – you probably won't be sure that you are pregnant, although you may have your suspicions. There are some pregnancy tests that will give you a positive result even at this early stage.

Symptoms   You will notice few, if any, symptoms at this stage, although you may feel slightly pre-menstrual and pass urine more frequently than usual. From a very early stage, your breasts will feel sore and heavy and the nipples tingle. Soon after, veins become visible under the skin on the surface of the breast. You may even feel sick at this stage.

Ovulation cycle   Once the embryo has implanted in the lining of your uterus, your normal ovula-tion cycle ceases. The corpus luteum (see p.26) in the ovary continues to secrete progesterone to keep the pregnancy healthy and viable, and to prevent menstrua-tion from occurring.

Cervix   Under the influence of progesterone, normal cervical mucus becomes very dense and thick, forming a plug. This mucus plug will remain in place until just before labor starts, when it will be expelled (the "show") as your cervix softens and dilates.

Uterus   The wall of your uterus softens so that the embryo can become firmly embedded. Your uterus enlarges almost from the moment of implantation.

FIRST 4 WEEKS
(Four weeks from conception; six weeks of pregnancy)

The fertilized egg becomes a ball of cells (blastocyst), which floats into the uterus and implants in the lining. The basis for your baby's future development is now laid down.

YOUR BABY'S PROGRESS

Once it has implanted, the embryo secretes chemicals that have two functions. First, they signal to your body that the embryo has arrived, and this triggers a number of changes in your body: your ovulation cycle and menses stop, the mucus in your cervix thickens, your uterine wall softens, and your breasts begin to grow. Second, your immune system is adjusted so that the embryo is not treated as foreign and rejected, but is allowed to grow. In addition, an outer layer of the blastocyst develops into a protective cocoon around the embryo. This cocoon will create the rudiments of the placenta and the support system in which the embryo will grow – the amniotic sac (the watery balloon in which it will float), the chorion (a safety cushion around the amniotic sac), and the yolk sac (which will manufacture blood cells until the liver takes over). The chorion then grows fingerlike projections, the chorionic villi, with which the cocoon burrows firmly into your uterine lining.

The cells specialize   Throughout these early weeks the embryo's cells become more specialized. There are now three layers of them, each destined to create different organs of the body. The innermost layer forms a primitive tube that will later develop into the lungs, liver, thyroid gland, pancreas, urinary tract, and bladder. The middle layer will become the skeleton, muscles (including the heart muscle), testes (or ovaries), kidneys, spleen, blood vessels, blood cells, and the deepest layer of skin, the dermis. The outer layer will provide the skin, sweat glands, nipples (and breasts, if it is a girl), hair, nails, tooth enamel, and the lenses of the eyes. These three cell layers differentiate to create an entire human body.

THE EMBRYO'S SUPPORT SYSTEM

The villi of the growing placenta intermingle with the maternal blood vessels of the uterine wall in such a way that they eventually become surrounded by "lakes" of blood. Maternal blood flows in and around these spaces and, because it is divided by only a cell or two from fetal blood, the exchange of nutrients and waste between fetus and mother can occur in these blood spaces. The placenta is a "hormone factory" pumping out hormones, such as human chorionic gonadotrophin (hCG), that are designed to sup-port a healthy pregnancy. Until the sixth week the embryo's blood cells are supplied by the yolk sac; after the end of the third week, his blood circulation is pumped by his own heart.

YOUR BABY AT FOUR WEEKS OF LIFE

YOUR BABY

The fourth week
Surrounding layers of chorion and amnion protect the embryo, and blocks of tissue, which will become the vertebrae can be seen forming. Between these grow bunches of nerves.

Before you may even know you are pregnant, the embryo reaches a critical stage in its development. It is therefore vital to plan for pregnancy.

Spinal cord *During the second week, a dark mark appears on the back of the embryo, denoting the position of the spinal cord.*

Heart *By the end of the third week, there is a heart that is now beginning to beat.*

Sensitivity *In the third week, the embryo enters a sensitive phase of development when all the major organs are forming. Embryos are generally robust but can be harmed by drugs, alcohol, smoking, infections, etc. Many embryos don't survive, largely because of serious chromosomal defects.*

The embryo has gill-like structures that will later become its jaw, neck, and part of the face

The rudimentary heart of the embryo bulges predominantly

The rudimentary spinal cord appears

BABY'S VITAL STATISTICS

By the end of this month, the embryo's length will be approximately $1/sin$ (4mm). It will weigh less than 0.03oz (1g).

Changing shape
By the end of this period, the embryo is no longer a hollow cluster of many cells. It is shrimp shaped – long and narrow with a slight waist in the middle. It has a top, a bottom, and sides. The bottom is shaped like a pointed tail. In the middle, the surface layer of cells, which will form the brain and nervous system, creases into 2 lengthwise folds. The groove that forms between them then closes over to form a tube that will become the spinal cord. The tube grows at the top end, and this will become the brain.

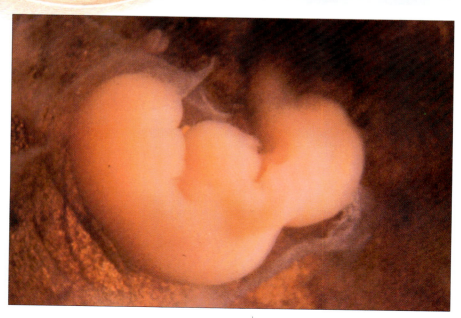

MOTHER

For some women, morning sickness, which can range from mild nausea to severe vomiting and can occur at any time (see also p.192), is one of the first signs that they are pregnant. Other changes happen now that may not be as discernible.

Metabolic requirements *Very early in pregnancy, the basal metabolic rate begins to increase and a woman who is pregnant requires a greater intake of protein and calories.*

Circulatory changes *The total blood volume begins to rise; about 25% of this is being used by the placental system.*

Genitals *The blood supply to the vagina and vulva increases quite rapidly, and they develop a purple coloration. The vaginal walls become softened and relaxed, and a watery substance is produced in increasing amounts. This, plus the shedding of vaginal cells, increases the total discharge from your vagina while you are pregnant.*

Breasts *Your breasts may start to swell or feel tender and heavier than usual. The skin around the areola begins to develop a softer, lighter area known as the secondary areola.*

Fatigue *You are likely to get tired more easily than usual and may even feel faint at times.*

Skin problems *If your face usually breaks out before your period, it is apt to do so again now. Alternatively, your skin may become dry and itchy.*

UP TO 8 WEEKS
(Eight weeks from conception; ten weeks of pregnancy)

This is a time of extremely rapid and crucial development as your baby quadruples in size. Lying at the center of a large placental cocoon, the embryo is still very tiny. Its cells are constantly differentiating to form new structures.

YOUR BABY'S PROGRESS

Within the tube that will ultimately become the brain and spinal cord, the embryo's cells multiply at a phenomenal rate, then move away to the areas where they will become active. Nerve cells that will form the brain travel along pathways that are being laid down by glial (glue) cells. These cells enable the nerve cells to move toward one another, connect, and become active.

The head is growing rapidly to accommodate the enlarging brain, and the body becomes less curved. A neck begins to develop and the primeval tail disappears.

The skin now starts to differentiate into its two layers, and the sweat glands and sebaceous (oil-producing) glands begin to develop. Hair then starts to grow from the hair follicles so that the skin becomes downy. All the major organs develop. The heart takes on its final form and beats strongly. Stomach, liver, spleen, appendix, and intestines develop. The intestine becomes so long it forms a loop, the circulatory system is established, and most muscles begin to attain their final form.

Facial features Under the skin on its face, primitive facial bones have now emerged and are fusing together. One of these goes down between the eyes and ends on either side of the nostrils, thus forming the nose and the middle of the upper lip. Two others appear under the eyes, forming the cheeks and sides of the upper lip. Two more grow under the mouth, fusing to form the lower lip and chin. All this provides the framework to which the facial muscles become attached, thus enabling the embryo's face to move. Some pigment can already be detected in the eyes, which are covered and are very far apart. The internal and external parts of the ears begin to form and the taste buds start developing. The tooth buds of all non-permanent teeth are now in place.

Arms and legs Embryonic limbs continue to develop. Wrists and fingers appear on the arm buds, which lengthen and project forward. The arms become bent at the elbow. Touchpads form on the fingertips. Leg buds sprout, then develop three distinct sections – thigh, calf, and foot. Toes start to appear. At this stage, the embryo's arms and hands develop faster than her legs and feet. This trend will continue after birth – your baby will be able to grasp objects long before she can walk.

YOUR BABY AT EIGHT WEEKS OF LIFE

YOUR BABY

Color-enhanced scan
The developing umbilical cord and placenta are clearly visible in the top right-hand corner of the sonogram.

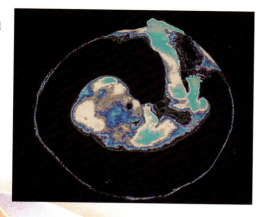

The face begins to develop, and eyes and nose appear

Fingers and toes are apparent

The heart beats and can now be heard

Body begins to straighten

The tail is reabsorbed

Nutrients pass from you into the placenta and the umbilical cord to feed the embryo, which needs more and more nourishment to support its rapid growth.

Heart rate *The heart beats at 140–150 per minute, approximately twice the rate of yours.*

Body shape *The embryo's head is still very large in comparison to the body and is bent forward on the chest. The body begins to straighten and elongate.*

Internal organs *All organs will now be present, and most major structures will have been formed.*

Reflexes *The embryo can respond to touch, though you won't be able to feel it move.*

BABY'S VITAL STATISTICS
By the end of this month, its crown-to-rump length will be 1in (2.5cm), and it will weigh approximately 0.1oz (3g).

External features
The embryo's eyes become pigmented, and the first visible signs of the nostrils, lips, and ears also appear. The rudimentary ears now divide into inner and outer sections, the eyelids form, and the tip of the nose can be seen. The embryo's muscles start to build, and by the seventh week of life the first embryonic movement can be detected using ultrasound. The picture shows the embryo at 6 weeks of development since conception.

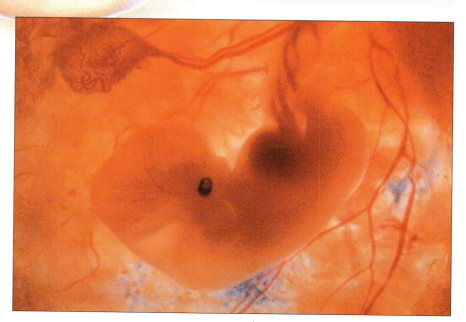

MOTHER

You will probably start to feel better during this month, particularly if you have been suffering very badly with nausea and vomiting.

Weight *You will probably begin to gain weight, as baby and baby's support system grow rapidly.*

Hormones *Your fluctuating hormones begin to settle down and you will probably feel much less emotionally unbalanced and vulnerable.*

Fundal height *Your developing baby is causing the fundus (see External examination p.160) of your uterus to rise through the pelvic brim where it can be felt. Your doctor will begin to gently palpate your abdomen to check how the baby is developing.*

Outlook *If you had been anxious about the pregnancy, you will now feel more relaxed, as the risk of miscarriage diminishes greatly.*

Circulatory system *Your cardiac output has reached almost the maximum level, which will be maintained throughout pregnancy. To lower your blood pressure, the arteries and veins in your extremities relax, so your hands and feet are nearly always warm.*

UP TO 12 WEEKS
(12 weeks from conception; 14 weeks of pregnancy)

Fourteen weeks after your LMP, all your baby's major organs have formed and his intestines are sealed in the abdominal cavity. He now starts to grow and mature.

YOUR BABY'S PROGRESS

Nine weeks after conception, your baby is recognizable as a human being, and he will now be called a fetus (offspring) rather than an embryo. His head is very large compared to the rest of his body, and by 12 weeks of life will be about one-third of his whole length. His eyes are completely formed, although the eyelids are still developing and remain closed. His face, too, is completely formed. His trunk has straightened, and the first bone tissue and ribs appear. The fingers and toes have nails and some hair may even have grown. His external genital organs are now growing and the sex of your baby may already be discernable by ultrasound. Internally, his heart is beating between 110 and 160 times per minute, and the circulatory system continues to develop. The fetus swallows amniotic fluid and excretes it as urine.

His sucking reflex is establishing itself – his lips purse, his head turns, and his forehead wrinkles. The muscles he will use after birth for breathing and swallowing are also being exercised.

In fact, by the end of this month your baby will have discovered movement and will begin to move vigorously, although you probably won't be able to feel his movements until the fourth month.

Blood cell production   While your baby will continue to rely on the placenta for nourishment, oxygen, and the clearance of waste until he is born, a system of blood cell formation that will eventually support independent life is essential. Toward the end of this month, the yolk sac becomes superfluous as its task of producing blood cells is taken over by your baby's developing bone marrow, liver, and spleen.

HIS SUPPORT SYSTEM

At this point, the placenta is developing very quickly, ensuring a rich network of blood vessels to provide your baby with vital nourishment. Now the layers thicken and grow until the chorion and membranes cover the entire inner surface area of the uterus. The umbilical cord is now completely mature and consists of three intertwined blood vessels in a fatty sheath. The large vein carries nutrients and oxygen-rich blood to the fetus, while the two smaller arteries carry waste products and oxygen-poor blood from the fetus to the placenta. The umbilical cord is coiled like a spring because the sheath is longer than the blood vessels, allowing him plenty of room for movement without the risk of damaging his lifeline.

YOUR BABY AT 12 WEEKS OF LIFE

YOUR BABY

Feet and hands
Your baby's fingers and toes are developing rapidly and becoming fully formed.

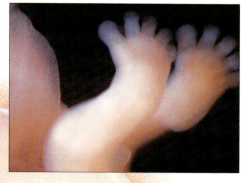

His head and neck extend and grow

His eyes move around to the front of his face but are still wide apart

Fine hair covers his whole body

His external ears move up from the neck (where they were gill-like growths) to their places on the side of his head

External genitals differentiate

Your baby is fully formed; now he needs to mature. He is very active at this stage, although you won't feel him yet.

Bones In the form of flexible cartilage, his bones are rapidly developing.

Movements He jerks his body, bends his arms and legs, and has an occasional hiccup.

Jaws These already show 32 permanent tooth buds.

Amniotic sac The fetus floats comfortably in a warm bath of amniotic fluid (the temperature of the amniotic fluid is higher than your own body temperature). He has plenty of space for movement.

BABY'S VITAL STATISTICS

By the end of this month, his crown-to-rump length will be 3.5in (9cm), and he will weigh 1.7oz (48g).

12-week-old fetus
The profile has become more human and the features are much more clearly defined. This fetus now has a definite chin, a large forehead, and a button nose. His eyelids have begun to develop across his fully formed eyes, and he is beginning to respond to external stimuli – if his mother's abdomen is poked, he will try to wriggle away. A sonogram would reveal fetal movements at this stage, but these cannot be felt by the mother until next month at the earliest.

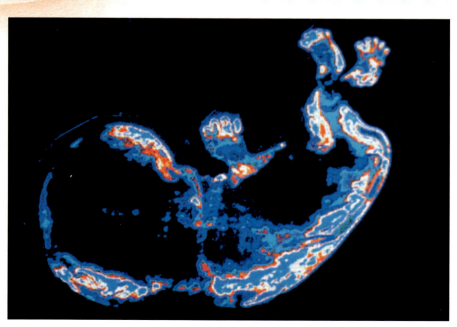

MOTHER

You are showing many signs that pregnancy is advancing well, although you may not have gained much weight. You will probably have extra vitality and energy.

Nipples *They are darkening in color as your skin becomes more deeply pigmented. They may tingle and feel sore; the surface veins are becoming more prominent.*

Heart *It is working twice as hard as before, putting out sufficient blood (over 6 quarts per minute) to maintain the increasing needs of your vital organs. The uterus and skin need twice as much blood as usual and the kidneys 25% more.*

Abdomen *A dark line, called the* linea nigra, *may develop down the center of your abdomen. Your uterus has been forced out of the pelvic cavity into your abdomen by your growing baby and can be felt on examination.*

Quickening *Toward the end of this month, you will probably feel your baby moving – a bubbling, fluttering sensation like butterflies, little fishes, or gas! First time mothers feel movements later than women in subsequent pregnancies (see p.176).*

UP TO 16 WEEKS
(16 weeks from conception; 18 weeks of pregnancy)

The second trimester of pregnancy starts from 12 weeks from conception – 14 weeks of pregnancy. Your baby is steadily growing. You will probably have a sonogram at this time, which may reveal the baby's sex. The diameter of her head will be measured to confirm the EDD.

YOUR BABY'S PROGRESS

Your baby is looking more and more human, with legs longer than arms and the parts of her legs in proportion. The fetal skeleton continues to produce more bone and those parts that contain sufficient calcium can be seen in an X-ray.

The fetus now contains the same number of nerve cells as an adult. The nerves from the brain begin to be coated in a layer of protective fat known as myelin. This is an important step in their maturation because it facilitates the passage of messages to and from the brain. Connections between nerves and muscles are established so that your baby's well-formed limbs will be able to move around their joints when muscles are stimulated to contract and relax. Now that her arms are long enough, her hands can grasp each other if they touch accidentally, and she can form fists. However, movements are not yet under the control of the brain. Nor do they register with you at first because the fetus is not big enough to activate the nerve endings on your uterine wall. Second-time mothers tend to feel fetal activity sooner (see p.176).

The fetus' external genital organs acquire a more distinctive appearance. A girl's vaginal plate, the precursor to her vagina, is clearly developing, and a boy's testes are at the deep inguinal ring, and well on their way to descending into the scrotum.

HER SUPPORT SYSTEM

The placenta is producing the increasing amounts of chorionic gonadotrophin, estrogen, and progesterone that are needed throughout pregnancy. It also produces an assortment of other hormones that maintain the health of the uterus, and play an essential part in the growth and development of the mother's breasts in preparation for lactation. The placenta forms a barrier against general infection, although not against viruses, such as rubella (German measles) and AIDS, and toxic substances such as alcohol and nicotine. By the end of the 16th week, the placenta has grown in thickness to about one-half inch and measures three and a half inches across.

Growth will continue until at term it reaches a weight of one pound, a thickness of an inch and a half, and a diameter of eight to ten inches. The placenta is firmly attached to the uterine wall (usually the upper part).

YOUR BABY AT 16 WEEKS OF LIFE

Sonogram

At this time, your baby's nose, fingers, and toes can be seen clearly. Her head is still large in comparison to her body.

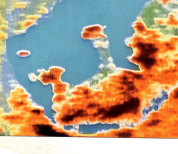

Tiny fingernails are visible

Respiratory movements can now be detected as can the protective "brown fat"

Eyelids have formed and are fused shut. They will open in the sixth month

YOUR BABY

Your baby's skin is transparent, and her blood vessels can be seen clearly, as can her bones, which are beginning to harden throughout her body.

Taste buds *They have begun to develop on her tongue.*

Ears *As the tiny bones inside her ears harden, she begins to hear sounds – your voice, your heart, and your digestion rumbling.*

Lungs *They are developing and she "breathes" the amniotic fluid. She will continue to receive oxygen via the placenta until she is born.*

BABY'S VITAL STATISTICS

By the end of this month, her crown-to-rump length will be about 5$\frac{1}{2}$in (13.5cm), and she will weigh 6oz (180g).

Head and face

Her face is developing and becoming more human in appearance, and she begins to make her first facial expressions. She can frown, squint, and grimace. Eyebrows and eyelashes start to grow; the hair on her head becomes slightly coarser and is colored by special pigment cells. Her ears stand away from the head, and her eyes now look straight ahead, although they are still widely spaced. The retinas of her eyes have become sensitive to light, although they remain covered by her eyelids, and she is aware of bright light from outside her mother's abdominal wall.

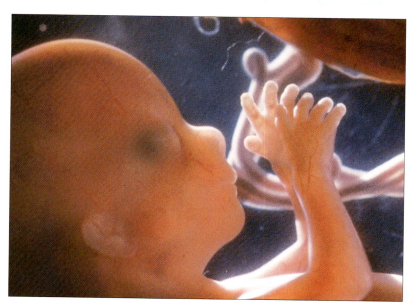

MOTHER

At this time, well into your second trimester, you'll probably notice a mood change. Any nausea should have disappeared, and your energy and sense of fun should have returned.

Movements *If you did not feel your baby move earlier, you will certainly feel him now. The experience of the baby "quickening" is wonderful.*

Abdomen *Your waistline has disappeared and you may notice stretch marks.*

Skin *Dilated blood vessels may cause tiny red marks (spider nevi) to appear on your face, shoulders, and arms. These should disappear after the birth.*

Minor complaints *The gums may become spongy, probably from hormonal influences. You may experience heartburn and constipation. The risk of bladder infections increases because of the relaxation of the smooth muscle in the urinary tract.*

Metabolic changes *Your thyroid gland becomes more active; one result can be a tendency to perspire more heavily than usual. Your breathing will become deeper, and there may be some shortness of breath when you exercise.*

UP TO 20 WEEKS
(20 weeks from conception; 22 weeks of pregnancy)

Your baby has developed enough to have a nervous system and muscles capable of allowing movement. Because he is still so small compared to the amount of amniotic fluid, he can swim up and down and be in any position at any particular time.

YOUR BABY'S PROGRESS

Starting now, from 19 weeks after your LMP, your baby's rapid growth rate, except for weight gain, starts to slow down and he matures in other ways. He begins to build up his defense systems.

A sheath begins to form around the nerves in his spinal cord to protect them from possible damage. He also has his own primitive immune system, with which he can partially defend himself against some infections. To produce body heat and maintain his temperature, your baby needs specialized fatty tissue. This is provided by a substance known as "brown fat," which began to form during the fourth month. Now, deposits of brown fat begin to build up in areas of his body such as his neck, chest, and crotch. This will continue until term. One of the reasons that premature babies are so vulnerable is that they have insufficient amounts of brown fat, and so are unable to keep themselves warm.

Your baby's skin will continue to grow, although it will be red and wrinkled because there is so little fat underneath it. His body begins to get plumper. The sebaceous glands become active and produce a waxy, greasy substance (known as the *vernix caseosa*), which provides his skin with a protective coating during its long immersion in the amniotic fluid.

Your baby's body is also covered with fine hair called lanugo. Nobody is quite sure of the purpose of this hair, but it may help to regulate his body temperature, or it may be there to hold the protective *vernix caseosa* in place.

His movements As his nerve fibers become connected and his muscle development and strength increase, his movements are more purposeful and coordinated. He embarks on his own exercise program – stretching, grasping, turning – to build up his muscles, improve his motor ability, and strengthen his bones. These movements can make your abdomen sore.

Sex organs A baby boy's scrotum is solid at this stage. A baby girl's vagina starts to become hollow, and her ovaries contain about 7 million ova, which will be reduced to approximately 2 million at birth. By the time she reaches puberty, between 200,000 and 500,000 ova will be left, and she will release only 400–500 of these during her adult life – approximately one per month. Nipples and underlying mammary glands develop in both sexes.

YOUR BABY AT 20 WEEKS OF LIFE

YOUR BABY

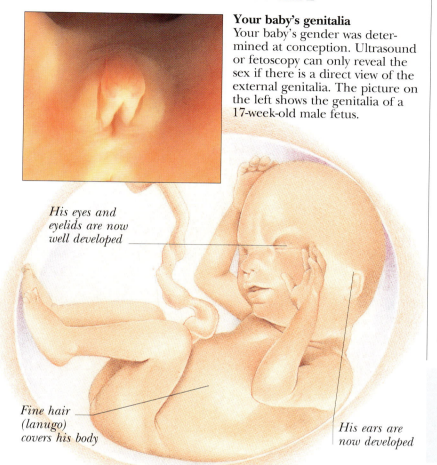

Your baby's genitalia
Your baby's gender was determined at conception. Ultrasound or fetoscopy can only reveal the sex if there is a direct view of the external genitalia. The picture on the left shows the genitalia of a 17-week-old male fetus.

His eyes and eyelids are now well developed

Fine hair (lanugo) covers his body

His ears are now developed

Although he is well developed, your baby cannot yet survive outside your uterus. His lungs and digestive system are not fully formed, nor is he fully able to maintain his own body heat.

Vernix caseosa *The waxy coating produced by your baby's oil glands keeps his skin supple.*

Taste *He can now distinguish sweet from bitter.*

Touch *His skin is sensitive to touch, and he will move in response to any pressure that is put on the abdomen.*

Teeth *Hidden in his gums, many of his "baby" teeth have already been formed.*

Heartbeat *This can now be heard by less sensitive stethoscopes.*

BABY'S VITAL STATISTICS

By the end of this month, his crown-to-rump length will be $7^{1}/_{3}$in (18.5cm), and he will weigh 1lb (0.5kg).

His hearing
He can hear the sounds of blood flowing through your blood vessels, your heart beating, and your stomach rumbling. He can hear sounds from outside the uterus and will respond to sound, rhythm, and melody from now on. You could try singing and talking to your unborn child. After he is born, he will probably be soothed by the same songs, finding them reassuring, and he will feel safe and secure when he hears his parents' voices.

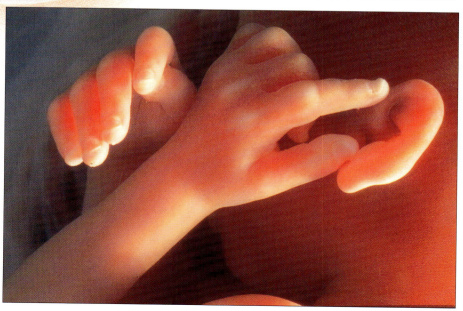

Now that fetal movements are well established, you should be feeling some every day. When she hiccups, for example, you may feel a sudden jerk.

Weight *You will be putting on weight at the rate of about 1lb (0.5kg) per week. Don't worry if you are told you look "small for dates." Your size will depend on many factors, such as your build, stature, carriage, and the amount of amniotic fluid inside.*

Aches and pains *As your baby grows, and your uterus along with her, they push upward against your rib cage so that it will rise by about 2in (5cm) and your lower ribs will spread outward. This can give you rib pain and, because your baby is now beginning to press up on your stomach, you may also start to have bouts of indigestion and heartburn (see p.190). As your uterine muscle stretches, you may get stitchlike pains down the sides of your abdomen.*

UP TO 24 WEEKS
(24 weeks from conception; 26 weeks of pregnancy)

Your baby is growing taller and stronger, while her movements are becoming more complex. She is also showing signs of sensitivity, awareness, and intelligence.

YOUR BABY'S PROGRESS

She is still red and skinny, but she will soon start to put on weight. Any extensive wrinkling of the skin is due to a lack of subcutaneous fat and a relative increase in the amount of skin.

Her body is growing faster than her head now, so that by the end of this month her proportions approximate those of a newborn baby. Her arms and legs now have their normal amount of muscle, her legs are in proportion to her body, and her bone centers are beginning to harden. The lines start to appear on the palms of her hands. The brain cells she will use for conscious thought now start to mature, and she begins to be able to remember and learn. (In one experiment, babies in the uterus were trained to kick in response to a specific vibration.)

The genitals are now completely differentiated; if the baby is a boy, testosterone-producing cells in the testes increase in number.

Her hearing Your baby can hear sound frequencies that are beyond your range, and she will move more in response to high frequencies than to low ones. She will also move her body in rhythm with your speech; and from this month on she will begin to respond to drumbeats by jumping up and down. Some mothers report having to leave concerts because their unborn babies would not keep still. If she hears a piece of music played frequently while she is in the uterus, she may discover that when she is grown up it is familiar to her – even if she can't remember ever hearing it before. Some musicians have said that they "knew" particular pieces of music and that they later discovered that these were played to them by their mothers while they were in the uterus.

She can also learn to recognize her father's voice from this month onward. A baby whose father talks to her while she is in the uterus can distinguish her father's voice in a roomful of people immediately after she is born, and will respond to it emotionally – for example, if she is upset, she will stop crying and calm down.

Her breathing Inside her lungs, air sacs are forming in ever-increasing numbers. They will continue to increase until eight years after she is born. Around them, the blood vessels that will help her to absorb oxygen and expel carbon dioxide are multiplying. In addition, her nostrils have now opened, and she is beginning to make breathing motions with her muscles, so that her system has plenty of breathing practice before she is born.

Your baby at 24 weeks of life

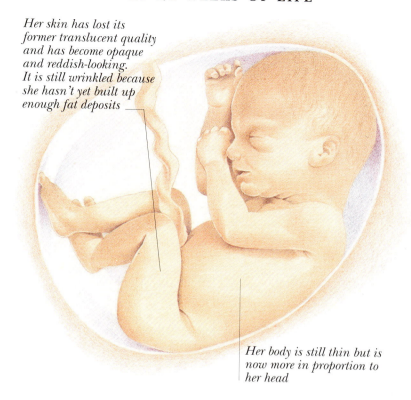

Her skin has lost its former translucent quality and has become opaque and reddish-looking. It is still wrinkled because she hasn't yet built up enough fat deposits

Her body is still thin but is now more in proportion to her head

Your baby

She continues to grow slowly and steadily. If she is born now, she would probably have a slim chance of survival.

Lungs The bronchi of her lungs are growing, although they are not yet mature.

Brain The patterns of her brain waves now resemble those of a full-term newborn child. The source of these brain waves is thought to be the cortex, the highly evolved part of the brain. She has now developed patterns of sleeping and waking.

Baby's vital statistics

By the end of this month, her crown-to-rump length will be 10in (25cm), and she will weigh just under 2lb (1kg).

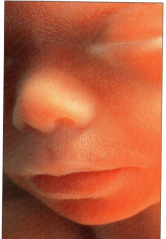

Facial features
The features of this 6-month-old fetus are very similar to those of an infant at birth. Lanugo, the downy hair, forms patterns because of the oblique way in which the hair roots are positioned in the skin.

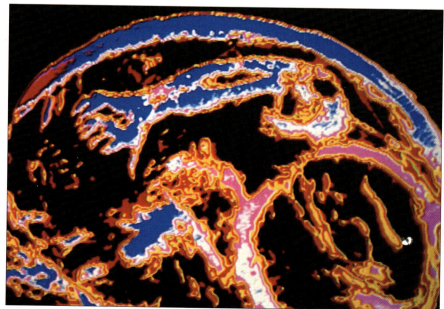

Ultrasound
The baby is growing bigger, putting on more weight, and taking up more and more of the uterus. At the top of the above view, which has been taken by ultrasound and then color enhanced, a fully formed arm, hand, and shoulder lie adjacent to the head.

This ends your second trimester. You may start to feel tired and, knowing that your baby just needs to mature, you may now begin to anticipate the birth.

Colostrum This sweet, watery fluid, less rich than breast milk and easier to digest, will probably have formed in your breasts. It will provide your baby with his first few meals before your milk comes through (see also p.304).

Urination Your growing baby will now be pressing against your bladder, causing you to pass urine more frequently.

Sleeping problems Few positions will be comfortable if you are very big. Lying on your side with one knee to your chest and the other stretched out will probably be most comfortable.

Low back pain Owing to a change in your center of gravity caused by the enlarged uterus, plus the slight loosening of the pelvic joints, you may experience backache. Wearing low-heeled shoes and sitting with a straight back on a hard chair or the floor will help. Avoid lifting if you can.

UP TO 28 WEEKS
(28 weeks from conception; 30 weeks of pregnancy)

Your baby is now so big that his position can be assessed by your doctor or midwife in an abdominal examination. This is the last month your baby will be able to turn a somersault.

YOUR BABY'S PROGRESS

Great changes take place in the nervous system this month. The brain grows larger (to fit inside the skull, it has to fold over and wrinkle up until it looks like a walnut), and the brain cells and nerve circuits are all fully linked and active. In addition, a protective fatty sheath begins to form around the nerve fibers, just as a similar sheath formed earlier around the spinal cord, and this fatty sheath will continue to develop until early adulthood. As a result, nerve impulses can travel faster, and your baby becomes capable of increasingly complex learning and movement.

Your baby starts preparing himself for birth. (If he were to be born prematurely, he would have an excellent chance of surviving. Even though such a baby may have some breathing problems and difficulty in keeping warm, modern special-care facilities should help him thrive.) Some fat is beginning to appear underneath his skin, which smoothes out, loses its wrinkles, and becomes more rounded. His coat of hairy lanugo may diminish to a patch on his back and shoulders. The membranes that sealed and protected his eyes during their growth will, by the beginning of this month, have fulfilled their function as his eyes are now fully formed and his eyelids have separated and allowed his eyes to open. He continues to develop his swallowing and sucking skills.

His breathing He has now developed his mature breathing rhythm, and the air sacs in his lungs start to prepare for the first breath he will take in the world outside the uterus. They line themselves with a coating of special cells and a fluid (surfactant) that will prevent them from collapsing.

His movements Over the course of this month, he will find he has less room to move around in, and will gradually give up moving around so much. He will wriggle uncomfortably if you have your body in a position that doesn't suit him (see p.176).

Orientation During his weeks of "gymnastics practice," he has done more than increase his muscle tone – he has developed the ability to orient himself in space. He will probably continue to lie in your uterus with his head upward during this month, although if he is maturing very fast he may turn upside down and settle into place for delivery slightly earlier than usual (engage). This is more common in first-born babies.

YOUR BABY AT 28 WEEKS OF LIFE

YOUR BABY

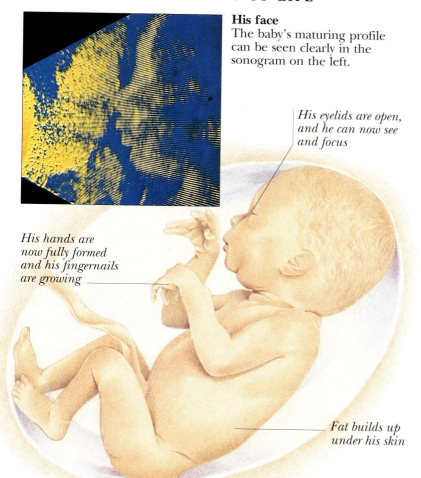

His face
The baby's maturing profile can be seen clearly in the sonogram on the left.

His eyelids are open, and he can now see and focus

His hands are now fully formed and his fingernails are growing

Fat builds up under his skin

Your baby continues to gain weight and to mature. He communicates with you by wriggling and kicking.

Temperature *He now begins to control his own body temperature.*

Fat *White fat begins to build up under his skin.*

Red blood cells *His bone marrow has now taken over full responsibility for the production of red blood cells.*

Urine *He passes urine into the amniotic fluid at the rate of about 1 pint ($^1/_2$ liter) every day.*

Genitals *The testes of boy babies descend into the groin and then into the scrotum (premature boy babies usually have undescended testicles when born).*

BABY'S VITAL STATISTICS

By the end of this month, his crown-to-rump length will be 11in (28cm), and he will weigh 3lb (1.5kg).

Your baby grows
His body is now growing plumper as the subcutaneous fat builds up under his skin, filling out the wrinkles. His eyebrows and eyelashes are fully developed, and the hair on his scalp is becoming longer. His eyelids have now opened, and he begins to practice seeing and focusing – the limitations of his field of vision (8–9in/20–25cm) at birth is thought to be related to how far he is able to see while he is in the uterus. As the sonogram on the right shows, his head and body look more balanced in size. He now has the proportions of a newborn baby.

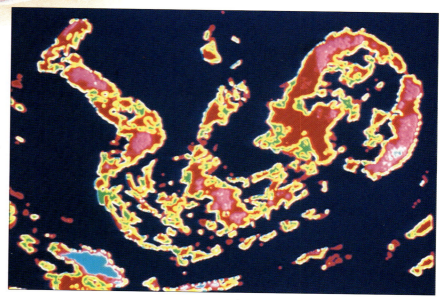

MOTHER

You will probably be having more frequent prenatal checks now. Your doctor will be monitoring your blood presure and urine as well as checking on the baby's position.

Contractions *Your uterus hardens and contracts as a practice for labor. Known as Braxton Hicks contractions, these last only about 30 seconds and you may not be aware of them.*

Pelvis *Your pelvis has expanded and may ache, especially at the back.*

Blood *You may have a low hemoglobin level at this stage in pregnancy.*

Abdomen *Your baby's size is increasing so that the uterus is pushed hard against your lower ribs, and your rib cage may become quite sore. Your abdomen is so stretched that your navel pushes out. The increased pigmentation of the* linea nigra *can make it look very prominent.*

UP TO 32 WEEKS
(32 weeks from conception; 34 weeks of pregnancy)

Thirty-four weeks after your LMP, your baby is perfectly formed. All her proportions are exactly as you would expect them to be at birth. Still, she has some maturing to do and some weight to gain before she is ready to be born.

YOUR BABY'S PROGRESS

Her organs are now almost fully mature, except for her lungs, which are still not completely developed, although they are secreting increasing quantities of surfactant. (This substance will keep them from collapsing once she begins to breathe air.) She can make strong movements that may be felt on the surface of your abdomen. Almost all babies born at this time survive.

Her skin, nails, and hair Her skin is now pink rather than red, due to the deposits of white fat underneath it. Fat deposits build up under her skin in order to provide energy and regulate her body temperature after she is born. The protective *vernix caseosa* that covers her skin is now very thick. Her fingernails reach the ends of her fingers, but her toenails are not yet fully grown. She may have quite a bit of hair on her head.

Her eyes Her irises can now dilate and contract. They will contract in response to bright light, and also to enable her to focus – although she will not need to develop this skill until after she is born. She can close her eyelids, and she has begun to blink.

Her position Some babies assume the head-down position about now, but there is still plenty of time – most engage after 36 weeks. However, she may remain in the breech (bottom-down) position until birth, although most babies do turn on their own.

HER SUPPORT SYSTEM

This month the layers of the placenta may start to thin. To make estrogen, the placenta converts a testosterone-like hormone that is produced by your baby's adrenal glands. By this month these glands have reached a size equivalent to those of an adolescent, and every day they produce ten times as much hormone as an adult's adrenal glands. They will decline after your baby is born.

The amniotic sac, or bag of waters, contains a large amount of fluid, most of which is the baby's urine; she can void as much as one pint of urine daily. Excess *vernix caseosa*, nutrients, and products necessary for lung maturation are also present.

The umbilical cord is large, strong, and tough. A firm, gelatinous substance surrounds the blood vessels; this prevents kinks or knots in the cord that could affect the baby's blood supply.

78

YOUR BABY AT 32 WEEKS OF LIFE

YOUR BABY

Her head and face
The sonogram on the left shows very clearly how both the shape of her head and her profile have developed, so she now looks like a "real baby."

Your baby's main activity now is to settle into a head-down position and adjust to her lack of space in the uterus.

Eyes She can now focus and blink.

Weight gain She will have gained at least 2lb since last month. This is made up primarily of increased muscle tissue and fat.

Lungs Her lungs are still developing so that she can adjust to respiration outside the uterus. If she were to be born at this stage, she would almost certainly have breathing difficulties, although she would stand an excellent chance of survival.

Her face is now smooth, with most of the wrinkles gone

Fingernails reach tips of her fingers

There may be a lot of hair on her head

BABY'S VITAL STATISTICS

By the end of this month, her crown-to-rump length will be about 12in (32cm), and she will weigh about 5lb (2.5kg).

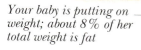
Your baby is putting on weight; about 8% of her total weight is fat

Your baby's size
It is now becoming rather a tight fit in the uterus, especially if your baby is large. As a consequence, her movements tend to decrease in frequency, although you should still be able to feel her moving (see pp.176 & 177). In addition, her body, like that of the baby in the sonogram on the right, will now start to become tightly curled as her elbow and knee room are restricted. Quite a few babies are in the bottom-down (breech) position at the start of this month (see column, p.239), but most will have tipped head-down by term.

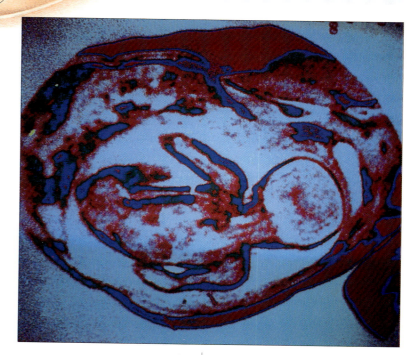

MOTHER

You will be seeing your doctor on a weekly basis now. He or she will be checking that everything is going well.

Engagement *In most first-time mothers, the baby's head drops down into the pelvis at about 36 weeks. You will feel more comfortable and your breathing will become easier. It is perfectly normal for the baby's head not to engage until later – sometimes not until labor has started.*

Posture *You may tend to compensate for the extra weight in the front of your body by leaning backward. This throws your head back so that your line of vision is different from usual. Your center of gravity has altered, so you may bump into walls or drop things by mistake.*

Sleeping and resting *It may be more and more difficult for you to get a good night's sleep, as your large abdomen makes finding a comfortable position difficult. However, rest as much as possible, with your feet up, if you can.*

Nesting instinct *Usually occurring during pre-labor (see p.250), this often seems to manifest itself in an urge to clean! Try to resist it – you'll need all your energy for giving birth.*

UP TO 38 WEEKS
(38 weeks from conception; 40 weeks of pregnancy)

The most precise way to calculate fetal development is from the date of conception, which adds up to 38 weeks. Doctors set an artificial but convenient time table of 40 weeks, calculated from your LMP. This is an estimate set by doctors, not by babies.

YOUR BABY'S PROGRESS

During this month your baby will probably shed almost all of the fine hair (lanugo) from his body. There may be some small patches left in odd places – perhaps on his shoulders, his arms and legs, and some in his body creases.

His skin is smooth and soft, and there is still some *vernix caseosa* left on it (mostly on his back), which will help his passage down the birth canal. He will be almost chubby prior to birth. His fingernails are long and may have scratched his face, and will need clipping soon after birth. His eyes are blue, although they may change in the weeks after birth, and when he is awake they are open.

In these last weeks, your baby produces increasing amounts of a hormone called cortisone from his adrenal glands. This helps his lungs mature in readiness for his first breath.

Meconium His intestine is filled with a dark green, almost black, substance called meconium. It is a mixture of the secretions from his alimentary glands together with lanugo, pigment, and cells from the wall of his bowel. Meconium will be his first bowel movement after he is born (see **Fetoscopy**, p.166), although he may pass it during the birth.

Immune system His own system is still immature, so to compensate for this he receives antibodies from you via the placenta. They will protect him against anything that you have antibodies for, such as flu, mumps, and German measles. After he is born, he will continue to receive antibodies from you via your breast milk.

HIS SUPPORT SYSTEM

The placenta now measures eight to ten inches (20 centimeters) in diameter and is just over one inch (three centimeters) thick, thus creating a wide area for the exchange of nourishment and waste products between yourself and your baby. There is now more than a quart of water in the amniotic sac.

The hormones produced by the placenta are stimulating your breasts to swell and fill with milk. This also causes swelling in your baby's breasts, whether it is a boy or a girl. This will recede after birth. If your baby is a girl, the cessation of these same hormones following delivery may cause her to have a light bleeding from her vagina (like a period) a few days after her birth, which is normal.

YOUR BABY AT TERM

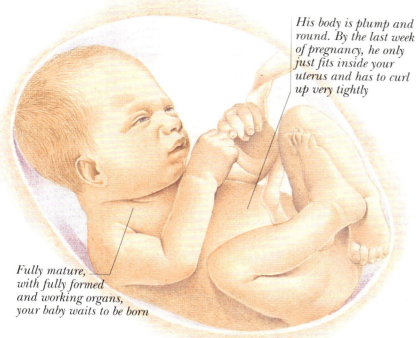

His body is plump and round. By the last week of pregnancy, he only just fits inside your uterus and has to curl up very tightly

Fully mature, with fully formed and working organs, your baby waits to be born

YOUR BABY

Your baby prepares for birth; his lungs mature and the last of his brown fat is laid down.

Reproductive organs The testes of most boy babies will have descended by now. In a girl baby, the ovaries are still above the pelvic brim and do not reach their final position until after birth.

Movements Although his movements will be only a fraction of what they were earlier, you should still be able to feel him kick.

BABY'S VITAL STATISTICS

At birth, his crown-to-rump length will probably be 14–15in (35–37cm), and he will weigh about 6–8lb (3–4kg).

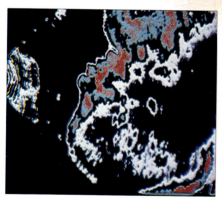

Engaged head
The above sonogram shows the baby lying head-down, with his head against his mother's cervix (bottom right-hand corner).

Prepared for birth
As your baby gets heavier and matures, he will tip head-down in your uterus. In the color-enhanced X-ray on the right, the baby's head can be seen settled deeply into the mother's pelvis.

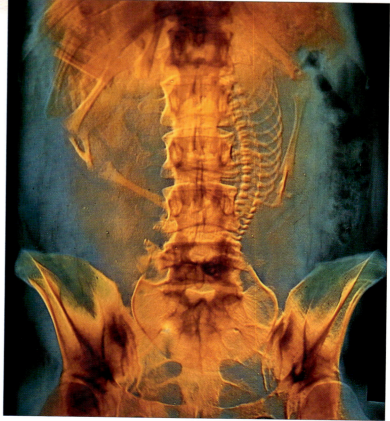

NAME *Karen Phillips*

AGE *36 years*

PAST MEDICAL HISTORY *Nothing abnormal*

FAMILY HISTORY *No history of twins known*

OBSTETRIC HISTORY *2 previous pregnancies. Edema in last month of both.*

Karen was diagnosed as expecting twins when she had a sonogram at 16 weeks. She knew from the beginning that there was something different about this pregnancy as she was constantly sick in the first couple of months, which she hadn't been in her previous pregnancies. She also looked huge – at 3 months she looked about 5! Consequently it wasn't a total surprise when her sonogram showed that she was carrying twins.

Twins shown by ultrasound
Ultrasound scanning can clearly show if you are carrying 2 babies. Sometimes, however, one may be behind the other and therefore not so easy to see. If twins are still suspected despite only one being visible on the ultrasound, you will probably have another sonogram several weeks later.

TWINS

Once they got over the initial shock of finding out that they were expecting twins, Karen and Joe were delighted, if a little bit apprehensive. Their primary concerns were the well-being of Karen and the twins throughout pregnancy, and how they would cope with the birth.

SUSPECTING A MULTIPLE PREGNANCY

Many women guess early on that there is something different about their pregnancy when they are carrying twins. Size is often the telling factor, as well as the shape – twins tend to push the abdomen out sideways as well as forward, so that it looks oval rather than round. Ultrasound will confirm the presence of two babies, and twins can be diagnosed by week eight of pregnancy.

KAREN'S SPECIAL NEEDS

Some women sail through a twin pregnancy with very few or no side effects. Some do not. The stresses imposed by carrying two babies can intensify feelings of tiredness and sickness as your body adjusts. In addition, twin pregnancies need to be watched carefully for raised blood pressure, anemia, edema, and preeclampsia (see p.204). Like all expectant mothers of twins, Karen should visit her

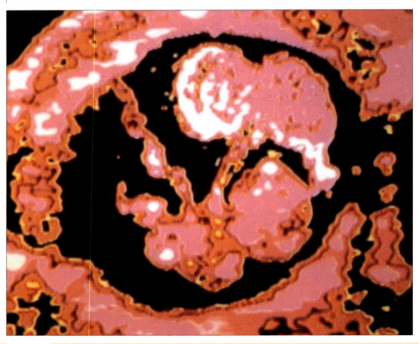

doctor or midwife more frequently than a woman expecting a single baby. Her doctor will be alert for the recurrence of edema and may hospitalize her if she seems likely to develop preeclampsia (see p.204). A good high-protein diet is essential.

Sheer size can be a problem in later pregnancy, and finding a comfortable position can be difficult. I told Karen that she might find that being in water helps, as it reduces the effects of gravity. Gentle swimming would be fine as long as her doctor agrees. Long warm (not hot) soaks in a large tub will help any expectant mother relax, and Karen should find them especially beneficial. Making love is not usually prohibited, although Karen should follow her doctor's advice and consult him or her immediately if she has any problems, such as discharge or bleeding or if she has contractions that might signal the onset of premature labor.

Women who are expecting twins and who do not have adequate rest are much more likely to go into premature labor than those expecting twins who have had complete rest from the fifth month. Work during pregnancy, inside, as well as outside, the home (especially caring for young children), should not be too strenuous. I advised Karen to arrange for child care and to have at least three hours bed rest a day.

LABOR AND TWINS

Labor is always managed in a hospital because of the risks (see column, right). As doctors and midwives are highly sensitive to the problems that might occur, 20 minutes is the most they will allow to elapse between births, and the second twin is always monitored closely for any signs of distress. An emergency Caesarean section may be necessary if either twin appears to be in any danger.

KAREN'S
BABIES

There are a number of differences between a twin pregnancy and delivery and a single birth.

A shorter gestation period *Twins are normally born at 37 weeks rather than 40 weeks. This is mostly due to space restrictions, although external factors are also important.*

A lower birthweight *Because of their shorter gestation period, twins weigh less than singletons.*

Extra risks for the second-born *She has to go through the intense contractions of expulsion (second stage) twice over. The second twin may also suffer from a diminished oxygen supply to the placenta because the uterus will start to contract once the first twin has been delivered.*

IDENTICAL OR FRATERNAL?

A third of all twins are identical. They are always the same sex and usually share the placenta, although this depends on how late the egg splits. Half of fraternal twins are boy–girl pairs and half are same sex. Their placentas are separate, but may be fused together. The incidence of identical twins appears to be completely random, while fraternal twins often run in families, inherited through the mother's side. There is no history of twins in Karen's family. However, the likelihood of having non-inherited, fraternal twins rises until a woman's mid-thirties, then declines, and seems to be higher if she is tall, strong and conceives easily. The chances of having fraternal twins also appear to increase with each subsequent child.

IDENTICAL TWINS

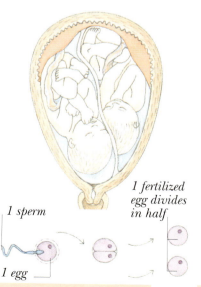

1 fertilized egg divides in half

1 sperm

1 egg

FRATERNAL TWINS

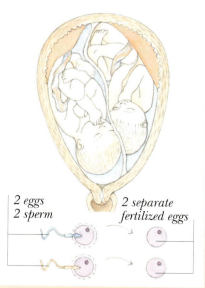

2 eggs 2 sperm

2 separate fertilized eggs

3

The birth of your CHOICE

There are many choices surrounding labor and birth, and you should be aware of all your options. In theory it's possible to have exactly the kind of birth you want, but it's up to women and their partners to take a more assertive, informed part in the way their labor and delivery will be handled.

 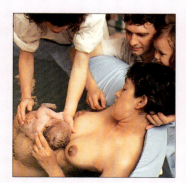 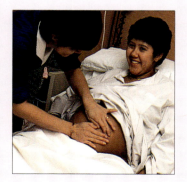

THOUGHTS ON
BIRTH

*The majority of the major
philosophers of birth (see p.94)
have been mainly concerned
with natural childbirth.*

*"Natural childbirth means
normal physiological childbirth.
When childbirth becomes associated with varying degrees of
fear and therefore varying
degrees of tension, it becomes in
varying degrees unphysiological
or pathological."*

Grantley Dick-Read

*"Doctors and midwives, once
they have become aware of the
ordeal it is to be born, will meet
the young newcomer with more
sensitivity, more intelligence,
and more respect."*

Frederick Leboyer

*"Everywhere around us, we saw
doctors increasing their use of
drugs and artificial intervention, while we have kept
intervention to an absolute
minimum, and considered
drugs unnecessary and
harmful."*

Michel Odent

*"Childbirth is not primarily a
medical process, but a psycho-
sexual experience. It is not
surprising that adapting your
responses to the stimuli it
presents should involve a subtle
and delicate working together
of mind and body."*

Sheila Kitzinger

THE CHOICES IN CHILDBIRTH

*Over the past few decades, women have been taking greater
control of their own health. In many cases, members of the
medical profession have responded enthusiastically to the
changing desires and needs of women, and the choices in
childbirth have never been greater, nor our wishes more
paramount. Today most of us ask to have our children more
naturally, and this option should be available to all of us,
whether the birth is at home or in the hospital. But we shouldn't
ignore the benefits a managed birth can provide, particularly
when childbirth doesn't go as smoothly as expected.*

THE MODERN MANAGED BIRTH

The modern managed birth (high-tech birth in a hospital) came
out of a justified concern for the mother and baby and from
increased medical knowledge of the physiological aspects of birth.
In a managed birth, labor is actively controlled by the obstetrician
according to hospital policy so that it fits into what is perceived as
being normal (this perception can differ, however, depending on
the hospital and the obstetrician).

A managed labor is the norm for most hospital births. In the
main, this is obstetrician-based care within a general hospital, and
it is essential for some women who may have complications during
pregnancy, labor, and birth – a pre-existing medical condition or
an anticipated breech birth, for example.

In this setting, too, you are most likely to experience medical
intervention involving some of the most modern procedures in
obstetrics. With this kind of labor, epidural anesthesia is literally
on tap and the use of electronic fetal monitoring is standard
practice. Your attendants will notice very small changes in your
baby's condition and may be pressured to act on them. Consequently, all types of medical intervention are more common with
this type of birth: there are more inductions and Caesarean sections, and more use of forceps.

Although these practices do indeed confer a benefit on a percentage of births where intervention is needed, the routine use of them
often cannot be justified by hard evidence. So women who want to
have complete control over their deliveries may feel very strongly
about their use (see **Childbirth's contentious issues,** p.90). Other
women find a hospital setting makes childbirth the event they
expect it to be and would feel cheated, nervous, and even second-
class if they didn't have an obstetrician in attendance with the high-
tech machinery close by.

THE MODERN NATURAL BIRTH

It seems a paradox that a natural birth should be something that you have to request well in advance of the event, but even in this day and age you may find that delivery practice is still dominated by obstetricians. Unless you make your preferences known early, a natural birth can be quite difficult to arrange.

It is completely reasonable for most women to want to have natural births: ones in which there is no fear because the whole process of birth and delivery is familiar; where there is no unnecessary medical intervention; where there is a calm, homey atmosphere; where mothers are allowed to do anything they desire – to take up any positions that are most comfortable for them; and where there is no undue pressure to take pain-relieving drugs. Female bodies are well designed for giving birth; all the soft tissues of the birth passage can open up so that a baby is gently squeezed out. But breathing and relaxation techniques can make birth even easier to manage, and a number of natural childbirth philosophies advocate these techniques.

Although there are individual differences, all birth philosophies share one common aim – to enable women to give birth in the way they want. Women are somewhat isolated from birth and death in modern society, and many remain ignorant about the process of childbirth. Inaccurate truisms and fearful myths lead many women to worry about intense pain and danger unnecessarily. However, tension and fear can actually prolong labor.

Most of the philosophies of childbirth adopt some form of a psychological re-learning so that your pain expectation is reduced and your pain threshold raised. In many cases, breathing techniques are central to the philosophy. There are slight differences in the type that each teaches, but all emphasize your intense concentration on breathing patterns and the learned ability to relax your body at will. The best way to experience a totally natural birth is in a dedicated center or at home (see below). The use of water pools and being free to give birth out of bed are options that are becoming more popular but are not always easy to obtain.

HOME BIRTH

In many European countries healthy women may opt for a home delivery if their pregnancy has been straightforward. In the United States it is more difficult. In order to consider a home birth, most doctors would like to see an obstetric history of one normal child, by a normal delivery before agreeing to a home birth for a second baby. Arranging a home birth can be difficult (see box), and you must be very sure that it is the best option for you. Always keep an open mind about transferring to a hospital if things are not progressing well. If you have difficulty arranging a home birth, contact the American College of Nurse-Midwives (see **Addresses**). It is essential that you have a midwife in attendance for a home birth. It is best to contact her early in pregnancy (a midwife is legally required to attend you if contacted while you are in labor – although this isn't really fair to her or you).

THE CASE FOR HOME BIRTH

A planned home birth can be one of the safest ways you can give birth.

A recent British report has concluded that although 94% of all births take place in hospitals, they are no safer and may be less safe, than home births.

In Australia, a study of 3,400 home births found that there was a lower perinatal mortality rate, and less need for Caesareans, forceps delivery, and suturing for an episiotomy or a tear, than in women delivering in hospitals. The mothers were not all "low risk": the figures included 15 multiple births, breech deliveries, women who had previous Caesareans, and women with previous stillbirths. The group as a whole was older than the national average. Less than 10% had to transfer to a hospital.

ARRANGING A HOME BIRTH

Arranging a home birth isn't always easy or straightforward, but it's always exciting!

* *Visit your doctor and request a home birth*

* *If your doctor says yes, arrange a schedule of prenatal visits*

* *If your doctor says no, find one who will agree (your doctor may be able to help), or contact the American College of Nurse-Midwives (see **Addresses**)*

* *Arrange prenatal visits as usual with your new carer, and make a plan of the type of labor you wish to have (see p.106)*

YOUR WATER BIRTH

If you choose to use a birthing pool during your labor, you may worry that your baby will drown if he is actually born under water.

As long as your baby is not kept under water for more than a few moments, he is safe while he is still receiving oxygen from the placenta. Most newborns make strong vigorous movements of their own accord, and while these may bring them to the surface, you should immediately lift your baby so that his body is clear of the water, to stimulate him to gasp for breath, and give him a welcoming cuddle.

Birth in water
Using a birthing pool during labor can help relax you and reduce the pain of contractions. You are much less likely to be subjected to interventionist procedures because of an imposed time limit. This in turn means that you will have the time needed for your tissues and muscles to open and stretch. Your partner can share in the intimacy of a water birth, and your baby can be welcomed with a skin-to-skin cuddle from both of you immediately afterward.

Risks Your doctor may tell you that a home birth is not safe, that it presents too many risks. But there is always some risk attached to giving birth, and statistics have proved that in some circumstances a hospital birth can actually be less safe than a planned home birth (see p.96). However, unplanned out-of-hospital births can be extremely dangerous, whether it is a teenager trying to conceal an unwanted pregnancy or a couple who do not make it to the hospital and whose baby is born *en route*.

WATER BIRTH

Over the past few decades, the use of water during labor has gained steadily in popularity. Dr. Michel Odent (see p.95) was one of the first obstetricians in the West to offer laboring mothers the use of a shallow birth pool in which to relax when their contractions were at their height. At first, it was never intended that the baby would be born under water but if, by chance, the birth occurred while the mother was still sitting in the pool, then it could be, and therefore was, accommodated.

Birthing pools are primarily a means of pain relief; the birth isn't necessarily under water, as many people have come to believe. There can be some danger to the baby if he or she is delivered under water and the head is not lifted out right away (see column, left).

Many hospitals now offer birthing pool facilities, and there are a few companies that have portable pools for rent. These can be taken to the hospital, if your hospital agrees, as well as being used at home, whether for pre-labor or labor. Water births must always be supervised by a qualified attendant.

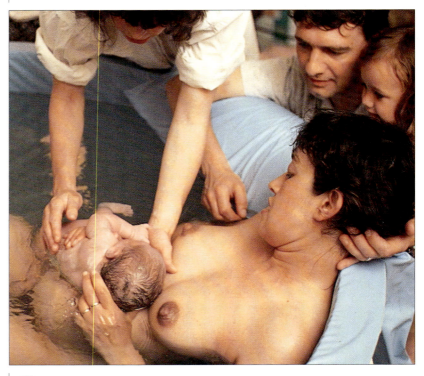

ACTIVE BIRTH

An active birth is basically one in which you are not in bed and you don't lie down for delivery – you're active. In the past, when the supervision of labor rooms and childbirth was a woman's responsibility, mothers were free to move about as they wanted and to take up any position for birth that they found comfortable. However, once doctors invaded the delivery room, women were confined to bed and made to lie on their backs because this made obstetrical maneuvers easier. Today, women are rediscovering more natural and mechanically efficient postures for labor and birth. Mothers, often supported by partners, are now encouraged to move about and become more actively involved in the process of childbirth, adopting whatever positions feel comfortable for labor and birth.

Methods of preparation for an active birth are widely incorporated in childbirth classes, as it has been proved that movements and positions that enable the uterine contractions to be aimed downward, thus pushing the baby toward the floor, make labor more efficient. Squatting, kneeling, sitting, or standing can all help reduce pain and ensure greater comfort, and a mother who is free to move around may reduce her risk of needing to have an episiotomy, forceps being applied, or a Caesarean section performed. Moreover, it has also been shown that lying on your back can prolong labor and result in other complications (see column, p.90), whereas assuming a vertical position may mean an easier and shorter progress through labor.

One other aid from the past that is enjoying a revival is the birthing stool. This is a low support that allows the mother to attain a vertical position in which, with the help of gravity, she can help push the baby out while at the same time staying sufficiently high above the floor's hard surface.

PARTNER-ASSISTED BIRTH

Every woman going into labor should have with her someone other than medical and nursing professionals to offer support and encouragement. The best assistant is your partner, especially if he has attended your prenatal classes with you, and knows how to help you through each stage of labor (see also pp.108 & 268).

However, it doesn't have to be your partner. Your mother, sister, or best friend would be an excellent choice, particularly if she's had children of her own and can stay calm when a situation does not go quite as planned. Whomever you choose (and you may want both your partner and a female friend to be with you) should be someone you trust, who can judge your physical and mental state, and, if necessary, make decisions on your behalf based on your preferences (make sure they know your views inside out).

For example, you may be determined not to accept analgesics, but you may find you can't handle the pain, and ask for medication. Your assistant may then be able to give you the support you need to carry on without drugs (see also p.266). Studies have shown that the full emotional and physical support of a trusted individual can reduce a laboring woman's need for pain-relieving drugs.

ENDORPHINS

The body's natural narcotics, endorphins, are usually produced in enormous quantities during labor.

Endorphins are small protein molecules with a chemical structure similar to morphine that are produced by cells in the body. They act as pain-reducing enzymes at specific sites in the brain, spinal cord, and all of the nerve endings. In addition, endorphins are thought to be involved in controlling the body's reaction to stress, regulating contractions of the intestinal and uterine walls, and determining mood.

Every person has a unique, individual endorphin response, which probably has a bearing on how different women handle the pain of giving birth.

In most women, the endorphin response appears to "kick in" at a certain point during childbirth, and from then on labor will be arduous, but bearable.

RECUMBENT DELIVERIES

Although fetal monitoring (see p.92) may confine you to bed, lying on your back for delivery can have many disadvantages.

- *You have to work harder, literally pushing the baby uphill, and become exhausted more quickly than in the upright position*

- *Pain may be greater in this position than in a vertical one*

- *The tissues of the birth canal may fail to be opened and stimulated by the descending baby, possibly prolonging labor*

- *There is a greater need for an episiotomy*

- *There may be an increased chance of a forceps delivery*

- *It inhibits spontaneous delivery of the placenta*

- *There is a greater possibility of lower back strain in this position*

CHILDBIRTH'S CONTENTIOUS ISSUES

Certain procedures historically associated with childbirth are being re-evaluated. Some have been found to be unnecessary, others unjustified. On the other hand, most of today's obstetricians believe that they can guarantee that childbirth is a safer and happier experience for the mother and the baby with the help of all the modern technology available. For example, in the first stage of labor this may include effective analgesia including epidural anesthesia; monitoring of the fetal heart with a rate meter and the uterine contractions with a tocograph; recording cervical dilatation on a partogram to make sure that progress is being made, and the occasional use of an oxytocin drip to ensure that uterine contractions are sufficiently strong, frequent, and regular.

While a fuller discussion of certain of the following subjects is given in other parts of the book, this is a good place to preview certain issues that may affect your choice of hospital and/or attendant. By drawing your attention to arguments in favor of going against some of these standard medical practices, this will help you question them assertively with your medical and nursing attendants. More often than not, your wishes will be complied with, especially if you give everyone concerned several weeks' notice, but occasionally you will be told that to continue with a particular option will put your baby and you at serious risk – for instance, if your baby is showing signs of distress and you fight to continue with totally natural childbirth. In this situation you should be prepared to change to your alternative birth plan (see column, p.106). This happens rarely, however, so don't accede to medical intervention unless you secure adequate answers to your questions.

Intervention sometimes occurs because of the desire of midwives and doctors to get the baby out quickly. An episiotomy, for instance, is often made necessary when you're encouraged to deliver your baby's head before the skin and muscles in the perineum have been given a chance to stretch. Here are some of the most often questioned areas in childbirth.

Shaving *"You don't need to be shaved."* Shaving became a standard part of obstetrics during the early twentieth century, when pubic hair was eliminated because it was thought to harbor infection, making it impossible to sterilize the perineum when an episiotomy was needed. Now, however, any chance of infection can be eliminated by wiping the vulva with gauze to remove any contaminant and simply spraying with an antiseptic. Nowadays, shaving is usually unnecessary unless you are having a Caesarean section. In careful hands there should be no cuts or bruises but hair regrowth is often accompanied by profound irritation.

Enemas *"Enemas are unnecessary."* Like shaving, enemas were introduced as part of the "clean childbirth" procedures in maternity hospitals. Modern hospitals have abandoned enemas as it has been found that they make no significant difference. Most women empty their bowels at the onset of labor.

Nothing by mouth *"Forbidding a laboring woman to eat or drink is illogical."* In cultures other than our own, a woman in labor is encouraged to eat and drink to keep up her strength. There is no medical nor scientific rationale for starving a woman during labor. In fact, quite the opposite. Sometimes a laboring woman has a sudden demand for energy and for this she needs sugar. Other women don't wish to eat, but they certainly need fluids; the hard work of labor uses up much energy, which causes sweating, and a woman must replace the fluids that she has lost through her skin.

To provide adequate fluids and nutrition, your doctor may insert an intravenous drip early in labor. This intravenous line can prove important if you need medications or anesthetics for pain relief in labor, or if a Caesarean section becomes necessary.

Moving to a delivery room *"Explore alternatives to this sterile environment."* In many hospitals the delivery room has a clinical and mechanical atmosphere. Moreover, you may be forced, at the most stressful time of your labor, to undergo the physical and emotional upheaval of leaving the room in which you have so far labored in order to have your baby there. Ideally, labor should proceed smoothly in peaceful surroundings, and as long as a room is equipped with good lighting, oxygen in some form, and a suction apparatus to clear out the baby's air passages, if necessary, I can see no reason why a woman in normal labor should be forced to give birth in such a delivery room. Discuss this with your doctor. Many progressive hospitals have more congenial birthing rooms and, if it is at all possible, you should choose a hospital that has one.

Induction *"Why am I being induced?"* Labor may have to be induced for medical reasons including preeclampsia, high blood pressure, or postmaturity – and induction can save the lives of mothers and babies. Induction may also be desirable if your labor contractions are weak and inefficient; in such a situation, induction can produce a shorter, more efficient labor. However, avoid letting your medical team induce birth for reasons of convenience. The intravenous drip used will restrict your movements somewhat and may increase your need for pain medication. More extensive fetal monitoring may be recommended once the drip is in; this too can restrict your ability to move around.

Amniotomy *"Is it absolutely necessary?"* This is when the membranes (the bag of waters) surrounding the baby are artificially ruptured. It is now fairly routine practice in a high-tech birth and is usually done early in labor.

Amniotomy is performed for three reasons. The first is so that electronic fetal monitoring equipment can be set in place; the second is to check if the amniotic fluid contains meconium (this is the baby's first bowel movement, and its presence may indicate fetal distress); the third is that once the bag of waters is removed, the baby's head can press hard on the cervix, facilitating dilation of the cervix and completion of labor's first stage.

EPISIOTOMY

An episiotomy is an incision, about the length of your little finger, in your perineum that allows more room for delivery of the baby's head and shoulders (see p.92).

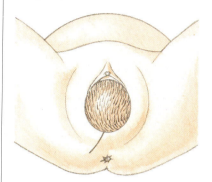

The mediolateral cut
This is angled down and away from the vagina and perineum into the muscle.

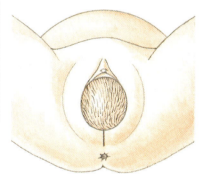

The mid-line cut
This is performed by cutting straight down into the perineum, between the vagina and anus.

If you have already had an epidural, you will probably not need any additional anesthetic. Otherwise, a local anesthetic in your perineum, known as a pudendal block, will be necessary.

WHEN YOU NEED AN EPISIOTOMY

There are certain circumstances when the safe delivery of your baby's head and body will require an episiotomy.

• *Birth is imminent and your perineum hasn't had time to stretch slowly*

• *Your baby's head may be too large for your vaginal opening*

• *You aren't able to control your pushing so that you can't stop when necessary and then push gradually and smoothly*

• *Your baby is in distress*

• *You are going to need a forceps or a vacuum extraction delivery (see pp.280 & 281)*

• *Your baby is a breech presentation, and there is a complication during delivery*

Fetal monitoring *"Ask for the minimum."* The traditional way to monitor your baby's heartbeat is for the nurse to listen, often with a stethoscope, through your abdomen, although many attendants now use portable sonicaids (see column, p.161). However, continuous electronic monitoring, where equipment is strapped to the mother's abdomen (see p.263) is becoming routine in some hospitals. If you wish to move around, then question the necessity of using electronic monitoring.

Obviously having a "window" into the uterus during labor is of great value, but it is very difficult to change positions once the equipment is attached (although a portable type is becoming more widely used), and this may slow labor. If machines are incorrect, or interpreted incorrectly, then unnecessary intervention can occur. In addition, using a machine to monitor the baby may switch attention from the mother to the machine; this can be distracting and upsetting for a woman in labor.

Forceps *"Ask to be consulted before they're applied."* These are tong-shaped instruments (like large sugar tongs) used to ease the baby's head out of the birth canal. Forceps have saved the lives of many babies and their mothers and can reduce the need for a Caesarean section for a baby that is stuck up in the pelvis. However, forceps are being applied more and more often, sometimes unnecessarily. Resist them! Ask for time (see **Time**, opposite). The use of forceps requires that an episiotomy, often quite large, be performed. Suction extraction (see pp.280 & 281), in which a cup is attached to the baby's head by suction, is often used instead of forceps.

Episiotomy *"This is an overdone, often unnecessary surgical procedure."* This is a surgical cut to enlarge the vaginal outlet at delivery to avoid tears, which have ragged edges and are difficult to stitch together, and to protect against possible injuries to your perineal or vaginal tissues. Tears, however, can be avoided if a woman stops pushing while the head is being born, and allows the uterus to ease out the head very gradually rather than suddenly. If the head is delivered suddenly, a tear is usually inevitable, so an episiotomy will be done if the perineum is under stress.

You are more likely to need an episiotomy during your first labor than during your subsequent labors. Episiotomy is the most commonly performed operation in the West.

If an episiotomy is done too early, before the perineum has thinned out, muscle, skin, and blood vessels are damaged and the bleeding may be heavy. Also, tissues are crushed by the scissors as they are cut; this leads to bruising, swelling, and slow healing and can result in the stitches becoming too tight. This tightness causes great discomfort in the postpartum period, and may even lead to a painful scar, which may prevent you from engaging in intercourse for months afterward. If you wish to avoid an episiotomy, it's as well to have it clearly stated on your notes that you wish to avoid an episiotomy unless entirely necessary. Common child-bearing myths have it that there are no nerve endings in the perineum and that a woman is bearing so much pain anyway as the head is born that she will not feel the pain of an episiotomy. This is utter nonsense and nothing less than brutal. You must have a local anesthetic in the perineum before an episiotomy is performed. Insist that you get it. It is your right to have an episiotomy without feeling any pain.

Breech birth *"Consider your options carefully."* Many women and midwives believe that a gentle and unhurried approach to birth, coupled with skilled midwife care, enables a breech baby to be born vaginally with the minimum of risk.

A recent issue of the *British Medical Journal*, however, reports that although there is a very small risk of a breech baby dying at or just after birth, whether born by a normal vaginal delivery or Caesarean, the risk is significantly greater in a vaginal delivery (1 percent compared to 1 in 3,000). Most obstetricians feel that a breech baby should be born by Caesarean section.

As it is now fairly common practice for a breech birth to have epidural anesthesia, should you need a Caesarean section, it can be done quickly and simply without further anesthesia and you will be able to hold your baby as soon as he or she is born. Nearly all breech births are normal, with healthy babies and mothers.

Time *"Don't let them hurry you."* What is considered to be the normal length of labor varies from hospital to hospital – for example, the "right" length for the second stage can be two hours or 30 minutes, or somewhere in between, depending on the obstetrician or mid-wife. The normal length of labor varies between women, and from birth to birth, and it is the marrying of what is normal for you with what is right for the doctor or hospital that may cause problems.

In most cases where the first stage is considered to have gone on too long, the membranes are ruptured (if they haven't done so already), or an oxytocin drip is set up to increase the rate and strength of contractions. Where the second stage is considered to take too long, episiotomies and forceps deliveries are often per-formed as routine. However, many midwives say that it is usually obvious when labor is proceeding well but is just taking some time, as opposed to when it is slow because something is wrong. Labor can usually be speeded up by moving around, or sitting in water. Appeal to your midwife or doctor for more time, but be willing to take medical opinion into consideration.

Being together *"Ask to be together as much as possible."* In some hospitals babies may be separated from their mothers, spending most of the time in the nursery. This is not common these days, and often it is assumed that your baby will sleep next to you. However, it is likely that your partner will not be allowed to stay with you in the hospital for even the first night, which can leave him feeling very depressed after the excitement and emotion of the birth. Most women say that they were too excited to sleep afterward and wished that they had someone to talk to about it. Before going to the hospital, ask if your partner can stay with you.

YOUR POSITION IN LABOR

Whatever the nursing staff or doctors say, you should be free to have your baby in whatever position you like.

A few hospitals still persist in delivering women in the lithotomy position, where their ankles are held in stirrups. This position was initially instigated to enable doctors to see how the baby was being born. The time for such practices is long gone. You, like most women, will probably find it more natural to take up a semi-vertical position (see p.278), not just because you find it more comfortable but because it is more mechanically efficient. And if you want to have the baby out of bed, squatting, standing, or on all fours, that is all right, too.

THE BRADLEY METHOD

This refinement of birth preparation was initiated by Dr. Robert Bradley and is also known as husband-coached childbirth.

The Bradley method teaches women to accept the pain and to go with the flow under the guidance of the husband or partner, friend, or counselor. The coach attends the prenatal classes with the mother, helps her with her exercise and breathing routine, and comforts, coaxes, and coaches her through labor and delivery.

The danger of this is that most women need to be distracted from the pain, to focus outside of themselves, in order to cope, and that going into the pain can be totally overwhelming.

In addition, each labor is completely individual and may be very dissimilar to what you have practiced, and a woman often reacts to giving birth in a different way than she imagined. Some birth partners can become so enthusiastic about the coaching that they lose sight of the woman and her needs.

CHILDBIRTH PHILOSOPHERS

There have been a number of people who have influenced the way women and their carers approach birth in the late twentieth century. Their teaching and ideas have altered prenatal and postnatal care, thus making childbirth an ever-evolving experience, and they are beginning to have an effect on the atmosphere and procedures surrounding childbirth in the Western world. Most seek to enable the woman to follow the lead of her own body, in a loving and intimate environment.

DR. GRANTLEY DICK-READ

The first obstetrician to realize that fear of giving birth is one of the main causes of pain during labor, Dr. Dick-Read brought the principles of natural childbirth not only to the attention of the medical world, but to mothers as well. He was the doctor who introduced proper education of mothers through prenatal classes and careful teaching, and also emotional support, in the hope of eliminating fear and tension. His teaching was so basic that it is now taken for granted by all, and there is no method of childbirth that does not rely on his teaching, including breathing exercises, breathing control, and complete relaxation. Dick-Read's watchword was preparation – not only with information, but also by seeking help, reassurance, and sympathy.

FREDERICK LEBOYER

The Leboyer method of delivery works best if it's seen as an attempt to help people understand what the newborn baby sees, hears, and feels. Leboyer was influenced by the psychiatrists Reich, Rank, and Janov, who shared the belief that later problems in life stem from birth's trauma. Leboyer's concern, therefore, is not primarily with the mother, but rather with the baby's experience of labor and delivery, and how this may affect the baby in adulthood.

In order to minimize this trauma he suggests, in his book *Birth Without Violence*, that the birthing room have soft lighting, and that noise and movement be kept to a minimum. Leboyer also believes that immediate skin-to-skin contact is essential to calm the baby, and that she should be laid on her mother's stomach as soon as she is born. He further suggests that the newborn then be bathed in warm water as this is the closest the baby can get to the nurturing environment of the uterus.

Not all of this fits in with the physiology of what actually occurs at birth. A baby needs to feel air on her face in order to stimulate her lungs to breathe for the first time: placing her in a warm liquid may not be sufficiently stimulating for her to continue breathing.

Many professionals say that there is no proof that his theories work. However, it is only right and fitting that every baby be welcomed into the world with reverence, so even if you don't agree with all of Leboyer's theories, you can still be interested in a gentler birth.

DR. MICHEL ODENT

As a general surgeon, Dr. Odent was extremely shocked when he first witnessed women pushing their babies uphill against the forces of gravity because their feet were held in stirrups. Consequently, stronger contractions were needed, which were more painful, labor was much slower and exhausting, and there were more complications because mothers were in a position where the baby was held back from being delivered.

This initial shock led him to devise his own methods of childbirth, broadly based on traditional midwifery in France. Odent believes that, given the opportunity, women in labor return to a primitive biological state, where they function at a new level of animal awareness, losing inhibitions, and entering a state of consciousness where they will follow their basic instincts. He believes that the body's natural narcotics, endorphins (see p.89), are responsible for this.

SHEILA KITZINGER

A very highly respected birth practitioner, who has an enormous amount of influence in the West, Kitzinger believes that birth is a very personal experience, and that the laboring mother should be an active "birth-giver," rather than a passive patient, a decision maker rather than a centerpiece.

She has likened the modern, managed birth in a modern, managed hospital to giving birth in captivity; in essence, to being in a zoo. She says that the zoo may be humanely and scientifically managed; the keepers may be kind and considerate, and pride themselves on a low mortality rate and the good condition of their charges; the visiting times may be frequent and the premises may be friendly and welcoming; there may be space to move around in the cage; those in charge may have tried to re-create the natural habitat, but the zoo still dictates the behavior of the captives.

Kitzinger believes that the challenges facing the maternity services today are as follows. First to enable parents to have a real choice, whether that be a totally managed birth, a totally natural birth, or somewhere in-between, and to respect their wishes concerning where, and how, their child is to be born. Second, she believes that birth is not an illness and that professionals must not treat a laboring mother and her partner as patients, but as intelligent adults whose right it is to have the final say in all the decisions surrounding the birth of their baby.

Kitzinger stresses that the goal of labor is not merely to produce a healthy child, but also to empower the mother. To achieve both of these goals, women must maintain control over their labors and understand the options that are available. An empowering birth will produce a sense of triumph in the new mother, no matter how difficult the labor.

THE LAMAZE METHOD

This method of psychological counseling was pioneered in Russia, and was then adopted in France by Dr. Lamaze.

More than 90% of women in Russia and 70% of French women are now taught variations of the Lamaze method. It has become equally popular in the United States, and still forms the basic teaching of the National Childbirth Trust in Britain.

Lamaze felt that no matter how relaxed a woman was, she almost certainly would experience a degree of pain, and that she would have to cope with it.

Following the reporting of Ivan Pavlov's research into stimulus-response conditioning in dogs, Lamaze saw the value of conditioned learning in helping women to cope with the pain of childbirth.

It has 3 mainstays. The first is that fear of labor is reduced or eliminated by information and understanding. Second, you learn how to relax and become aware of your body, and therefore how to cope with pain. Third, you consciously use rhythmic breathing patterns through each contraction as a distraction from the pain.

HOME BIRTH

At home, pre-labor (see p.250) will shift imperceptibly into full labor, without changes in location or attendants.

- *You will remain in familiar surroundings with no need to travel while in labor*

- *Once notified, your midwife will come to your house and stay with you throughout*

- *You will be free to move around, and get into any position that feels comfortable*

- *You will be encouraged to follow your body's own schedule during labor*

- *Your membranes will normally be left to rupture spontaneously*

- *You will be encouraged to seek relief of pain without drugs (see p.266) although if you require pain medication, it will be available from your midwife*

- *Your midwife will try hard to help you retain an intact perineum thus avoiding an episiotomy*

- *Your partner and family can be an integral part of the birth*

- *You will have your baby with you at all times*

- *After the birth you will be free to celebrate as you choose*

The main difference between home and hospital birth is that at home the birth is your responsibility, and it's you who leads the way. You are the team captain, and everyone else is there to support you. The major drawback is that if anything does go seriously wrong, medical backup is not immediately at hand – although the chances of this happening are very small because of the relaxed environment. The "birthing" room should be properly prepared with your midwife's guidance and necessary supplies should be available.

WHAT TO EXPECT

During the early stages of labor, you will probably find it is more comfortable if you move around. Many women feel a burst of energy, and some get an overwhelming urge to clean the kitchen or sort out a closet. This is an expression of nesting and is a subconscious urge to prepare for the imminent birth. Use this time to arrange your birthing room, gathering sheets and newspapers and readying all the things you, your midwife, and the baby will need. Once labor has become really established, you or your partner should phone the midwife if she isn't already on her way, as well as any other people whom you want to be present.

Throughout labor, your midwife will be with you continuously and will monitor the baby every five minutes with a stethoscope or sonicaid (see column, p.161). She and your partner will encourage you and help you into the most comfortable positions; some pain relief will be available if you need it.

As the baby is being born you will probably find it helpful to squat. Your partner may catch the baby before putting him to your breast and your baby may breastfeed immediately. His cord will be clamped and cut once it has stopped pulsating, he will be quickly checked over (Apgar score – see p.290), and the midwife will help you deliver the placenta. The baby will then be given a thorough examination and weighed. You will be cleaned up and, if necessary, sutured. Then you will be ready to become intimately acquainted with your new family member.

THE ADVANTAGES

There are certain clear advantages to having your baby at home, such as the security of knowing you are in familiar surroundings with all the privacy you require. Your partner can play an integral part in the birth, and your other children may also be present. You will have the major say in your labor, avoiding routine medical intervention. At home you don't have to perform according to preconceived medical ideas of what is normal. You create your own normal labor in your own home. You will have the same midwife throughout and you will not be separated from your baby or your partner afterward. You will avoid the possibility of cross-infection from medical staff and other mothers and babies: bonding and breastfeeding usually happen spontaneously. One of the biggest bonuses of this type of delivery is that your partner can be an integral part of the birth of his baby – holding, cuddling, and looking after the baby while your needs are being attended to.

THE DISADVANTAGES

Rest assured that the vast majority of home births go without a hitch. However, if something does go seriously wrong, you will have to go to the hospital. Your midwife will always accompany you. There are three main problems that can occur – your baby may have problems being born and get "stuck"; he may have difficulties breathing at birth (although breathing difficulties in the newborn are often due to pain-relieving drugs – one risk that does not occur at home), or you may have a retained placenta.

Not all of these problems require immediate emergency hospitalization. Most breathing difficulties for example, can usually be eased by clearing the airways, giving oxygen, and massage. All midwives carry oxygen just in case. A retained placenta will mean that you and your baby will have to travel to the hospital.

A very few babies will be too weak or disabled to fend for themselves. They will need the attention of a special-care baby unit. If your baby is needy, you and he will have to travel to the nearest obstetrical unit – although special care seldom affects the final outcome for newborns with severe birth defects. Some mothers feel that if their babies are too handicapped to survive, they would rather they died peacefully at home.

You should also bear in mind that childbirth is very messy and noisy, and some preparation is needed in advance (see p.240).

YOUR BABY'S EXPERIENCE

Your baby will benefit from the relaxed atmosphere at home and will have the same care from your midwife as if he'd been born in hospital.

- *Your baby's heart rate will be monitored by a fetal stethoscope or a hand-held sonicaid*

- *He will emerge into the skilled hands of the midwife, or be caught by your birth partner*

- *Once breathing he will be given to you immediately after his birth and may suckle spontaneously*

- *His umbilical cord will be clamped and cut once it has stopped pulsating*

- *The skin-to-skin contact he experiences as you give him a welcoming cuddle may help him to start breathing*

- *He will be weighed and examined by the midwife; there will be no hurry to clean him up*

Birth at home
Your baby's birth will be a private celebration as he is born into the intimate environment of his family. The absence of bright lights and noise will allow you to greet your baby calmly and gently. If you have other children they can get to know this new member of the family immediately and you can have them present at the moment of birth if you wish.

HOSPITAL BIRTH

Most babies are born in a hospital. Though more and more women are choosing to have babies at home, the majority of women, encouraged by their medical advisers or their own predilections, will give birth in a hospital.

Your experience of giving birth in a hospital varies depending on your choice of hospital and professional attendants (see p.102), but will probably include the following procedures. If you wish your experience to be different, you must talk to your doctor or midwife.

- *You will probably travel to the hospital while you are in labor*

- *You will go through brief hospital admitting procedures*

- *You may be put into bed*

- *Your membranes may be ruptured and fetal monitoring equipment set in place (see p.263)*

- *If labor slows down, or stops, you will probably be given oxytocin in order to stimulate uterine contractions*

- *Pain-relieving drugs of different types will be available*

- *Your birth partner will usually be allowed to stay with you during labor and the birth*

- *You will probably be attended by shifts of different midwives and doctors, especially if you are in labor during the night*

- *An episiotomy may be performed to ease the delivery of your baby's head and to protect against possible injuries to your perineal or vaginal tissues*

- *You may be given medication (see p.289) to help you deliver the placenta*

- *You will be given your baby to hold after birth and be encouraged to start breastfeeding*

- *You may be separated from your baby at night and be subject to certain hospital routines*

WHAT TO EXPECT

The unfamiliarity of hospital surroundings can add to the drama of the occasion. Here are some tips on making the experience more pleasurable. You will probably have been advised to leave all valuables at home but on entering the hospital you may be requested to remove your remaining personal effects including jewelry. This can be depersonalizing, so ask if you can keep your personal belongings with you in a bag. Trading your own clothes for a hospital gown can have the same effect so, if this bothers you, find out beforehand if you can wear your own nightgown or nightshirt. If you wear contact lenses, ask about the hospital's policy as they may prefer you bring in a pair of glasses.

Even now, confinement to bed is the rule in some hospitals. If getting into bed bothers you, make it clear that you wish to walk about as necessary. However in some hospitals it can be physically difficult to find space in which to move, so make sure you know the set-up well in advance. If the bed rails are raised, making you feel hemmed in, ask for them to be lowered.

After admission   On arrival, your doctor or midwife will ask you about the progress of labor – the frequency of contractions and whether your waters have broken, for example. Then a member of the obstetric team will examine your abdomen to confirm the situation, the baby's position will be felt and the baby's heart checked. Your blood pressure and temperature will be taken and you'll be given an internal examination to see how far your cervix has dilated. Fetal monitoring equipment is often then set in place. It can be difficult to move once the equipment is set up, so make sure you are comfortable before you start.

Giving birth   If you wish to manage without drugs for as long as possible during labor, the nurses will usually be more than happy to help you cope using other methods (see p.266). Drug relief, however, is available and you can ask for smaller doses if you don't feel you need the full measure.

Once the baby is descending, you will be assisted into a semi-reclining position for support. An episiotomy (see p.92) is usually performed as the baby's head is crowning, if you are in any danger of tearing. Forceps always necessitate an episiotomy (see p.280). Your baby will be delivered onto your abdomen; while you take your first look at each other you may be given an injection of medication so that your uterus will contract, thus helping expel the placenta. Your baby will then be given an Apgar rating (see p.290) while you are cleaned up. You are usually sutured by the doctor at this point.

THE ADVANTAGES

In certain situations a hospital birth offers the best chance of a happy outcome. It is the birth of choice if you suffer from a medical condition such as heart disease or diabetes, if you are expecting twins or any other multiple birth, if your baby is known to be breech, or if as a first-time mother, your obstetrical history just presents too many unknown factors.

Should anything go wrong, skilled emergency medical assistance will be immediately at hand and pain medication during labor is readily available. You may feel more confident knowing that your baby can be given treatment in a special-care baby unit if the need arises. By staying in the hospital for a few hours or days after the birth, you may be able to have a more complete rest that could be difficult to arrange at home.

THE DISADVANTAGES

Once you enter the hospital it's easy to feel overpowered by the businesslike atmosphere, although some hospitals are getting more relaxed. Bear in mind that everybody in the hospital is following rules and routines and that you're going to have to fit in with them. That doesn't mean, however, that you have to do anything you aren't happy about.

YOUR BABY'S EXPERIENCE

Your baby will be born surrounded by medical staff with the expertise to handle any problems that arise.

• *An electrode to measure her heart rate may be attached to her scalp during labor*

• *With the exception of epidural anesthesia she will experience any drugs that you are given, and this may mean that she feels drowsy or is slower to feed once she is born*

• *She will be handed to you to cuddle and get acquainted with for a few minutes*

• *Her umbilical cord will be clamped and cut as soon as she has been born*

• *She may have her mouth and nose suctioned routinely to clear them of any mucus*

• *She will be weighed and examined (Apgar score) by the doctor or nurse (see p.290)*

• *She will be returned to you, possibly cleaned and wrapped in blankets, to begin bonding and breastfeeding*

• *At a later time, she will be thoroughly examined by a doctor for any abnormalities*

Birth in hospital
As far as possible you should be allowed to assume positions that are comfortable and to have your birth partner close at hand.

*There are many things that you
need to think about or investigate when you are choosing a
hospital in which to give birth.
Here are some questions to
ask yourself or others, before
you decide.*

• *What sort of birth do I want?*

• *What birth facilities are offered
in my area?*

• *Am I prepared, or able, to
travel for prenatal care? Can it be
provided by my doctor?*

• *What sort of reputations do the
hospitals in my area have? Have I
gotten as many different opinions,
from as many different sources, as
I possibly can?*

• *What are the staff members at
the different hospitals actually like?
What are their views on labor and
birth? Do I agree with them? There
may be a difference between a
hospital's policies and the way the
staff actually approaches birth*

• *Do I want a special-care baby
unit to be immediately on hand?*

• *How long do I want to be in
hospital for, and what sort of
rooming-in facilities are available?*

• *Do I want to feed my baby when
and how I feel like it?*

• *Do I want my baby with me at
night? All night?*

• *What are the visiting hours?*

• *Can my partner (and children)
be with me whenever I want?*

• *Can my partner stay with me the
first night after the birth?*

CHOOSING A DOCTOR

Pregnancy is a major life event, both physically and emotionally.
When you plan in advance, you can make decisions that will benefit both your health and that of your baby. Good general health
prior to pregnancy lets you cope better with the stresses of pregnancy, labor, and delivery, and can help ensure that neither you
nor your baby will be exposed to harm. Before you try to conceive,
visit your family physician or an obstetrician-gynecologist (Ob-Gyn)
who has treated you in the past. He will review your medical history
to determine whether you may need special care during pregnancy,
when special demands are placed on your body.

FINDING THE RIGHT DOCTOR

The doctor who cares for you during pregnancy and delivery may
be one you already know and like – a family physician who practices
obstetrics or an Ob-Gyn you have visited. If you haven't found a
suitable doctor, try asking friends and co-workers who have young
children for recommendations. Many hospitals have referral lines.
You can ask other physicians, or call your local medical society for
names of obstetricians practicing in your area.

   If you are choosing a new doctor, you may wish to interview him
or her before making a final decision; physicians today are familiar
with this approach and should welcome your interest in planning
and discussing your prenatal care. Feel free to raise questions or
concerns that could affect your choice of a doctor, including:

• At what hospital(s) does the doctor perform deliveries?

• Is the office close to your home and work? Are office hours
convenient?

• How is emergency care provided outside normal office hours?

• What are the doctor's fees, and how are they covered by your
insurance plan, if you have one? Does your plan limit your choice
to certain physicians?

• What is the doctor's attitude about questions which concern you,
such as breastfeeding, pain relief during labor, presence of fathers
in labor and delivery rooms, and the use of birthing rooms? What
are his or her views on each, and how willing is the doctor to
accommodate your personal wishes?

OTHER FACTORS

Find out if the doctor practices as part of a group, collaborative,
or alone. In a group practice, you will probably have a primary
doctor and receive care from others throughout your pregnancy.
By the time you go into labor, all the doctors will know you and the
details of your pregnancy. Your delivery will be performed by your
primary doctor, unless he or she is ill, on vacation, or off duty at
the time. In a collaborative practice, a doctor and a certified

nurse-midwife work as a team to provide your prenatal care and labor-delivery care. A solo practitioner provides your complete care; during illnesses or vacations, another doctor – who you may or may not have met – will cover.

CHANGING YOUR DOCTORS

No matter how intensively you research doctors, no matter how closely you question them, no matter how glowing their reviews from other patients, you may find, some time into your pregnancy, that you don't get along with your doctor. In that case, the patient-doctor relationship must be terminated and you will have to find another doctor. Before breaking away, try to have a forthright discussion of your views. If after that you still feel uncomfortable in his or her care, and you see no ready solution, advise the doctor (in person, on the phone, or by letter) of your decision, settle your outstanding bill or insurance claim, and seek another doctor promptly, so as not to interfere with your continuing prenatal care. Switching doctors can be very stressful, so it's best to make every effort to choose the right one the first time.

BECOMING FAMILIAR WITH YOUR HOSPITAL

Visit the hopsital or hospitals where your labor and delivery could occur. At your first visit, ask questions about hospital policies, practices, and facilities. If your doctor practices at more than one hospital, find out what differences exist between them (see **Your Considerations**). A tour of the hospital is often part of childbirth classes, or you can arrange a private tour. It's a good idea to take your partner, so both of you will be familiar with the hospital.

TYPES OF HOSPITAL

Several types of hospital offer maternity care. The most modern are often found in teaching hospitals, staffed by resident obstetricians who are always on duty. Smaller community hospitals tend to be more friendly and more flexible about policies and procedures – although you may be forfeiting some of the equipment, facilities, and trained support staff found at a teaching institution. Although a major provider of quality maternity care, Roman Catholic hospitals may be more restrictive in their policies, particularly those concerning postpartum sterilization and contraception.

Teaching and community hospitals frequently offer what has become known as "Family-Centered Maternity Care" (or some similar term), which means that they have eliminated certain routine procedures and added other options, such as Leboyer delivery; breastfeeding on the delivery table; nonseparation of parents and baby; rooming-in; early discharge.

Many hospitals have responded to parents' wishes by providing birthing rooms where the family can participate. Birthing rooms share the specialized staff and services of the usual labor and delivery suite. They provide a comfortable setting for labor, delivery, recovery and, sometimes, the entire postpartum stay, so that the birth process can take place in one room.

QUESTIONS TO ASK

Once you have chosen a doctor or midwife, find out as much about the hospital as you can by asking questions.

- *Will I be able to wear my own clothes and personal effects (rings, contact lenses, spectacles)?*

- *Can my partner or friend stay with me all the time? Will he or she ever be asked to leave?*

- *Will I be able to move around freely during labor and give birth in any position I choose?*

- *Will I be able to have the same attendants throughout labor?*

- *Can I bring in my own midwife to attend to me throughout labor?*

- *Does the hospital have a birthing room? Are beanbags, birthing chairs, and stools provided?*

- *Does the hospital offer tubs or showers for patients in labor?*

- *What is the hospital policy on pain relief, routine electronic monitoring, and induction?*

- *What kind of pain relief is available? Is this at all times?*

- *Will I be able to eat and drink if I want to?*

- *What is the hospital policy on enemas and the shaving of pubic hair?*

- *What is the hospital policy on episiotomies, Caesareans, and the expulsion of the placenta?*

- *If I tear or have an episiotomy, are midwives or nurses allowed to suture me, or will I have to wait for a doctor to attend to me?*

- *What is the hospital policy on separation of parents and child in the first hour? What about during the rest of the stay?*

YOUR ATTENDANTS

There are many different approaches to birth, so ask your doctor, Ob-Gyn, or nurse-midwife the following questions to find out exactly what you can expect from him or her.

- *Do you think enemas and shaving are useful?*

- *What are your views on inducing labor and birth?*

- *Under what circumstances would you consider it necessary to rupture the membranes?*

- *Do you believe electronic fetal monitoring is a valuable aid in every birth?*

- *Would you be concerned if labor were slower than normal?*

- *What are your views on moving around and breathing techniques to help relieve pain? What drugs do you normally give to control pain during labor?*

- *Would you be concerned if the lights were dimmed during labor?*

- *How often do you perform episiotomies?*

- *Are you happy for me to stand or squat to deliver my child?*

- *Under what conditions would you consider a Caesarean section to be necessary?*

- *Will we be able to have some time alone with our baby immediately after his birth?*

- *What are your fees?*

PROFESSIONAL ATTENDANTS

You have many choices regarding the team of health-care professionals who can guide and support you through your pregnancy, labor, and delivery. Wherever you decide to have your baby – usually in a hospital, but sometimes at home – remember that the system can usually be tailored to meet your individual preferences and needs. Of course, your professional attendants are not the only ones who surround you during pregnancy. Most women are supported by their partners during childbirth, as well as their close friends, sisters, and parents.

Babies can be delivered by family physicians who do obstetrics, by obstetrician-gynecologists, or by certified nurse-midwives. There may also be a team of health-care specialists to assist your doctor.

YOUR FAMILY DOCTOR

Doctors in family practice provide general care for most medical conditions, and many of them do obstetrics. This doctor is often the first professional you will visit, to test for and confirm your pregnancy. He or she may have treated you before your pregnancy, and so will be very familiar with your health history, just as you may be familiar with the doctor's views on childbirth. If you choose your family practitioner to deliver your baby, he or she will most always want to conduct your delivery in a hospital, but some are amenable to alternatives such as home birth, depending on your history and the progress of your pregnancy.

THE OBSTETRICIAN-GYNECOLOGIST

Obstetrician-gynecologists are physicians who specialize in the care of women's health problems. After medical school, they usually complete a four-year course of specialized training called residency. Then they must pass intensive examinations to document their competency in the special knowledge and skills required for the medical and surgical care of the female reproductive system and related disorders.

THE CERTIFIED NURSE-MIDWIFE

Certified nurse-midwives are registered nurses who are educated and experienced in providing health care to women and their babies from early pregnancy through labor, delivery, and the period after birth. In most states, nurse-midwives must practice in collaboration with a doctor, and they must refer patients to a doctor if complications occur. The nurse-midwife has special skills to support you throughout your pregnancy and delivery. Some midwives are associated with freestanding birthing centers, others are based in hospitals. Many will come to your home to deliver your baby – and if all goes well, neither you nor the baby have to enter the hospital. However, if a problem arises, the nurse-midwife will escort you to the hospital for appropriate treatment.

TEAM OF ATTENDANTS

Many doctors coordinate a team of health-care professionals to meet a woman's needs. This team may include:

• Nurses, who assist the doctor by gathering information needed to diagnose and treat medical conditions. Nurses are often the main providers of patient education

• Childbirth educators, who teach prospective parents about conception, pregnancy, childbirth, and family life

• Certified nurse-midwives, who are specially trained to care for women during pregnancy and childbirth

• Labor and delivery nurses, who care for patients in labor and for the baby immediately after birth

• Postpartum nurses, who help care for the mother after birth

• Neonatal nurses, who help care for the newborn

• Social workers, who provide counseling and information

• Nutritionists, who give advice and guidance on diet, nutrition, and any special dietary needs both before and after delivery

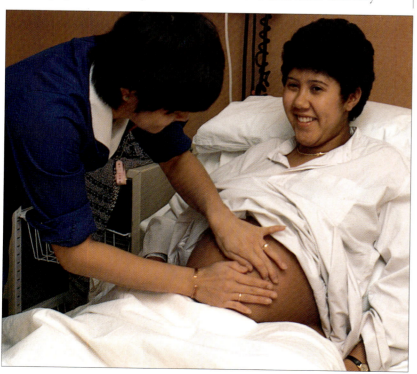

CHOOSING YOUR NURSE-MIDWIFE

Because she will be your primary caregiver, you will need to get to know her. You may like to know the following:

• *What training and experience has she had?*

• *Does she work alone, or with other midwives? Will you be able to meet them?*

• *What are her considerations in managing labor?*

• *What is her back-up system? Does she work closely with a doctor and a hospital?*

• *What equipment, drugs, and resuscitation equipment for you and the baby does she carry?*

• *What prenatal care does she provide? Are there home visits?*

• *Under what conditions would she transfer a mother or baby to the hospital?*

• *What does she charge?*

Your birth attendant
The professional who assists you to give birth should be someone you know and trust, who will give you the kind of support that you and your partner need. The best attendant is one who helps create an intimate atmosphere so you can work with your body to bring a new life into the world.

THE SINGLE MOTHER

NAME *Rosemary Hutchinson*

AGE *38 years*

PAST MEDICAL HISTORY *Appendix removed at age 15*

OBSTETRIC HISTORY *One abortion at 11 weeks, 10 years ago. She is now 14 weeks pregnant*

Ros never considered motherhood to be the most pleasurable aspect of being a woman. She always felt that work would be more fulfilling and that the pursuit of a career would be more satisfying. Even as a small girl, Ros was determined not to "dwindle" into marriage or adopt the role of housewife. She has always taken the responsibility for contraception in her relationships and believes fervently that she has the right to decide whether or not to have a baby. Indeed, Ros made the decision to abort an 11-week pregnancy when she was 28 years old because she did not wish to interrupt her career.

Ros is a lawyer. She studied political science, philosophy, and economics in college and went on to study law at a distinguished school. She is now a highly respected attorney, specializing in family law and working for a noted law firm.

Ros has had two long-term relationships but in neither case felt she had found a partner with whom she could settle down. She did not wish to make any form of long-term commitment to a partnership that would force her to relinquish any independence.

However, this independence had its price. As she got older, Ros began to fear that her fertility was diminishing, and she sensed that time was running out. She began to want a baby very much, but remained reluctant to commit herself to a man. She began to think about the possibilities of having IVF, but didn't like the idea of not knowing who the father was. During a recent passionate and whirlwind affair with a younger man, Ros decided that she would be more than happy if her lover, Timothy, was the father of her baby, although she couldn't see the relationship lasting and didn't particularly want it to. She talked it over with Timothy, who agreed that he didn't want to make any long-term commitment to Ros either, although he was willing to father her baby. The affair has now ended, although Ros and Timothy have remained firm friends, and Ros has just entered the second trimester of her pregnancy.

A HEALTHY BABY

This will be Ros's only child and she wants to do everything she can in order to ensure that the baby will be healthy. To this end, she went to a genetic counselor before she became pregnant because a cousin on her father's side suffers from hemophilia (see p.20). However, because her father had not suffered from the disease, the counselor was able to reassure Ros that she was not carrying the gene. After she had discussed the possibility of pregnancy with Timothy, Ros also asked him about his family background. Happily, everything seemed to be normal.

Prenatal care On her first visit, Ros was told that her lifestyle is more important than her age in determining the smoothness of her pregnancy and her delivery. She is therefore being very careful about her diet (see p.112), exercise (see p.126), not smoking, drinking, or taking any medication. All of her medical tests have proved normal and she is aware that she should not gain too much weight, that her blood pressure will be meticulously checked, and that she must be on the lookout for signs of water retention (tight rings, swollen ankles), as this could herald preeclampsia (see p.204). Ros had a sonogram at her last prenatal visit in order to find out, among other things, if there are any obvious abnormalities with the baby. Everything appeared to be normal. Although ultrasound scanning revealed no abnormality, Ros is eager to have the added reassurance of the information about genetic or chromosomal diseases that can be revealed only by amniocentesis (see p.164). She will also have a specimen of blood examined to check her alpha-fetoprotein (AFP) levels (see p.159).

PREGNANCY AND LABOR

Ros hopes that by careful reduction and flexibility in working hours and workload, she will be able to work right up until labor begins. Despite being allowed up to 28 weeks maternity leave, she intends to return to the office part-time after only two weeks at home with her newborn baby. Given her demanding working schedule, Ros knows the importance of rest. Already she rests with her feet up for 20 minutes during her lunch hour and in the late afternoon is quite likely to snatch a nap in her office or in the car. She is rigorous about getting enough sleep, has stopped socializing except on weekends, and is in bed by 9.30 p.m. I advised her to learn deep muscle and mental relaxation and to continue with her yoga.

Ros is determined to have the very best medical care available during labor and has made the choice to be delivered at a large teaching hospital that is at the forefront of technology. She has decided that she wants to have an active birth and is pleased that she will be supervised by a team of midwives as she will not have a birth partner and will therefore be relying on her carers for emotional support. She has made a birth plan (see p.106), which has been attached to the front of her hospital records.

AFTER THE BIRTH

Being able to afford it, Ros has opted for a full-time nanny who will live in with her and the baby as soon as she returns from her hospital delivery. The nanny will be on night duty from the end of the first two weeks so that Ros can get a full night's rest in preparation for returning to work. Ros has decided to breastfeed for as long as possible and is prepared to express milk and store or freeze it so that her baby has the benefits of breast milk even though she herself is absent. I warned Ros that one of the hardest things about being a single parent is that she will have no one with whom she can share the memorable events, such as when her baby first smiles or speaks. I also warned her that although her baby would not suffer from having only one parent, it would mean that the demands on Ros herself would be very high. While work will bring her great satisfaction, I encouraged Ros to have as active a social life as her commitments will allow because it's so easy to become isolated at home with a small child.

ROS'S BABY

Ros's baby will only have one parent right from the start, which means that her experience will be somewhat different from that of a child who has both parents present.

Feeding She will have the advantage of having Ros's breast milk, despite the fact that Ros will be at work. However, this does mean that she will have to get used to being bottlefed by her nanny and breastfed by her mother.

Care Ros will be able to provide her baby with just as much care as two parents would. Her baby will also become very attached to her nanny, who will be a very important person in her life, but there is nothing wrong in this.

Time Ros's baby will not see her mother all the time, but when she does, it will be quality time.

Relationships Ros and her child will tend to be everything to each other, which may lead to a very intense relationship.

COVERING YOUR ALTERNATIVES

Although you will make your plan according to the kind of birth you would like to have, it is a good idea to have another one on stand-by.

This alternative plan can set out the procedures that you would prefer to be followed should complications arise. On rare occasions, labor may become unexpectedly prolonged or difficult, or the baby may need special attention. By considering all the possibilities, you enable your birth attendants to take care of any situation as you wish.

Planning your labor
Make a note of all the issues that are important to you, and discuss them with your doctor.

BIRTH PLAN

Making a plan of your baby's birth will help ensure you have active involvement in the way he is born and what happens to you as a family after the birth. By carefully considering all your ideas and preferences, and by discussing them with your birth attendants and partner, you will be able to establish a bond of trust and create a happier and more comfortable labor.

A CONSENSUS PLAN

Think about the issues that are important to you and then find out as much as you can to see if what you want is feasible (see pp.100 & 102, and column, right). There is no point in making a plan that cannot be used once you are in labor.

Discuss your plan with your doctor early in your pregnancy so that you can make sure he or she would be most likely to accord with your wishes. You should make specific inquiries about the routines followed where you intend to give birth, as some hospitals will not be able to meet your requirements. Discuss your requirements with your midwife, the teacher of your childbirth education-class, and other members of your prenatal team as they will be able to advise you about the kinds of experiences mothers have had in local hospitals and with particular doctors.

Hospital response Your hospital team may be pleased to see how well you have prepared yourself for the labor, and then your full participation will probably be encouraged. Some mothers have experienced negativity from hospital staff on the grounds that a birth plan may interfere with their standard practices. Don't be intimidated – just remember your baby is your responsibility and so is the way in which you give birth to him.

Working together Cooperation is an important feature of the birth plan. By working it out in detail with all your attendants, including your partner, you should be able to alleviate any anxieties and feel more in control of your baby's birth. Make sure, too, that staff know of any alternatives.

Try to maintain a friendly relationship with your caregivers – but be firm about your wishes. Bear in mind that your goal is to create a warm and supportive atmosphere. Once the details of your plan have been finalized, give a copy to your primary caregiver.

Special considerations Make a note on your birth plan of any special needs, such as diet, which may be applicable during your time in the hospital. Allergies and religious beliefs could also be mentioned.

PRESENTING YOUR BIRTH PLAN

These 2 examples of a birth plan outline different choices of birth – there are many variations. The plan may be laid out as a list, a letter, or a document such as that from the Chelsea and Westminster Hospital, London.

Thank you for all the information that you provided in the prenatal classes and at the childbirth classes. I have thought carefully about how I would like my labor and delivery to be.

My partner, John, will be my companion during labor. He has attended childbirth classes with me.

I understand that electronic fetal monitoring is routinely used, and I am happy for this to be done.

If I need pain relief I would prefer an epidural, with as low an epidural dose as possible so that I still have feeling in my legs and am aware of contractions. I would prefer for it to wear off for the second stage, as I would like to push out the baby myself.

If everything goes well and I do not need pain relief, I would prefer to be able to walk around and give birth using a birthing stool, which I will provide myself.

If I have to have a Caesarean section I would like my partner, John, to be with me throughout the operation.

I intend to breastfeed on demand and want the baby to sleep next to me if at all possible. I would also like my partner, John, to be able to stay with us for the first night.

Jenny Lewis

I am looking forward to coming into Central Hospital. I would like to record a few points about the birth as the midwives have suggested. They are:

Support person	I will be accompanied by my sister, Sarah.
Shaving and enemas	I would prefer not to be shaved or to have an enema.
Monitoring	I would prefer to be monitored by a sonicaid or Pinnard stethoscope.
Positions	I will probably want to deliver the baby in a semi-upright position, as this is how I had my other two babies.
Pain relief	It is likely that I will need Demerol, as I did last time.
Episiotomy	I would prefer not to be cut if it can be avoided. I would welcome help in order to help prevent it.

Paula Bell

When?
Make sure your plan is with your carers by your eighth month.

IT'S YOUR CHOICE

Look at all the possibilities that will help you to approach your labor with confidence. Don't feel that labor has to be totally managed, or natural; it can be a blend of many things. Here are some alternatives:

- *Hospital/home birth*

- *Partner not allowed for certain procedures/allowed throughout*

- *Shave pubic hair/no shaving*

- *Use of enemas or suppositories/neither given*

- *Medical induction of labor/spontaneous start*

- *Amniotomy/spontaneous rupture of membranes*

- *Fetus monitored electronically/by midwife or doctor with a Pinnard stethoscope (see p.161)*

- *Confined to bed in first stage of labor/free to move*

- *Nothing by mouth/eat and drink as and when desired*

- *Types of pain relief: injection, epidural, breathing exercises*

- *Catheterization/empty own bladder as necessary*

- *Commanded pushing/spontaneous pushing*

- *Passive position/position of your own choice*

- *Elective episiotomy/episiotomy only if absolutely necessary*

- *Mother not touching vaginal area/touching baby's head as it crowns, lifting baby out*

- *Use of medication to speed delivery of placenta/natural expulsion of placenta*

CHILDBIRTH TEACHERS

You'll probably choose a childbirth teacher fairly early in your pregnancy; make plans to start classes in your seventh month or earlier.

Both the quality and approach of classes can vary – some are tightly structured with little question-and-answer time, others allow plenty of time to practice techniques. Some depend mainly on lectures, others on class participation. The teacher is very often the determining factor, so do check with other couples you know who have attended classes before you make your final choice.

Try to select a teacher whose philosophy of birth fits in with the type of birth you'd like to have. Conflicts and confusion can arise if what you learn in class does not accord with your later experience in the hospital or at home.

Find out how many couples are taught in each class. Half a dozen couples is ideal as you will receive plenty of attention from the teacher while being intimate with your fellow participants.

Childbirth teachers are, by their very nature, aware and sensitive to the needs and problems of pregnancy. Yours will probably be more than happy to talk to you – even if you are not yet attending childbirth classes.

CHILDBIRTH CLASSES

As an enthusiastic proponent of prepared childbirth, I believe that everyone can benefit from childbirth classes. These classes are tremendously enjoyable. The camaraderie is wonderful and you may find the other members of the group act as a substitute for your extended family as you exchange folklore; certainly they will make you feel less alone and isolated. It's a great help to be able to share feelings and experiences with people who are in the same position and it helps to relieve tension and anxiety. Strong personal bonds are often formed with others in the class; these can be the basis of lasting friendships.

PARENTING CLASSES

These are particularly useful for first-time parents because they're designed to give you information that will make you both feel more confident. They work in three ways:

First, they cover the processes of pregnancy and birth, including female anatomy and physiology, and the changes that occur throughout pregnancy. This is done so you will have a clearer understanding of what is involved and why things are happening. The teachers will also talk to you about the sort of medical procedures that you can expect, and why these will be done.

Second, they provide instruction in relaxation, breathing, and exercise techniques that will help you to control your own labor, reduce pain, and give you the confidence that only comes with being familiar with what's happening. Bear in mind that bodies, not brains, give birth, so anything that helps you tune into your body is going to be useful. Your partner should learn how to give you a massage to help relieve your pain (see p.267).

Third, the teachers will talk you through the stages of labor and birth, advise on breastfeeding, and will offer practice in bathing and dressing the baby, changing diapers, bottlefeeding, and making up formula. This will help you cope with the practicalities of caring for your newborn baby.

EXERCISE CLASSES

Strengthening the muscles used in childbirth often results in an easier delivery. Many hospitals offer prenatal classes that incorporate exercise and relaxation classes, and there are independent organizations as well – some are even for specific types of birth. If you tell your instructor that you would like to have your baby while you are standing or squatting, you will be given suitable exercises to help strengthen your back, hips, pelvis, and thighs.

YOGA

With its emphasis on muscular control of the body, breathing, relaxation, and tranquility of mind, yoga is an excellent resource to use as a preparation for pregnancy. However, yoga is a philosophy that pervades the whole of life and, though special exercises for pregnancy exist, they are only a small part of the system. Consequently, it is not something that you can do casually – to have any benefit, it must be practiced regularly, preferably starting long before you conceive.

TECHNIQUES OF CHILDBIRTH CLASSES

Many studies have shown that taking a childbirth class shortens the length of labor. In one study, the average duration of labor for a group of women who had taken classes was 13.56 hours, compared with the average labor of 18.33 hours in the control group, which had no training. This is probably because knowing how to deal with pain produces a more relaxed labor. Strategies taught by childbirth classes to deal with pain include the following:

Cognitive control You disassociate your mind from the pain by visualizing a pleasant scenario in which to experience the pain. For example, you will feel happier about experiencing contractions if, every time you have a pain, you imagine your baby moving further down the birth canal, closer to emerging. In this way, you will be concentrating on the non-painful part of the sensation.

You can also use distraction to cope with pain during labor, though this works best in the early stages. Counting to 20, going through a list of possible names for your new baby, or concentrating on a beautiful picture or piece of music should enable you to take your mind off the pain, and keep it from completely filling your consciousness and overwhelming you. Focusing your attention on your breathing techniques and becoming consciously aware of your breathing pattern is another way of forcing your mind away from focusing on pain.

Systematic relaxation In order to decrease your fear of pain and thus increase your tolerance for it, you will be taught exercises to relax the various muscles of the body. In this way you will be able to isolate pain from the contracting uterus rather than allowing it to pervade other parts of your body.

Hawthorne rehearsal You receive enhanced attention from a birth assistant. Psychological research has shown that the more attention you are given, the less pain you feel.

Systematic desensitization You gradually become more tolerant of pain. An example used in many classes is your coach pinching your leg very hard to illustrate how painful a contraction will be. This pinching is repeated every time you attend a prenatal class, and by the end of the course you will be able to tolerate harder squeezing for longer periods.

FATHER'S ROLE

In a prenatal class you may be able to show your partner for the first time just how central a role he is going to play.

Classes will make a supportive man a more effective birth assistant by familiarizing him with the processes of labor and delivery.

Some courses have father-only sessions where the men can talk freely about any problems or anxieties they have about the forthcoming event. A worried man should find security and support in the teacher, as well as in the company of other fathers-to-be.

Team effort
Childbirth classes give a couple a unique opportunity to work as a team toward a common goal – the birth of their baby – and very often this results in a special closeness.

CHAPTER

4

FOOD

and eating in pregnancy

Eating healthfully in pregnancy is mainly a question of eating a wide variety of the right kind of foods – those rich in essential nutrients. Concentrating on fresh fruit and vegetables, whole grains, organically grown meat, and low-fat dairy products will ensure a healthy environment in which your baby will develop.

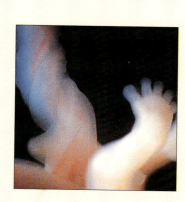

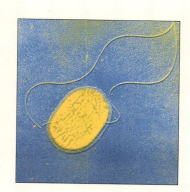

EATING FOR YOURSELF

Your body will never work harder than it does during pregnancy and childbirth. To cope with the increased demands, maintain your strength, and enjoy your pregnancy, you must eat well.

- *Increase your intake by 500 Calories per day*
- *Start to eat 5-6 small meals a day instead of 2-3 big ones*
- *Make certain you get sufficient protein and carbohydrates (see p.116); the former supplies essential nutrients for your developing baby, the latter meets your energy needs*
- *Eat foods that contain vitamins, such as vitamin C, and minerals, particularly iron (see p.117). These are essential for the healthy functioning of all your organs*

Gaining weight

Doctors recommend that a woman of average weight, experiencing an average pregnancy, should gain approximately 20–30lb (10–15kg) in the total 40 weeks gestation as shown in the chart on the right. This allows 6–8lb (3–4kg) for the baby and 14–24lb (7–12kg) for the baby-support system (placenta, amniotic fluid, increased blood, fluid, fat, and breast tissue). It is usual to gain very little, if anything, during the first trimester, approximately 1–2lb (5–10kg) each week between months 4 and 8, then very little, or none at all, in the last month. A steady gain like this means that your body can adapt more easily to your increasing size, and your baby will have a continuous flow of nourishment.

FOOD IN PREGNANCY

Pregnant women, like most people, rarely have the time or inclination to sit around measuring out ounces of this and portions of that and trying to remember the calorific value of everything. In fact, there's no need to do that as long as you follow some basic guidelines about healthy eating in pregnancy. One important rule is that the nearer food is to its natural state, the more nutritious it is. So fresh is best, frozen is next best, and you should always make canned foods your last choice. In many ways, good nutrition is just common sense.

EATING FOR TWO?

As your pregnancy progresses your appetite will increase; this is nature's way of making certain you eat enough for you and your baby. Your energy requirements will increase only by 15 percent, or 500 calories per day, far less than if you ate twice your normal amount of food. (Certain mothers-to-be, however, such as those who previously ate an inadequate or unbalanced diet, may be nutritionally at risk and have special requirements – see also column, p.122.) The saying "eating for two", therefore, underlines

AVERAGE WEIGHT GAIN DURING PREGNANCY

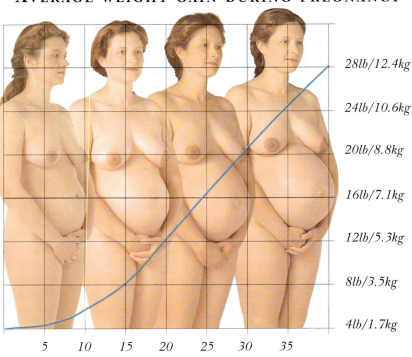

28lb/12.4kg

24lb/10.6kg

20lb/8.8kg

16lb/7.1kg

12lb/5.3kg

8lb/3.5kg

4lb/1.7kg

5   10   15   20   25   30   35

your responsibility to provide for the nutritional needs of your developing baby. Everything you eat should be good for you and your baby; more problems develop if you eat too little rather than too much. Pregnancy is not the time for dieting. Research has shown that when mothers-to-be eat poor diets, there is a higher incidence of spontaneous abortions, neonatal death, and low-birthweight babies than normal.

However, you do need to beware of really excess weight gain; fat that is deposited at the tops of the arms and the thighs is very difficult to get rid of after pregnancy. Junk food, from chocolate bars to hamburgers and fries, tends to be made up mainly of fat and sugar, which are of little value to your growing baby, and your body converts it to maternal fat.

A quite substantial amount of fat will be lost by breastfeeding your baby, as it is accumulated specifically to be converted to milk during lactation. However, some will remain and this will be difficult to lose once you have finished breastfeeding.

You therefore owe it to yourself, as well as your baby, to eat a diet that is best for both of you. While you should adhere to the nutritional recommendations on page 119, you can balance your food intake over a 24- to 48-hour period rather than at each meal. Make sure that you don't miss meals – your baby grows all day, every day, and suffers if you starve.

BABY'S REQUIREMENTS

During pregnancy, you are your baby's only source of nourishment. Every calorie, vitamin, or gram of protein that your baby needs must be eaten by you. You are the sole manager of your unborn child's nutrition; you, and only you, can make sure that the best-quality food reaches her.

You will fulfill all of your baby's requirements if you eat lots of fresh fruit, vegetables, beans, peas, whole-grain cereals, fish, fowl, and low-fat dairy products. (A Danish study, recently released, shows that eating oil-rich fish – salmon, herring, sardines – may help lessen the risk of preterm birth.) Make your diet as varied as possible, choosing from a wide range of foodstuffs.

DON'T FORGET MOM

The other important person you must eat for during pregnancy is yourself. A good diet will mean that you have better reserves to cope with, and recover from, the indisputable strain of pregnancy, and the hard physical work of labor. Anemia and preeclampsia (see p.204) are much more common in those mothers who have a poor diet, and the common complaints such as morning sickness and leg cramps are often exacerbated by what you don't eat; for example, not enough salt may cause leg cramps.

Overall, good nutrition will help minimize excessive mood swings, fatigue, and many common complaints (see pp.188–195). In addition, a sensible eating regimen that cuts out or restricts the amount of empty calories you consume will mean that you will be left with less excess fat to lose after your child has been born.

EMPTY CALORIES

The following foods should be avoided in pregnancy; they usually contain nothing more than sugar or sugar substitutes and refined flour.

- *Any form of sweetener – including white or brown sugar, maple syrup, molasses, and artificial products such as saccharine and aspartame*

- *Candies and chocolate bars*

- *Soft drinks, such as cola and sweetened fruit juices*

- *Commercially produced cookies, cakes, pastries, doughnuts, and pies, as well as jam and marmalade*

- *Canned fruit in syrup*

- *Sweetened breakfast cereal*

- *Ice cream and frozen desserts that contain added sugar. Freeze fruit juice or puréed fruit instead*

- *Foods that contain sugar, such as peanut butter, relishes, pickles, salad dressings, mayonnaise, spaghetti sauces, and many others – read the label*

YOUR OFFICE SUPPLIES

The average nine-to-five job can wreak havoc with your nutritional intake. However, advance planning and a few strategically situated supplies can help.

In the office refrigerator

- *Mineral water*
- *Unsweetened fruit juice*
- *Plain live-culture yogurt*
- *Dutch or Swiss cheese*
- *Hard-boiled eggs*
- *Fresh fruit*
- *"Snack" vegetables – carrot sticks and red pepper slices, tomatoes*
- *Whole-grain bread*
- *Jar of wheat germ*

In your desk drawer

- *Whole-grain crackers, crispbreads, or breadsticks, perhaps with seeds*
- *Dried fruit*
- *Nuts or seeds*
- *Decaffeinated instant coffee and decaffeinated tea bags*
- *Powdered skim milk for extra calcium in drinks*

In your handbag

- *Whole-grain crackers, crispbreads, or breadsticks, perhaps with seeds*
- *Dried fruit, nuts, and seeds*
- *Fresh fruit or "snack" vegetables*
- *Small thermos of unsweetened juice or milk*
- *Hard candy for emergencies*

Make sure everything is securely wrapped and sealed.

THE BEST FOOD TO EAT

Quality food is as close to its original state as possible and offers you and your baby good nutritional value. Eating quality food should be your goal throughout, as well as after, pregnancy.

When shopping, select fresh produce; seasonal fruit and vegetables will be fresher as well as cheaper. Always select sound fruit and vegetables; reject any that look tired or are going bad. Buy your meat and fish from reputable groceries, butchers, and fish markets – don't run the risk of contracting a food-related illness (see p.123). If you can afford it, opt for free-range or organic foods to avoid pesticides and hormones (especially pertinent in the case of organ meats). Some stores label foods as natural or organic as a sales ploy when they are nothing of the sort.

Frozen packages of vegetables, such as peas and green beans, are good standbys – particularly when vegetables are out of season. Avoid cans, except for tomatoes and fish. Always read labels – the nearer an ingredient is to the top of the list, the more there is of that one ingredient. Bear in mind that sugar has many different names (see **Carbohydrates and calories**, p.116) and can appear on a list more than once, hence adding up to be the major ingredient.

Foods that have been over-refined, such as white flour and white sugar, have had all of the natural goodness stripped out of them and can offer you and your baby nothing but excess calories. Instead, choose whole-grain bread, pastry, and flour, rather than "enriched" refined products, as it is highly unlikely that the enrichment puts back in all that has been taken out. The two "waste" products of refining are bran (the fiber) and wheat germ (the heart of the wheat), and these contain most of the goodness. Bran is probably an unnecessary addition for the average pregnant woman (although it will help prevent constipation), but everyone can benefit from the multitude of vitamins and minerals in wheat germ. Wheat germ tastes a bit like cashews – crunchy and nutty – and can be added to salads, sandwiches, and pizzas, as well as to cooked and baked dishes. Wheat germ is often available in bulk from health food stores as well as in jars from grocery stores. It should be kept in the refrigerator after opening.

GOOD EATING HABITS

The first thing to acknowledge is that willpower alone will probably not be enough to achieve your aims; willpower has a nasty habit of letting you down in the face of temptation. The first step is to avoid temptations like chocolate-chip cookies in the afternoon or take-out for dinner. Have a homemade, sugar-free fruit-and-nut bar, and always keep a decaffeinated tea bag on hand. Cook up a large batch of meals over the weekend when you are feeling energetic, and store the resulting goodies in the freezer or pantry, to be there when you're too tired to cook. Banish junk food from your kitchen.

Learn to snack on nutritious foods and eat little and often if your appetite is quickly extinguished. Toward the end of pregnancy, eating substantial amounts will become a bit of a problem, so you really have to make every mouthful count. Eating a piece of cake, for example, washed down with a soda will fill you up to the extent that you won't be able to compensate nutritionally with tuna salad and a glass of milk later on. Think before you eat – a roast chicken sandwich on whole-grain bread is much better for you and your baby than bacon and avocado on white. Invest in a healthy-eating cookbook and learn how to make dishes that are lower in fat and sugar but still taste delicious. If you do slip up and cheat, don't give up in despair; forgive yourself and continue eating healthfully.

VEGETARIANISM

A large number of people do not eat meat; many more people who aren't strict vegetarians limit their intake of meat, particularly red meat. If you fall into one of these categories, you need to take special precautions to ensure that you eat enough protein, vitamins, and iron to meet your own and your baby's needs.

There are complementary plant protein sources such as dried beans and grains. These, if eaten in combination, will provide you with most of the necessary amino acids normally found complete in animal forms of protein (see below).

All vegetarians need to make sure they take in sufficient iron as there is relatively little in vegetable matter and certain substances interfere with its absorption (see p.117). If you eat no animal products at all, you will have to work harder to make sure that you are not deficient in any nutrient – particularly calcium, vitamins B_6, B_{12}, and D, all of which are provided by dairy products. Vitamin B_{12} is only found in animal sources. Although very little is needed, lack of it will eventually lead to pernicious anemia. If your diet contains no animal products, you need to take vitamin B_{12} supplements.

(see p.117)

SHORTCUTS

When time, energy, or money are short, eating nutritiously can often seem to be too much hassle. Here are some tips that will help you do the best for you and your baby, without too much effort:

- *Keep a supply of various frozen vegetables*

- *Buy meat and fish in bulk, and freeze in meal-size portions*

- *Cook ahead and freeze*

- *Buy ready-made fresh salads*

- *A microwave cooks food quickly and retains nutrients*

- *Keep it simple – eat raw vegetables and fruit; steam, stir fry, or grill for speed, or bake so you can leave food to cook on its own*

- *Enlist help – many grandparents-to-be will be itching to give you a hand*

COMPLEMENTARY PROTEINS

Grains

Milk products

Nuts and seeds

Beans, peas, and lentils

Combining proteins
All animal products contribute first-class proteins, so called because they contain all the essential amino acids that the body needs in the right proportions. Plant products contribute second-class proteins because the amino acids that they provide are not of the right proportions. In order to receive the full complement of necessary amino acids, you would have to eat certain foods in combination. For example, peas could be served with rice or corns; a handful of nuts could be added to rice and sweetcorn salad.

◀▶ *Generally complementary*

◀▶ *Sometimes complementary*

CHOOSING
PROTEINS

*Due to the intensive develop-
ment of your growing baby,
your protein requirement
increases by 30% from the onset
of pregnancy.*

*This means your needs jump from
1 3/4–2 1/4oz (45–60g) to 3–4oz
(75–100g) of protein daily,
depending on how active you are.*

*Proteins are made up of amino
acids, which are vital to individual body cells and tissues. A
total of 20 different amino acids
are required. The body can
synthesize 12 of these, the non-
essential amino acids, but 8
others, the essential acids, must be
supplied by food you eat. These
latter are first-class proteins and
are found only in animal products
such as meat, dairy products, fish,
poultry, and eggs. Always choose
organically grown produce especially poultry, eggs, beef, and
organ meats, whenever possible.*

*Your choice of proteins, however,
also needs to be guided by what
else you are getting from protein-
rich food. Organ meats and meat
are the richest sources of first-class
proteins and contain vital B
vitamins. However, some meat,
particularly red meat, can be very
high in animal fat, while liver
shouldn't be eaten during pregnancy (see column, right), so you
could choose fish instead.*

*Fish is a first-class protein that is
high in vitamins and nutrious
fish oils, and low in fat.*

*Equivalent amounts of protein are
1 egg, 1 slice of hard cheese, 2
tablespoons peanut butter, 2 tablespoons cottage cheese, 1/2 cup peas
or beans.*

ESSENTIAL NUTRITION

Research has found that what you eat when you are pregnant not
only affects your baby at birth, but also appears to have a long-term
effect throughout your child's life – even into old age.

PROTEIN

Protein is probably the most essential nutrient for your baby; the
amino acids that make up protein are literally the building blocks
of the body. Proteins form the main structural elements of the cells
and tissues that make up muscles, bones, connective tissues, and
many of your organ walls.

The type and quality of protein in food varies (see column, left).
Generally, the more expensive foodstuffs like meat, fish, and
poultry are the best sources, but less expensive products eaten
together can also supply you with adequate protein. Wholewheat
bread or noodles with beans, cheese, or peanut butter; or cornmeal
or noodles with sesame seeds, nuts, and milk are cheaper ingredients that will keep your protein intake high. You need at least three
servings of protein foods daily (see p.118).

CARBOHYDRATES AND CALORIES

These should provide the largest part of your daily calorie intake.
As you need to increase your calorie intake by 500 calories during
pregnancy, you should make certain that you eat the best kind of
carbohydrates you can and avoid empty calories (see p.113).

Simple carbohydrates are sugars in various forms. The most
common types and sources are sucrose (cane sugar), glucose
(honey), fructose (fruit), and maltose, lactose, and galactose (milk).
Because they are absorbed quickly from the stomach, all provide
"instant energy." This is useful when you are in dire need (hard
candies may be helpful in case of nausea).

Complex carbohydrates are the starches contained in grains,
potatoes, lentils, beans, and peas. The body has to break them down
into simple carbohydrates before it can use them, so they provide
a steady supply of energy over a period of time. In addition,
complex unrefined carbohydrates (such as whole-grain oats and
brown rice) are wonderful sources of essential nutrients, like fiber,
vitamins, and minerals.

VITAMINS

Vitamins are essential for health. Good sources of many vitamins
(and minerals) are vegetables and fruits. Some are rich in vitamin
C and others contain vitamins A, B, E, minerals, and folic acid; you
must include all in your daily diet. Vitamins are fragile, and are
quickly destroyed by exposure to light, air, and heat. Many cannot
be stored by the body, so good levels are necessary every day. Leafy
green vegetables, yellow/red vegetables, and fruit supply vitamins
A, E, B_6, riboflavin, iron, zinc, and magnesium. Choose spinach,
watercress, carrots, tomatoes, bananas, apricots, and cherries.

There are some vegetables, such as watercress, that are rich in many vitamins, so you can do yourself and your baby a lot of good if you eat them. Other vegetables and fruit may not give you a big dose of any individual vitamin, but they will provide a selection of vitamins and minerals, as well as fiber.

Although some B vitamins are supplied by vegetables and fruit, the bulk of our vitamin B intake is usually supplied by meat, fish, dairy products, grains, and nuts. Some are entirely animal-sourced, and so vegetarians must take extra care.

If you don't eat dairy products you will definitely need to take vitamin B_{12} supplements. You should always get these from your doctor: never self-prescribe in pregnancy because vitamins can be toxic in large quantities.

MINERALS

A good diet should supply you with sufficient amounts of minerals and trace elements, those essential chemicals that contribute to proper functioning of the body but cannot be synthesized by it. Two in particular, iron and calcium, must be maintained at high levels to support your baby's development.

Iron Essential for the production of hemoglobin (the oxygen-carrying part of the red-blood cells) its intake must not only be adequate (see column, right) but continuous during pregnancy. It is vital to support the large increase in your blood volume, and you should bear in mind that iron is cleared from your baby's blood in seconds. Iron, particularly iron supplements, can block the absorption of zinc, which is essential for the development of your baby's brain and nervous system, so eat zinc-rich food, such as fish and wheat germ, separately from iron-rich food.

Calcium Your baby's bones begin to form between weeks four and six, so it's absolutely crucial that your intake of calcium be high prior to pregnancy and that it remain high for the rest of pregnancy. Foods rich in calcium include all dairy products (choose low-fat ones), leafy green vegetables, and soy products, broccoli, and any fish containing bones, e.g. sardines and canned salmon. If for some reason you can't drink milk or eat dairy products, you may need supplements. Vitamin D (see box) is required to help calcium absorption, so some of your daily intake really should come from cheese and eggs – foods in which both are present.

FLUID

During pregnancy your blood volume and blood fluids will expand by nearly half, so it's very important to keep up your fluid intake. Do not restrict it at all except for cutting out high calorie drinks. Water is best, although fruit juices are good, too. If you suffer from mild swelling of the ankles, face, or fingers, it will not help to limit your fluid intake. However, because your body fluids are increasing, it is essential to keep up your salt intake, to prevent any possible side effects of salt depletion to you or your baby.

MAINTAINING IRON INTAKE

Necessary iron intake varies from woman to woman and the form in which it is best taken in is open to debate.

The preferred way of ingesting iron is from foods such as organic free-range red meat and eggs. These animal sources of iron are more easily absorbed than iron from fruit and vegetables. However, it is advisable to avoid liver during pregnancy as recent health guidelines say that the high levels of vitamin A that liver contains may be toxic to the fetus.

Iron-rich foods, besides the above, include fish, string beans, apricots, raisins, and prunes.

Alkaline medicines for indigestion cut down the absorption of iron. So make sure that you increase your iron-rich food intake if you need to take antacids.

If you are iron-deficient when you become pregnant, or develop iron deficiency later on, iron tablets or injections will be prescribed by your doctor in order to prevent you from developing anemia.

VITAMIN D
Vitamin D can be manufactured by the body if it is triggered by the action of light on the skin.

• *Most pale-skinned people need about 40 minutes of light (it is not necessary for it to be sunlight) a day to produce adequate amounts*

• *Dark-skinned people who live far from the equator need progressively more depending on their skin tones*

A balanced meal
The above meal of cold trout
and salad, melon with yogurt,
nectarines, and a glass of milk is
tasty and nutritious.

NUTRITIONAL VALUES

Although there is no need for you to devote the whole of your
pregnancy to measuring out portions and calculating your intake,
it is good to have a guide so that you can be sure you are eating as
well as you possibly can. You can balance your nutritional intake
over the course of one or two days, rather than balancing each meal.

DAILY REQUIREMENTS

To give yourself and your baby the best possible diet, try to eat the
following portions each day – each of the suggested sources represents a single portion. You should vary the food you choose.

- First-class proteins – 3 servings
- Vitamin C foods – 2 servings
- Calcium foods – 4 servings in pregnancy, 5 during lactation
- Green leafy and yellow vegetables and fruits – 3 servings
- Other fruit and vegetables – 1 or 2 servings
- Whole grains and complex carbohydrates – 4 or 5 servings
- Iron-rich food – 2 servings
- Fluids – 8 glasses a day, not coffee or alcohol. Water is best

REQUIREMENTS	SUGGESTED SOURCES	
Calcium foods	*2oz/50g hard cheese* *4oz/100g soft cheese* *13oz/325g cottage cheese* *9fl oz/250ml yogurt*	*¹/₃ pint/200ml milk or milk made* *up from powdered milk* *3oz/75g canned sardines, with* *bones*
First-class protein foods	*3oz/75g hard cheese* *4oz/100g soft cheese* *1pint/500ml milk* *12fl oz/340ml yogurt* *3 large eggs*	*4oz/100g fresh or canned fish* *4oz/100g shrimp* *3oz/75g beef, lamb, pork, poultry,* *without the fat*
Green leafy and yellow/red vegetables and fruits	*1oz/25g spinach, broccoli florets* *¹/₂oz/13g carrots* *10oz/250g peas, beans* *1oz/25g sweet pepper* *6oz/150g tomatoes*	*2oz/50g melon* *6 plums* *1 mango, orange, grapefruit* *2 apricots* *4 peaches, apples, pears*
Whole grains and complex carbohydrates	*3oz/75g cooked barley, brown rice,* *millet, bulgur* *1oz/25g whole-grain or soy flour* *1 slice whole-grain bread* *6 whole-grain breadsticks*	*3oz/75g kidney beans, soy beans,* *chick peas* *100g/4oz lentils, peas* *1 whole-grain pita or tortilla* *6 whole-grain crackers*
Vitamin C foods	*1oz/25g sweet peppers* *9oz/225g tomatoes* *8oz/200g blackberries or raspberries* *4fl oz/100ml citrus juice*	*1 pomegranate* *3oz/75g strawberries* *1 large lemon or orange* *¹/₂ medium grapefruit*

VITAMIN AND MINERAL SOURCES

We are dependent on food sources for all our vitamin and mineral needs, except for vitamin D. The chart below is a guide to the best sources of essential vitamins and minerals. These tend to be fragile, so always try to eat the foods as fresh as possible. As you can see, some foods contain a variety of vitamins and minerals.

NAME	FOOD SOURCE
Vitamin A (retinol & carotene)	Whole milk, butter, cheese, egg yolk, oily fish, liver, green and yellow fruits and vegetables
Vitamin B₁ (thiamine)	Whole grains, nuts, beans, organ meats, pork, brewer's yeast, wheat germ
Vitamin B₂ (riboflavin)	Brewer's yeast, wheat germ, whole grains, green vegetables, milk, cheese, eggs
Vitamin B₃ (niacin)	Whole grains, wheat germ, organ meats, green vegetables, oily fish, eggs, milk
Vitamin B₅ (pantothenic acid)	Organ meats, eggs, peanuts, cheese
Vitamin B₆ (pyridoxine)	Brewer's yeast, whole grains, soy flour, organ meats, wheat germ, mushrooms, potatoes
Vitamin B₁₂ (cyanocobalamin)	Kidneys, fish, milk, eggs
Folic acid (part of B complex)	Raw leafy vegetables, soy flour, oranges, bananas, walnuts
Vitamin C (ascorbic acid)	Red and green peppers, citrus fruits, pomegranates, strawberries, tomatoes
Vitamin D (calciferol)	Fortified milk, oily fish, eggs (particularly yolks), butter
Vitamin E	Wheat germ, egg yolk, peanuts, seeds, vegetable oils, broccoli
Calcium	Milk, cheese, small fish with bones, peanuts, walnuts, sunflower seeds, soy, yogurt, broccoli
Iron	Kidneys, fish, egg yolks, red meat, cereals, molasses, apricots
Zinc	Wheat bran, eggs, nuts, onions, shellfish, sunflower seeds, wheat germ, whole wheat

PREPARING FOOD

Try to develop some good cooking habits that will promote healthy eating habits.

- *Trim off any fat from meat before cooking*

- *Skim fat off the surface of casseroles and soups*

- *Bake, steam, microwave, or grill rather than fry*

- *Stir-fry in a teaspoon of olive oil, plus a little water, or with a stock cube dissolved in a cup of water*

- *Use nonstick pans and the minimum of fat when cooking omelettes or scrambled eggs*

- *Use flavored vinegars, such as raspberry, basil, thyme, or garlic (home-made ones are better than store-bought), or yogurt for salad dressings, rather than mayonnaise, or sour cream*

- *Add dried skim milk to milky drinks, or when baking, for extra servings of calcium*

- *Always choose low-fat, rather than full-fat, dairy products*

- *Eat fruit and vegetables raw wherever possible*

NAME *Anne Watkins*

AGE *31 years*

PAST MEDICAL HISTORY *Nothing abnormal*

OBSTETRIC HISTORY *2 full-term pregnancies, normal deliveries, boy aged 5, girl aged 3*

Anne became a vegetarian two years ago, a year after the birth of her second child, Katie. Although she feels very healthy eating a vegetarian diet that includes dairy produce and eggs, she is concerned about the additional nutritional needs of pregnancy. She is worried that her obstetrician may oppose vegetarianism and that she may be pressured into eating meat. She turned to me for advice and support.

Your baby's lifeline
The umbilical cord links your baby with the placenta. Everything, including all the necessary nutrients for growth and development, passes to your baby through the cord.

A CASE STUDY

VEGETARIAN MOTHER

Anne had a number of anxieties about the ability of her vegetarian diet to maintain her baby's healthy growth and development. We looked at her various concerns and, having identified possible protein and calcium deficiencies, I offered advice on how she could go about obtaining sufficient supplies.

SPECIAL NEEDS FOR VEGETARIANS?

Having had two previous babies, Anne was aware that certain dietary changes might have been necessary even with her previous eating habits, but now that she was a vegetarian, she wanted to clarify certain things. For example, she had heard that a vegetarian diet might be short of vitamin B_{12}; if so, would that harm her baby? She had read something about folic acid and spina bifida. Was her diet short in folic acid, and should she take supplements? She knew that many pregnant women are given iron supplements; would she be a candidate?

Anne knew that the main change she had to make to her diet would be to increase the protein content, but what kind of protein and which foods provide it? Pregnancy demands increased calcium intake, should she take calcium tablets or could she get enough from calcium-rich and calcium-fortified foods?

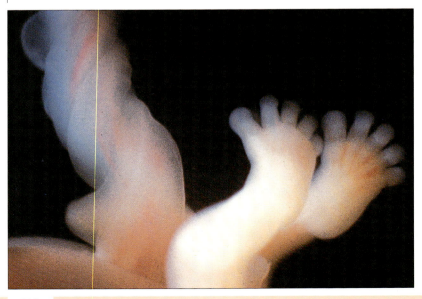

SUGGESTED DAILY MENU

BREAKFAST

2 slices of whole-grain toast with peanut butter

Cup of decaffeinated tea with skim milk

1 banana

MID-MORNING SNACK

Raw vegetables with hummus and whole-grain pita bread

LUNCH

Baked potato topped with cottage cheese, red bell pepper, tomatoes, and watercress

Glass of tomato juice

Chopped nuts and dried fruit

AFTERNOON SNACK

Broccoli and cheese soup, with chopped walnuts and low-fat ricotta

2 slices of rye bread

DINNER

Mushroom and tofu lasagne, spinach, steamed snow peas, and whole-grain garlic bread

Fresh fruit with low-fat yogurt

Grapefruit juice

BEDTIME SNACK

Boiled egg, with whole-grain toast

Orange juice with brewer's yeast

Glass of skim milk

EASY WAYS TO MEET HER INCREASED NEEDS

Opinions on vegetarianism in pregnancy are widely divergent and encompass those of vegans who believe that women taking in no animal protein can carry a healthy baby to term without even vitamin B_{12} supplements, to inflexible doctors who preach that meat and fish are essential ingredients in a pregnant woman's diet. Both of these views are wrong.

In the case of veganism, where no animal products, including dairy products, are eaten, vitamin B_{12} supplements are absolutely mandatory. B_{12} is vital to the healthy growth and development of the fetus, as well as that of a breastfed baby. Therefore, vegan mothers have to add milk and eggs to their diet, or take synthetic B_{12}, during pregnancy and while they are breastfeeding.

A vegetarian diet in which dairy products are also eaten can properly support a pregnancy, and later breastfeeding, as long as calcium and protein intake is increased. All pregnant women should increase their milk intake to at least a pint a day; up to a quart is fine (choose skim). Anne can also boost her protein and vitamin intake by drinking vitamin-fortified soy milk and eating lots of other soy and dairy products. However, the simplest expedient in increasing the protein and vitamin content of Anne's diet would be if she ate at least four eggs a week. Eggs will provide iron, too, although not as much as red meat. While some vegetarians claim that they can get the same amount of iron that red meat provides by eating more green, leafy vegetables, they would, in fact, have to eat almost five pounds of these vegetables per day to do so!

I advised Anne to ask her obstetrician to prescribe a suitable prenatal multivitamin/multimineral supplement for daily consumption during the course of her pregnancy. She will probably want to continue taking supplements during breastfeeding.

ANNE'S BABY

In pregnancy, nature provides preferentially for the nutritional needs of Anne's baby by ensuring he receives what he needs from her body's stores. The baby, therefore, could be better nourished than she.

Iron *A baby's iron needs are high to support blood formation and organ growth. This can be supplied by eating iron-rich foods.*

Calcium *The cornerstone of healthy bones and teeth, a diet that is rich in calcium is necessary to support the needs of Anne's baby as well as her own.*

Protein *To nourish fast-growing muscles, bones, skin, and vital organs, Anne should eat a wide variety of protein-containing foods.*

Vitamin B_{12} *The development of the baby's brain and nervous system depends on sufficient supplies. Therefore, Anne, like every other mother, cannot afford to be deficient.*

Folic acid *The development of the brain, spinal cord, and spine depends on sufficient intake.*

Calories *The blood sugar of the fetus is always lower than that of its mother because energy is used so quickly. A constant supply is needed for healthy growth.*

TAKE CARE

B_{12} is frequently deficient in vegetarian diets, as it only exists naturally in animal products and brewer's yeast. Supplements are necessary to ensure the healthy growth and development of the fetus.

*If you fall into any of the
following groups, then you
could be nutritionally
vulnerable and your baby may
be at risk. You will need special
advice and help from your
doctor or your prenatal clinic.*

• *If you've had a recent miscarriage or stillbirth, or your children
are coming very quickly after one
another (there should be a minimum of 18 months between babies)*

• *If you smoke cigarettes, or drink
alcohol heavily*

• *If you're allergic to certain key
foods, such as cow's milk or wheat*

• *If you suffer from a chronic
medical condition that means you
are regularly taking long-term
medication*

• *If you are under the age of 18,
your own body is growing quickly
and you have more than average
nutritional requirements*

• *If you are carrying more than a
single baby*

• *If you have been subjected to
a great deal of stress or any
physical injury*

• *If you work at a job that entails
hard labor or is in a potentially
dangerous environment (see
Avoiding hazards, p.150)*

• *If before conception you were
generally run-down, underweight,
or eating an inadequate or
unbalanced diet*

NUTRITIONAL AND FOOD-RELATED PROBLEMS

A pregnant woman can put herself and her developing baby at risk if she eats insufficient good food to fulfill her nutritional needs; she is nutritionally at risk. Quite apart from this, the food itself may constitute a hazard to her and her baby if it is contaminated with bacteria that cause disease; an example would be chicken or eggs contaminated with salmonella.

MALNUTRITION

Inadequate food intake by a mother can have serious consequences for her baby. There is a higher risk of miscarriage, and having a premature or low-birthweight baby that will be more vulnerable at birth and throughout its life. (Having a low-birthweight baby does not mean labor will be easier.) Maternal malnutrition also retards the growth of the placenta, and low placental weight is related to a higher infant mortality rate. The most rapid brain development takes place in the last trimester of pregnancy (and in the first month of life after birth) so a severely undernourished mother may prevent optimal brain function.

Inadequate nutrition during pregnancy can have an effect throughout your child's life and may be a contributory factor to such middle-aged diseases as high blood pressure and coronary artery disease, and obesity. Apparently, if nutrition is restricted, the fetus will divert what is available to those cells that are immediately important, and away from those cells that will not be important until later in life – in effect, the fetus trades long life for survival.

On the other hand, when a mother is adequately nourished and produces a good-sized baby, such larger babies prove easier to care for and are more vigorous, active, mentally alert, and suffer from less colic, diarrhea, anemia, and infection.

While the foods necessary for a healthy pregnancy and baby are rarely expensive, there is help available if you have financial difficulties. Your department of health can assist you with supplements and unborn-child allowances.

As a general rule, fresher foods are better, so we can all lower risks of poor nutrition by trying to avoid foods that may contain high levels of undesirable chemicals, such as processed foods, and those containing additives, flavorings, and colorings.

Processed foods A great many of these foods contain chemicals to improve flavor, nutritional value, and shelf life. As a general rule, these should be avoided – in particular, processed cheese and meats, cheese spreads, and sausages.

Additives in foods can be easily identified when ingredients are listed on labels. Always read the labels on packaging to ensure the food is well within the use-by date, and avoid foods that don't list their ingredients. It is a good rule to avoid highly salted foods, particularly those containing monosodium glutamate (MSG). For example, salty soy sauce can cause dehydration; MSG can cause headaches. Both are widely used in Chinese cooking.

Preserved food Smoked fish, meat and cheese, sausages, and pickled food often contain nitrate as the active agent. These should be avoided because nitrates can react with the hemoglobin in your blood, thus reducing its oxygen-carrying power.

Drinks Caffeine (in tea, coffee, and chocolate) is a stimulant; drinks containing it should be avoided in pregnancy. The tannin in tea affects iron absorption, so organic herbal teas should be drunk instead. Soft drinks always contain sugar or artificial sweeteners, so limit your intake of them. Mineral water is fine.

FOOD HAZARDS

We now know that certain foods are contaminated with large enough numbers of bacteria to cause illness, particularly in vulnerable people – such as pregnant women and babies.

Listeriosis Foods found to contain large numbers of listeria bacteria include soft cheese, unpasteurized milk, ready-made coleslaw, cooked chilled foods, pâtés, and improperly cooked meat. The listeria bacteria is normally destroyed at pasteurizing temperatures, but if food is infected and refrigerated, the bacteria may continue to multiply. For this reason, chilled food should not be eaten after the "best-by" date. Listeriosis can also spread through direct contact with infected live animals, such as sheep.

Symptoms are a bit like flu – a high temperature and generalized aches and pains. There may also be a sore throat and eyes, diarrhea, and stomach pain. An unborn child that is affected through its maternal blood supply may be stillborn, and listeriosis may be a cause of recurrent miscarriage.

Salmonella Infection with salmonella can often be traced to eggs and chicken meat so, in general, it's advisable to avoid foods that contain raw eggs, cook eggs and chicken sufficiently well, and always choose free-range eggs and fowl whenever possible. Symptoms, including headache, nausea, abdominal pain, diarrhea, shivering, and fever, develop suddenly about 12–48 hours after infection and last about two or three days. Only if the infection has spread into the bloodstream will antibiotic treatment be required.

Toxoplasmosis This is a common infection that can be picked up by eating raw or undercooked pork or steak, or by coming into contact with the feces of infected cats and dogs (see p.151).

Botulism This very rare but severe, form of food poisoning is caused by eating improperly canned or preserved food such as cured pork or ham. The toxin causes progressive degeneration of the nervous system and muscular paralysis.

FOOD SAFETY

Never take unnecessary risks when handling and storing food; bacteria can multiply rapidly.

- *Always use clean utensils between jobs or tastings*

- *Always wash hands after going to the lavatory and before touching food, and take care to bandage any infections or cuts*

- *Ensure food, especially poultry, is completely defrosted and thoroughly cooked*

- *Never let raw meat or eggs come into contact with other foods*

- *Avoid dented and rusty cans and any food that appears "off"*

- *Make sure dairy products have been pasteurized*

- *Do not refreeze food that has already been defrosted*

- *Reheat food thoroughly only once, then throw away*

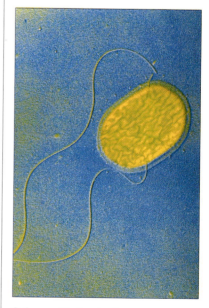

Salmonella bacteria
The above picture shows one of the many hundreds of different strains of salmonella bacteria that may contaminate food.

5

A

FIT

pregnancy

Keeping fit during pregnancy, both physically and mentally, is of prime importance. Exercising will help you maintain a sound mind in a sound body. Everyone is exposed to certain levels of stress and anxiety, and even to potentially hazardous situations and substances. Learning how to cope with, and avoid, problems will ensure a truly fit pregnancy.

Exercising regularly can be emotionally as well as physically satisfying. It's an enjoyable way of preparing for the months of change ahead.

- *You will receive an emotional lift from the release of internal hormones such as endorphins*

- *You will feel more contented, as the release of tranquilizing hormones that follows exercise aids relaxation*

- *You can improve your self-awareness as you learn how to use your body in new ways*

- *Backache, leg cramps, constipation, and breathlessness can be alleviated by regular exercise*

- *Your level of energy will be increased*

- *You will be better prepared for the work of labor*

- *You will regain your shape more quickly after delivery*

- *You can make new friends by meeting other mothers at prenatal exercise classes*

- *You can share the exercise routine with your partner or other members of your family*

EXERCISE FOR A FIT PREGNANCY

The physical benefits of exercise – improving your stamina, suppleness, and strength – will help you face the extra strain placed on your body as it adapts to meet the demands of pregnancy and childbirth. By exercising you can also develop a better understanding of your body's capabilities and learn different ways of relaxing.

Psychologically, exercising counteracts the tendency to feel fat or ungainly, particularly in the last three months. It increases your circulation, and that can help ease any tension. Labor may be easier and more comfortable if you have good muscle tone, and many of the exercises taught in prenatal classes, combined with relaxation and breathing techniques, will help you trust your body during labor. Staying in condition during pregnancy will also mean that you should regain your normal shape sooner after delivery.

YOUR EXERCISE PROGRAM

Incorporating a daily exercise routine into your busy schedule may not be very appealing. But many of the exercises recommended during pregnancy, as shown on the following pages, can usually be performed while you do other activities: pelvic floor exercises may be performed while brushing your teeth; foot and ankle exercises while sitting at your desk or on the bus; and tailor sitting while reading a book or watching television.

Begin your routine at a gentle pace, gradually building up to what feels right for you. Before each exercise, try a few deep breaths. This gets the blood flowing around your body and gives all your muscles a good supply of oxygen. If you suffer any pain, cramping, or shortness of breath, stop exercising; when you resume, make sure it is at a slower pace. If you are out of breath, your baby is also being deprived of oxygen.

Normally a woman can restore her energy by lying down for half an hour, but it can take a pregnant woman several hours to recover from exhaustion properly. So be kind to yourself and choose an activity that you will find both enjoyable and relaxing.

RECOMMENDED ACTIVITIES

You are free to be involved in most sports during pregnancy (until the last trimester), as long as it is a sport you have been doing regularly beforehand, and you pursue it regularly once you are pregnant so that your body remains in condition. There are also sports (see right) that are particularly recommended during pregnancy. For activities to avoid, see **Practice with Caution**.

Swimming This sport tones muscles and is excellent for improving stamina. Because your weight is supported by the water, it is very difficult to strain muscles and joints, so swimming rarely results in physical injury. Some health clubs offer special prenatal classes.

Yoga This has many benefits, such as increasing suppleness and reducing tension. It also teaches you to control your breathing and concentration during labor, which is very useful.

Walking Even if you are not usually an active person, you could at least take up regular walks of a mile or more. Walking is good for the digestion, the circulation, and your figure. Try to walk tall, with your buttocks tucked under your spine, your shoulders back, and your head up, not hanging down. Toward the end of pregnancy, however, you may find that the cartilage in the pelvic joint softens so much that you get a backache if you walk more than a short distance. Always wear well-cushioned flat shoes.

Dancing This can be a very enjoyable way of toning your body. As long as you are not too energetic, you can dance as often as you wish throughout pregnancy.

PRACTICE WITH CAUTION

Any sport requiring precision balance, for example skiing and horseback riding, should be given up after 20 weeks. Sports that involve body contact – basketball, hang-gliding, motorcycling, and others – are also best avoided. Don't scuba dive at all during pregnancy – it could affect the oxygen supply to your baby. Other activities, including those listed below, should be avoided because they put your body under unnecessary stress that could harm both you and your baby.

Jogging This is very hard on your breasts and jarring for your back, spine, pelvis, hips, and knees. Don't jog while pregnant.

Backpacking Weight-bearing sports like this one are harmful because they put a severe strain on the ligaments in your back. Bear in mind that during pregnancy, progesterone relaxes your ligaments and, unlike muscles, which can go back to their old shapes, ligaments remain stretched.

Sit-ups Any exercise that pulls on the abdominal muscles is a very bad idea. The longitudinal muscles of the abdomen are designed to separate in the middle to allow room for the enlarging uterus, and sitting straight up from a lying position encourages them to part even further. The strain may slow down the recovery of abdominal tone after delivery. Leg lifts while you are on your back can have the same effect. In order to sit up from a lying position (see also p.143), you should always roll over onto your side and use your arms to push you up sideways. This way your abdomen will not be working and stretching as you get up.

GOOD FOR YOUR BABY

Every time you exercise within your limits, your baby gets a surge of oxygen into her blood that sets her metabolism alight and gives her a real high. All her tissues, especially her brain, function at their best.

- *The hormones that are released during your exercise pass across the placenta and reach your baby. At the beginning of exercise, therefore, your baby receives an emotional lift from your adrenaline*

- *During exercise, your baby also experiences the effect of endorphins, our own natural morphinelike substances that make us feel extremely good and happy*

- *When exercise is over, endorphins have a profound tranquilizing effect that can last up to 8 hours, and your baby also experiences this*

- *The motion of exercise is extremely soothing and your baby feels comforted from the rocking movements*

- *As you exercise, your abdominal muscles exert a kind of massage on your baby that is comforting and soothing*

- *During exercise, blood flow is optimum and so your baby's growth and development proceeds at a good pace*

STRETCHING

Before beginning any exercise routine, always warm up gently (see left) with these few stretching exercises. They will stimulate your blood circulation, giving you and your baby a good supply of oxygen. Repeat each exercise five to ten times; make sure you are comfortable and that your posture is good.

Head and neck

Gently tilt your head over to one side, then lift your chin and rotate your head gently over to the other side and down. Repeat, starting from the other side. Keeping your head straight, turn it slowly to the right, back to the front, and then back to the left. Return to face the front.

Always treat your neck carefully. Rotate your head slowly

Place hands loosely in front of your legs

Keep your neck and back straight

Waist

Sitting comfortably with your legs crossed, straighten your back and gently stretch your neck upward. Breathe out and turn your upper body to the right, placing your right hand behind you. Place your left hand on your right knee and use this hand as a lever to twist your body a little farther, gently stretching the muscles of your waist. Repeat in the other direction.

Place your hand on your knee to help control the stretch

128

Clasp your hands together lightly if you can; if you can't reach, don't worry

Arms and shoulders

Sitting with your legs tucked underneath, lift your right arm up and slowly stretch it toward the ceiling. Bend it at the elbow and drop your hand down behind your back. Put your left hand on your right elbow, pushing it farther down your back. Put your left arm down behind your back and reach up to grasp the right hand. Stretch for 20 seconds, then relax. Repeat with other arm.

Legs and feet

Sit with your back straight and your legs stretched out in front of you. Place your hands on the floor next to your hips to support your weight. Bend your knee slowly and then straighten. Repeat with other leg. This will tone the muscles in your calf and thigh. Helps alleviate cramps.

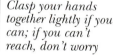

Keep your back straight and your weight central

Improving circulation

Raise your foot off the floor and flex it outward. Then draw large circles in the air by moving only your ankles.

Bend your foot toward you to make the muscles work harder; take care not to strain

129

YOUR PELVIC FLOOR

The pelvic floor muscles form a funnel that supports the uterus, bowel, and bladder and serves to close the entrances to the vagina, rectum, and urethra.

During pregnancy, an increase in progesterone causes the muscles to soften and relax. To counter this there is an exercise you can do to keep the pelvic floor well-toned.

Pull in and tense the muscles around your vagina and anus, as if you were stopping the flow of urine. Hold as long as you can without straining. Relax. Repeat 25 times or more each day.

You should restart this exercise, often called the Kegel exercise, as soon as you can after delivery to minimize the risk of any kind of prolapse. Early exercise will tone up the vagina for sexual inter-course, too – an extra benefit!

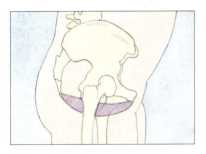

The pelvic floor
This is made up of the hammock of muscles that lie in 2 main groups forming a figure of 8 around the urethra, vagina, and anus. The layers of muscle are at their thickest at the perineum.

BODY EXERCISES

By performing exercises for your whole body, you will relieve the strain caused by your extra weight and strengthen major muscle groups. Also, if you learn to move your pelvis easily during pregnancy, you will be better able to find the most comfortable position during labor. A major proponent of active birth, Janet Balaskas, specializes in prenatal exercises using modified yoga positions. Some of her suggestions are shown here.

Make sure your back is straight

Forward bend
1. Place your feet about 12in (30cm) apart, keeping them parallel. Clasp your hands behind your back. Bend slowly forward from the hips, keeping your back straight. Breathe deeply for a few breaths, then rise slowly.
2. You should do this exercise only if you are able to do Step 1 comfortably. After bending forward, slowly raise your hands until they are as far above your head as possible.

Make the same movements while rocking your pelvis gently up and down

Pelvic tuck-in
Kneel down on all fours with your knees about 12in (30cm) apart. Clench your buttock muscles and tuck in your pelvis so that your back arches upward into a hump. Hold for a few seconds, and then release, making sure you do not let your back sink downward. Repeat several times.

Inhale, then breathe out as you lower your back onto the floor

Raise yourself on supported arms to strengthen thighs and lower back

Lower back release

1. Lie flat with your arms by your sides, palms down. Press your feet into the floor. Lift your pelvis so that your spine rises as high as your neck. Come down one vertebra at a time.

2. Keeping your sacrum in contact with the floor, gently hug your knees. Hold for a few minutes, breathing deeply.

3. Straighten your right leg on the floor and gently hug your left knee. Repeat with the other leg.

4. Bend both knees and cross your feet at the ankles. Then rotate your hips clockwise, making tiny circles with your lower back on the floor. Repeat the motion in the other direction.

Hold your knee for a few moments, breathing deeply

Uncross ankles, place feet together, keeping knees bent

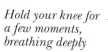

Spread arms out at shoulder height, palms down

Spinal twist

Keep your shoulders and arms flat on the ground and, as you breathe out, slowly turn your knees over to the right and your head to the left. This gently twists the spine. Hold for a few seconds. Come back to the center, keeping your knees bent, and relax. Then roll your knees to the left and your head to the right. Repeat.

131

SHAPING UP FOR LABOR

Your labor may be a more comfortable experience if you have prepared your body and mind in advance. The following exercises are very useful during pregnancy. You may find it easier to give birth while squatting, and tailor sitting will strengthen your thigh muscles and increase circulation to your pelvis, making the joints more supple. By performing this exercise you will also fully stretch your pelvis and help relax the tissues of your perineum.

After every exercise session, spend 20–30 minutes relaxing and, if possible, arrange a routine break during the day. Five or ten minutes with your eyes closed and your feet up can be sufficiently refreshing (it is not necessary to actually sleep), and learning relaxation techniques will be particularly beneficial during labor, when tension can exacerbate the pain. By concentrating on the rhythm of your breathing, you will be able to alleviate anxiety and conserve your energy.

If, as below, you find it difficult to pull your feet close to your groin, start with them about 12in (30cm) away from your body and gradually bring them nearer. Continual practice will loosen the muscles

Tailor sitting
Sit on the floor and stretch your legs out in front. Make sure your back is straight. Bend your knees and bring the soles of your feet together, then pull them as close as possible toward your groin. Open your thighs and lower your knees toward the floor. Relax your shoulders and the back of your neck. Breathe deeply for a few breaths. Concentrate on breathing down toward your pelvis resting on the floor, relaxing when you breathe out. As you breathe in, lift up and stretch your spine while keeping your pelvis on the floor.

Support your thighs with some cushions or blankets, or sit with a wall behind you at first if you find it easier

Correct   *Incorrect*

Safe balance

If necessary, hold on to something secure, such as a chair, low stool, or window ledge, to support your back as you squat, and use a towel underneath your heels. You can also lean against a wall.

Squat to make your pelvis more flexible, stretch and strengthen the thigh and back muscles, and relieve back pain

Squatting

Stand with your back lengthened and straight, and your feet 18in (45cm) apart. Squat down as low as you can. Linking your hands, spread and hold your knees apart with your elbows. Try to get your heels on the ground with your weight evenly distributed between heels and toes; don't worry if you have to raise your heels. Hold for a few minutes or for as long as you like, if you are comfortable. Then come forward to kneel or stand up. Squatting can become a natural part of your daily life, especially when you're lifting an object.

RELAXATION

As your abdomen gets bigger you may find it more comfortable to lie on your back with your head supported by a cushion. Raise your feet and lower legs onto a chair or bed. You can relax in this position while your other children are playing nearby.

Lie with your feet up to relieve swollen ankles and feet

Clear your mind and breathe in deeply. Hold to a count of 5 and breathe out. Relax all parts of your body

Alleviate pressure on the major blood vessels and the abdomen by lying in this way

Lying down

Lie on your side with a pillow under your head. Bend your upper arm and leg upward and place a pillow under this knee; keep your lower leg straightened. Close your eyes and concentrate on your breathing.

MASSAGE AIDS

A variety of different items can add greatly to the experience. Make sure you have everything ready before beginning the massage so you can avoid breaking the rhythm.

Scented oils are available that will help your hands glide over the skin, leaving it soft and smooth. Their fragrance will add to the atmosphere, making each occasion special.

Feathers, fabric, and other soft, textured materials can be rubbed against the skin to leave it tingling.

Warm, fluffy towels are ideal for covering areas of exposed skin.

Use spinal rolls for firm, smooth counter-pressure (see p.256).

A soft bristle hair-brush applied to the hair with light strokes can be very relaxing.

MASSAGE FOR RELAXATION

A massage from a partner, or one that you give yourself, is an ideal way to relax and unwind. It stimulates the nerve endings in your skin, improves your circulation, and soothes tired muscles, creating an overall sense of peace and well-being.

SOOTHING TOUCH

Use a good-quality massage oil (one with a vegetable oil base) to reduce friction between hands and skin and make the massage more pleasurable. Try to create a comfortable atmosphere: dim the lighting, put on some soft music, and place pillows or cushions around and underneath yourself. In the later months, you may find it more comfortable to lie on your side supported by pillows, or to sit astride a chair and lean against the back.

Apart from your back, you can massage most parts of your body quite effectively yourself. Work clockwise around each breast, stroking with the palms and fingers of one hand, from the base

SELF-MASSAGE

Soothing your forehead
Cover your face with your hands. Place your fingertips on your forehead and rest the heels of your hands on your chin. After a few seconds, draw your hands toward your ears.

Toning your chin
Stimulate the blood circulation under your chin with brisk movements. Using the back of both hands, one after the other, gently slap upward.

Firming your neck
Make gentle pinching movements around your jawbone. Softly squeeze the skin between your thumb and the knuckles of your index finger. Be careful not to drag the skin.

toward the nipple; gently knead the nipple between your fingers and thumb. Massage your abdomen, hips, and thighs with the palms of your hands, using a smooth, circular motion.

If you are to be massaged by a partner or a friend, make sure the masseur's hands are warm before starting the massage, and he or she should remove any rings, bracelets, or watches that may scratch or jangle. When you are both in comfortable positions, take a few deep breaths to help you relax. The masseur should begin the massage gently and gradually increase the pressure if it is comfortable for you, but he or she should always keep the movements slow.

Circling Use the palms of both hands simultaneously to make circling strokes in the same direction away from the spine. Lighten the pressure when massaging over the abdomen and breasts.

Effleurage Make light, feathery, circular movements with the fingertips as though tickling the skin. This can be done all over the abdomen during pregnancy.

Gliding Place the palms of both hands on either side of the sacrum (lower back), with the fingers pointing toward the head. Push the hands up toward the shoulders, without putting weight on the hands. Slowly glide the hands down the sides of the body back to the starting point.

MASSAGE BY A PARTNER

ESSENTIAL OILS

Aromatic oils can greatly enhance your massage, helping you feel relaxed and refreshed. Their diverse scents also help conjure up wonderful images.

These oils are distilled from flowers, trees, and herbs, and are said to have therapeutic qualities. For example, lavender oil relieves headaches and insomnia, and jasmine helps treat postpartum depression. Always blend an essential oil with a carrier oil, such as almond.

Gently press your fingers against the temples to ease tension

Supporting her head
Kneel behind her to massage her neck muscles. Gently turn her head, keeping it well supported. With the heel of your hand, slowly massage downward, from her face.

Relaxing her neck
Slowly stroke up the back of her neck with both thumbs. Make circular movements away from the center of the neck. Massage all around the base of the skull.

Stroking her brow
Gently massage her forehead and temples with both hands simultaneously. Using your fingers, make light, circular movements from the center of her forehead outward. Run your fingers out over her hair.

EMOTIONAL CHANGES

It is not only your body that alters during pregnancy – your emotions will fluctuate rapidly and you will experience feelings you have never had before. It is important to recognize that you will feel upset from time to time, that all pregnant women do, and that there are things that you can do that will help with your mood swings.

Your swinging hormone levels lead to mood changes from elation to depression. Your changing body shape disturbs your image of yourself. And then we are all occasionally beset by fears about our suitability as parents. Emotionally, pregnancy can be very difficult.

HORMONAL CHANGES

Enormous changes occur in your body during pregnancy and, because of this, your mood is likely to swing frequently. It is not unusual to find yourself becoming hypercritical and irritable, your reactions to minor events will be exaggerated, you will feel unsure of yourself and panicky sometimes, and you may even have bouts of depression and crying.

It is normal to feel all of these things, because you are less in control of your feelings than usual. The swinging levels of hormones have taken over and are controlling your moods the way a conductor controls an orchestra. So there is no reason to feel guilty or ashamed if you show irritation, anger, or frustration. If you explain the situation, most people will be understanding. At work, you may have to struggle to preserve a veneer of calm. This effort will definitely pay off, especially if you plan to return to your job after the birth of your baby.

CHANGING BODY SHAPE

Under normal circumstances it takes quite a long time to adjust to a change in body image, such as going from blond to brunette or losing or gaining weight. In pregnancy you are not given time to adjust to the shape of your body, and you may feel strange, even unrelated to the body in which you find yourself. You may also worry about putting on too much weight and of becoming fat and unattractive during and after pregnancy.

Thinking of pregnant women as fat, and therefore ugly, is essentially an Anglo-Saxon attitude: many other cultures regard pregnant women as sensuous and beautiful. Instead of viewing your increasing curves with despair, think of them as a reaffirmation of life; see the roundness as ripeness, and glory in the fertility of your body. Feel confident and proud of your shape and fertility.

Your changing shape
A positive attitude to your appearance is important because it will help keep you buoyant.

CONFLICTING FEELINGS

Even with the most positive attitudes about pregnancy, it is normal to have conflicting feelings. One moment you are thrilled at the prospect of a new baby, the next minute you are terrified of your new responsibilities. Becoming a parent is a time of reassessment and change, worries and fears.

The first and most important psychological task you have is to accept the pregnancy. This may sound obvious, but there are women who blithely sail through the early months of pregnancy giving it as little thought as possible, which is especially easy until the baby begins to show.

You and the baby's father have to come to terms with the pregnancy and begin to think about the reality. Until now your thoughts about a baby and parenthood have probably all been in soft focus, a pastel picture of a loving threesome.

Conflicting feelings are sure to surface once you begin to accept the pending realities. Let me reassure you that it's good to have conflicting feelings. It is normal to feel this way and you shouldn't worry about it. It means that you are genuinely coming to terms with the situation. You won't have the horrible shock some people do, the ones who wait to face all this until the baby is at home.

FEARS

You may be worried about labor – whether you will be able to cope with the pain, whether you will scream or defecate, or lose control, or need an episiotomy or emergency Caesarean. Most women worry about these things, but there is really no need. Labor is usually straightforward and how you behave will be of little or no importance. You may be surprised at how calm you are; you may not be calm at all, and that's okay, too. Just remember that your birth attendants have seen it all before, so there is nothing for you to feel embarrassed about.

You may worry about how good a parent you'll be, whether you will hurt or harm your baby, or not care for her properly. These kinds of feelings are quite common and represent legitimate fears. Like many modern women, you probably do not know much about baby care and are worried about doing a good job. The answer is to get some hands-on experience – handle and care for a newborn baby if you can. Perhaps you could baby-sit for a friend's baby, or spend some time with her. If you change and bottlefeed her, you will probably gain confidence. Try to get these fears into perspective – you probably had similar worries about starting a job.

DREAMS

Dreams may become more frequent, and even frightening in the last trimester. There are many common themes reported by pregnant women and all express deep feelings and concerns that are entirely natural – everybody worries at one time or another that something will be wrong or go wrong with their baby. You may have dreams about losing the baby, and this is usually an expression of fear about miscarrying or having a stillborn baby. Dreams like

WILL MY MOOD AFFECT MY BABY?

You may worry that your swinging emotional changes will somehow affect your baby.

Although your baby reacts to your moods, such as kicking when you are angry or upset, your change-able emotions appear to have no detrimental effect on your baby (see A Mother's influence, p.174).

Dreams and nightmares can be very vivid, and you may find that you wake up abruptly – hot, drenched in sweat, and with your heart racing. Be reassured that this will not harm your baby.

On the other hand, your baby really enjoys your good moods – your excitement, your happiness, and your elation. When you feel good, your baby feels good. When you're relaxed, your baby is also feeling tranquil.

If some activity makes you content and happy – listening to music, dancing gently, painting – do as much of it as you can and share the feeling with your baby.

KEEPING A DIARY

Keeping a diary at any time of your life can give you information and insights about yourself that you might not have the time to recognize.

It is a place where you can let go of those thoughts and feelings that you may not want to share, and it will also help you to focus on yourself. Your child will also enjoy reading it herself – especially when she is about to start her own family.

Pregnancy journal
Taking the time to keep a pregnancy journal means that you will have a cherished record of this special time in your life.

these may be a psychological preparation for a possible unwanted outcome, as well as a way of bringing these feelings to the surface. In a way, they act as a release for your anxieties.

Dreams, nightmares, and thoughts in general may be a way of expressing hostility to your unborn child. She is going to dominate your life, disrupt your privacy and comfortable routine. They may express feelings you may not be able to cope with or may not be consciously aware of. Again, don't make the mistake of taking dreams literally and then feeling guilty or frightened.

SUPERSTITIONS

It is likely that you may be more superstitious than normal. Superstition and old wives' tales were, in the past, ways of explaining an inexplicable world. With the excellent medical care now available, your chances of having a "damaged" child are very low, and what you might interpret as a bad omen certainly does not mean that anything will go wrong with your baby.

COPING WITH EMOTIONAL CHANGES

Try to see the emotional turmoil you are experiencing as a positive force as you adjust to being pregnant and becoming a mother. Don't imagine that having second thoughts or fears means that you've made a mistake. You're tossing this around in your head the way one wrestles with any big life decision. Yet social conditioning makes us feel guilty if we don't walk around with a madonna-like expression and saintly attitude to everything. That is absurd. Being pregnant isn't all fun. Accepting the reality is the best thing you can do for yourself and your child.

Spend time daydreaming Imagining and thinking about your baby helps you to form a relationship with her even before she is born, and you shouldn't feel silly if you find that you spend a couple of hours doing nothing but thinking about the baby. Making that connection with the tiny person growing inside you is the first step in accepting your child.

The daydreams of pregnant mothers are notoriously sexist, with many having an undisguised preference for a girl or a boy. Although it isn't usually a problem if your newborn turns out to be the opposite sex from the one you wanted, it can mean readjusting, so try not to get too carried away with your plans!

Consider your parents Your parents are about to become grandparents, perhaps for the first time. They may be delighted, they may be upset, and they may feel a combination of both. In other words, it is possible that they are feeling nearly as ambiguous about their new role as you are about yours. Becoming a grandparent is often seen as being synonymous with becoming old, and can be unsettling for a person who perhaps feels only just middle-aged. Try to be understanding and loving, include them in your pregnancy, talk to them, and share your feelings with them.

Confront your isolation It is quite common for a pregnant woman to feel isolated nowadays. Many women are postponing having children, and some are deciding against it altogether. You may find that you are the first in your social circle to start a family and that you don't know any other pregnant women or full-fledged mothers. It can be lonely. There is so much that you want to know, that you want to discuss. You may have little niggles and worries that you feel are too irrelevant or silly to talk about at your prenatal clinic, and you may wish that you knew someone who was going through the same thing or who had already had a child. If so, find people to whom you can talk – join parent groups, approach other pregnant women in your childbirth classes, and ask your friends or family if they know any pregnant women, or parents with young children, whom you could get to know. These relationships may provide support long after your baby is born. Don't forget your partner either – if you are feeling isolated, he probably is too, so talk to him, include him, and expand your social circle together.

Communicate Wanting to talk and share what you are feeling and thinking during your pregnancy is natural. Your partner is the logical first choice and will probably be anxious to talk to you. There are bound to be things that he would like to talk about: worries, things that he may have refrained from discussing with you because he thought that he might upset you, or you might think him silly, or because you were too busy, or too tired. Keep talking. You need each other more now than ever before. Denying or ignoring your fears and feelings will not make them go away. Suppressed feelings have a nasty way of festering and then surfacing when you are least equipped to deal with them, thus becoming full-blown, often difficult to resolve, problems. You should be able to avoid these problems if you bring them out in the open when they first occur and then get on with your lives.

COPING WITH MATERIAL CHANGES

Everyday difficulties that you would normally deal with quite calmly can turn into dramas during pregnancy. Keep a level head, and try not to overreact if you can help it.

Finances One of the major causes of marital strife, financial problems, can become especially troubling during pregnancy. You may find it difficult to cope with an inevitable reduction in income, even if you plan to return to work, but remember that you are in this together. Work out before the birth how you will cope on your income once the baby has arrived.

Housing Moving or expanding your home may be something that you are forced to consider – perhaps you need the extra space, or it may be because of the lack of facilities in your area. This can be stressful, and tends to be worse when you are expecting. If you must move – and it's not really recommended from a physical standpoint – do it before your pregnancy is too advanced.

GRANDPARENTS

A new baby means a new role not only for you but possibly also for your parents.

While they will, no doubt, revel in their roles as doting grandparents once the baby is born, they may feel they are still too young when you first tell them the glad tidings.

A source of help
Even before the baby is born, your parents are often invaluable sources of information, expertise, and reassurance.

MAKEUP TIPS

Pregnancy can change the tone and color of your skin, and you may want to adjust your make-up to counteract the effects.

Fine lines or wrinkles *These will become more accentuated if your skin becomes drier than usual, so stop using products that make them look more obvious. Shiny or glittering eye shadows, heavy foundations, and colored powders will make them more prominent.*

Extra greasy skin *To help combat this, use an astringent lotion, oil-free foundation, and cover with translucent powder.*

Extra dry skin *This is very rare in pregnancy, but if your skin becomes so dry that it flakes, it should be left makeup free. You should continue to moisturize it well. Otherwise, use an oil-based film of foundation and powder to help slow water loss. Thick, creamy moisturizers will also act as a barrier to water loss.*

High color and spider veins *Stipple a thin, light coat of matte beige foundation, free of any pink, onto your cheeks. When dry, cover with your regular foundation and a transparent powder.*

Dark circles *On top of a thin layer of foundation, stipple an under-eye coverup cream and leave to dry. Cover with another thin layer of foundation and blend carefully. Finish with a dusting of transparent powder.*

BODY CARE

The pregnancy hormones bring about changes to almost every part of your body, including your breasts, skin, hair, teeth, and gums. To ensure that your body is kept in the best condition, a new daily routine may be necessary. Moreover, your enlarging abdomen may affect your posture, so you should pay closer attention to the way you stand or move (see p.142).

SKIN

Your skin will probably "bloom" during pregnancy because the hormones encourage it to retain moisture that plumps it out, making it more supple, less oily, and less prone to pimples. However, the opposite can sometimes happen. Red patches may enlarge, acne may worsen, areas may become dry and scaly, and you may notice deeper pigmentation across your face.

Skin care Here are a few general tips during pregnancy. Soap removes the natural oils from the skin, so use it as infrequently as possible. Try using baby lotion, or glycerine-based soap and body wash. Always use oils in the bath to minimize the dehydrating effects of hard water, and do not lie in a bath for long periods of time because prolonged contact with water particularly dehydrates the skin. Makeup is very good for your morale and can act as a good moisturizer for the skin, as it prevents the loss of water (see column, left). Aromatherapy oils can also have a wonderful effect, relaxing and invigorating you, and will leave a film of protective oil on your skin that will keep it supple, and prevent dehydration and damage due to water loss.

Deeper pigmentation This affects nearly every woman, especially the areas of the body that are pigmented to begin with, such as freckles, moles, and the areolae of the breasts. Your genitalia, the skin of the inner sides of the thighs, underneath your eyes, and in your armpits may become darker too. A dark line, called the *linea nigra*, often appears down the center of your abdomen. It marks the division of your abdominal muscles, which separate slightly to accommodate your expanding uterus, and you should be very careful when getting up from a lying down position (see p.143) to avoid straining the muscles. Even after birth the *linea nigra* and the areolae usually remain darker for some time, but the extra pigmentation will gradually fade and disappear.

Sunlight intensifies areas of skin that are already pigmented, and many women find that they tan more easily during pregnancy. Since ultraviolet A (UVA) rays can lead to skin cancer, and the effect they have on the unborn baby is unknown, it is best to avoid sunlamps. Keep your skin covered up in hot sunshine, or use a sun block, especially on pigmented areas such as your nipples.

Chloasma This is a special form of pigmentation, also called the mask of pregnancy, which appears as brown patches on the bridge of the nose, cheeks, and neck. The only way to handle chloasma is to camouflage it with a blemish stick or the cover-up cosmetics used for birthmarks. Never attempt to bleach out the pigment; the patches will begin to fade within three months of labor. Conversely, some black women develop patches of paler skin on their faces and necks. These will probably disappear after delivery and can be camouflaged during pregnancy.

Spider veins All the blood vessels in pregnancy become sensitive – rapidly dilating when you are hot, and constricting quickly when you are cold. Consequently, tiny broken blood vessels called spider veins may appear on your face, particularly on your cheeks. Do not worry; these will fade soon after delivery, and will probably have disappeared altogether within three months.

Pimples If your skin has a tendency to become oily before periods, you may get pimples now, particularly in the first trimester when the pregnancy hormones stimulating the sebaceous glands in the skin have not yet reached a balanced level. Try to keep your skin as clean as possible, and use a cleanser two or three times a day to prevent pimples altogether. If one appears, apply a tiny smear of antiseptic cream. Never squeeze pimples as this only spreads the infection into the deeper layers of the skin.

Stretch marks About 90 percent of pregnant women get stretch marks. These usually appear across the abdomen, although they can also be seen on the thighs, hips, breasts, and the upper arms. Nothing you can apply to the skin (including oil), and nothing you can eat will prevent stretch marks because they are due to the breakdown of protein in the skin by the high levels of pregnancy hormones. Gradual weight gain should allow the skin to stretch without tearing, although some women are blessed with more elastic skin than others. While the reddish streaks may look prominent during pregnancy, during the weeks after delivery they will become paler and shrink until they are nothing more than faint silvery streaks that are barely noticeable.

TEETH

During pregnancy, you will be more susceptible than normal to gum problems owing to the increased blood supply and to the high level of progesterone, which softens all of your body's tissues. The increased blood volume also puts pressure on the tiny capillaries around the gum margin, which often bleed easily. A balanced diet helps prevent tooth and gum problems. Sufficient calcium and high-quality protein, along with a good supply of vitamins B, C, and D, helps protect you. You should see your dentist at least once during your pregnancy and have your teeth cleaned professionally to reduce the risk of gum infections, but be sure to tell him or her you are pregnant because you should avoid X-rays.

YOUR HAIR

During pregnancy, it is very common for the hair to change in quality, quantity, and manageability.

The high levels of hormones arrest the usual cycle of hair growth and loss. Usually some hair grows and some is lost every day. In pregnancy, little hair is lost while growth continues.

After delivery, the cycle passes into a resting phase when masses of hair can be lost. Hair loss can go on for up to 2 years and may be alarming, but rest assured, it will stop – pregnancy never causes baldness. The hair you will lose once your baby is born is simply the hair you would normally have lost throughout the whole 9 months of pregnancy.

If your hair becomes more difficult to manage, this may be a good time to try a simpler hair style that is easier to care for. Use a mild shampoo and apply the shampoo only once – massage gently to a lather, leave for 30 seconds, and rinse off.

Body and facial hair also may increase in quantity and may even darken in color.

MAINTAINING YOUR POSTURE

Adopting good posture will help you to minimize the backache and fatigue that can easily arise as your pregnancy advances.

Bad posture is a common problem in pregnancy, caused by the increasing weight of your baby. Your enlarging abdomen thrusts your center of gravity forward; to balance this you tend to arch your back backward, putting your back muscles under constant strain – hence the backache.

When you are standing, sitting, or walking with the correct posture, your neck and back will be in a straight line.

Always keep your back straight, and lift by straightening your legs

AVOIDING PROBLEMS

The pregnancy hormones stretch and soften your ligaments, particularly in the lower back, making them more vulnerable to strain. But with a little care you can avoid the unnecessary problems and fatigue that many women suffer during pregnancy.

Don't bend down
When you are doing household chores or working in the garden and you need to work on something at floor level, sit or kneel to bring it within easy reach. Whenever possible, avoid bending or stooping.

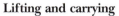

Keep the weight close to you and hold it with both hands

Sit back on your heels, but try to avoid making your legs go numb

Lifting and carrying
To lift something from the floor, reach down to it by bending your knees, keeping your back as straight as you can. When you pick it up, hold it close in to your body, and lift it by straightening your legs, so that you use the strength of your leg and thigh muscles to do the actual lifting. Never struggle to lift objects that are too heavy – get someone to help you. Don't try lifting heavy things to or from high shelves or upward. If you are carrying heavy bags, try to divide the weight equally between both your hands.

Getting up

When you have been lying down on the floor, for instance, if you have been exercising, get up in easy stages. First, turn onto your side (see below), then use your hands to support yourself as you move yourself into a kneeling position (see top right). From there, keeping your back straight and using the strength of your thigh muscles, push yourself up into a sitting position (see bottom right). From here you can stand up without straining your abdomen.

Use your hands to support yourself

Use your hands for support

Cross your upper leg over the lower

Push up with your thighs

SKIN AND NAIL PROBLEMS

POSSIBLE PROBLEMS	WHAT TO DO
Itching or chafed skin The skin of your extended abdomen may become quite itchy, and the area between your thighs may become chafed.	*Massage your skin with baby lotion to stimulate the blood supply and ease irritation. Keep the thigh area dry; dust with powder, and wear cotton underwear.*
Rashes These are not uncommon in the groin and under the breasts, and are a result of excess weight gain and sweat that accumulates in the skinfolds. Poor hygiene will increase the risk.	*Keep your groin area and the skin under your breasts clean, and apply calamine or other drying lotion. Take care to keep your weight under control. Wear a firm, supporting bra to hold the breasts up.*
Pigmentation Many women find that their skin pigmentation alters when they are pregnant; this particularly affects already-darkened areas such as moles, and the areolae of the breasts.	*Use sunblock to protect your skin from the ultra-violet rays in sunlight. The pigmentation effects will disappear following the birth.*
Nails Your fingernails will grow faster than usual during pregnancy but they may also become brittle and split, or break more easily than they did before you became pregnant.	*Keep your nails short, and wear gloves for housework and gardening.*

Maternity underwear
A pregnancy bra and girdle can
be invaluable for your comfort
during pregnancy – and your
figure afterward.

MATERNITY WEAR

*Comfort is the watchword during pregnancy as far as clothes are
concerned. As your size increases, try to stay one step ahead –
there's nothing more demoralizing than feeling constricted and
too big for your clothes. Because the blood is circulating around
your body at a faster rate, you'll probably be warmer during
pregnancy than you expect. Feet and legs tend to swell,
particularly toward the end of the day, so footwear and hosiery
should be chosen with care.*

CLOTHES

Pregnancy does not have to mean lots of expensive maternity
clothes. A few specially bought basics, such as a pair of maternity
jeans with an expandable front panel, a selection of properly fitted
maternity bras, some maternity cotton or wool tights and leggings
with expandable gussets, and one or two pretty maternity dresses
for special occasions, can be happily supplemented with inexpensive ethnic dresses, drawstring cotton trousers, leggings, and man-
size tops and jumpers – all of which can be worn when you are no
longer pregnant. Before you splurge on any special outfits, ask
around to see if friends or neighbors have pregnancy clothes that
you could borrow. There are also stores that specialize in nearly-
new maternity clothes, where you can find clothes at bargain prices.
Avoid synthetic fabrics whenever you can as they're not as comfortable as natural fabrics. Stretch fabrics, for example, can become
unpleasantly clingy and tight; polyester tends to trap moisture,
causing discomfort in hot weather.

Work clothes   Depending on where you work, you may be able to
get away with wearing smarter versions of your casual wear, such
as leggings with an elegant top or a loose cotton skirt with a crisp
cotton blouse. However, if you work in an environment where chic
clothes are worn, you may have to invest in higher-priced maternity
clothes. Ordinary long-line jackets, large-size skirts and blouses,
and drop-waist dresses may suffice. If you wear a uniform, make
sure that you tell your employers that you are pregnant as soon as
you can, as they may be able to offer you financial help even if they
don't provide uniforms. Make sure that you change to flat shoes
if you normally wear heels to work.

SHOES

The bigger you get, the more unstable you become, so it's
a good idea to wear flat or low-heeled, comfortable, easy-fitting
shoes. They should give your feet good support, be sufficiently
roomy, and preferably have a nonslip sole for safety. Sneakers fulfill
all the criteria, and you should choose a pair with a Velcro fastening
because later in pregnancy it may be difficult for you to bend down

to tie the laces. There are lots of stylish flats available that are versatile and durable. Your feet will swell during pregnancy, so choose a size bigger than normal, and avoid anything with a heel. Best of all, go barefoot whenever you can.

UNDERWEAR

Bra This is one item that is essential in pregnancy. Your breasts may enlarge substantially, particularly during the first three months, and if you don't support them, they are likely to sag later. This is because the sling of fibrous tissue to which they are attached can never regain its former shape once it is stretched. A good, well-fitting bra will help prevent stretching in the first place.

When you buy a bra, it is best to have it properly fitted. A store specializing in maternity clothes or lingerie, or a large department store, is the most likely to have specially trained staff. Make sure that the bra of your choice gives you good support with a deep band underneath the cups and wide shoulder straps that don't cut into your skin. Fastening should be adjustable for comfort, so back-fastening bras may be better than front-fastening. Buy only a couple of bras to begin with, as your breasts will continue to grow and you'll have to get larger sizes later in pregnancy.

If your breasts become very big it is a good idea to wear a light bra in bed at night to give them extra support, and just before your due date you should get a nursing bra, with flaps on the cups, so that you can breastfeed. They can be bought in any maternity or department store. You will also need to get a nighttime bra for after the birth. Leakages in bed are not much fun.

Girdles Wearing a maternity girdle during the second and third trimester will give you much-needed support – especially if you are expecting more than one baby. By relieving your back of some of the strain, a girdle can also help prevent backache.

Socks These should be made of cotton and be loose-fitting; synthetic materials don't give and can cut really deeply into swollen feet. In addition, they don't draw sweat away, so the skin may become waterlogged and soft. Avoid knee-high socks because they can form a restricting band around the top of your calf, encouraging varicose veins (see p.194).

Pantyhose Even sheer maternity pantyhose give a lot of support. There are many different types available in a variety of colors. You will find them in maternity shops and most department stores.

Stockings If you suffer with severe yeast infections, you may prefer thigh-high stockings. Support stockings, or ones containing a high percentage of spandex, will probably be the most comfortable, although they obviously don't offer the same amount of support as maternity pantyhose. Garter belts will be most comfortable if they fit on your hips under your abdomen, so choose one that is big enough, and shorten the straps if necessary.

Maternity outerwear
Choose cotton leggings, big cotton tops, and flat shoes for comfort and style throughout your pregnancy.

TIPS FOR YOUR DAY

There are a few minor adjustments that you can make to your normal work habits that will make your day more comfortable.

Put your feet up *Sit down as much as possible, and put your feet up whenever you can. Convert a piece of furniture, such as an overturned trash can, or an extended drawer, into a footstool.*

Relaxation exercises *Practice a few simple neck, shoulder, pelvic, and foot exercises as often as possible when traveling and at work. These will release any tension and help improve your circulation.*

Practice squatting *Use the squatting position whenever you have to bend down, or if there is no chair available. You will strengthen your thighs, and prepare yourself to use this position at the delivery.*

Eat well *Keep a supply of nutritious snacks close at hand (see p.114). Although you may still experience nausea, your urge for food may strike at inconvenient moments. A cracker and a glass of skim milk will be filling and help relieve attacks of nausea.*

Take it easy *In general, you should just try to take things more slowly. Stop and rest whenever you feel fatigued.*

A WORKING PREGNANCY

Whether you are working because of financial necessity or you find your career stimulating and intend to continue after your baby is born, make sure you are fully aware of information that will protect both your health and your job. You may wish to continue working well into your pregnancy, and there is no reason why you shouldn't unless your environment will pose a danger to your baby. Harmful materials or fumes, or heavy physical labor, for example, can be deleterious.

Pregnancy brings with it a variety of physical changes and discomforts, but working can confer the psychological benefit of reaffirming that it is a normal state. By continuing to work, you can maintain this important and stable aspect of your life at a time when you may be feeling disoriented owing to the physical and emotional changes created by your pregnancy.

PUTTING YOUR RIGHTS INTO PLAY

Most employers will cooperate with your wish to continue working during, and after, your pregnancy, provided you keep them well informed of your plans for stopping work before your baby is born and possibly resuming it afterward.

Protect your job Discuss with your employer or your trade union representative your entitlements concerning maternity leave and pay. You are usually allowed time off with pay for prenatal care. You may be entitled to paid, or unpaid, maternity leave.

Protect your health If there is the possibility of your work causing harm to your baby for example, if X-rays or heavy lifting fall within your area of responsibility, your employer should make every effort to find you an alternative job while you are pregnant, provided you have worked with him or her for an adequate period.

ADAPTING YOUR ROUTINE

Coping with fatigue while working is an uphill battle when you are pregnant. Bouts of morning sickness, particularly in early pregnancy, can make the situation even more difficult. As your pregnancy progresses, you will lose some of your agility, so that working long hours may leave you feeling very tired. Overtiredness will exacerbate your feelings of nausea, and you could also find yourself losing concentration and falling asleep. Added to this, the stress of traveling to and from your job, especially if you use public transportation during the rush hours, can prove exhausting.

Seek flexibility If aspects of your job make you uncomfortable, find out whether you can alter them until your baby is born. You may be able to change the times you start and finish work to avoid traveling during the rush hours. If you have to do a lot of standing or walking, see whether you can get a more sedentary position.

Take it easy Don't push yourself too hard. Adopt a more lenient attitude toward household chores, letting domestic priorities slide. Your health and that of your baby are far more important than an immaculate house. Relaxation is vital during pregnancy, and you should allow yourself enough free time to look after your body, including an exercise routine and massage.

Request support If he doesn't already help with the cooking and cleaning, ask your partner to do so. Maybe you could leave most of the chores until the weekend and do them together. Let your colleagues know you're pregnant. They will be more likely to be understanding of your emotional and physical changes, such as mood swings, lack of energy, and need for a more comfortable environment.

DECIDING WHEN TO STOP

Some women happily continue working until they near labor. However, most medical authorities believe that you should not continue up to your due date, preferably not after the 36th week. It is around this time that your heart, lungs, and other vital organs will have to work harder, and when a great deal of physical stress will be placed on your spine, joints, and muscles. This is the time when you should allow your body to rest whenever possible, and that may be difficult if you continue working.

DECIDING WHEN TO RETURN

It's very important that you think carefully about when you will want to return to work after your baby is born, and about what you will do when you do return.

You may wish to go back under different working conditions, and you will have to discuss this with your employer. There may be provision for part-time employment in your work, or a phased return that allows you to be, in effect, a part-time worker for a certain period after your baby's birth. You may also like to investigate job sharing, flexi-time, or going it on your own in some freelance activity that will enable you to work from home. Try to consider these options early in your pregnancy. Advance planning makes it easier to work with your employer to map out a postpartum schedule, or to lay the groundwork for freelancing.

When deciding whether or not to continue working after your baby is born, try to consider your partner's feelings along with your own. It can only lead to unhappiness and resentment if you decide to return to work when your partner is reluctant for you to do so. If he does feel this way, talking about it openly together may lead to a suitable compromise and to a solution for your working future.

YOUR BABY'S SAFETY

Try to be aware of any chemicals in your workplace that may potentially harm your baby. If you are worried, talk to your doctor and employer about the risks, and take steps to avoid them.

Many mothers working in an office environment are particularly concerned about hazards posed by exposure to radiation from copying machines and computer video display terminals. However, recent reports state that these very low levels of radiation will not harm the developing baby.

If you are in a smoking environment, find out whether it is possible for you to transfer to a smoke-free zone, at least until you have finished breastfeeding.

NAME *Vicky Dyson*

AGE *29 years*

PAST MEDICAL HISTORY *Nothing abnormal*

OBSTETRIC HISTORY *One son aged 6; everything normal and straightforward*

Vicky, a junior partner in a firm of accountants, is very anxious to go on working during her pregnancy. She passed her accountancy exams while she was expecting her first child, so she knows that she can cope with being pregnant and doing a full-time job. She also knows that she can combine work and mothering, as she has worked since shortly after the birth of her son 6 years ago. Her challenge now is to combine everything – pregnancy, the job, and being the mother of a schoolboy, while still maintaining a good relationship with her partner. The secret lies in time management and being sensitive to her own needs.

THE WORKING MOTHER

Vicky has to fit the pieces of her life together like a jigsaw puzzle – when to leave work, when to return, child care, her family, and her health. She needs to make the well-being of herself and her baby the top priority in all her plans.

VICKY'S WORK SITUATION

Vicky's colleagues and senior partners are all men, and she fears they will resent her taking a lot of time off either before or after the birth. I advised her to inform her senior partners that she is pregnant at three months and to make an appointment with them, for some time within the next few days, to discuss when she might leave work and when she might return (see p.54). I also advised her to make sure her diet gives her all the energy and nutrition she needs to keep working while her baby grows inside her. In addition, she will need extra rest and therefore should, if possible, take a nap in the afternoon – or at least rest with her feet up.

When to leave No two pregnancies are alike, so Vicky cannot know in advance how she will feel this time around. I advised her that she would be unwise to commit herself to staying at work beyond the 36th week, but perhaps she could arrange an informal option to do so if she feels well enough.

When to return This is a more complicated decision, as there are so many things to take into account. Vicky's menstrual cycle may take only three months to get back to normal, but her muscles and various organs need more time. The process takes a year altogether. Vicky has to make special feeding plans if she wants to go back to work before her baby is four months old. Because she doesn't want to give her baby formula, she will have to express her breast milk and freeze it (see **At the office**, opposite, and p.305). She'll need to allow time to build up an initial stock of milk, then a further six weeks for the baby to get used to the new arrangement.

I suggested that Vicky could choose a provisional date for her return to work, bearing in mind that she may feel quite different after the birth, and should consult her doctor as the date approaches.

Choosing a carer When choosing a carer, she will need to check out all the available options well in advance – day care, baby-sitters, daytime nannies, au pairs – until she finds a carer who's just right.

MAKING TIME

Once she is back at work, running her home, looking after her family, and mothering her new baby, Vicky will probably feel that time is very precious – and that she hasn't got enough of it.

She must have some time alone with her new baby every day, and her son, Jack, will need lots of reassurance at this stage. The best way to give him this is to let him have his own special time with her, so that he doesn't feel shut out. Vicky will also want to have time alone with her partner Peter, so that their relationship doesn't suffer. She and Peter, with or without the children, will also want to spend time with their friends. Above all, Vicky will need some time to herself – even if it's only one free hour a week when nobody is making any demands upon her. Many mothers feel guilty about taking time for themselves, but it's essential for a more relaxed mother and, therefore, a happier family.

Getting into a routine I suggested that Vicky would be likely to feel less overwhelmed if she has a routine to work with, and that the rest of her family would also feel happier. For example, her time with the baby could be when Vicky gets back from work. She could encourage Peter and Jack to bring her a cup of tea, make sure she is comfortable, then leave her alone with the baby while they go off and play together. Her special time with her son could be his bedtime, when she reads him a story and listens to him talk about his day. She and Peter could then have their evening meal together and chat, before the baby requires her late evening feeding.

EXPRESSING HER MILK

I explained to Vicky that the main factor in maintaining a good supply of breast milk is the removal of milk from the breasts, either by feeding her baby or by expressing it regularly. Leaving milk in the breast discourages further milk production and supplies quickly dwindle. Vicky feels sure that she will have enough milk for her to be able to express some just after a feeding for gradual stockpiling.

At the office I told Vicky she will probably find that her breasts will become full twice during the day, so she will have to make the time to express it during her working day.

Vicky told me that she intended to use a breast pump and, although her firm is predominately male, there is a comfortable, clean ladies room where she can express her milk in private, as well as a refrigerator in her office where she can store it until she goes home in the evening, so she anticipates few problems. I reminded her that all containers must be sterilized and that breast milk can only be kept for up to 48 hours in the refrigerator (up to six months in the freezer).

As Vicky will be at work all day, the carer will be responsible for defrosting each day's supply of breast milk. This should usually be done in the refrigerator although to defrost breast milk quickly, you can place the container under running lukewarm tap water. The baby's leftovers must be thrown away, never refrozen.

VICKY'S BABY

As her mother is working, Vicky's baby will also have to adjust to a routine.

- *She will have to accept the bottles of expressed milk; this is done more easily if she's introduced to them before she is 5 weeks old*

- *If she persistently refuses to accept them, she may want bottles with a different type of nipple*

- *About 6 weeks before Vicky returns to work, the baby will start being weaned off the breast for her daytime feedings. To start, one daytime feeding will be replaced by a bottle, until she is used to it*

- *She will have to accept the person who looks after her all day while Vicky is at work*

- *She will bond with her carer, who will be an important person in her life, but this will not affect her relationship with her parents*

- *She must make the most of her time with her mother. The best time is when Vicky gets home from work; her breasts will be full and the baby will be ready for a feeding*

- *She'll be quick to figure out that mommy is there all night and may become a wakeful baby as 2 of my own sons did*

DRUGS AND YOUR BABY

AVOIDING HAZARDS

Consult your doctor before taking any drug – prescription or non-prescription – and don't consult a doctor about anything without saying you're pregnant.

It is best to avoid taking anything during pregnancy unless your doctor determines that the benefit to you outweighs any risk to the fetus. The long-term effects of many drugs on the unborn child are still largely unknown. Other drugs have been proved to be hazardous to the fetus and should be completely avoided (see below).

Many of our normal activities may pose dangers during pregnancy. Things we do at home, such as cleaning out cat litter, or contact with harmful chemicals in the work environment, passive smoking while socializing, or vaccinations for traveling, may affect the development of the unborn baby, and certain precautions should be taken.

AT HOME

Very few of us can move to a perfect environment while pregnant, but you should try to avoid handling raw meat, touching other people's pets and cleaning out litter boxes, breathing in exhaust gases from cars, and working with pesticides in the garden.

DRUG	USE	EFFECTS
Amphetamines	Stimulant	May cause heart defects and blood diseases
Anabolic steroids	Body building	Can have a masculinizing effect on a female fetus
Tetracycline	Treats acne	Can discolor both first and permanent teeth
Streptomycin	Treats tuberculosis	Can cause deafness in infants
Antihistamines	Allergies/motion sickness	Some cause fetal malformations
Antinausea drugs	Combats nausea	May cause fetal malformations
Aspirin	Treats pain	Can cause problems with blood clotting
Diuretics	Rids body of excess fluid	Can cause fetal blood disorders
Narcotics (Codeine, etc.)	Treats pain	Addictive; baby may suffer withdrawal symptoms
Retin-A	Treats acne	Can cause birth defects
LSD, marijuana	For "fun"	Risk of chromosomal damage, and miscarriage
Sulfonamides	Treats infections	Can cause jaundice in the baby at birth

Alcohol, coffee, and teas containing caffeine are also best avoided. Herbal teas are generally safe (avoid raspberry leaf, which is said to cause contractions) but always choose organic ones in order to avoid the risks of pesticides.

Harmful chemicals You should limit your use of aerosol sprays in the home, and there are alternatives to most aerosols on the market today. Although modern aerosols contain halogenated hydrocarbons (rather than CFCs), which have not been implicated in causing harm to fetus or mother, my feeling is that we are all exposed to invisible sources of potentially harmful chemicals, and it's wise to take every possible precaution.

Avoid substances that give off vapors, such as glue and gasoline, as they may be toxic and should never be inhaled, whether you are pregnant or not. Read the label of any material you use, and avoid those which are potentially harmful. Some examples are cleaning fluids, contact cement, creosote, volatile paint, lacquers, thinners, some glues, and oven cleaner. Perms are apparently safe in pregnancy, but if you have fears about their long-term effects, I would advise you to wait, at least until after the first three months, when the most crucial organs in your baby's body have formed.

Hot baths Saunas and hot whirlpools have been implicated in fetal abnormalities, particularly those of the baby's nervous system, in exactly the same way as fever. When your body is subjected to extreme heat over a lengthy period you can become overheated and this may affect your baby. Avoid saunas and whirlpools, especially in the first trimester, and keep bath temperatures moderate.

Television rays Rays, even from color television, have not been shown to form ionizing radiation. It is not harmful to sit within several feet of the screen, even for long periods. However, make sure you are sitting comfortably to avoid backstrain.

Immunizations Because your entire immune system is changing under the influence of your pregnancy and may be weakened, your responses to immunizations can be unpredictable.

Your doctor will discuss with you any immunizations that are necessary if you have been exposed to infectious diseases or if you have to travel outside the US. In general, vaccinations that are prepared using live viruses – including measles, rubella (German measles), mumps, and yellow fever vaccinations – are avoided. It is recommended that women not have the flu vaccine during pregnancy, unless there is a high risk of heart or lung disease.

AT WORK

If you work outside the home, you may have many questions that have no simple answers: How safe is my workplace? Will the demands of my job put my pregnancy as risk? How long can I work? If your job is strenuous, involving a lot of standing, walking, or lifting, it may deprive you of the extra rest you need during

TOXOPLASMOSIS AND YOUR BABY

This is a parasite that normally produces only mild flulike symptoms in an adult, but it can seriously damage the unborn child.

It can cause fetal brain damage and blindness, and is fatal in certain cases. The greatest danger is during the third trimester.

Toxoplasma is carried in the feces of infected animals, particularly cats, but most people contract it by eating undercooked meat, particularly poultry. About 80% of the population have had it and have developed antibodies, but the younger you are, the less likely you are to be immune. You can ask your doctor to do a blood test.

Guidelines to follow:

• *Don't eat raw or undercooked meat, especially pork, rare steak, or steak tartare*

• *Don't feed raw meat to your cat or dog. Keep their food bowls away from everything else*

• *Don't garden in soil used by cats*

• *Do wear gloves when gardening*

• *Don't stroke other people's pets*

• *Don't empty your cat's litter box or use your dog's pooper-scooper. If it is unavoidable, always wear gloves and wash your hands thoroughly in disinfectant immediately afterward*

• *Do wash your hands after gardening or petting your animals*

• *Do cook meat to an internal temperature of at least 140°F/ 54°C – the temperature at which bacteria are killed. Use a meat thermometer to be sure*

• *Do try to keep your cat indoors as much as possible if it hunts; the parasite lives in infected mice and birds*

151

YOUR RISK OF INFECTION

In the first 12 weeks of pregnancy, you must try to avoid contact with anyone, expecially a child, who has a high fever, even if the fever is not thought to be caused by German measles (see p.19).

If you contract mumps in pregnancy, it will run the same course as if you were not pregnant. There is a minimal risk of increased miscarriage if you get the disease in the first 12 weeks of pregnancy.

The mumps vaccine will not be given during pregnancy because it is live and could therefore affect the fetus adversely.

Chickenpox is an uncommon disease in adults and is similarly uncommon in pregnancy. There is some evidence that it can cause fetal malformation.

Infection
If you have small children, there is obviously not much you can do to keep away from them. If you are a schoolteacher, be fairly strict about sending home any feverish child.

pregnancy and aggravate fatigue. Your doctor may suggest that you reduce your work hours, transfer to less strenuous work or stop working several weeks before your EDD. In all circumstances, pregnant women must avoid jobs that expose them to physical danger, including some police work, motorcycle racing, and so on.

Your doctor may also advise you to stop working if you have certain diseases, such as heart disease, if you have a history of more than one premature baby or miscarriage, or if you're expecting more than one baby.

Be alert to jobs that could expose you to potentially harmful environmental factors and make sure that your employer transfers you to a working place or alternative job that does not present possible hazards (see also p.146). Especially avoid:

• Anesthetic gases (nurses, physicians, dentists, anesthesiologists)

• Chemicals used in manufacturing and other industries – for example, lead, mercury, vinyl chloride, dry cleaning fluids, paint fumes, and solvents

• Animals, which present a risk of toxoplasmosis

• Exposure to infectious diseases, especially childhood rashes

• Exposure to toxic wastes of any kind

• Exposure to excessive levels of cigarette smoke, including passive smoking, such as in offices without smoking restrictions

• Unacceptable levels of ionizing radiation (although these are now strictly monitored by government regulation). It is generally accepted that day-to-day exposure to ultraviolet or infrared radiation emitted by office equipment such as laser printers, copying machines, and computer video display terminals is not dangerous to you or your baby. To be extra careful, women who work with photocopying machines every day should always keep the top closed when the machine is copying.

Otherwise, if you are a healthy woman having a normal pregnancy, and you work in a job presenting hazards no greater than those you encounter in daily life, you can usually work until close to your expected delivery date.

SOCIALIZING

Infections are caught from people with whom we come into contact. Although being pregnant doesn't mean that you should become a hermit, or wear a gauze mask when talking to people, it pays to be cautious – especially around children (see column, left), or adults who are running an elevated temperature. Colds and flu will not harm your baby, but do your best to avoid running a fever. If your temperature is very high, your doctor will advise what medications are safe (no aspirin in pregnancy) and a damp sponge and a fan might help to cool the skin. Don't take any cold or flu medicines that contain antihistamines. There is some evidence that virulent flu viruses can cause miscarriage.

TRAVELING

There is absolutely no evidence that travel precipitates labor, or leads to miscarriage, or any other complication of pregnancy. You should be extra cautious if you have miscarried before, or have a history of premature labor. Ask your doctor for the name of an obstetrician in the area you are visiting and, in the last trimester, limit yourself to trips within 30 miles of home.

Trains Reserve a seat if possible, and make sure that it is not next to the café car – the smell may make you feel nauseous. Eat lightly to minimize motion sickness. Do not lean on, or stand close to, outside doors as they have been known to fly open (this obviously applies even when you are not pregnant).

Cars Traveling by car can be exhausting, so limit your journeys. Get out of the car at regular intervals and take a short walk to ensure good circulation. Always fasten your seatbelt, but buckle it low, across your pelvis, and use a shoulder harness if you have one. You can do the driving as long as you are comfortable behind the wheel, but you must stop as soon as you begin to feel cramped. In addition, it may seem an obvious point, but don't drive yourself to the hospital if you are in labor!

Air travel After your seventh month, air travel is not a good idea because of pressure changes in the cabin. If you must fly at this time, check with the airline about whether it requires a doctor's letter to let you on the plane after your seventh month. Do not fly in small private planes that have unpressurized cabins. If you sit over the wings or toward the front of the plane, you will feel less of the plane's motion.

While flying, eat lightly because pregnancy makes you more prone to motion sickness. Make sure that you empty your bladder before you board because there may be a delay in takeoff, or the seatbelt sign may stay on a long time. When fastening your seatbelt, make sure that you buckle it low on your hips.

Foreign travel Take care when eating out that you follow the guidelines I've given to protect against listeria and other food-related diseases (see p.122). Drink bottled water when in doubt.

Check with your doctor about possible immunizations. Typhoid fever vaccinations could harm the baby. Even if you have been exposed or are in an epidemic, the bad effects of the live vaccine will have to be weighed against the risk to your baby. You should refuse to have a yellow fever vaccination unless there has been direct exposure. However, you can be vaccinated against cholera, as the vaccine is probably not harmful and you may need it to satisfy travel requirements in Southeast Asia. Rabies and tetanus vaccinations may be necessary, particularly if there is any indication of exposure. Chloroquine may be used for malaria but only if you're going to an endemic area. Polio vaccine may be administered in pregnancy if you are not already immune.

GOOD TRAVELING

Bearing in mind a few important points when you are traveling will make it a more comfortable experience.

- *Leave more than enough time for your journey*

- *Try to leave yourself a comfortable margin between any connections you have to make*

- *Travel in short bursts rather than a long stretch*

- *Travel safely (see main text)*

- *Carry a drink, such as milk or fruit juice, in a thermos*

- *Take adequate amounts of nutritious portable food, such as whole-grain crackers, cold hard-boiled eggs, raw fruit or vegetables, and nibbles like dried fruit, nuts, and seeds*

- *Carry hard candies so that you can prevent nausea due to low blood sugar*

- *Make use of an eye mask and ear plugs so that you can get some sleep when you are traveling by train or plane*

153

6

Your prenatal

CARE

Excellent prenatal care should be rewarded with healthy mothers and babies. Routine tests will usually pinpoint many problems as soon as they arise, while special tests are available for mothers and babies with particular needs. The doctor's or midwife's office also provides opportunities to ask questions and to meet other mothers-to-be.

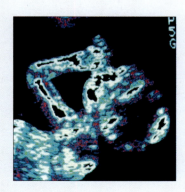
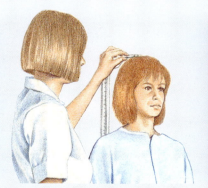
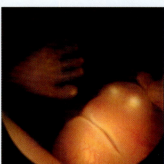

YOUR FIRST VISIT

On your first visit to your doctor or midwife, you will be asked various questions on the following subjects:

• *Your personal details and circumstances*

• *Childhood illnesses or serious illnesses you have had*

• *Illnesses that run in your family or in your partner's family*

• *If there are twins in your family*

• *Your menstrual history – when you started, how long your average cycle is, how many days you bleed, and the date of LMP (see p.52)*

• *What symptoms of pregnancy you have, and your general health*

• *Details of previous births, pregnancies, or problems in conceiving*

• *If you are taking any prescription medicine or if you suffer from any allergies*

Discussing your pregnancy
Don't hesitate to request more time if you have questions that need answering.

PRENATAL CARE

Consultations, checkups, and tests will be carried out throughout your pregnancy to monitor your health and that of your baby. Although most pregnancies proceed normally, these visits and investigations are vital to monitor progress and spot problems early before any harm is done.

VISITING YOUR CAREGIVER

A program of prenatal care allows your doctor or midwife to monitor your health and that of your baby throughout pregnancy. Most pregnancies proceed normally, but each one has the potential of risk. Assessing the risk on an ongoing basis is the vital part of prenatal care. Complications can arise without warning, so early and regular visits are important.

Most women are asked to visit once a month until week 28, then every two weeks until week 36, then once a week until delivery. However, if there are complications, such as multiple fetuses or medical illnesses, you may need to go more frequently.

Your first prenatal visit will be longer and more involved than subsequent ones. It will include a detailed history of your own health, your past obstetrical history, your family's history of such things as multiple births or inherited diseases, and your work, family life, and habits. You will undergo a physical examination and confirmation of your expected date of delivery – your EDD or "due date." Several laboratory tests will be done then and/or at subsequent visits, such as:

• Blood tests to identify your blood type, Rh factor, and other antibodies; complete blood count (CBC) for anemia and sexually transmitted diseases

• Tests for rubella (German measles) or hepatitis

• Urine tests to check your levels of sugar and albumin, and to detect possible urinary tract infections

• A Pap test to check for cervical cancer

• Depending on your history, age, race, or family background, other tests may also be needed, such as screening for diabetes or genetic defects

After your first visit, your prenatal appointments will usually be shorter. These visits are designed to find out how you are feeling, how the fetus is growing, and to discuss any special problems you may be having or your concerns about labor and delivery. At every visit, your weight and blood pressure will be checked, and a urine sample is tested.

TALKING WITH YOUR CAREGIVER

Answering your questions and addressing any concerns that you and your partner have are essential ingredients of good prenatal care. Write down your questions – the reality of the office or examining room can drive them out of your head. If you need moral support, take along your partner or a close friend.

It's also important to make notes of any unusual signs or symptoms that appear between visits. At your first visit, ask the doctor or midwife to explain to you any such events that should be brought immediately to his or her attention through a phone call.

EXPRESSIONS USED IN THE DOCTOR'S OFFICE

Here are some common expressions you may overhear during your visits to your pregnancy caregivers or during labor and delivery. If there is something you don't understand, ask your caregiver.

TERMS YOUR DOCTOR MAY USE

LMP *Last menstrual period*

EDC/EDD *Estimated date of confinement or delivery – your due date*

BP *Blood pressure*

HT *Hypertension*

Edema *Swelling/water retention of fingers, legs, or ankles*

Toxemia (or preeclampsia) *Presence of increased blood pressure, swelling, and albumin in urine, sometimes occurring in last trimester*

CBC *Complete blood count (measures your hemoglobin, red and white cell counts, and appearance of your blood platelets)*

Hb/Hgb *Hemoglobin*

STS test *Test for syphilis*

HIV test *Test for presence of the AIDS virus*

Albumin *One of the proteins found in a urine sample*

Section *Caesarean section*

hCG *Human chorionic gonadotrophin – the hormone manufactured by the embryo and measured in pregnancy tests*

FH *Fetal heart*

Head engaged *Baby's head has dropped into the bony pelvis, ready for birth*

Head "floating" *Baby's head is not yet engaged*

Vertex *Baby is head-down*

Breech *Baby is bottom-down*

Lie *The relationship of the baby's spine to your spine. In a longitudinal lie (see middle pictures, right), the baby's spine is parallel with yours; in a transverse lie, his spine is at right angles to yours*

High-risk *Any pregnancy complicated by problems found in your medical history or occurring during your pregnancy*

Height of fundus *The height of the top of the uterus, measured with a tape measure or calipers in centimeters, above the bony pelvis*

Primigravida *Your first pregnancy*

Multigravida *Second or later pregnancy*

Femur length *A measurement of the baby's "thigh bone"; helps estimate fetal growth*

THE LIE OF YOUR BABY

Certain abbreviations describe how the baby is lying, and refer to where the back of the baby's head (occiput) is in relation to your body – on the right or left, to the front (anterior) or back (posterior). ROA, for example, means the back of his head is to the front on your right.

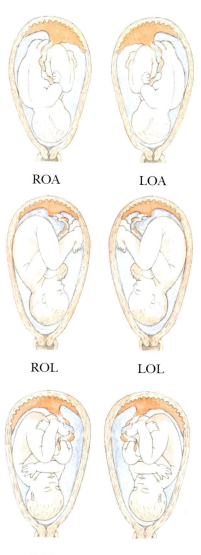

ROA   LOA

ROL   LOL

ROP   LOP

ROUTINE TESTS

Every pregnant woman undergoes certain routine tests to keep a check on her health and the development of her baby. These tests may be performed on every visit, or at different times during her pregnancy. Some are performed only once. If the tests indicate that there is, or that there may be, a problem, you will be monitored closely and prompt action will be taken if necessary.

HEIGHT

Your height will be measured at your first visit. If you are very petite, you may have a small pelvic inlet and outlet, both of which need to be assessed. However, the chances are that your baby will be closely tailored to suit your particular physical build.

WEIGHT

This is noted at every visit and gives an indication of the growth of the fetus. You should try to wear the same sort of clothing each time, so that your weight does not fluctuate unnecessarily. In the first trimester, a loss of weight usually reflects nausea and vomiting due to morning sickness and is usually nothing to worry about. But sudden weight gain may reflect fluid retention and indicate preeclampsia. In the past, maternal weight gain was taken as a reliable indicator of the growth of the baby. Research now indicates, however, that maternal weight gain should not be relied upon on its own, but viewed in conjunction with external and internal examinations, blood and urinary tests, sonograms, and other information.

LEGS AND HANDS

On every visit your legs will be checked for varicose veins, and your ankles and hands will be checked for swelling and puffiness (edema).

A little swelling in the final weeks of pregnancy is normal, particularly in the evening, but excessive puffiness may give an early warning of preeclampsia (see p.204).

BREASTS

Your breasts will be examined, and the condition of your nipples will be noted. A very few women have dimpled (known as inverted) nipples, and these may have to be corrected by wearing a breast shield inside your bra, although inverted nipples do usually correct themselves during pregnancy.

YOUR BABY'S HEAD SIZE RELATIVE TO YOUR PELVIS

The shape and size of your pelvis are important because of the risk of disproportion between it and your baby's head size. This could become apparent during labor, delaying the baby's descent through the birth canal.

Disproportion means that your pelvis is too small for your baby's head to pass through it easily, or your baby's head is too large.

To avoid delays in delivering your baby, it's important for your doctor or midwife to make an assessment of the size of your pelvic outlet.

Your doctor or midwife can also get a good idea by doing an internal examination of your pelvis (see p.160). If difficulties are suspected, your baby's exact head size will be determined using ultrasound (see p.162). Severe disproportion may necessitate a Caesarean section (see p.284).

Measuring your height
Potential problems may be indicated if you are very short in comparison to the average height for your type and build.

URINE

At your first visit a sample of midstream urine will be taken to test for a kidney infection. At every subsequent visit your urine will be tested for protein, which is a sign of urinary infection; for sugar, to check that you are not developing diabetes; and for ketones, which are the classic sign that diabetes is established and needs urgent treatment. A rare cause of ketonuria is severe vomiting in pregancy, called hyperemesis gravidarum, which requires urgent hospitalization. Urine testing in pregnancy can also unmask underlying diabetes (see p.205). Diabetes may disappear completely after this pregnancy but return in future pregnancies.

A trace of protein in your urine in late pregnancy is a strong indication of preeclampsia. This will be treated promptly because of the associated risks of miscarriage, a small-for-dates baby, and premature delivery.

BLOOD TESTS

At your first visit, a routine blood sample will be taken, usually from a vein in your arm, to find out your basic blood group (A,B,O), and your Rhesus (Rh) blood group (positive or negative), in case a blood transfusion becomes necessary. If you are Rh negative, you will be tested for Rhesus incompatibility (see p.184).

You will also have a complete blood count, measuring the levels of your red and white blood cells, blood platelets (which aid in blood clotting), and hemoglobin. Hemoglobin is a measure of the oxygen-carrying power of your red blood cells. The normal level is between 12 and 14 grams; if it falls below 10 grams, treatment

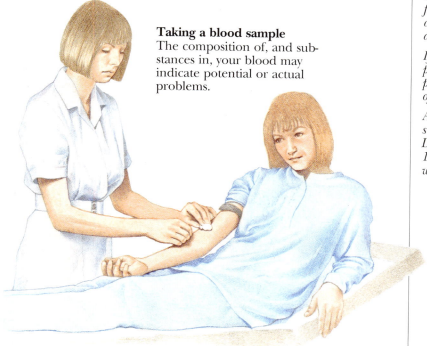

Taking a blood sample
The composition of, and substances in, your blood may indicate potential or actual problems.

ALPHA-FETOPROTEIN

This is a protein that is first produced by the embryo's yolk sac, and then later by the fetal liver. Doctors use alpha-fetoprotein (AFP) as an indicator of what is going on inside the uterus.

AFP is found in varying amounts in your blood throughout pregnancy. Between 16–18 weeks, the levels are usually low, so if a blood test is performed and the levels are 2–3 times higher than the average of a sample group, it may indicate a neurological problem such as spina bifida or hydrocephalus (see p.179).

However, the levels may be raised because of a multiple pregnancy, inaccurate dating of the pregnancy, abnormalities of the baby's kidneys or digestive tract, or if there is a threat of miscarriage. Therefore, a sonogram (see p.162) will be taken to check for multiple fetuses or to confirm your dates in case your pregnancy is more advanced than you think.

If the sonogram rules out either possibility, another AFP test will be performed, and then you will be offered amniocentesis (see p.164).

An abnormally low level of AFP suggests that the fetus may have Down's syndrome (see pp.20 & 180) and, again, amniocentesis will be offered.

ASSESSING YOUR PELVIS

Your doctor can make a fairly accurate assessment of your pelvis by internal examination (see also main text) and will note any potential problems.

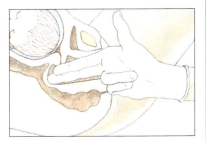

The pelvic inlet
Using 2 gloved fingers, the doctor will try to feel your sacrum through the back of your vagina.

The ischial spines
The doctor will feel left and right for the 2 ischial spines. They may be blunt or sharp, barely noticeable or quite distinct.

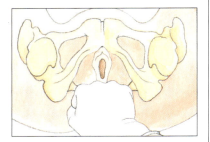

The pelvic outlet
The doctor will measure the distance between the ischial tuberosities. It is normally over 5in (11cm).

for anemia will be given. (Iron and folic acid raise the oxygen-carrying power of your blood, so it is essential that you make sure you are eating healthfully.)

German measles (rubella) antibodies (see p.19) will be looked for, to see whether or not you are immune. Additionally, the presence of sexually transmitted diseases, such as syphilis, will be revealed. Certain genetic disorders, such as sickle cell anemia and thalassemia (see pp.20 & 21), are detectable in blood. At 16 weeks, tests for alpha-fetoprotein may be done (see column, p.159).

EXTERNAL EXAMINATION

At every visit your abdomen will be gently felt to determine the size of your growing baby. This examination gives a good idea of whether your baby is approximately the right size for your dates and also means that the series of measurements that are taken over the course of your pregnancy will give an accurate picture of your baby's rate of progress.

The top (fundus) of your uterus will be felt (it normally enters your abdomen at 12 weeks and rises until just prior to term), and a measurement taken of the distance between your pelvic bone and the top of your uterus. The amount of amniotic fluid, as well as your individual size and weight, can have an effect on the reading, so after 26–28 weeks the doctor or midwife will also feel for your baby's "poles" (head and rump). This gives a good indication of the "lie" of your baby (see p.157).

Checking your weight
You will be weighed at every visit. This can give an early indication of problems such as preeclampsia and slow fetal growth.

INTERNAL EXAMINATION

By no means will everyone have an internal examination at their first prenatal visit, but if done the doctor will confirm the pregnancy, check your cervix, and assess your pelvic size (see also column, left). If an internal examination is to be performed, you will be asked to lie down and raise your knees. Your uterus will be checked to see that it is the right size for your dates; your cervix will be looked at to see if it's tightly closed, and a cervical smear may be carried out to test for precancerous cells; and your pelvis may be checked to ensure that the outlet is adequate for a vaginal delivery – although this check may be done at about 36 weeks. This is carried out so that doctors and midwives can check for pelvic disproportion (see box, p.158). It will not be uncomfortable as long as you relax, and it will not harm your baby.

The doctor or midwife will insert two gloved fingers of one hand into your vagina and press your abdomen with the other hand to check the size of your uterus. He or she will see if your sacrum can be felt (usually it can't) at the back of your vagina, then feel sideways for the ischial spines (two small protruding bones) to check that there is enough room for your baby to pass through at birth. The doctor will then check the dimensions of your pubic arch and, after removing his or her hand and making a loose fist, will finish by estimating the distance across your pelvic outlet (see column, left). If you were checked early in pregnancy, some doctors and midwives will perform another internal examination at 36 weeks on first-time mothers to check pelvic dimensions. Further internal examinations will be carried out once you are in labor.

BLOOD PRESSURE

This reading is taken at every visit, and measures the pressure at which your heart is pumping blood through your body. The reading is made up of two numbers: the upper one is the systolic pressure – when the heart contracts it pushes out blood and "beats." This is measured when the armband is tight. As the pressure is released, the lower, or diastolic, reading is made. This is the resting pressure between beats. The statistically average reading in pregnancy is about 120 over 70, although blood pressure differs with age, and there is a range of blood pressures at any one age that are considered normal. A higher reading than normal may indicate preeclampsia, and bed rest may be advised. Constant checks ensure that changes are quickly noted.

External palpitation
Your abdomen will be felt at every visit to check fetal growth and position.

FETAL HEARTBEAT

Your baby's heartbeat will be monitored at every visit from week 14. The baby's heartbeat is almost twice as fast as your own (approximately 140 beats per minute, compared with 72 beats per minute), and sounds like a tiny galloping horse.

Pinnard stethoscope *The doctor or midwife may listen to your baby's heartbeat using a traditional ear trumpet known as a Pinnard stethoscope.*

Sonicaid *It is more likely, however, that the carer will use a sonicaid, a small portable instrument that is placed on your stomach and uses ultrasound (see also p.162) to pick up the fetal heartbeat. The sonicaid magnifies the sound of your baby's heartbeat, so you can listen to it.*

Electronic monitor *If your baby is stressed for any reason, the heart rate dips. This occurs during labor during each contraction, and the hospital staff will record the baby's progress using an electronic fetal monitor (see p.263).*

ULTRASOUND

*Sonograms are normally done
to check the baby's progress, but
certain problems may also
necessitate ultrasound.*

- *As part of infertility assessment*
- *To identify abdominal problems,
such as an ectopic pregnancy*
- *If the doctors suspect an
imminent miscarriage*
- *To check for a multiple
pregnancy*

With the aid of an ultrasound scan you can see a picture of your
unborn baby. An ultrasound scan, or sonogram, checks the baby's
general well-being and position, and guides doctors performing
special tests and operations. Most women will be offered a scan at
least once during their pregnancy. It is usually performed between
16 – 18 weeks when the baby can be seen at various angles. If any
problems are detected, repeat scans may be performed several
times before the birth.

HOW IT WORKS

The process is based on a sonar device that reveals objects in fluid.
It was first used by the US Navy to detect submarines during World
War II. A crystal, inside a device called a transducer, converts an
electrical current into high frequency sound waves, inaudible to the
human ear. The sound waves form a beam that penetrates the
abdomen as the transducer is moved back and forth. The beam

HAVING A SONOGRAM

An ultrasound scan is
painless and usually lasts
about 15 minutes. You
may be asked to drink
about a pint of water
and not urinate before
arriving at the clinic.
This may cause
some discomfort,
but a full bladder
will provide a
clearer picture of
the fetus on the
screen. At the
clinic, you may be
asked to remove
your clothes and
put on a hospital
gown before lying
on a bed beside
the scanner. An
oil or jelly that acts
as a conductor of
the sound waves is
rubbed on your
abdomen, and the
transducer is passed
over this area in
different directions.
As the image
appears on the
screen, you can just
relax and enjoy this
first view of your baby.

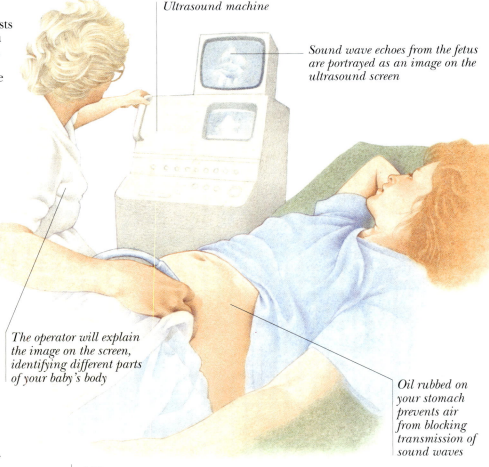

Ultrasound machine

*Sound wave echoes from the fetus
are portrayed as an image on the
ultrasound screen*

*The operator will explain
the image on the screen,
identifying different parts
of your baby's body*

*Oil rubbed on
your stomach
prevents air
from blocking
transmission of
sound waves*

reflects off material in its path, and the transducer records these echoes. The echoes are converted into electrical signals, which produce an image that can be displayed on a television-like screen. The beam can only penetrate fluids and soft tissue such as the amniotic sac, kidneys, and liver. It cannot pass through bone, or register gas. Sonograms are increasingly used to assess threatened miscarriage, exclude ectopic pregnancies, for infertility treatments, such as IVF, and for fetal surgery (see p.182).

YOUR FIRST SONOGRAM

The sophisticated equipment used for an ultrasound scan may at first appear rather daunting, but don't be intimidated. The sonogram offers an exciting opportunity for you and your partner to see your baby for the very first time.

You should be able to hear her heartbeat and to distinguish the gentle movement of hands and feet, waving and kicking, as she floats around in the amniotic fluid. Ask the ultrasound operator to explain the image on the screen as some detail may be difficult to interpret. Many clinics will give you a print of the image of your baby as a memento to cherish.

IS IT SAFE?

Ultrasound scanning poses no known risk to the fetus. Questions have been raised about long-term effects, such as hearing impairment caused by the impact of sound waves. However, recent research seems to indicate that ultrasound is not harmful to the mother or baby, as the waves are of a very low intensity, and so it is safe for sonograms to be performed repeatedly. But, if you are worried, avoid having a scan before ten weeks, and discuss any concerns with your doctor.

WHY BABY HAS IT DONE

Routine sonograms will reveal a great deal about your baby's health. They may be used at different stages of your pregnancy.

- *To check the baby's location and development of the placenta*

- *To check on growth rate of the baby, particularly when date of conception is unknown*

- *To find out whether the baby is ready to be born, if it is overdue*

- *To confirm your baby is in the normal head-down position, and not bottom-down, after week 38*

- *To detect certain fetal abnormalities, such as spina bifida*

- *To monitor the fetus throughout special tests such as amniocentesis and fetoscopy*

- *To assist in operations performed on the fetus in the uterus*

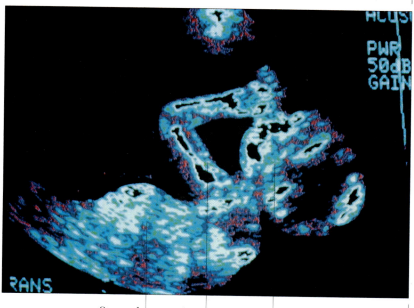

Fetus at 22 weeks
An ultrasound scan will clearly show your baby's size, its position, and whether there is more than one fetus. This portrait shows the baby in its mother's uterus. The fetus floats and moves around continuously in the amniotic sac, developing day by day, sucking its thumb, blinking, and urinating.

Stomach   Arm   Head

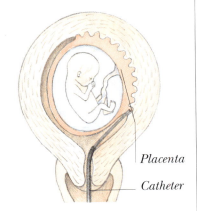

Chorionic sampling
A small amount of chorion
(placental tissue) is withdrawn
from the uterus through the
cervix with the aid of a catheter.

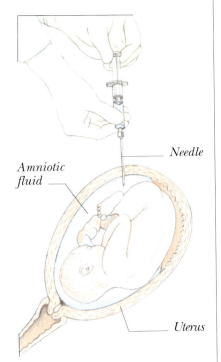

Amniocentesis
Amniotic fluid is extracted only
after a sonogram has determined
the position of the fetus and the
placenta. Using ultrasound, the
doctor will pass a needle through
the abdominal wall, which has
been numbed with local
anesthetic, and into the uterus.
A small amount of amniotic
fluid is withdrawn.

SPECIAL TESTS

If your doctor suspects a problem that cannot be detected by
simple routine tests, you will have special tests. These will enable
doctors to check for various complications, and may include invasive techniques, such as chorionic villus sampling. The tests can
perform two useful services for you and your partner: they can be
reassuring by failing to detect a suspected weakness such as the gene
for cystic fibrosis, or they may provide you with information that
makes you question whether your pregnancy should proceed. Have
full discussions with your doctor about the tests and their results.

AMNIOCENTESIS
Amniotic fluid contains cells from the baby's skin and other organs
which provide clues to his condition. Amniocentesis is the simple
procedure that withdraws this fluid from the uterus.

Why is it done? You will be offered an amniocentesis if you are
over the age of 35, when the risk of chromosomal abnormalities
(such as Down's syndrome) is slightly higher, particularly if blood
tests reveal a very low level of alpha-fetoprotein (see p.159). In
addition, amniocentesis can reveal other important information.
Where there is cause for concern, the test shows:

• The sex of the baby: cells sloughed off by the fetus accumulate
in the amniotic fluid. Under the microscope, male cells can be
distinguished from female cells and the baby's sex ascertained. In
genetically linked disorders such as hemophilia, a male child will
have a 50 percent chance of being affected

• The age of the fetus: if the lecithin/sphingomyelin (L/S) ratio
in the fluid is measured, the maturity of the lungs can be assessed,
which is in itself an indication of fetal age

• The chemical composition of the fluid: this can reveal metabolic
disorders caused by missing or defective enzymes

• The bilirubin content of the fluid: this helps to determine if a
Rhesus-positive baby needs an intrauterine transfusion

• The amount of oxygen the baby is getting: gases dissolved in the
amniotic fluid can be measured, revealing whether the baby is at
risk from lack of oxygen

• The acidity of the fluid: this is another indication of fetal distress
often caused by inadequate oxygen flow to the fetus

• The chromosome count: determined by examining discarded
cells. Any deviation from the normal chromosomal structure usually means that the child will be handicapped

How is it done? Amniocentesis is usually performed from the 14th
week, although it can be done earlier. A hollow needle is inserted
into the amniotic sac through the front of the abdominal wall.

About half an ounce (14 grams) is usually withdrawn and this is then spun in a centrifuge to separate the cells shed by the baby from the rest of the liquid. The cells are cultured for about two to five weeks, and therefore results take some time.

Amniocentesis is only undertaken with ultrasound monitoring to guide the needle into the amniotic sac, so that neither the placenta nor the fetus is harmed. The risk of the procedure inducing a miscarriage in early pregnancy is about one in 200. It has also been suggested that there may be a very small risk (less than 1 percent) of respiratory difficulties in babies after amniocentesis.

CHORIONIC VILLUS SAMPLING (CVS)

The chorionic villi, fingerlike outgrowths on the edge of the chorion, are genetically identical to the fetus. They develop earlier than the amniotic fluid, so examining a sample of chorionic villi will provide valuable information about your baby's genes and chromosomes before amniocentesis is possible.

Why is it done? The most important group of mothers needing CVS are those at risk of having a Down's syndrome baby. An abnormality of hemoglobin, such as sickle cell disease or thalassemia, can be diagnosed with CVS. Inborn errors of metabolism are fortunately rare, but if a family is afflicted, the incidence may be as high as one in four. The basic defect is an enzyme deficiency, and direct enzyme analysis on the chorionic tissue will provide the diagnosis within two days. Single gene disorders, such as cystic fibrosis, hemophilia, Huntington's chorea, and muscular dystrophy, can be detected.

How is it done? CVS is also carried out under ultrasound control, usually between 10 and 12 weeks, before the amniotic sac completely fills the uterine cavity. Two routes are employed: the transcervical route and the transabdominal route. For the former, the cervix is first examined. A plastic or metal catheter is then introduced through the cervical canal, across the uterine cavity, and into the outside edge of the placenta. A small amount of chorionic villi tissue is then removed. The latter procedure follows that of amniocentesis, but taking a sample of the placental tissue rather than amniotic fluid. The risk of miscarriage following CVS is about 2 percent higher than the spontaneous miscarriage rate. CVS has also recently been implicated in certain birth defects. Discuss the risks with your doctor. CVS gives a result within 24–48 hours.

UMBILICAL VEIN SAMPLING (CORDOCENTESIS)

This procedure is used to examine the constituents of fetal blood. and, in the case of fetal anemia, for intrauterine blood transfusion. It is vital in four other situations.

Infection detection Rubella, toxoplasmosis, and the herpes virus may be detected by performing a specific analysis of certain proteins that are present in the blood of the fetus.

Your age is important, but it's just one of several factors that can affect the outcome of your pregnancy. Your nutrition is much more important.

With increasing age you are more likely to fall into a group requiring special attention. You'll be asked questions to identify your special needs. Potential problems will be identified and appropriate tests done. After this, your prenatal care will be fairly routine.

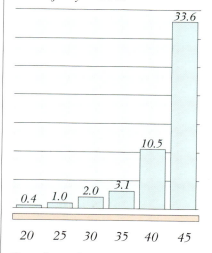

Down's syndrome and your age
Exactly why the chromosomal abnormality occurs that results in Down's syndrome is not known, but maternal age seems to be an important factor. As you can see from the graph, the risk of having a baby with this condition rises with advancing maternal age. However, as a Down's syndrome baby is born every 2,000 births, and as most babies are born to women under 35 who don't undergo screening for Down's syndrome, there are now more Down's babies born to the pre-35 age group than to the post-35 age group.

FETOSCOPY

This is done by passing a very small, tubular, light-bearing device into the vagina or abdomen for a good view of the amniotic fluid or fetus.

The appearance of the amniotic fluid can give many clues. If the fluid is greenish-yellow, instead of clear or amber as it is normally, the fetus has passed a substance called meconium.

This is noteworthy because when a baby is in distress (e.g. from lack of oxygen) the anal sphincter muscle relaxes and releases meconium from the fetus' large intestine into the amniotic fluid.

The fetoscope also contains a powerful lens so that the developing baby can be seen clearly and any abnormalities noted. Under local anesthetic the fetoscope is passed through the abdominal wall via a small incision just above the pubic bone. The whole procedure is constantly monitored on the ultrasound screen.

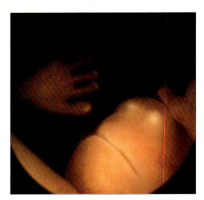

A fetoscopic view
The picture above shows a close-up of the nose and the mouth of a 16-week-old baby. Fetoscopy provides a closer look at the fetus, particularly his limbs, genitals, and spine. It is a radical mechanical intervention and is only used in exceptional circumstances.

Rhesus iso-immunization In cases of Rhesus incompatibility (see p.184) the direct assessment of fetal hemoglobin is the best way to determine the severity of blood cell destruction and whether an intrauterine blood transfusion (also done through the umbilical vein) needs to be carried out.

Chromosome count Certain white blood cells (fetal lymphocytes) will provide a chromosome count in a few days. Such information is desirable if the fetus is found to have a congenital abnormality known to be associated with trisomies (see p.180).

Suspected growth retardation If the fetus is considered to be growth-retarded, cordocentesis may be used to measure the degree of acidity or alkalinity of the blood, and the amounts of oxygen, carbon dioxide, and bicarbonate in the blood. In addition, plasma levels of glucose can be estimated.

How is it done? Under ultrasonic control, a hollow needle is passed through the front wall of the abdomen and uterus into a blood vessel in the umbilical cord, about one half-inch from where it emerges from the placenta. A small quantity of blood can then be removed for testing.

The risk to the fetus appears to be about 1–2 percent. In theory, cordocentesis can replace any investigation currently undertaken on a blood sample.

OTHER TESTS FOR CHROMOSOMAL DEFECTS

The Bart's "triple test" A new test that has been developed by St. Bartholomew's Hospital in London. In this test a maternal blood sample is taken at 16 weeks to measure the levels of three substances – estriol, human chorionic gonadotrophin, and alpha-fetoprotein. The results can be assessed along with your age to predict the chance of your baby suffering from Down's syndrome. If the chances seem high, amniocentesis will be offered. The Bart's triple test is not yet offered automatically, although you can request it.

Ultrasound scanning New research seems to indicate that Down's syndrome can be identified using ultrasound. A shadow, of a particular size and shape that is present at the back of the fetus's neck, denotes Down's syndrome. If this shadow is present, amniocentesis will be offered.

FETAL HEART MONITORING

This is an efficient method of monitoring the well-being of the fetus during pregnancy. A healthy fetus that is receiving adequate supplies of oxygen and nutrients will generally be more active than a malnourished, oxygen-starved fetus, and the heart rate will respond to stress more effectively. Hand-held monitors are used to check the presence of the heartbeat; electronic fetal monitors are also available. When a healthy, active fetus moves, the heart rate accelerates by approximately 15 beats per minute for 15 seconds.

Continuous electronic monitoring This is used to detect early fetal distress during labor. It is done by strapping the monitor across your abdomen. As the strap has to be firmly attached to provide a good reading, this may be slightly uncomfortable. The baby's heartbeat is recorded using ultrasound, and a printout gives a graph of the baby's heartbeat. If during this time a normal uterine contraction does not occur, then one may be obtained by gently pressing on the abdomen.

Stress to the fetus in labor does occur during a uterine contraction, and the fetal heart rate shows this by slowing down a little (see below). A normal fetus overcomes this stress quickly and the heart rate returns to normal soon after the contraction ends. However, when the fetus is distressed, both the slowing down, and the return to normal, of the fetal heart rate are delayed.

MONITORING THE FETAL HEARTBEAT DURING LABOR

In picture (A) you can see a printout of the normal fetal heart rate (measured in beats per minute – bpm). In pictures (B) and (C) are printouts of the baby's heart rate during contractions. The baby's heart rate will usually slow down at the beginning of a uterine contraction, and then quickly return to normal (type 1 dips – B). This doesn't indicate fetal distress. However, if the baby's heart rate starts to dip later during a contraction, and takes longer to return to normal (type 2 dips – C), fetal distress is indicated.

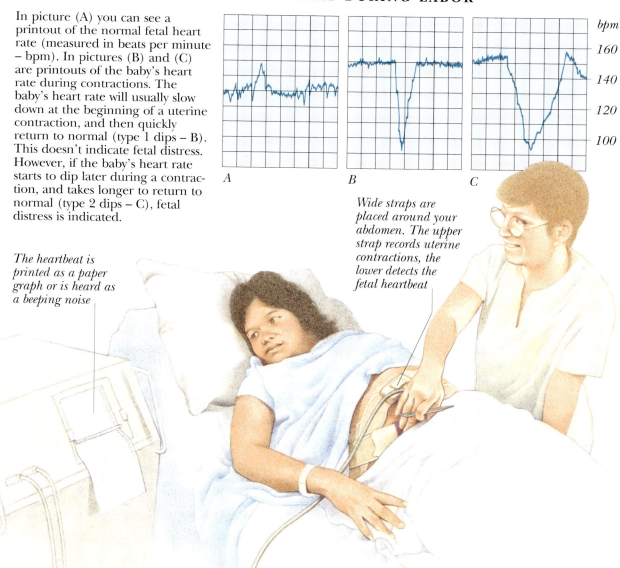

A   *B*   *C*

bpm
160
140
120
100

Wide straps are placed around your abdomen. The upper strap records uterine contractions, the lower detects the fetal heartbeat

The heartbeat is printed as a paper graph or is heard as a beeping noise

NAME *Jill Dalton*

AGE *27 years*

PAST MEDICAL
HISTORY *Developed insulin-dependent diabetes at age 25 after having had 2 children*

OBSTETRIC
HISTORY *At 23 years, a son, normal vaginal delivery, weight 10lb 10oz. At 25 years, second son, normal pregnancy, normal vaginal delivery, weight 11lb 4oz*

Jill developed diabetes relatively late, at 25 while she was pregnant with her second child, and has had the disease for only a couple of years. Both these factors give a good prognosis for her pregnancy. Nonetheless, she is highly motivated to seek outstanding prenatal care. She realizes that uncontrolled diabetes could lead to complications for her and to more serious ones for the baby.

THE DIABETIC MOTHER

Having or developing diabetes during pregnancy does not mean that pregnancy will be difficult or that the chance of producing a normal, healthy baby is less likely. As long as diabetes is very carefully managed, with the obstetrician and internist in close cooperation, the outcome should be satisfactory.

PREGNANCY AND DIABETES

As well as being 50 percent more likely than men to become diabetic, women have a tendency to develop the disease during pregnancy. Certain women are recognized as being potential diabetics. They usually have had at least one heavy baby or have a family history of diabetes in parents or siblings. Other women, known as gestational diabetics, develop diabetes during pregnancy. Some may remain diabetic after pregnancy, but others revert to normal. All these diabetics are treated in the same way.

Pregnancy can complicate established diabetes. While most sufferers will have been treated with insulin, some women with diabetes may have been treated by means of diet alone or with dietary measures and blood sugar lowering (hypoglycemic) tablets. The extra demands of pregnancy may lead to insulin having to be prescribed or the prescribed dosage being increased.

JILL'S PREPARATIONS FOR PREGNANCY

Having been an insulin-dependent diabetic for two years, Jill was meticulous about her pre-pregnancy preparations. She planned this present baby and made sure she had a full assessment of her diabetes well before she became pregnant. In particular, she was concerned about controlling blood sugar levels, the functioning of her kidneys, and the health of her eyes. In the months before conceiving, she maintained careful control of her diabetes.

KEEPING CONTROL DURING PREGNANCY

Jill knows that careful control of her diabetes during the first trimester should greatly reduce the risk of her baby having any kind of abnormality (see **Possible prenatal complications**). Therefore, she came to seek my advice very early in the pregnancy.

I told Jill that now she is pregnant, she may need less insulin for the first three months. Then her body will start to produce hormones with an anti-insulin effect, so she will need more insulin than before. Ketosis (see box) is more apt to occur during pregnancy,

168

so Jill has to test for ketones in her urine every day. However, urine testing will no longer be a reliable way to monitor her blood sugar, because the level at which the kidneys allow sugar into the urine tends to be lower in pregnant women, so that a urine test can give a false result. I therefore advised Jill to buy a blood-glucose meter that she can use in her own home. She is aware that maintenance of normal glucose concentration in her blood brings the best results for herself and her baby. However, this may occasionally be difficult. I told her that she may require hospitalization, perhaps more than once, in order to stabilize her diabetes, but that she shouldn't let this worry her unduly.

POSSIBLE PRENATAL COMPLICATIONS

As an established diabetic, Jill is susceptible to a number of disorders while she is pregnant, owing to fluctuations in her blood sugar levels. She may suffer from urinary tract infections, yeast infections (see p.194), high blood pressure, preeclampsia (see p.204) and polyhydramnios (an excess of amniotic fluid, present in one out of five diabetic pregnancies). She may also go into premature labor.

Her baby, too, may be subject to several problems if the diabetes gets out of control. If maternal blood sugar levels become high, sugar crosses the placenta and is converted into fat, muscle, and enlarged organs. The resulting baby is overweight. The baby produces large quantities of insulin to cope with the high sugar levels. At birth, suddenly cut off from the source of sugar, the baby experiences a sudden drop in blood sugar while insulin production is still high. If left untreated, this causes profound hypoglycemia (shortage of blood sugar), which can ultimately result in coma and death. This situation, however, should never happen if the mother has good prenatal care.

Shortly before his birth, Jill's baby will have his lecithin/sphingomyelin (L/S) ratio measured from the amniotic fluid. This will give a good indication of how mature his lungs are so that he can be induced as soon as his lungs are mature enough, if necessary.

A GOOD OUTLOOK FOR JILL

The good news for Jill is that her careful control of her diabetes will make a big difference. Diabetic women used to be warned of the risks of having babies at all. Now they are helped to exercise control of their condition, with specialist assistance from both their obstetrician and their internist, to ensure a healthy and normal baby. Unless there are obstetric complications, such as high blood pressure or pelvic disproportion and, as long as her diabetes remains under control, she can hope for a normal vaginal delivery. I told her that she would have a glucose and insulin intravenous drip to control the diabetes during labor, as well as continuous fetal heart monitoring and fetal blood sampling to detect any early fetal distress. After careful and comprehensive checks in a neonatal special-care unit to rule out the need for immediate treatment, her baby should be returned to her so she can breastfeed him – this will counteract the shortage of blood sugar in her newborn baby.

JILL'S BABY

As long as Jill remains under a doctor's constant care, the risks to her baby will not pose too great a threat. Her doctor will be aware of the following:

• *At birth, Jill's baby may be very large so he may have to be delivered with the help of forceps or by Caesarean section*

• *He may suffer from mild hypoxia (a shortage of oxygen supply to the tissues) shortly before birth, and this can lead to an increased incidence of neonatal jaundice (see p.318) – a condition that can be successfully treated once he is born*

• *He will be carefully checked after birth for any complications*

• *Jill should breastfeed him as soon as possible in order to counteract any hypoglycemia (shortage of blood sugar) in her baby after birth*

KETONES

When carbohydrates are not available for energy, fatty acids are burned instead. This produces ketones.

Ketones are chemically related to acetone, which is found in solvents such as nail polish. The presence of ketones (ketosis) can be detected by urine testing.

Ketosis is a rare but dangerous condition that can occur in uncontrolled diabetes.

Ketosis can lead to vomiting, stomach pains, and ultimately to loss of consciousness and death.

TIME AND YOUR BABY'S PLACENTA

At term the placenta looks like a piece of raw liver about the size of a dinner plate and about 1in (2.5cm) in thickness. The maternal side is divided into wedge shaped chunks called cotyledons.

The placenta has substantial functional reserves, readily adjusts to injury, repairs damages due to ischemia (lack of oxygen) and does not undergo aging. The widely held view that aging occurs progressively during the course of a normal pregnancy is due to a misinterpretation of the appearance of different placental components over time.

Unquestionably, however, there are changes in the character of the villi around the placenta as pregnancy advances, and by the 36th week there may be deposition of calcium within the walls of the small blood vessels, and a protein deposit may appear on the surface of many of the villi. Both of these occurrences have the effect of reducing the exchanges of substances, but this is countered by the smaller distance between fetal vessels and the thin cover of the villi, both factors enhancing the exchange of nutrients.

If labor does not start at the right time (this varies from woman to woman and from pregnancy to pregnancy, but is usually 2 weeks either side of the EDD), the placenta may become relatively inefficient. This happens slowly, and at 42 weeks it should still be capable of supplying your baby with nutrients. However, sometimes it may fail to nourish and support your baby adequately. This placental insufficiency would be a reason for inducing labor.

ARE YOU OVERDUE?

Only about 5 percent of all babies actually arrive on the date that they are expected. The expected date of delivery (EDD – see p.53) is only a statistical average; studies have shown that as many as 40 percent of babies are born after the 41st week of pregnancy – more than a week after the EDD, and up to 10 percent are born after the 42nd week of pregnancy.

BEING OVERDUE

One of the main difficulties in deciding whether a baby is actually overdue or not is that the precise date of conception in any particular pregnancy is unknown. Even if you have a regular menstrual cycle of 28 days (the standard on which the EDD chart is based by doctors), the date of ovulation is only known approximately (see p.53).

Apart from this uncertainty about the date of ovulation, every baby is different and therefore it is unrealistic to expect all babies to mature in precisely the same number of days. Moreover, since labor is initiated by your baby producing certain hormones as he reaches full maturity, it follows that the actual date of delivery can vary fairly widely – even in "textbook" pregnancies.

However, doctors do become concerned if a pregnancy continues much beyond the estimated date of delivery. This is because postmaturity and possible placental insufficiency pose risks to the health of your baby (see **Risks**, opposite). The longer the baby continues to grow in the uterus, the larger he is likely to be, which will increase the chances of a difficult labor, and the possibility that the placenta will not be able to continue to support the baby over an extended period (see column, left).

If you have a personal or maternal family history of longer-than-average gestations (43 or 44 weeks for example), your doctor will probably be more willing to allow you to go more than two weeks overdue without inducing labor – although you will be closely monitored in case any problems develop.

Breech babies If you are only a week or so past your EDD, and your baby is still in the breech position, it may be an indication that he is not yet ready to be born. Babies do not usually tip head down until they are fully mature (see column, p.239).

Pelvic disproportion Labor may be delayed if your baby's head is too big to pass through your pelvis. This disproportion may prevent the baby's head from becoming engaged. If this is the case (see column, right) a Caesarean section may be required.

POSTMATURITY

An overdue baby is in danger of being postmature. A postmature baby is one that has lost fat from all over his body, particularly his tummy. Consequently, his skin will look red and wrinkled as if it doesn't fit him, and it may have begun to peel. Very few babies are actually postmature, but because postmaturity depends not only on the baby, but also on his placenta, it is difficult to predict which babies will be at risk.

Risks These include a longer and more difficult labor, because the postmature baby tends to be bigger and the bones in his skull tend to be harder, which means that his descent through the birth canal is likely to be more traumatic for both him and for you and an increased risk of stillbirth (the risk doubles by the 43rd week and triples by the 44th week). A further risk is that a uterus that is slow to begin labor may also be relatively inefficient during labor itself.

MONITORING THE OVERDUE BABY

Babies past their EDDs are monitored closely, and there are a number of different ways of keeping a check on your baby.

Fetal movement recording The most accurate sign that all is well with your baby is if you can detect regular fetal movements. Since mothers, and babies, are different, the amount of movement that is normal for each individual pregnancy varies. You are the best judge of whether your unborn baby is acting normally, and you can monitor his activity using a kick chart (see p.177).

Electronic fetal monitoring This may be used to check the baby's heartbeat by providing a continuous sound or paper recording (see p.167). If the heartbeat is satisfactory, it is usually judged unnecessary to perform other tests or to induce labor.

Urinary estriol tests These measure the amount of estriol (a form of estrogen) in your urine. The placenta produces estriol in increasing amounts throughout pregnancy until just before labor begins, when estriol production drops off. A lower estriol level than might be expected suggests that the placenta is not functioning as well as it should. However, estriol levels in your urine can vary by as much as 30 percent from day to day, even when everything is normal, so a series of readings will be taken.

Oxytocin test Oxytocin is the hormone that causes your uterus to contract, and is often used to induce labor. Occasionally it is used to check on your baby's well-being. A needle is inserted in your arm, and a small amount of oxytocin is dripped in, making your uterus contract. The fetal heart is monitored throughout the contraction – it is usual for it to show type 1 dips (see p.167) during a contraction. Any deviation from this is considered to indicate fetal distress, and almost certainly induction will be advised.

LATE ENGAGEMENT

When engagement is late, doctors worry in case disproportion is preventing your baby's head from engaging, as this could obstruct labor.

In order to check whether your baby's head will actually engage in, and pass through, your pelvis, your doctor will perform a simple test as follows:

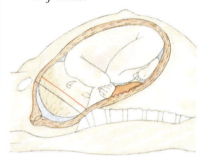

Step 1
You will be asked to lie on your back. When you are in this position, your doctor will be able to feel your baby's head resting just at the pelvic brim.

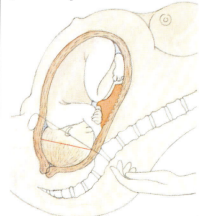

Step 2
When you are propped up on your elbows, however, your baby's head slips easily into your pelvis, so showing there is no problem with pelvic disproportion.

7

Caring for your
UNBORN
baby

*By being observant and aware, you and your partner can be
in touch with your unborn baby throughout pregnancy. Your
baby can hear you talk and sing, and can feel your touch
through your abdominal wall. And while not all babies have
the friendliest of uterine environments, and not all develop
normally, modern medical techniques mean that even these
babies have the best possible chance.*

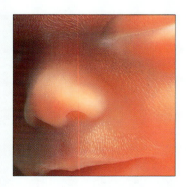
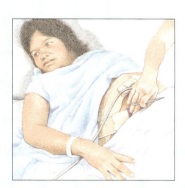

WHAT YOU
CAN DO

Communication can begin early on. What you say, do, think, or experience, and the way you move may be transmitted to your baby.

Talk and sing *Get in the habit of talking out loud to your baby, and singing to her, when possible. Some children have recognized lullabies played to them while in the uterus.*

Touching *Stroking your baby through your abdominal wall is another way of keeping in touch and will usually quiet her down. This soothing effect of stroking may continue after she is born. In the final months you may be able to distinguish her foot or hand through your skin.*

Thinking *Be aware of your baby. Think positive, happy thoughts about her. If you are upset about something, don't shut her out.*

Moving *Try to move in a relaxed manner whenever you can. The gentle movement of your uterus as you walk soothes her. Rocking and swinging will remain a favorite relaxing activity after she is born.*

Feeling *When you feel happy and excited, so does your baby. When you feel depressed, so does she – so reassure her that you still love her. Share feelings with her consciously.*

IN TOUCH WITH YOUR BABY

A constant awareness of your unborn baby is a first stage in bonding with her and ensuring a good future relationship. Keeping in touch means you will be aware of what's best for your baby's physical and emotional health.

WHAT YOUR BABY EXPERIENCES

While she is still in your uterus, your baby feels, hears, sees, tastes, responds, and even learns and remembers. She is not, contrary to decades of medical opinion, an inert, unformed, blank personality. She has firm likes and dislikes. She enjoys soothing voices, simple music with a single melody line (lullabies, flute music), rhythmic movements, and feeling you stroke her through your abdomen. Her dislikes include strident voices; music with an insistent beat (hard rock); strong, flashing lights; rapid, jerky movements; and being cramped by you sitting or lying in an awkward position.

Sight Although your baby is shielded by the walls of your uterus and abdomen, light that is sufficiently strong can get through to her; for instance, she can detect sunlight if you are sunbathing. What she sees is probably just a reddish glow, but from about the fourth month, she will respond to it, usually by turning away if it is too bright. The limits of her sight at birth (she will be able to see faces within one foot of her own) may be a consequence of the parameters of her "home" before she was born.

Sound Your baby's sense of hearing develops at about the third month, and by midterm she is able to respond to sounds from the outside world (see above). The amniotic fluid in which she is suspended conducts sound well, although what she hears will be muffled in the same way that sounds are when you are under water. She is also able to distinguish the emotional tone of voices and moves her body in rhythm to your speech, so she will be soothed if you use a soft, reassuring tone.

The sound of your heartbeat is a continual presence in her world and this seems to be something that will leave a profound influence on her. One study found that when newborn babies were played a tape of maternal heart sounds, they gained more weight and slept better than a control group who did not hear the tape.

A MOTHER'S INFLUENCE

The unborn baby first experiences the world through her mother. Your baby experiences not only external stimuli (see above), but also your feelings, because our different emotions trigger the release of certain chemicals into our bloodstream – anger releases adrenaline, fear releases cholamines, elation releases endorphins. These chemicals pass across the placenta to your baby within seconds of you experiencing that particular emotion.

Babies dislike being exposed to prolonged levels of negative maternal emotions, such as anger, anxiety, or fear. However, short periods of intense anxiety or anger (caused by a missing child or an argument with your partner, for example) do not appear to have any long-term negative effect on your unborn child. In fact, they may even be beneficial as they may help her to begin to develop the ability to cope with future stressful situations. On the other hand, research indicates that long-term festering anger or anxiety, such as you might experience in an unsatisfactory, unsupportive relationship or poor social conditions, can have detrimental effects on your baby. These effects appear to include a problematic birth, a low birthweight, being a colicky baby, and future learning problems. However, studies have found that long-term negative maternal emotions appear to have far less effect on the baby if the mother feels generally happy and positive about being pregnant and doesn't shut out her unborn child.

A FATHER'S INFLUENCE

As the expectant father, you are the second-most important factor in your unborn baby's life. Your attitude toward your partner, the pregnancy, and your child is crucial. If you are happy and looking forward to your newborn baby, your partner is much more likely to be happy and to enjoy her pregnancy. This, in turn, means that your baby is much more likely to be a happy, contented, healthy child. In addition, you should talk directly to your unborn baby as often as possible because research has shown that newborn babies can recognize the voices of their mothers *and* their fathers.

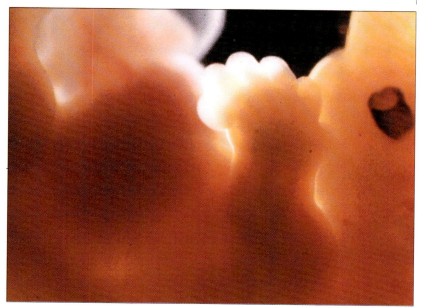

WHAT YOUR BABY DOES

There are a variety of ways in which your unborn baby interacts with her world.

Movement She moves constantly while she is awake. She will kick and wriggle her body in response to external stimuli, such as if you sit in a position that she finds uncomfortable.

Hearing From the sixth month your baby begins to respond to external sounds. She moves her body and limbs in rhythm to your voice. She may jump and kick when you raise your voice.

Seeing She dislikes bright light, especially if it flashes, and will move away, put her hands up to her face, or become agitated.

Feelings She will experience changes in mood to match yours when the chemicals your emotions release into your bloodstream cross the placenta into her body.

Her secure world
If she finds the world she experiences through you a reassuring place, she is likely to develop a generally trusting, positive personality. If she finds the uterus stressful, she may develop a generally anxious approach to life.

SENSING THE MOVEMENTS

When you begin to feel your baby's movements, it is because they are being transmitted through the wall of the uterus to the sensitive nerve endings in your abdominal wall.

The reason you do not feel any of your baby's movements until several weeks after they actually begin is partly because they are very weak at first, and partly because the uterus does not transmit them. Only when it has grown sufficiently to touch your abdominal wall will any movements within it be felt.

On average, most women can feel around 9 out of every 10 of their baby's movements, although for some women the proportion is only 6 out of every 10. Whether you feel a movement or not depends on its direction and strength and on the position your baby is in when she makes it. For instance, if she is facing and kicking in toward your spine, you will not feel the sort of short, sharp jab that you will get if she kicks out toward your belly or up toward your ribs.

If your baby kicks or squirms more than she usually does, sit down in a comfortable, quiet place and try to calm her. Playing her gentle, relaxing music, singing her a lullaby, or humming to her are often very effective, partly because the sound will be pleasant to her and partly because you will become more relaxed and she will tend to do the same. Reading to her, or just talking, is also soothing, as is gently stroking your abdomen.

YOUR BABY'S MOVEMENTS

For most pregnant women, the first awareness of movement within the uterus is exciting, tangible proof that the baby actually exists. If you are a first-time mother, you will probably begin to notice the movements of your baby within the uterus at about 18–20 weeks, but if you already have had a child, the first movements may be apparent at 16–18 weeks or even before. This is because the earliest noticeable movements of the baby – the "quickening" – produce a delicate sensation that has been likened to the fluttering of wings or the darting movements of fish. This feeling is easily mistaken for indigestion, gas, or hunger pangs, but the experienced mother knows what to expect, and is usually adept at identifying these sensations as movements of her baby.

WHY YOUR BABY MOVES

Your baby continually stretches and flexes her limbs as she develops. This activity, vital for the proper development of her muscles, starts at around the eighth week, when she begins making very tiny movements of her spine. At that stage, and for several weeks to come, her movements will go unnoticed, but by about the end of the sixteenth week, the vigorous movements of the now fully-formed limbs may occasionally be felt, although you might not recognize them for what they are.

Your baby's movements – which include kicking, pushing, punching, squirming, and turning somersaults – can often be seen as well as felt. They will steadily increase as she grows, reaching their maximum between weeks 30 and 32. The typical fetus averages 200 movements per day at week 20, rising to 375 per day at week 32, but the number of movements per day can range from 100 to about 700 over a period of several days. After week 32, your baby's movements become steadily more restricted as she grows to fill the uterus. Although restricted, she will still be able to give plenty of sharp kicks. When her engaged head bounces on your pelvic floor muscles, you will feel a jolt.

Changing position and emotional reactions Your baby will move about in your uterus for reasons other than the need to exercise and coordinate her growing muscles.

If you feel her moving she may, for instance, be shifting her position because she feels like a change, or because you are sitting or lying in a position that causes her discomfort. Or she may be trying to relocate the thumb that she had been happily sucking before she decided on a change of position.

However, she may also be moving about in response to your emotions. Hormones, such as adrenaline, are released into your bloodstream when you are physically or emotionally stimulated. Pleasure, excitement, anger, stress, anxiety, or fear also stimulate the production of chemicals in your body that will pass across the placenta and into your baby's bloodstream. These hormones make your baby react in a way that corresponds to your emotions, so if you get angry or very anxious, she may become agitated and start kicking and squirming. If you can, sit down in a quiet place and practice your relaxation techniques (see p.238). This will help calm both you and your baby.

COUNTING THE KICKS

Just like the rest of us, your baby will feel and be more active on some days than on others, but her daily pattern of movements will become more consistent after about week 28. From then on you can monitor your baby's movements.

There are several ways of counting fetal movements, but one of the easiest is to use a kick chart like the one shown below, which is easily drawn up on a piece of graph paper. Down the left of the chart, mark out a convenient six-hour period during which you will count the number of movements, say from 9 a.m. to 3 p.m. or from 4 p.m. to 10 p.m., and fill in the weeks and days across the top. Each day, starting at your chosen time, count the number of fetal movements until they reach five, and then mark the time of the fifth movement on your chart.

Some hospitals now have their own kick charts that they will give you at your prenatal clinic. You can use this to record your baby's movements during the final months of your pregnancy.

If you notice any significant change in your baby's movements as term approaches advise your doctor without delay. You must do this without fail if there are no movements during a six-hour period, and it is also advisable to do so if there are fewer than five movements in six hours. Even if your baby's movements seem to have ceased altogether, don't panic. Your doctor can quickly assess your baby's well-being and decide whether everything is all right or if induction or Caesarean intervention will be necessary.

Monitoring fetal movements
This is a useful way of checking your baby's well-being, especially if you are overdue. Only you can tell if your baby is moving in a way that is normal for her, and if there is a significant drop in the number of her movements, you should contact your doctor, midwife, or the hospital.

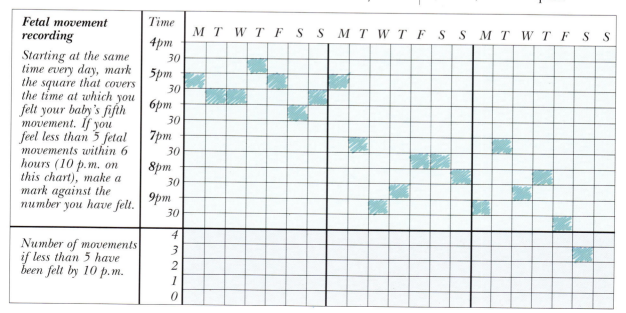

Fetal movement recording	Time	M	T	W	T	F	S	S	M	T	W	T	F	S	S	M	T	W	T	F	S	S
Starting at the same time every day, mark the square that covers the time at which you felt your baby's fifth movement. If you feel less than 5 fetal movements within 6 hours (10 p.m. on this chart), make a mark against the number you have felt.	**4pm**																						
	30																						
	5pm																						
	30																						
	6pm																						
	30																						
	7pm																						
	30																						
	8pm																						
	30																						
	9pm																						
	30																						
Number of movements if less than 5 have been felt by 10 p.m.	4																						
	3																						
	2																						
	1																						
	0																						

NEONATAL HEART SCANS

Congenital heart disease is diagnosed in a number of ways, such as by the use of chest X-rays or by a form of ultrasound scan called echocardiography.

A congenital heart condition, such as ventricular septal defect (hole in the heart – see main text) some-times isn't detected until the baby is about 4 weeks old. Both chest X-rays and echocardiograms are used to confirm the diagnosis and to give an indication of the extent of the problem, so that the appropriate treatment can be given.

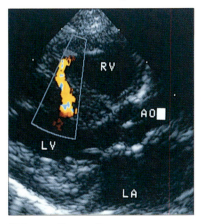

Echocardiography
The above shows a baby's heart that has a ventricular septal defect. Echocardiograms are taken by an ultrasound scan and displayed as a series of lines on the screen. Color-enhancement shows the defect as red. The abbreviations used are: Ao = aorta (main artery); RV = right ventricle (pumping chamber that pumps blood in to the lungs to be oxygenated); LA = left atrium (collecting chamber that collects reoxygenated blood from the lungs); LV = left ventricle (pumps reoxygenated blood back into the body).

FETAL PROBLEMS

I am aware that this subject is an emotive one that may cause you to worry. However, I cannot stress strongly enough that fetal handicaps are extremely rare, so please try not to be too anxious. The cause of many fetal defects is still unknown. Some are genetically determined (see p.20), while others may be due to the adverse effects of drugs, radiation, fetal infections, or metabolic disturbances.

The types of malformations that may occur are numerous and varied, although most are very rare. The fetal tissues that are most actively growing at the time when the adverse factor operates are the most likely to show the defect. Some malformations are incompatible with life, and no treatment is possible. The defects that are especially important to recognize just after birth are those that endanger life but, with prompt intervention, can be treated very successfully. An increasing number of problems are now recognized before birth by ultrasound scan (see p.162), and many can be treated just after birth or later in infancy.

Imperforate anus This is when the anus is sealed, either because of a thin membrane of skin over the anal opening or because the anal canal that links the rectum with the anus has not developed. The rectal pouch may be connected to the vagina, urethra, or bladder, and so the baby must be referred for surgical treatment at once. Although rare, this condition is carefully looked for at every birth, and is treated immediately if found.

Umbilical hernia The gap in the muscle sheath in your baby's abdominal cavity, where the umbilical cord entered his or her abdomen, normally closes up in time. Sometimes, however, a soft swelling called an umbilical hernia forms when the abdominal contents bulge through this weak spot in the abdomen. In most cases the hernia eventually disappears, although a few will require surgical treatment later in childhood.

Congenital heart disease The most common form of congenital heart disease is ventricular septal defect (hole in the heart). In this disease there is a hole in the septum, the thin dividing wall between the right and left ventricles (pumping chambers) of the heart, and so the ventricles are connected instead of being divided. It does not usually produce symptoms or signs in a newborn baby, because it may take as long as four weeks for the blood vessels in the lungs to relax sufficiently to allow pressure differences to develop between the ventricles. Consequently, there may not be an appreciable left-to-right shunt of blood through the hole for a month or so, and symptoms will be absent. Symptoms to look for are a bluish tinge to the skin, especially around the mouth, floppiness, and breathlessness. One of the first signs may be breathlessness while feeding. An operation is not always required because the hole may seal spontaneously.

Congenital dislocation of the hip Dislocation of the hip happens when the ball at the head of the thighbone does not fit snugly into the socket of the hip joint. In the newborn infant this is a potential, rather than an actual, problem. It is more common in girls.

As part of the routine examination of newborn babies (see p.291), the hips are examined for excessive mobility, or for a characteristic "clunk" felt when the legs are spread apart and the thighs are flexed. Orthopedic advice must be sought if there is any doubt, and early follow-up and treatment such as manipulation and splinting may prevent trouble in later infancy, although an operation may be required in severe cases.

Spina bifida It is important that babies with a good prognosis should be sent to a special center where appropriate surgery can be performed without delay. Spina bifida is when the vertebral bones of the spine do not fuse so that the meninges (the coverings of the brain and spinal cord) bulge through at some level in the spinal column. The area may be covered with skin, or only by a bluish membrane. It may contain nerve roots, or the spinal cord itself may be exposed. In many cases, the place where the bones of the vertebrae are not fused is covered with skin and is only marked by a small, dark, hairy mole.

The absence of the various coverings that normally protect the cord means that meningeal infection can occur very easily, but this can be prevented by immediate surgery to cover the defect. However, the overall prognosis is poor for babies with more severe defects. Problems may include complete paralysis of the legs, incontinence of urine and feces, mental retardation, and the probable appearance of hydrocephalus (see below).

Hydrocephalus (water on the brain) In hydrocephalus there is an excessive amount of cerebrospinal fluid within the skull. Hydrocephalus often occurs with other neurological defects such as spina bifida and it is caused by restricted circulation of the cerebrospinal fluid in the brain. It is most common following brain hemorrhage in the preterm baby. The head swells, and the soft tissues between the skull bones and the fontanelles become wide and bulging. The condition may be present before birth owing to congenital malformations, and will obstruct labor, or the baby's head may show excessive enlargement after birth. If hydrocephalus is suspected before birth, frequent ultrasound checks are performed, and the head circumference is measured every two or three days. If the rate of growth is much faster than normal, a neurosurgical opinion is sought, as it is possible to prevent progression of the hydrocephalus by repeated lumbar punctures or by inserting a drainage tube and valve into a tiny hole made in the skull.

CLEFT LIP AND CLEFT PALATE

These conditions are due to the incomplete development of the upper lip or of the palate or, in some cases, both.

A cleft lip, sometimes known as a harelip, occurs when the halves of the upper lip fail to join properly during fetal development. Similarly, a cleft palate is the result of the halves of the fetal palate failing to join.

These defects can cause surprisingly little difficulty in feeding – breastfeeding can often be successfully achieved but bottlefeeding may be more difficult, and it may be necessary to resort to cup and spoon. Care is necessary when feeding a baby who has a cleft palate, because the cleft may permit milk to enter the nose and cause him to gag.

Early consultation with a plastic surgeon is advisable so that treatment can be planned. Some hospitals are now performing immediate closure of the cleft lip at birth. However, if a cleft palate is closed too early, it may mean a major operation during early adulthood, as the palate may be unable to develop fully.

TRISOMIES

Trisomy is a chromosomal disorder in which a pair of chromosomes has an extra chromosome, making 3. This defect exists in all the cells of the body.

The most common trisomy is Down's syndrome (see p.20), also known as trisomy 21, in which there are 3 number 21 chromosomes.

The infant is born with small features, a tongue that tends to protrude, and slanting eyes that have folds of skin at their inner corners. The head is flat at the back, and the ears are unusual. He or she is rather floppy, and the hands and feet are usually short and wide, with a single transverse crease across the palms and soles. In addition congenital heart disease may be detected.

Down's syndrome sufferers are usually mentally handicapped, although the degree of handicap varies, and many Down's syndrome children are near normal.

Children with Down's syndrome are very rewarding. They're affectionate, outgoing, and have a great sense of humor. With careful attention and early education they often do very well. Some manage to live independently.

Other trisomies include trisomy 13 (Patau's syndrome) and trisomy 18 (Edwards's syndrome), both of which produce a number of severe physical and mental abnormalities but which are much rarer than Down's syndrome.

Neural tube defects such as spina bifida and hydrocephalus may be diagnosed by ultrasound (see p.162) and amniocentesis (see p.164) well before the child is born. High alpha-fetoprotein (AFP) levels can indicate a need for more investigation (see p.159).

Cerebral palsy This is muscular paralysis, stiffness, or incoordination that occurs because of damage to the brain before, during, or after birth, for instance, because of a poor supply of oxygen to the brain during late pregnancy or a difficult labor. Premature babies are particularly vulnerable. An infection of the mother's uterus may also result in cerebral palsy, as may meningitis or a severe injury to the baby's head after birth. It is not possible to detect cerebral palsy before birth. The symptoms are usually not obvious until the baby is several months old and his development appears to be delayed. He may not be sitting, or making normal progress as expected; there may be a stiffness in the arms or legs, or a persistent abnormal posture. The degree of disability ranges from slight – where the child may just be very clumsy or unsteady – to severe, where at the very worst the child is totally immobile.

If there are muscular spasms and the limbs are abnormally stiff, the baby is termed spastic. Rigidity may affect the arm and leg on one side (hemiplegia), the legs only (paraplegia), or all four limbs and trunk (quadriplegia). A child may display unintentional writhing movements, which is termed athetosis, or a loss of coordination and balance, known as ataxia. Very often, a child's other abilities – speech, vision, or hearing – may be detrimentally affected. Unfortunately, a number of children may suffer severe mental handicaps, particularly quadriplegics, but a significant number do have normal intelligence. Cerebral palsy is incurable but it is not progressive – it does not get worse as the child grows older. Physiotherapy will help prevent deformities caused by stiffness and spasms, and develop muscular balance and control; speech therapy will help ease communication problems.

Respiratory distress syndrome In this condition, the baby's lungs are deficient in surfactant, a substance that keeps open the minute air sacs within the lungs through which oxygen is absorbed into the blood. This is due to immaturity of the lungs, or because the function of crucial lung cells is temporarily depressed because of a lack of oxygen. Respiratory distress syndrome is most commonly found in small preterm babies, but also occurs in the infants of diabetic mothers whose diabetes is not sufficiently well controlled. A low fetal oxygen level just prior to birth is a predisposing factor and it is very rare in full-term infants.

With increasing skill in detecting immaturity of the baby's lungs before birth and in the management of preterm deliveries and early and effective resuscitation, the incidence of the disorder has fallen in recent years. Infants that are born with the established disease require full support in an intensive care unit. Where RDS is suspected, the L/S ratio (see p.169) of the amniotic fluid indicates the maturity of the lungs so that precautions can be taken.

Pyloric stenosis   The narrowing of the pylorus, the passage leading from the stomach into the small intestine, because of thickening of the pyloric muscle, is more common in males than females. The cause is unknown, but the symptoms typically first appear when the baby is two to four weeks old, although they can start earlier.

Food builds up in the stomach, which then contracts powerfully in an attempt to force the food through the narrow pylorus. Because this is impossible, milk is vomited up violently after feeding. This is known as projectile vomiting, when the vomit may be propelled several feet. The baby may suffer constipation and dehydration, but a simple operation to widen the pylorus will be performed, giving a complete cure.

Epispadias and hypospadias   About one in every 1,000 male babies has an abnormality of the penile opening of the urethra. In epispadias, the opening is on the upper surface of the penis, and the penis may curve upward. In hypospadias, the opening of the urethra is on the underside of the glans (head), and the penis sometimes curves downward.

In extreme forms of hypospadias, which are very rare, the urethral opening lies between the genitals and the anus, and the genitals may appear to be female. The necessary surgery is straightforward and is usually successful, enabling normal passage of urine and, later, satisfactory sexual intercourse. Neither epispadias nor hypospadias (even the severe form) are a cause of infertility.

CLUBFOOT (TALIPES)

This is when a child is born with the sole of 1 foot, or both feet, facing down and inward or up and outward.

The exact causes of the many varieties of clubfoot are not fully understood, but it is known that the condition can be inherited, and on rare occasions may spontaneously recover.

In most cases, though, treatment is necessary if the defect is to be corrected. The most common remedy is repeated manipulation of the child's foot over a period of many months. In the intervals between manipulations, the foot is held in the required position by some form of bracing such as splints or a plaster cast. In some cases, surgery may be required.

FETAL DEFECTS PER 10,000 BIRTHS

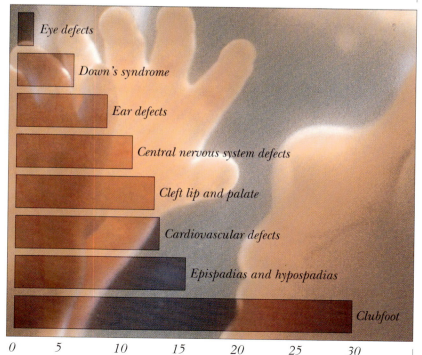

Eye defects

Down's syndrome

Ear defects

Central nervous system defects

Cleft lip and palate

Cardiovascular defects

Epispadias and hypospadias

Clubfoot

0   5   10   15   20   25   30

Incidence of fetal defects
This chart summarizes typical incidences of birth defects. The most common is clubfoot, which affects both boys and girls. Epispadias and hypospadias, together the second most common, are defects of the urethra and affect only boys. Cardiovascular defects are those of the heart and circulatory system, including congenital heart disease, and the defects of the central nervous system include spina bifida and hydrocephalus.

Despite the physical and emotional stresses involved in fetal surgery, most parents cope extremely well.

When an unborn baby is diagnosed as having a serious illness or defect, and the doctors contemplate fetal surgery, the parents are given extensive counseling to help them decide whether or not to agree to it. Fetal surgery, although advancing rapidly, is still at the experimental stage. The most complicated techniques are only attempted if there is nothing to lose. At some experienced centers, however, simple procedures like exchange transfusions are performed routinely.

If the surgery succeeds, the rewards are immense, and there appears to be little or no effect on the mother's fertility. Many women subsequently become pregnant again, and their pregnancies are normal. With less successful surgery, there is the possibility of subsequent miscarriage, premature birth, and the necessity of a Caesarean section. There may also be complications for the mother after the operation, which can be extremely stressful for all concerned.

FETAL SURGERY

Thanks to the development of specialized surgical techniques, it is now sometimes possible to correct a congenital defect while a baby is still in the uterus. Fetal surgeons are pioneering techniques that are breathtaking in their delicacy and near miraculous in their results.

As yet, only a small number of pioneering surgeons are involved in fetal surgery, and the number of defects they can help is limited, but research continues. New methods are constantly being tried and evaluated, and advances in the diagnosis of fetal defects make it easier for doctors to decide whether surgery is appropriate.

ULTRASOUND-GUIDED SURGERY

The more straightforward types of fetal surgery are carried out by thin needles inserted through the mother's abdomen and uterus and into the amniotic sac.

Ultrasound provides the surgeon with a view of the fetus, and enables him or her to manipulate the needles (only one at a time is used), with which blood or tissue samples are taken from the fetus and drugs or blood transfusions are given.

Using ultrasound-guided techniques, surgeons are able to treat a growing number of life-threatening conditions. Rhesus and other incompatibilities between the immune systems of mother and baby may be corrected through intrauterine blood transfusions. Drugs that will correct fetal heartbeat irregularities and destroy tumors may be injected into the fetus; small drainage tubes (shunts) that prevent further build-up of fluids may be inserted to drain excess fluids from the baby – for instance, from the brain in cases of hydrocephalus – and to clear urinary tract blockages. Ultrasound is also used to guide the tiny forceps and scalpels with which surgery can be carried out.

Intrauterine blood transfusions In some cases of Rhesus incompatibility (see p.184), where a mother's blood is Rhesus (Rh) negative and her baby's is Rh positive, the baby may become dangerously anemic. In this case he will be given one or more blood transfusions into one of the blood vessels in the umbilical cord to sustain him until he can be delivered safely. Fresh Rh-negative blood will be injected slowly, in volumes related to the estimated weight of the fetus and the degree of anemia.

Fetal blood transfusions have a good success rate, but in some very severe cases, Rh incompatibility will result in miscarriage or stillbirth, despite numerous transfusions. Until recently, if transfusions were unsuccessful there was nothing more that could be done, but now research is under way to investigate whether injecting the baby with donated Rh-negative bone marrow will stimulate him to become Rh negative and so remove the incompatibility.

A more uncommon type of incompatibility between mother and child results in the mother producing antibodies that destroy the baby's blood platelets. These platelets help blood to clot, and without them the baby could be in danger of suffering a hemorrhage and die. This can now be prevented by giving the fetus transfusions of platelets and, in severe cases, donor antibodies that counteract those of his mother.

Shunts for urinary tract problems Hydronephrosis, where a kidney becomes swollen with urine because the ureter that drains it is narrow or blocked, sometimes occurs in unborn babies. If it is left untreated, it can lead to severe kidney damage; if it affects both kidneys, it can cause kidney failure. Hydronephrosis can some–times be corrected by the insertion of shunts.

OPEN FETAL SURGERY

Some fetal defects that cannot be treated by ultrasound-guided techniques can be corrected by open fetal surgery. This involves opening up the uterus and partially removing the baby so that he can be operated on.

Open fetal surgery has been used to repair diaphragmatic hernias, where a hole in the baby's diaphragm allows his intestines to protrude into his chest cavity and damage his lungs, and to remove certain types of tumor.

The operation Unlike ultrasound-guided techniques, which are always carried out under local anesthesia, open fetal surgery requires a general anesthetic for both mother and baby. When the anesthetic has taken effect, an incision is made in the mother's abdomen to expose the uterus, and an ultrasound scan is used to locate the exact position of the placenta. The amniotic fluid is then drawn off and kept warm, and an incision about five inches (12 centimeters) long is made in the uterus and amniotic membranes, well away from the placenta to avoid damaging it. The baby is eased out of the uterus through this opening just far enough for the surgeon to be able to repair the defect.

After the operation Once the surgeon has finished, the baby is carefully replaced in the uterus along with the amniotic fluid (to which is added a small amount of antibiotic). The incisions in the amniotic membranes and the uterus are closed with absorbable stitches and surgical glue, and the incision in the abdomen is stitched together. The mother rests in bed for a few days after the operation, during which time both she and her baby are intensively monitored, and she usually leaves the hospital within ten days. Contractions of her uterus, caused by irritation following the operation, must be suppressed by drugs to prevent her going into labor at this early stage. These drugs are given intravenously while she is in the hospital, and she is switched to oral medication when she leaves. Most babies who undergo open fetal surgery are born before term, usually by Caesarean section.

PROSPECTS FOR THE BABY

Fetal surgery is used to help babies who have defects that are easier to correct before they are born than afterward, or who will die without it.

In general, the earlier in pregnancy that fetal surgery is performed, the better the baby's prospects of survival. This is partly because wounds will heal relatively quickly in a developing baby, and partly because organs that are unable to grow until the defect is repaired can complete their normal development. For instance, if a baby's lungs cannot grow properly because of a diaphragmatic hernia, they will need time to mature so that he will be able to use them when he is born.

The exact time when a baby can be operated on depends on a number of factors, one of the most important being the point at which the defect can be diagnosed. Blood and antibody problems are usually diagnosable in the earliest weeks of pregnancy, and often, as in many cases of Rh incompatibility, they are predictable. One baby who was given 25 transfusions of anti-bodies received the first at 11 weeks, when she was only about 2in (5cm) long. Most physical malformations, however, are not diagnosable until the organ or organs they affect have grown enough for the defect to be apparent. As a result, surgery to correct defects of this type is typically carried out after about week 18.

NAME *Gemma Duncan*

AGE *27 years*

PAST MEDICAL
HISTORY *Nothing
abnormal*

OBSTETRIC
HISTORY *One daughter
aged 2 years;
normal birth,
no postpartum
complications;
child's blood
group Rhesus
positive*

Gemma's blood group is Rhesus negative while that of her partner, Chris, is Rhesus positive. Their second baby has a 1 in 4 chance of being a Rhesus-negative baby if Chris passes on to the baby a recessive Rhesus-negative gene. Their first baby was Rhesus positive, which means that Gemma may have developed some anti-Rhesus-positive antibodies. If this second baby is also Rhesus positive, her red blood cells may be in danger from her mother's antibodies. To prevent any of the baby's red blood cells being destroyed, Gemma will have special care throughout her pregnancy.

A CASE STUDY

RH-NEGATIVE MOTHER

About 85 percent of the population has a protein-like substance called the Rhesus factor in their red blood cells. These people are known as Rhesus positive. The remaining 15 percent, whose blood cells lack the Rhesus factor, are known as Rhesus negative (Rh negative). Rhesus positivity is always dominant; negativity will only exist when only negative genes are inherited. Being Rhesus negative does not affect you unless you are pregnant.

AN INCOMPATIBLE MOTHER AND BABY

Gemma's first pregnancy went without a hitch. This is usual with first pregnancies where the mother has Rhesus-negative blood and the baby Rhesus-positive (an incompatible pregnancy).

However, when fetal blood cells mix with maternal cells, for example during delivery, the mother's blood becomes sensitized. When the Rh factor from the baby's blood enters the mother's blood stream, it acts as an antigen and stimulates production of anti-Rh-positive antibodies. These will attack and destroy the blood cells of her next Rhesus-positive (incompatible) baby. This causes hemolytic disease of the newborn (see p.318) and infants affected with blood conditions ranging from mild jaundice to serious, possibly fatal, anemia. Fetuses who develop the disease can often be saved by intrauterine blood transfusion (see p.182).

Not all Rh-negative women with Rh-positive babies become sensitized, but there is no way of predicting which women will. All of these women, therefore, should have a Rhogam injection.

DESENSITIZING GEMMA

Within 48 hours of delivering her first baby, Gemma was injected intramuscularly with Rhogam (Rh immune globulin) to help prevent the destructive antibodies from forming. Had this pregnancy miscarried, she would have also needed the injection, because her blood and that of the baby's would have mixed.

CAREFUL MONITORING

Gemma is hoping that she will be only mildly affected by Rhesus incompatibility. However, if antibodies have already formed, the Rhogam injection will be ineffective. Therefore, Gemma's blood will be monitored throughout her pregnancy. At each visit, Gemma will have a special specimen of blood taken to examine for increasing levels of antibodies. Only if they increase beyond a certain point is her developing baby in any danger. If increasing antibodies are noted, she will have an ultrasound scan at 18 weeks. This can check for the presence of fetal bilirubin (a by-product of red blood cell destruction) in the amniotic fluid.

In the third trimester, a direct test for the presence of bilirubin can be done by a process called cordocentesis (see p.165). This will enable the doctors to assess the severity of the condition and determine whether blood transfusions are necessary.

GEMMA'S EXPECTATIONS OF THE BIRTH

If her antibody count remains low, Gemma will not require further special care. However, if the count rises moderately, her baby may be induced early to prevent serious consequences. In this case, a home birth is out of the question and she will need to deliver in a hospital with an experienced obstetric department.

RHESUS DISEASE IN PREGNANCY

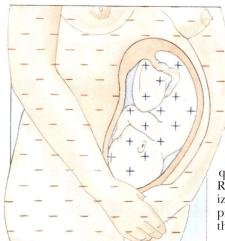

Rhesus disease only occurs when a woman who has Rhesus-negative blood (symbolized by red minus signs in the picture) is pregnant with a Rhesus-positive (symbolized by blue plus signs) baby. Most Rhesus-negative mothers carry their first babies without any problems – just as Gemma did. However, if they subsequently develop antibodies to Rhesus-positive blood (symbolized by green triangles in the pictures below) any babies that they have later could be at risk.

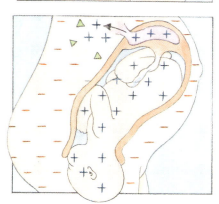

Mother is sensitized
If the mother is not given a Rhogam injection within 48 hours of giving birth, she may develop antibodies to Rhesus-positive blood.

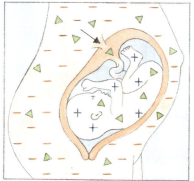

A future pregnancy
If she becomes pregnant with another Rhesus-positive baby, her antibodies may attack this baby's red blood cells.

GEMMA'S BABY

Gemma's baby is likely to be fit and healthy, owing to the Rhogam injections and the special care she receives during her pregnancy.

• *Immediately after birth he will have a Coombs' test, to reveal the presence of maternal anti-Rhesus-positive antibodies*

• *If the baby is affected by Rh incompatibility, his levels of bilirubin will rise very quickly after birth because his liver is unable to cope with the substance*

• *The high level of bilirubin in his blood and tissues will make him look yellow. This can be treated by placing him under "bililights" that convert the bilirubin into a substance harmless to the brain*

HAVING A RHOGAM INJECTION

Women who are Rhesus negative are also given a Rhogam injection after:

• *an abortion*

• *chorionic villus sampling*

• *an amniocentesis or cordocentesis, especially if there is blood on the needle after it has been withdrawn*

8

Common

COMPLAINTS

*Very few women go through pregnancy without suffering
a few complaints that are, for the most part,
uncomfortable rather than serious. Being prepared for
these difficulties is half the battle and also enables you to
differentiate between those that are just uncomfortable
and those that are potentially serious.*

COMMON COMMON COMPLAINTS

COMPLAINT	WHY IT HAPPENS
Backache is usually a general discomfort across the lower part of the back, often with pain across the buttocks and down the legs. It can occur when you have been standing for too long with bad posture or after lifting a heavy weight, especially during the third trimester.	High progesterone levels cause softening and stretching of the ligaments of the pelvic bones, allowing the baby to be born. The ligaments of the spine also relax, putting extra strain on the joints of the back and hips.
Intensely painful low backache may also occur when you rotate your spine and pelvis in opposite directions, such as when you turn over sideways in bed.	The baby is resting against your sacroiliac joint, which is located some 3in (7 1/2cm) in from the top of your buttocks. Rotary movements of the spine and pelvis open and close the sacroiliac joint, causing pain.
Carpal tunnel syndrome is a sensation of pins and needles, mainly in the thumb and first finger, with numbness and sometimes weakness. Occasionally the whole hand and forearm are affected. It can occur from conception onward.	Pressure on the nerve that passes from the arm to the hand along the front of the wrist. The pressure is caused by swelling of the carpal tunnel (a ring of fibers around the wrist under which the nerve passes) owing to water retention.
Constipation is when you have dry, hard stools that are difficult to pass. It can occur from conception onward.	Progesterone relaxes the muscles in the intestinal walls, so there are fewer contractions to push the food along. Consequently much more water than usual is absorbed from the stool in the colon, making it hard and dry. Stools may be less frequent, too.
Cramps are a sudden pain in the thigh, calf, and/or foot, followed by a general ache that lasts for some time. They tend to be more common in the third trimester, and usually wake you from sleep.	Cramps are thought to be caused by low calcium levels in the blood, or they may be due to salt deficiency. Check with your doctor.

Protecting your back
When lifting heavy weights, such as a toddler, always use your thighs to do the work. Don't treat your back as a crane.

During pregnancy you may experience a number of discomforts that are often no more than irritating. Most are caused by a combination of hormonal changes and the extra strain that your body is experiencing, can be treated very simply, and are nothing to worry about. A few, however, can be serious, so be aware of the symptoms and be prepared to act promptly if you suspect all may not be well.

WHAT CAN BE DONE

RISK TO BABY

Massage may help (see p.134). Do exercises to strengthen your spine. Make sure your mattress is firm. Lift heavy weights correctly (see bottom left, opposite). Try to improve your posture (see p.142), and avoid high-heels. If the pain runs down your leg toward your foot, consult your doctor just in case it's a slipped disc.

None.

Osteopathic manipulation can help you in even the most severe cases. Backache usually eases by itself in the fifth month when the fetus tips forward –although you may not be able to wait that long!

Diuretics prescribed by your doctor may alleviate the symptoms. A splint on the wrist at night may help, as may holding your hand above your head and wiggling your fingers. Acupuncture may help. Sleep with your arm on a pillow. Symptoms usually disappear soon after delivery.

None.

Drink lots of water. Eat as much roughage in the form of fruit, vegetables, and fiber as you can. Walk briskly for 20 minutes once a day or more. Don't take a laxative without consulting your doctor. Natural fiber laxatives are best, as they simply increase the amount of water in the stool, making it soft. Figs and prunes will also do the job.

None.

Massage the area very firmly. Flex your foot up and push into the heel. You may be prescribed calcium or salt tablets if your levels are low, but don't self-prescribe without first consulting your doctor.

None.

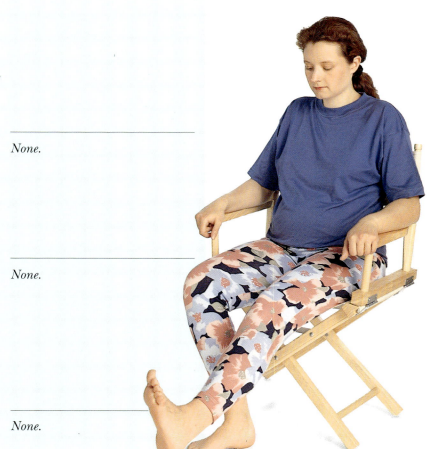

Relieving leg cramps
Keeping your foot flexed up, carefully make circling movements with your lower leg.

Coping with faintness
If you do feel faint, put your head as far down as you can – between your knees if you can still manage it! Get up slowly.

Avoiding heartburn
To prevent stomach overfilling, eat smaller meals. Learn to snack on nutritious food and split meals if they fill you up.

COMPLAINT	WHY IT HAPPENS
Diarrhea *is when you have soft, watery stools, requiring frequent visits to the toilet. It can occur at any time.*	*Usually because an infection by bacteria or a virus is present.*
Faintness *is a feeling of dizziness or vertigo that occurs suddenly, making you unsteady on your feet. It can come on if you stand up too quickly, or have been on your feet for too long, especially in hot weather.*	*A lack of blood supply to the brain, often caused by pooling of the blood in the legs and feet when standing, together with the demands of the uterus for an increased blood supply.*
Heartburn *is a burning sensation just behind the breastbone, sometimes with regurgitation of stomach acid into the mouth. It happens most commonly on lying down, coughing, straining when passing a stool, and when you are lifting heavy weights.*	*Early in pregnancy, the muscular valve at the entrance to the stomach relaxes under the influence of progesterone. This allows stomach acid to flow up into the esophagus, causing a burning sensation. Later in pregnancy, the baby can press up on the stomach forcing the contents back into the esophagus.*
Hemorrhoids or piles *are dilated rectal veins (varicose veins – see p.194) that may protrude through the anus. Usually they do not occur until the second trimester.*	*Your increasingly larger baby presses down on your rectum and impedes venous flow to the heart. The blood therefore pools, causing the veins to dilate to accommodate the dammed-up blood.*
High blood pressure (hypertension) *is an increase in blood pressure and is most likely near term. It can be mild or severe, and there may be no, few, or many symptoms including frontal headaches, visual disturbances, and vomiting.* *It is more common in women who are having their first baby, especially if they are over 35, and also in women who are having more than one baby. It is always looked for as it may herald Preeclampsia (see p.204).*	*The cause is not fully understood. In some women, cells from the placenta produce chemicals called vasoconstrictors that may cause the blood vessels to constrict. This may cause the blood pressure to rise, and the kidneys to retain sodium, leading to water retention.*

WHAT CAN BE DONE

RISK TO BABY

Increase your water intake to 12–14 glasses a day to replace lost fluid. This will ensure that your blood pressure remains normal. Consult your doctor, who will test your stools for infection and give you the appropriate treatment.

Diarrhea can cause dehydration and loss of calories that can put your baby at risk if left untreated for a long time. If diarrhea is profuse and protracted, you will need to be hospitalized for intravenous feeding.

Avoid standing for long periods. Always sit or lie down when you feel dizzy. Don't get up suddenly from sitting or get out of a hot bath too quickly. Keep cool in hot weather. If dizzy, sit with head between knees – if you still can – or lie down with your feet higher than your head.

None, unless you fall very heavily onto your abdomen.

Keep meals small so that the stomach is never overfilled. Sleep propped up with several pillows. A glass of milk at bedtime will help neutralize stomach acid. Your doctor may prescribe antacids, but only in the later stages of pregnancy.

None.

Keep your bowels regular and the stools soft by eating sufficient fiber – this will help you avoid straining down. Don't lift heavy objects, as this increases intra-abdominal pressure and back pressure in the rectal veins. Have coughs treated promptly for the same reasons. Aromatherapy oil may be able to relieve symptoms.

None.

If you suffered from high blood pressure before you were pregnant, tell your doctor. Keep an eye on your weight. Always report persistent headaches and nausea.

If your blood pressure goes up at any stage of your pregnancy, you will be advised to stay in bed and rest. If the rise is severe, you will be admitted to the hospital for monitoring. If the baby appears to be suffering, labor may be induced or you may have a Caesarean section. Your blood pressure will return to normal once the baby has been born.

*Pregnancy-induced hypertension (see **Preeclampsia**, p.204) can slow the baby's growth rate, owing to a reduced blood flow to the uterus. The baby may also be short of oxygen. Both factors may lead to low birthweight. There is a severe form called eclampsia (see **Eclampsia**, p.204), which can be life-threatening. Fortunately this is now very rare in the West, owing to excellent prenatal care that spots the signs very early.*

Monitor your weight
Gaining a lot of weight suddenly may indicate the onset of preeclampsia.

Complaint	Why it happens

Insomnia is the inability to sleep at night, making you tired and irritable during the day. It can happen at any time from conception onward.

Your baby lives on a 24-hour clock, and his or her metabolism keeps going even when you want to sleep. This can affect your body's responses. Other causes include night sweats and a desire to empty your bladder more frequently, particularly during the third trimester.

Mood swings describes rapid, uncharacteristic changes in mood, often with unexplained crying and anxiety attacks. They are common from conception onward, but are especially likely to occur in the third trimester.

Changes in your hormone balance during pregnancy have a depressant effect on the nervous system, causing symptoms similar to those that can occur pre-menstrually. Body image changes and identity crises may have a profound effect on you as your pregnancy progresses, and mixed feelings about pregnancy and parenthood can cause sudden shifts in your moods.

Morning sickness is a feeling of sickness and nausea, sometimes with vomiting. Contrary to its name, it can occur at any time of the day, but generally happens when you haven't eaten, or after a long night's sleep. These symptoms usually occur in the first trimester, then abate.

The main cause is low blood sugar, but pregnancy hormones may irritate the stomach directly.

Pigmentation, or excess pigmentation, usually means darkening of the skin around the nipples, down the center of the abdomen (linea nigra), plus deepening of any pigmentation in freckles or birth marks (see p.140).

During pregnancy, the body releases higher levels of the melanocyte stimulating hormone (MSH). This stimulates the skin to produce extra pigment.

Self-massage
Massaging your face, especially your temples and neck, is a wonderful and effective way of relieving tension and will help dispel insomnia.

Coping with mood swings
A reassuring hug is probably just what you need when you're feeling anxious and upset.

WHAT CAN BE DONE

RISK TO BABY

A warm bath and a hot milky drink may help, as may a relaxing massage (see p.134). Watch television or read until you feel tired and sleepy. Find a comfortable position, and try to stay cool. Your doctor will not prescribe sleeping pills until the third trimester, and then only if you are exhausted by lack of sleep, because they can cross the placenta and affect the baby (see also p.238).

None.

*You should consider these feelings natural. Depression, anxiety, and confusion can occur even in the easiest of pregnancies. Analyzing such feelings may only serve to prolong them. (See also **Emotional Changes**, p.136.)*

None.

Food will provide relief from nausea, so eat little and often. Eat high-carbohydrate foods such as whole-grain bread, potatoes, rice, and cereals, and avoid fried food and coffee, which trigger nausea.

Keep hard candy in your car, desk, or handbag. To prevent sickness in the morning, put a glass of water and a cracker by your bed before sleeping, and have them as a snack 15 minutes before you get out of bed.

Cigarette smoke and other strong smells may also trigger nausea. Drink extra fluids such as water, fruit juice, or skim milk – if you can keep them down.

In its severe form (called hyperemesis gravidarum), *vomiting can deplete you of fluid and minerals, leading to low blood pressure. This is always harmful to your baby. Inform your doctor if you vomit more than 3 times a day for 3 days. In very severe cases, hospitalization may be necessary to replace lost fluid.*

Use sunblock when out in strong sunshine. Never bleach the skin. The pigmentation will fade within a few months of delivery.

None.

Reducing nausea
Dry crackers can help relieve feelings of nausea. Skim milk makes the snack nutritious.

193

COMPLAINT	WHY IT HAPPENS
Rib pain can be felt as extreme soreness and tenderness of the ribs, usually on the right side, just below the breasts. The pain is more severe on sitting down. It tends to occur mainly during the third trimester.	It is caused by compression of the ribs as the uterus rises in the abdomen. In addition, the baby can bruise your lower ribs with his or her head, or by excessive punching and kicking.
Tender painful breasts, with a feeling of heaviness and discomfort, and a tingling sensation in the nipples, can be one of the first signs of pregnancy. Tenderness is present throughout but usually increases toward term.	Hormones are preparing your breasts for lactation. The milk ducts are growing and being stretched as they fill with milk.
Varicose veins are swollen veins just below the skin. Although most common in the legs or anus, they can also occur in the vulva.	See **Hemorrhoids** p.190.
Water retention happens when there is an increase in the amount of fluid present in the tissues. This causes swelling (edema), especially of the feet, face, and hands. Your rings may become tight.	Standing all day, especially in hot weather, can cause fluid to pool in the ankles. High blood pressure (see p.190), which is often associated with pregnancy, can force fluid from the bloodstream into the tissues, causing edema. Pregnancy hormones can cause retention of sodium by the kidneys, which in turn causes the body to retain fluid.
Yeast infection is characterized by a thick, white, curdy discharge from the vagina, accompanied by dryness and intense itching around your vagina, vulva, perineum, and, sometimes, your anus. You may also have pain when passing urine. Yeast infections can happen at any time.	It is an infection by the yeast Candida albicans, which normally occurs in the bowel. Infection occurs when the yeast grows uncontrolled by other bacteria, perhaps following a course of antibiotics. It is particularly common in pregnancy, probably because of the leakage of sugar into your body fluids due to increased vaginal blood flow. Excess sugar intake often aggravates it.

Wear comfortable clothes
Loose fitting, comfortable outerwear is essential during pregnancy. Tight-fitting tops will constrict you.

WHAT CAN BE DONE

RISK TO BABY

Wear loose clothes that won't compress your ribs. Improve your posture. Prop yourself up on cushions when you lie down. The pain ceases when the baby's head drops into the pelvic cavity prior to birth.

None.

Wear a good supportive bra from early in pregnancy. If your breasts are large, wear a bra at night as well (see p.145). Wash your breasts gently once a day with a mild soap, and pat dry. Apply moisturizing cream or oil if your nipples are sore.

None.

Avoid standing for too long. Put your feet up as often as possible. Wear pregnancy support stockings. Gentle massage may help prevent varicose veins, but do not massage the area if they develop.

None.

Avoid standing for prolonged periods, particularly in hot weather. Put your feet up. Avoid salty foods. Your doctor will check your hands, face, and ankles for any swelling at each prenatal visit, and occasionally diuretics may be prescribed.

Your doctor will always check for edema. It can be a sign of high blood pressure, which must be treated as it can lead to potentially dangerous complications (see p.204).

Take time to relax
Remember to make time to put your feet up; this will help prevent water retention and varicose veins.

Avoid wearing tight pants as this encourages infection. Choose cotton instead of manmade fibers. The doctor will prescribe suppositories that you should place in your vagina at night, as directed. You will also be prescribed a cream that should be gently rubbed into the skin surrounding the vaginal opening, the anus, and on the thighs. This will stop the itching. Avoid sugar.

The baby's mouth can become infected at birth.

Kathy Dixon

AGE *29 years*

PAST MEDICAL *Developed*
HISTORY *multiple sclerosis*
at the age of
23 years

OBSTETRIC *14 weeks*
HISTORY *pregnant*

When Kathy developed multiple sclerosis a year after her marriage to Tom, both were devastated. Each had dreamed of having children. Kathy and Tom came to believe that Kathy's MS reduced the possibility of her conceiving, even rendering her infertile, and that pregnancy was not advisable for women suffering from MS because it causes a deterioration of the condition with serious relapses and increased disability.

A CASE STUDY

MOTHER WHO HAS MS

Kathy has always longed to have children, but because of her multiple sclerosis (MS), she and Tom believed that their chances of having a family were nil. Every so often they talked things over with their rather elderly family doctor who, to their dismay, continued to advise them against attempting pregnancy. However, some months ago they were recommended to see an obstetrician with experience in similar cases.

A NEW PICTURE

As Kathy's walking was steady, her eyesight was hardly affected, and she had no troublesome urinary symptoms or vertigo, she and Tom eventually decided to press for a second opinion. They saw a modern obstetrician who had monitored several patients with MS through successful pregnancies, and who enlisted the help of a neurologist throughout prenatal care. This way, both the baby and the mother received optimum care.

To their delight, Kathy and Tom were given an entirely new and encouraging picture by the obstetrician. Multiple sclerosis, he told them, does not affect a woman's fertility in any way and has no apparent effect on the course of pregnancy, labor, or delivery. Women with MS have very few complications during the course of pregnancy. In a study of recent 36 pregnant women with MS, the only complications mentioned were two cases of mild vomiting. There is no increase in spontaneous abortions, complications in pregnancy or delivery, malformations, or stillbirths.

A GOOD PROGNOSIS

Kathy wondered whether pregnancy would make her MS worse. I told her that many research studies suggest that pregnancy is a *protection* for women with MS. This is probably because the natural state of immunosuppression that occurs in pregnancy to prevent a woman from rejecting her baby also suppresses the inflammation that causes nerve and brain damage in MS. On the other hand, there is a slightly increased risk of a flare-up for three to six months after the birth. Between 40 and 60 percent of women have a relapse during this time – 20 percent of these suffer from permanent side effects while 80 percent go back to the state of MS they were in before their pregnancy. The long-term course of MS does not appear to be affected by pregnancy. I reassured Kathy that the management of her labor and delivery would follow normal medical routine. She could be given analgesics without hesitation – any pain relief that would normally be used – and these would have no effect on her MS. A Caesarean section would not affect her MS, nor would forceps if they proved to be necessary.

MS and the baby   Tom was concerned that Kathy's MS might be passed on to their child. I explained that in an area with a high prevalence of MS, one person in 1,000 out of the normal population would be likely to develop the disease. One study has shown that among children of people with MS, the figure could rise to one in 100. Dietary and genetic factors appear to be involved, although nothing has as yet been proved conclusively. However, most people feel that the risk of their child having MS is not great enough to stop them from choosing to conceive.

MS medication and the developing baby   Kathy was worried that the drugs she is given for MS might harm the baby in the uterus. I told her that in the first 12 weeks of pregnancy a woman is never given drugs, even if she does have MS, unless her life or the life of the baby is in danger. Drugs to stop painful muscle spasms would be discontinued before conception, as would long-term anti-inflammatory therapies. Drugs that help control urinary frequency or incontinence would also be stopped. As MS rarely worsens during pregnancy, very powerful drugs like steroids, which are only given if either the mother or the baby's life is in danger, are hardly ever needed during pregnancy.

After the birth   Kathy wanted to know whether MS would affect her ability to feed and care for her baby. I told her that there are no medical reasons for her not to breastfeed and that she should insist on doing so if she enjoys it.

Rest, however, is extremely important, so she should make arrangements to have nursery help and express enough milk for the night feedings so that they can be given by others. Also, if she was already feeling insecure because of her MS, having a baby to look after might increase her sense of insecurity. I told Tom that he would be the best person to calm Kathy's fears in that situation.

Happily pregnant

Kathy and Tom thought about what they'd been told, and read the many articles about multiple sclerosis, which they found very helpful. They were a little bit stunned that after all the years that they had spent hoping for a miracle, there didn't appear to be much of a risk for Kathy after all. They decided to try for a baby, and Kathy is now 14 weeks pregnant. She is having routine prenatal care and seeing her neurologist once a month. Her doctors have told her that there is no need for special testing or monitoring of her pregnancy. She is being given iron to avoid anemia and her doctors are on the alert for warning signs of a urinary tract infection, which must be treated promptly if it occurs. Her pregnancy is proceeding normally and her MS remains unchanged.

Kathy's baby

There is every expectation that she will develop and be born in the normal way, with no need for special medical intervention.

• *She cannot inherit MS from her mother by transmission across the placenta, and the risk of transmission through genes appears to be very small*

• *While she is in the uterus, she will not be at risk from the drugs given for MS because her mother will cease taking medication*

• *After she is born, her mother should be able to breastfeed, or to express milk so that her father can feed her by bottle*

• *As long as her mother consults the doctor before she resumes any drug treatment, the baby won't be at any risks from drugs contained in the breast milk*

9

Medical
EMERGENCIES

Medical emergencies in pregnancy tend to be concentrated
in the first and third trimesters. In the first trimester,
most emergencies are associated with the loss of the fetus
(miscarriage), or with the blastocyst being wrongly
implanted, as in an ectopic pregnancy. In the third
trimester, there may be complications such as
preeclampsia or problems with the placenta. Nonetheless,
the majority of babies are delivered safely.

VAGINAL BLEEDING

Vaginal bleeding at any stage of pregnancy should be taken seriously. It may indicate an abnormally placed placenta, placenta previa (see p.202), or it may be a warning of imminent miscarriage. Both of these conditions require prompt medical treatment.

Vaginal bleeding occurs in the first trimester in about a quarter of all pregnancies. Over half of these pregnancies continue, with delivery of a healthy baby at term.

If at any time during your pregnancy vaginal bleeding occurs:

- *Call your doctor and go to bed*
- *Lie flat with your legs and hips higher than your shoulders*
- *If you pass any clots, they should be examined by your doctor*
- *Don't take any medicine or drink any alcohol*
- *Keep the room and yourself cool*

MEDICAL EMERGENCIES

The vast majority of pregnancies continue to term with no problems or emergencies. However, it is wise to be fully aware of the danger signs so that medical care can be sought if necessary.

MISCARRIAGE

Medically known as spontaneous abortion, miscarriage is when the fetus aborts before the 28th week. After the 28th week, it is called a stillbirth. In the first few weeks about a third of all pregnancies end in miscarriage, but a quarter of these occur before pregnancy has been diagnosed or even suspected, so women are often unaware that they have miscarried.

Miscarriages increase in frequency with age and with the number of previous pregnancies. They usually happen during the first trimester, the most common symptom being bleeding, which occurs in 95 percent of cases. *If bleeding occurs at any time in your pregnancy you must consult your doctor.*

Most early miscarriages are due to a seriously abnormal fetus failing to implant in the uterine wall. Maternal causes of miscarriage include uterine abnormalities such as large fibroids and hormonal imbalances. Some bacterial and viral infections can also cause miscarriage. Cervical incompetence (see p.203) accounts for only 1 percent of spontaneous abortions. Paternal factors include abnormal sperm, or incompatible blood type, which causes the mother to produce antibodies to her partner's blood. These antibodies then attack and kill her fetus. Doctors divide spontaneous abortion – miscarriage – into:

Threatened abortion Miscarriage is possible but not inevitable. There is vaginal bleeding and sometimes pain. This occurs in about 10 percent of all pregnancies and may be confused with the slight bleeding that can occur at the time of the first missed period.

Inevitable abortion Vaginal bleeding is accompanied by pain owing to the uterus contracting. If there is dilation of the cervix, the loss of the embryo, unfortunately, is bound to occur.

Incomplete abortion This is when abortion has occurred but some of the products of conception, such as the amniotic sac or placenta, remain within the uterus.

Complete abortion The fetus and placenta are expelled from the uterus, sometimes without any symptoms. This can be confirmed by ultrasound examination.

Missed abortion The fetus and placenta die, but remain in the uterus for some time, even months, before being expelled. The symptoms of pregnancy disappear, but there is no other indication of fetal death until much later.

Habitual abortion Three or more miscarriages have occurred at the same stage of pregnancy, possibly for the same reason.

Recurrent abortion Miscarriage has occurred on three or more occasions, for different reasons at different stages of pregnancy.

Treatment If you are bleeding, go to bed and stay there until the bleeding ceases. Stop activities such as strenuous exercise and sexual intercourse. If the bleeding and pain subside, you are quite likely to go on to deliver a healthy baby.

If miscarriage appears to be inevitable there is little doctors can do to prevent it. Complete and incomplete abortions should always be treated in a hospital. If incomplete abortion occurs, the uterus will be cleaned out by dilatation and curettage (D and C). Painkillers are given, along with drugs, to stop the bleeding. If a lot of blood was lost, a transfusion may be necessary.

There is no urgency in treating a missed abortion, but if, after a time, a spontaneous abortion hasn't occurred, a D and C procedure will be carried out. If fetal death occurs later in pregnancy, prostaglandin vaginal suppositories or an oxytocin injection will be given to stimulate delivery (see also p.292).

Habitual abortion that has occurred because of cervical incompetence (see p.203) can be treated by stitching the cervix shut at the beginning of the next pregnancy.

Other possible reasons for habitual abortion are genetic or hormonal disorders, which often can be pinpointed (see pp.40 & 42); long-term infections, such as listeria, may sometimes cause repeated miscarriages, but can be difficult to diagnose and treat; poor nutrition; chronic disease, such as renal disease; tumors in the uterus (particularly fibroids) or abnormalities such as partial or complete septums (see column, right) that can usually be corrected by surgery; and immune disorders.

This last happens when the mother's immune system identifies the fetus as foreign, and attacks it – Rhesus blood incompatibility (see Case study, p.184) is one example. Other immune problems can sometimes be treated by using medication to suppress the mother's immune reaction, or the fetus can occasionally be injected with antibodies, either via the umbilical cord or directly into the fetus if the cord is underdeveloped.

PLACENTAL SEPARATION

Bleeding can occur from the placental bed owing to partial or complete separation of the placenta from the uterus. Blood builds up in the spaces, and eventually escapes around the membranes and through the cervix into the vagina. Known as placental abruption (*abruptio placentae*), it occurs in about one in 200 pregnancies.

UTERINE SEPTUMS

In all mammals, the uterus develops from 2 separate tubes in the embryo.

In some, such as monkeys, horses, and human beings, the 2 tubes fuse to form 1 uterus. In others, such as cats and dogs, the tubes develop into 2 separate uteri.

Problems arise in women when the tubes have not fused completely, thus leaving a partition in the uterus. A birth complicated by a uterine septum usually requires a Caesarean section.

Bicornuate (horn-shaped) uterus
The baby is forced to lie in a transverse position from the second trimester.

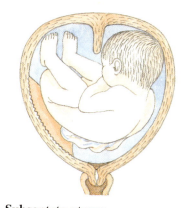

Subseptate uterus
The septum restricts the baby's movements, which will probably hinder his birth.

ABNORMAL POSITION OF THE PLACENTA

If the placenta has implanted incorrectly, it can obstruct the baby's birth.

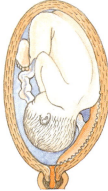

Side position
The placenta implants on the side and extends to the cervix, but does not cover it.

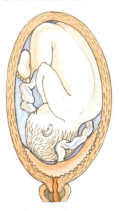

Blocking the cervix
The placenta implants centrally, completely covering the cervix – even when it is fully dilated.

The cause is unknown, but it is more common in women who have had two or more children and is divided into three types according to the severity of the separation.

In mild separation, blood loss can be slight. Bed rest is the best treatment, with ultrasound examination to monitor the situation. If it occurs late in pregnancy, labor may be induced.

In moderate separation, a quarter of the placenta separates and between one and two pints of blood may be lost. This requires a blood transfusion, and if the pregnancy is at or approaching term, a Caesarean section is usually performed.

Severe separation is an acute emergency, when at least two-thirds of the placenta shears off the uterine wall, and up to four pints of blood are lost. This causes severe shock, disturbance of blood coagulation, and full kidney shutdown. A rapid blood transfusion will be given, and if the pregnancy is approaching term, a Caesarean section will be performed to save the baby. If placental abruption occurs before the third trimester, fetal death is inevitable.

PLACENTA PREVIA

This occurs when the placenta is implanted in the lower segment of the uterus instead of the upper part (see column, left). It therefore lies in front of the baby as she comes to descend the birth canal at the onset of labor. The baby cannot pass down the canal without dislodging the placenta, thereby interrupting her own blood supply. Placenta previa is a major cause of bleeding after the 20th week and of hemorrhage in the final two months of pregnancy. It is more common in women who have had several children, although the cause is unknown.

The greater the proportion of the placenta lying in the lower uterine segment, the greater the likelihood of complications during delivery. Even though the growth of the placenta in both size and weight slows down after the 30th week of pregnancy, the lower segment of the uterus is increasing in length quite rapidly. Therefore, shearing stresses between the placenta and the uterine wall may occur, leading to episodes of bleeding.

This extremely dangerous condition can be diagnosed well ahead of delivery by ultrasound (see p.162). Early symptoms include episodes of bleeding, with bright red blood, which may occur after sexual intercourse. If this happens, the doctor will advise hospital admission for ultrasound examination and bed rest, with blood transfusion if necessary. Bed rest should continue, if possible, until the 37th week, at which time the baby will be delivered by Caesarean section (see p.284).

Postpartum hemorrhage may occur after the delivery of the baby and is usually anticipated. Drugs to prevent it will be given as soon as the baby is born. In a very few cases, hemorrhage will continue despite treatment and then a hysterectomy may have to be considered. For these reasons, placenta previa should only be treated by obstetricians, who are qualified to cope with these complications. Delivery in a well-equipped hospital is vital, where a blood transfusion service is on hand.

PLACENTAL INSUFFICIENCY

During pregnancy the fetus receives oxygen and nourishment, and excretes carbon dioxide and waste products, via the placenta and the umbilical blood vessels. A healthy placenta, one that is able to act as an effective organ of transfer, is therefore crucial in maintaining the health of the fetus. The placenta may be unable to support the fetus sufficiently for a number of reasons:

• The placenta may have developed abnormally

• Blood flow through the placenta may be restricted, or placental tissue lost because of a blood clot

• The placenta may separate, or partly separate, from the uterine wall (see also **Placental separation**, p.201)

• The placenta may be too small

• The placenta may be poorly developed

• The pregnancy may go beyond dates, so that the placenta becomes relatively inadequate for the fetus (see p.170)

• If maternal diabetes (see also pp.168 & 205) is present, this can affect the placenta adversely

Assessment and treatment There is no reliable test for placental function. However, insufficiency may be signaled if you show less than normal weight gain, if your uterus is growing too slowly, or if your baby's development is below normal.

Ultrasound is the most reliable way to measure the growth of the fetus. If it shows that the baby is not growing adequately, your doctor will carry out tests that measure placental hormone and enzyme levels in the blood. A biophysical profile that takes account of fetal breathing, body movement, tone and quantity of amniotic fluid, and a non-stress test may also be compiled. As the most useful sign in the last months, however, is the baby's activity level, you may be asked to keep a kick count (see p.177). Placental insufficiency may warrant the induction of labor, and even Caesarean section.

INCOMPETENT CERVIX

Fortunately, this condition is rare, unless the cervix has been damaged during previous surgery or pregnancy. During pregnancy, the cervix normally remains tightly shut and is sealed with a plug of mucus. This means that the fetus is safely held in the uterus until labor begins, when the cervix begins to dilate.

Occasionally, however, the cervical canal is "incompetent" and begins to open before term, usually in the third or fourth month. This allows the amniotic sac containing the fetus to sag through into the vagina, and rupture, with a sudden loss of amniotic fluid followed by miscarriage. Unfortunately, an incompetent cervix is usually diagnosed only after a first miscarriage has occurred.

If cervical incompetence is thought to be the cause of previous miscarriage, a soft nonabsorbable thread will be inserted around your cervix to tighten it (see column, right).

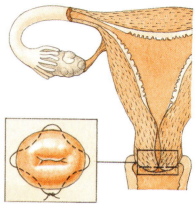

Suturing the cervix
The cervix is kept closed by passing a suture right around it – like the strings of a purse. The thread is normally cut approximately 7 days before the expected date of delivery.

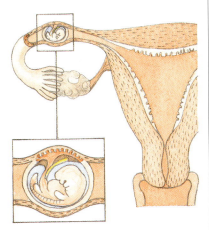

Tubal implantation
Ectopic pregnancy occurs in about 1 in every 300 pregnancies. The blastocyst (see p.30) usually (in 99% of ectopic pregnancies) implants in the Fallopian tube. Very rarely, it may implant in the abdominal cavity, the cervix, or on one of the ovaries.

After bed rest in the hospital you will be able to go home, but you should rest adequately throughout the remainder of your pregnancy. The thread will be cut approximately seven days before term and your baby probably delivered vaginally in the normal way.

PREECLAMPSIA

Pregnancy-induced hypertension, or preeclampsia, occurs in about 15 percent of all pregnant women. It is particularly common in women having their first baby, women over 35, and women carrying multiple fetuses. The cause is not fully understood.

Symptoms The signs of preeclampsia include elevated blood pressure, protein in the urine due to kidney malfunction, and swelling (edema) of the face, feet, and hands. The latter is often the first warning sign and will be looked for by your doctor. You may experience headaches and dizziness, and sometimes nausea.

Preeclampsia itself rarely occurs before the 20th week, but your blood pressure may start to rise progressively before this. This is why it is very important to have your blood pressure checked regularly at each prenatal visit. If preeclampsia develops, you will be admitted to the hospital for observation.

Treatment This includes bed rest and sedation, with constant monitoring of your kidney function. Blood pressure usually returns to normal with treatment, but if your condition doesn't improve the baby will be at risk from decreased blood and oxygen flow. Very rarely, preeclampsia can develop into eclampsia, one of the most dangerous complications of pregnancy, which causes coma and convulsions. Eclampsia is life-threatening to both you and your baby. However, this condition is nearly always preceded by preeclampsia, which acts as an early warning signal, and eclampsia can be prevented by rigorous treatment.

ECLAMPSIA

The word eclampsia derives from the Greek words meaning "like a flash of lightening" because it seemed to strike from out of the blue with seizures and, eventually, coma. Eclampsia is a potentially life-threatening condition for both mother and baby and it used to be quite common. However, it is now extremely rare due to the ability of doctors to diagnose the condition in its earliest phase, preeclampsia (see above), and because doctors and midwives are constantly alert for the warning signs. When eclampsia does occur, it is a full-blown medical emergency.

Symptoms Eclampsia is an emergency because blood vessels in the uterus go into spasm (vasospasm), thereby cutting down the blood flow to the fetus with dangerous tissue hypoxia (low oxygen).

Your own life is threatened because vasospasm leads to kidney failure. Brain oxygen is also lowered, causing heightened brain sensitivity, which appears as seizures. Tissues become waterlogged because of fluid retention and hemorrhages can occur in some

204

tissues including the liver. The earliest signs of eclampsia are drowsiness, headache, and dimness of vision, all of which are accompanied by rising blood pressure, edema (see p.194), and protein in the urine (see **Urine**, p.159).

Treatment High blood pressure always preceeds eclampsia, so your blood pressure will be taken at every prenatal visit. Even slightly raised blood pressure is treated with complete bedrest and sedation. Where eclampsia develops, treatment is aimed at increasing blood flow to the brain, sedating the brain, reducing high blood pressure, and delivering the baby – usually by Caesarian section. As soon as the baby is born the condition subsides.

ECTOPIC PREGNANCY

In ectopic pregnancy, the fertilized ovum implants somewhere other than in the cavity of the uterus, usually in a Fallopian tube. The rapidly growing embryo causes the tube to distend, and the invading placenta weakens its walls, causing bleeding. Eventually the tube bursts under the strain.

However, before a Fallopian tube bursts, certain symptoms that signal all is not well usually occur around the sixth week of pregnancy. They must be reported to your doctor immediately. Doctors define two forms of ectopic pregnancy:

Subacute form After a positive pregnancy test, the ectopic pregnancy may be signaled by pain in the abdomen, usually only on one side, sometimes with vaginal bleeding, fainting, and pain in the shoulder (on the same side as any pain in the abdomen). There is leakage but no rupture as yet, and it may not be detected until eight to ten weeks gestation. This form can sometimes be treated by injecting a drug into the embryo, causing it to die and be reabsorbed, which can save the Fallopian tube.

Acute form This occurs when the tube bursts, leading to severe pain and shock, with extreme paleness, weak but rapid pulse, and falling blood pressure. This acute form requires immediate hospital admission and treatment is by surgical removal of the pregnancy from the Fallopian tube. The tube itself may also have to be removed, depending on the degree of damage, and a blood transfusion is sometimes necessary.

Ectopic pregnancy is becoming more common in developed countries. The reasons for this are unknown, but some doctors think there could be a link with the increases in pelvic inflammatory disease, which causes scarring and blockage of the Fallopian tubes. However, the apparent increase may be due to improved diagnosis made possible by the advent of ultrasound.

Outlook Almost 60 percent of women who have had an ectopic pregnancy become pregnant again. 30 percent avoid further pregnancy voluntarily; the rest are infertile.

POSTPARTUM INFECTION

Postpartum infection, which used to be known as childbed fever, is now very rare indeed, although before the advent of antibiotics it was a primary cause of maternal mortality.

Postpartum infection is normally caused by remnants of the placenta remaining in the uterus. If one should occur, the first symptoms are a high temperature, acute stomach pains, and unpleasant-smelling lochia (see p.332).

If any of these symptoms develop, it is important to notify the doctor immediately; medical staff will promptly remove any remaining tissue and give you drugs to treat the infection.

NAME *Liz Turner*

AGE *27 years*

PAST MEDICAL HISTORY *Nothing abnormal*

OBSTETRIC HISTORY *Became pregnant for the first time a year ago; pregnancy miscarried in 11th week. She is now 8 weeks pregnant*

Liz and her partner, Alan, desperately wanted their first baby and both were upset by the miscarriage 9 months ago. Alan buried himself in work while Liz struggled with her feelings of bereavement. Liz is now 8 weeks into her second pregnancy and is determined to keep this baby. Her pleasure at being pregnant is marred by fears that the same thing might happen again.

MOTHER WHO HAS MISCARRIED

Liz was deeply distressed by her miscarriage. What made the situation harder to bear was that there didn't seem to be a cause and no one seemed to understand how she felt. She is now pregnant again and is naturally concerned about the outcome.

FIRST REACTIONS

When she miscarried nine months ago, Liz found herself fighting back guilt, despair, and anger in seeming isolation. Her doctor couldn't look her in the eye or talk openly about her lost baby. Her family and friends were sympathetic but their attempts to console her were rather clumsy. Some suggested that it was all for the best, because there must have been something wrong with the baby. Others reassured her that she could soon have another one. The unborn baby was not real to them as it had been to Liz, and they did not understand her sense of loss. She began to wonder if her reactions were normal – perhaps she was not justified in grieving for a baby who had never really existed? I reassured Liz that it is natural for a mother to mourn the loss of a child, even if the child has not been born. Her emotions as well as her body needed time to readjust. I also encouraged her to share her feelings with Alan, so that they could grieve together.

Accepting their loss At first, Alan was reluctant to share his feelings with Liz, and she felt she had to force him to talk to her. She knew that it would be impossible to care for another baby until she had given up this one, and this was something that they had to do together. I encouraged them to share their anxieties and frustration, talk through their feelings, and cry together. It was important that they did not deny their grief. I also suggested that it might help if they had a private memorial ceremony – perhaps something as simple as planting a tree in memory of their miscarried baby.

Something wrong with the baby? After her miscarriage, Liz was taken to the hospital and examined to make sure that no fragments of the placenta were left in her uterus, where they could create a site for infection. Following her doctor's advice, she collected everything her body had expelled and took it with her so that the fetus could be tested for chromosomal abnormalities. None were found. Liz was reassured by this, but then began to blame herself – perhaps the miscarriage was her fault? I explained that a first pregnancy is more likely to abort than any other – in fact one in three does. There are thought to be two reasons for this: an immature uterus needs to mature by having a trial run before it is fit to carry a pregnancy to term and defects in the sperm or ova can produce an abnormal fetus.

THE CHANCES OF ANOTHER MISCARRIAGE

Recent studies of early pregnancy loss show that a woman who has had one miscarriage is more likely to miscarry again. The risk seems to increase if conception occurs too soon after the miscarriage. Fortunately I had warned Liz and Alan about this, so they had waited for four months before trying to conceive again.

A simple predictive test, carried out before pregnancy, can help to identify women who are likely to miscarry again. During the menstrual cycle, too high a level of luteinizing hormone (LH) before ovulation increases the risk of miscarriage. Liz's LH levels were tested and proved to be normal.

RECURRENT MISCARRIAGES

Some women do, however, miscarry repeatedly, but even for them the chance of a successful pregnancy after three previous miscarriages is about 60 percent. Women who miscarry repeatedly are tested for uterine abnormalities, hormone imbalances, and disorders of the immunological system. Recently, scientific investigations have focused on a woman's immunological system and hormones as causes of recurrent miscarriage.

Immunologically induced miscarriages The immune system is designed to repel foreign bodies. Pregnancy normally overrides this, so that the woman's body protects the baby rather than rejecting it. In some mothers, for unknown reasons, the override fails, the immune system reasserts itself, and the baby is aborted. One treatment, still experimental, is to *immunize* women so that they do not produce antibodies hostile to their babies.

Hormonally induced miscarriages It has been found that 80 percent of repeat miscarriers suffer from polycystic ovary syndrome and need frequent monitoring of their hormone balance.

PREGNANT AGAIN

Now that Liz is pregnant again, she's being extremely careful in every aspect of her life (see **Avoiding hazards**, p.150). She goes to relaxation classes to help reduce her levels of stress, and Alan has learned how to give her a relaxing massage (see p.134). Most importantly, she has stopped blaming herself for the miscarriage and is taking a positive attitude toward her new pregnancy. I told Liz that although she can't be certain what the outcome will be, she can relax in the knowledge that her body is better prepared for pregnancy than it was last time. Alan is "sure it's going to be all right this time" but is reluctant to talk to his unborn child or make plans for its future as he did with the first one.

LIZ'S BABY

Liz is fit and healthy and doesn't appear to have any condition that predisposes her to miscarry again. Her baby has every chance of developing perfectly in the uterus.

In some ways, Liz's baby will actually benefit from her mother's previous miscarriage:

• *She will be very healthy because Liz is paying such careful attention to diet and exercise*

• *She should be comforted by the positive feelings that Liz is directing toward her*

• *When she is born, she will be greeted with relief and delight because she is making up for a previous disappointment. She represents success*

10

A

SENSUAL

pregnancy

The very high levels of female hormones present in your body during pregnancy mean that you have the potential to enjoy all aspects of sex, from massage to sexual intercourse, far more than ever before. However, you may experience sexual problems. These can easily color other aspects of your lives, but the majority can be eased or resolved with open communication.

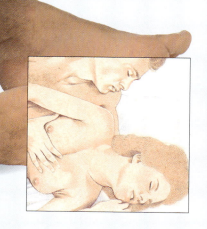

YOUR HORMONES

A woman undergoes many physical, emotional, and psychological changes during pregnancy, which will influence her attitude to sex and her enjoyment of it. These changes are due mainly to the vastly increased levels of hormones circulating in her body.

The most important hormones involved in maintaining pregnancy are progesterone and estrogen. In the early days of a pregnancy, these are produced by the corpus luteum in the ovary. However, once the embryo has implanted in the uterine lining, the embryo and the developing placenta quickly take over as the primary sources of progesterone and estrogen.

The increase in the amounts of progesterone and estrogen circulating in the body is swift and dramatic. The level of progesterone rises to 10 times what it was before conception, while the amount of estrogen produced in a single day is equivalent to that generated by a non-pregnant woman's ovaries in 3 years. In fact, during the course of a single pregnancy, a woman will produce as much estrogen as a non-pregnant woman could in 150 years.

Progesterone and estrogen induce a sense of well-being and also lead to shining hair, supple and glowing skin, and an aura of tranquility and contentment.

A SENSUAL PREGNANCY

Unless there are medical reasons for abstaining from it, sexual intercourse is safe and permissible during pregnancy. Moreover, every pregnant woman has the potential to enjoy sex – perhaps more than she ever has before.

The desire for sex and the enjoyment of it varies widely, not only from one woman to another during pregnancy, but also in the same woman at different times throughout its duration. Typically, though, there is a decline in interest in sex during the first trimester (especially if you are suffering from tiredness and nausea), followed by an increase in the second trimester, and then another decline in the third trimester.

When a pregnant woman does have sex, she may find it far more exciting and satisfying than it was before she conceived. In fact, a woman will sometimes achieve orgasm or multiple orgasms for the first time when she is pregnant. This enhanced sexuality is principally because of the high levels of female hormones and pregnancy hormones that circulate throughout her body when she is pregnant (see column, left). These cause a number of important changes to her breasts and sexual organs, making them more sensitive and responsive. In addition, because being pregnant is such an affirmation of being female, a woman may find her condition leads to enhanced sensuality.

EROTICISM DURING PREGNANCY

One of the effects of the rise in estrogen levels during pregnancy is an increase in blood flow, especially in the pelvic area. Because of this, the vagina and its folds, the labia, become slightly stretched and swollen. This stretching and swelling, which normally occur only during sexual excitement, make the sensory nerve endings hypersensitive, resulting in rapid arousal.

The breasts start to enlarge almost as soon as pregnancy occurs, one of the classic signs of pregnancy is sensitive, enlarged breasts with nipples that may tingle or even feel painful. The increased sensitivity of the breasts makes them a focus of sensory arousal, and a woman can feel the most exquisite sensations when her nipples and breasts are caressed and kissed by her partner. This sexual foreplay can result also in the arousal of the clitoris and the vagina, which will swell very readily.

Because of the increased blood flow the vaginal secretions are quite profuse, so a pregnant woman usually becomes ready for penetration much earlier than usual. Penetration is particularly easy because of the abundance of vaginal fluid, and a climax can be achieved quite quickly if the clitoris is stimulated simultaneously. The intensity of orgasm may reach new heights and the time taken to "come down" from an orgasm can be greatly extended. This is evident in the labia minora and the lower end of the vagina, which can remain swollen for up to two hours after orgasm, particularly in the last trimester.

In addition to stimulating the whole of the genital tract, the pregnancy hormones stimulate the production of a hormone within the brain called melanocyte-stimulating hormone (or MSH), which results in deeper skin pigmentation – as in the darkening of the nipple area. Darkening of the nipples can act as a sexual signal to a man, making his partner's breasts very attractive to him.

WHEN TO MAKE LOVE

You can make love whenever you want to, given that it's not too athletic and that there are no medical reasons for you to forego it (see p.218). Good sex in pregnancy is very enjoyable, and it helps prepare you for childbirth by keeping your pelvic muscles strong and supple. It also bonds you closer to your partner, which will help you cope much better with the stresses of parenthood.

There is absolutely no physical reason why a woman having a normal pregnancy should not enjoy sexual relations with her partner, and sex need not stop any earlier than the onset of labor, both partners being willing. In a low-risk pregnancy, the uterine spasms that accompany orgasms are perfectly safe, and in late pregnancy may be beneficial because they help prepare the uterus for the rigors of labor.

It is a fallacy that sex can *cause* an infection during pregnancy and may harm the baby – infection is virtually impossible because the cervix is plugged with a tough mucus that prevents the ascent of bacteria into the uterus. In addition, the baby is completely enclosed within the amniotic sac, which resists rupture even when under great pressure and cushions the baby against all external forces (including the weight of a partner during intercourse). However, extremely athletic sex is not a good idea, because it may cause soreness and abrasions and a pregnant woman should be free of these unnecessary discomforts.

Lovemaking positions   There are several lovemaking positions that you can use to enhance your enjoyment – without in any way diminishing that of your partner – once the missionary position becomes too awkward and uncomfortable. Side-by-side positions are often pleasurable, as are rear-entry positions, because in these positions your abdomen is not under any pressure from the weight of your partner. Sitting positions are particularly enjoyable in the middle months of pregnancy, and enable you to adjust your position but still see your partner's face and feel close to him.

If you are feeling sexy, but you don't really want intercourse, you and your partner could explore other forms of sensual and sexual pleasuring, such as erotically stroking and kissing each other, massage (see p.212), mutual masturbation, and oral sex.

BUILDING YOUR RELATIONSHIP

The physical and emotional changes that take place during pregnancy will inevitably have an impact on your sexual relationship with your partner. Love and understanding will help you to minimize any problems that may arise.

As pregnancy advances, you may find that you have to change your sexual habits, and the best way to approach this change is to realize that it is a chance to build on and enhance the physical side of your relationship. For instance, it might prompt you to explore (perhaps for the first time) the pleasures of new lovemaking positions and of other forms of sexual activity such as mutual masturbation and oral sex.

Try to understand any changes in your own and your partner's sexual desires, and be open with each other when discussing your needs, but never allow your sex life to become the dominant feature of your overall relationship. Concentrate on loving rather than lovemaking, and if at any time you or your partner don't feel like sex, rediscover the intimacy and joy of simply being with the one you love.

SENSUAL MASSAGE

When you and your partner give each other a loving, sensual massage, you will find it both relaxing and highly erotic, and it will reinforce the feelings of love you have for each other. Begin with tender hugs, cuddles, and stroking, and then take turns massaging each other all over, from head to toe, using slow, sensuous hand movements and plenty of massage oil.

Use sensual massage as a source of pleasure in itself, or use it as a form of foreplay.

Sensual massage is a highly enjoyable way of maintaining a close physical relationship with your partner during your pregnancy, especially if intercourse is not possible for medical reasons, or if you find it uncomfortable or undesirable. If you make the massage as sexy as you can, and masturbate each other while you do it, both of you will probably be able to reach orgasm without penetration. Alternatively, if you are still having intercourse, you can use sensual massage as a loving, prolonged, and highly effective method of foreplay.

A SHARED PLEASURE

Massage is a way of discovering what gives you pleasure, and you should approach it with a completely open mind. You may both be surprised at how sexy it feels to have certain parts of your bodies caressed. You may never have thought of these as erotic areas.

Preparing for massage Choose a time when you are not likely to be disturbed (taking the phone off the hook is a wise precaution), and prepare your bedroom beforehand, making sure it is warm and comfortable. If your bed is too soft for giving a massage, put a mattress, comforter, or folded blankets on the floor, covered by a large, clean towel or sheet. Dim the lighting if necessary, and play some soft music to create a soothing atmosphere.

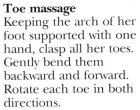

Make sure you are well supported; then lie back and enjoy being massaged

Foot massage
Press upward into her foot with the heel of your hand and work downward. Avoid massaging her heel and ankles, as this can cause uterine contractions.

Toe massage
Keeping the arch of her foot supported with one hand, clasp all her toes. Gently bend them backward and forward. Rotate each toe in both directions.

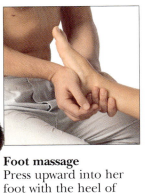

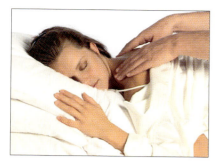

Shoulder and back massage
Knead the back of her neck, and then her shoulder muscles, between your palms, thumbs, and fingers. Massage her lower back with the heel of your hand.

Always take your time, using slow and sensuous movements. Make sure her body is comfortably supported by pillows or cushions

GOOD FOR YOUR BABY

Your baby may also respond with pleasure as your body is stroked and caressed. He can share some of the benefits you receive through massage.

- *From about the fifth month onward your baby may feel stroking movements through your abdomen, which she will find very comforting and soothing*

- *Learning to massage your own and your partner's body during pregnancy will help you to soothe your baby through touch after she is born*

- *Continue to massage your baby after she's born – babies find massage soothing too*

Lubricating the skin Use a massage oil or lotion made for the purpose, because substitutes such as hand cream or body lotion will be absorbed into the skin too quickly, while baby oil will leave an oily film on the skin. Warm the oil before you use it (by putting the bottle in a bowl of warm water, for instance) and make sure your hands are warm and your fingernails short and smooth. When you are giving the massage, put the oil on your hands and then smooth it onto your partner's skin. Never just pour the oil directly onto your partner because that can be distracting as well as wasteful and messy.

Touching intimately Lightly coat your fingertips with massage oil and delicately trace the outlines of each other's lips, cheeks, jaws, ears, and neck. Then, using plenty of oil, work your fingers and the palm of your hands sensuously over breasts, chest, sides, and abdomen, and across the shoulders and down the arms. Stroke firmly up the inside of each thigh in turn, using the lightest of finger pressure on the return stroke. Always handle her breasts carefully as they will be tender.

Abdominal massage
Make light, circular movements with your fingertips all over her abdomen as she leans back.

213

PARTNER'S
DO'S AND
DON'TS

By making a few adjustments to your lovemaking you can make the experience happier for the mother-to-be.

Do:

• *Be tender, romantic, patient, and understanding*

• *Use different kinds of stroking, such as using a firm hand over her abdomen if the baby kicks*

• *Keep your weight off her when making love*

• *Use lots of pillows for greater comfort and to get the right angles around the curves of her body*

• *Take your time when lovemaking, and don't be afraid to experiment*

Don't:

• *Force her to make love if she doesn't feel like it*

• *Expect her to have simultaneous orgasms – or even one orgasm*

MAKING LOVE

You can continue making love as late into pregnancy as you wish, as long as there are no medical reasons for abstaining from it (see p.218). Your baby, safe within your uterus, cannot be harmed by any normal sexual activity (see column, right), and probably enjoys sex as much as you do because your hormones reach him through the placenta (see also p.174).

In the early months you can use any lovemaking position you choose, but as your abdomen swells you will probably find that making love in some positions, particularly the missionary position, with your partner on top, becomes uncomfortable.

When this happens, there are plenty of other erotic and exciting positions to use. In addition, these alternatives are often the best positions to use when you first resume lovemaking after the birth of your baby (see p.338).

WOMAN-ON-TOP POSITIONS

You will probably find these most comfortable from the second trimester onward. As your abdomen enlarges, you can lift yourself further off his stomach by supporting yourself on your bent legs. In this way, you can avoid putting too much pressure on your abdomen and breasts. In these positions, too, you can better control the depth of your partner's penetration and the speed and rhythm of your lovemaking.

These positions allow a great deal of intimacy. You and your partner have your hands free to caress and stroke each other and he can easily reach your breasts with his mouth. Alternatively, you can brush his chest with your breasts to stimulate him further.

The "spoons" position
Your partner cuddles up to your back, making this one of the most comfortable and affectionate of all sexual positions.

KNEELING AND SIDE-BY-SIDE POSITIONS

These positions, many of which involve entering from behind, are useful during pregnancy, particularly if you don't feel very comfortable lying flat on your back or if you do not want to take too active a part in the lovemaking.

Kneeling positions allow your partner much freedom of movement and let him vary the amount of penetration. Side-by-side positions, like those illustrated below, are not only comfortable but permit plenty of passionate kissing and caressing. The "spoons" position (see page opposite), so called because the partners nestle together like a pair of spoons, will also be useful if you experience any soreness or discomfort when you resume lovemaking after you have given birth, especially if you have an episiotomy.

A variation on this position, with the woman lying on her back, frees her from any pressure on her abdomen while her partner has complete access to her vagina. He can continue to stimulate her either with his hand or his penis.

SITTING POSITIONS

Most useful in the middle and late months, these positions don't allow a lot of movement, but they are comfortable for both partners and alleviate pressure on the abdomen. In addition, the depth of penetration can be controlled. In these positions, your partner sits on a sturdy, comfortable chair or the edge of the bed and you sit on his lap, either facing him (if your abdomen is not too big), facing to one side, or facing away from him.

When you are facing to one side or away from your partner, he can use his hands to caress your body and breasts, and stimulate your clitoris. In addition, because his range of movement is limited, you have control of the sexual tempo.

Side-by-side
Maneuver yourself onto your partner's penis, if necessary holding it between your clenched legs, so he is free to caress your genital area.

SEX AND YOUR BABY

There is no risk of you harming your baby when having sex during a normal pregnancy.

Your baby is well protected by the amniotic membranes and fluid that surround him, acting as a cushion, and the mucus plug sealing your cervix acts as a barrier to infection.

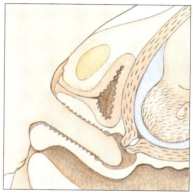

Penile thrusting
During intercourse, your partner's thrusting penis is guided safely away from your uterus by the angle of your vagina.

THE FIRST-TIME FATHER

NAME *Tony Hoggs*

AGE *33 years*

FAMILY HISTORY *Nothing abnormal in either family*

PARTNER'S OBSTETRIC HISTORY *This is his partner's first baby – she is 29*

Tony is absolutely determined not to miss the greatest event of his life; he wants to be a really active father. Research shows that men who are involved from the moment pregnancy is confirmed become enthusiastic fathers. Being involved means a lot of effort for Tony – taking part in all the preparations, going along for prenatal visits and classes, sharing in decisions on where and how to have the baby, and helping care for the baby after she is born.

Many modern fathers don't regard pregnancy and birth as exclusively women's business. They want to participate and contribute in every way they can, so that they are involved with their children from the start.

AN EAGERLY EXPECTANT FATHER

Tony was delighted when his partner, Sally, told him that she was pregnant. He believes that her pregnancy and labor will be profound experiences for him, too, and wants to share in them as much as possible. He is Sally's first choice of personal birth attendant and is excited at the prospect of assisting with the delivery of their baby. As he supports Sally through the various stages of pregnancy and joins in all the activities it entails, Tony is finding that their relationship is becoming richer than ever before. His unborn baby has given a new dimension to his life and he is really looking forward to becoming a father.

Sally is eager for Tony to be an interested and sympathetic partner and they have been attending prenatal classes together (see p.108). In addition, they have been practicing the different breathing patterns and the relaxation techniques at home, and this feeling of team spirit is extremely exciting for both of them.

However, there will be ups and downs during pregnancy, and sometimes a man finds it difficult to balance his own needs with those of his partner, or to know just what it is that his partner needs. Mothers-to-be often feel alone if they don't get the support and strength they need from their partners. However, the tensions that arise from approaching parenthood can usually be diffused if both are frank about their feelings.

WHAT HAPPENS AFTERWARD?

Much as he is enjoying Sally's pregnancy, Tony sometimes feels worried about what life will be like once the baby is born. Will he feel that he has lost his freedom; will he make a good father; will his relationship with Sally suffer?

Three's a crowd? I warned Tony that a new father can feel resentful about the fact that he is no longer the most important person in his partner's life. Having been a member of a couple, he now finds himself playing a supporting role to a new couple – the mother and baby. Tony will feel less shut out if he bonds with the baby himself, holding her, talking to her, and establishing their relationship. Sally and he have talked about it, and he is certain that he will be welcomed and made to feel as important to her as he always has been, as they share in caring for their baby.

A good parent   I reassured Tony that there is no right or wrong way to be a parent. He will have to be ready to grow, change, admit mistakes, but most importantly, make time available for his partner and baby. Fatherhood always involves hard work, a lot of responsibility, and a considerable amount of time, but I assured him that he would be repaid with immeasurable joy and satisfaction.

Postpartum blues   Tony can cope with Sally's changes of mood during her pregnancy, but these are mild compared with postpartum depression (see p.328), which can affect any new mother no matter how supportive her partner may be. I advised Tony to find out all he could about the subject well in advance. If Sally is unfortunate enough to suffer from it, Tony will be able to recognize what is going on and can encourage her to ask for help.

POSTPARTUM SEX

Some men who have watched the birth may find that they are turned off sex for a while. This is normal and I told Tony that if it happens he should not worry about it; his sex drive will return. Many new mothers lose interest in sex completely after the baby is born. This may last for two months, but it can last for much longer – up to ten months or even two years in some cases (see also p.218).

Take it easy   I advised Tony to be as gentle and understanding as possible with Sally, to take things easy at first – especially if she had an episiotomy during the birth – and not to expect sex to be marvelous right away.

I reminded him, too, that sex doesn't have to be penetrative and that he could use cuddling, touching, massage, and mutual masturbation to reestablish their sexual bond. Telling Sally how he feels and asking her to be equally open with him can help prevent an emotional rift; and, if problems persist, he would be well advised to ask for help from a counselor, childbirth teachers, or doctor.

Never the same   Some couples find that sex is better than ever after the birth of their baby, perhaps due to the mother's conscientious pelvic-floor exercises. I warned Tony, though, that even if their sex drive returns with all its former vigor, making love will never be the same as it used to be. They may be interrupted at any moment by a baby crying, and Sally's instincts will act immediately to switch her attention off Tony and onto the baby. The old spontaneity will be gone when lovemaking has to be fitted in with feeding and diaper-changing. But they will be able to work through any problems if they put their relationship high on their list of priorities. I also suggested that Tony and Sally might set up a babysitting exchange with a group of other young parents.

TONY'S BABY

The baby will happily respond to Tony's attempts to bond with her; this can start before birth, and continue at birth and once she is home.

- *As soon as she is born, Tony should hold her and make eye contact. Pressing her to his bare skin will enable her to come in contact with his individual smell, which will help them to bond*

- *If he begins to talk to her while she is in the uterus, she will recognize his voice even before she is born*

- *Tony's baby will bond to sound very quickly, so he should talk to her right away. Later she will associate his voice with security and love*

- *She will enjoy being given her bath by him and bottlefed by him with her mother's expressed milk or formula*

- *She will recognize him, by his voice and his smell, as a familiar and loving presence*

- *She will release in Tony some of the strongest emotions he will ever feel. Tony shouldn't be afraid of fondling and caressing her, even just after birth. Kissing, cooing, and hugging her will be enjoyable to them both*

- *She will form her own relationship with her father as a source of love and security*

- *She will start to make conversational advances toward Tony in early life, and he should talk to her a great deal, keeping up a running commentary, so that his voice becomes fully imprinted in her mind*

WHEN SEX MAY BE DANGEROUS

In some high-risk pregnancies, intercourse must be avoided at certain times or sometimes completely.

Your doctor will warn you if there is any risk of sexual activity being a danger to your pregnancy and will advise you about what (and when) is safe. You should always make sure that he or she explains the problem fully, and that you are completely clear about what you can and cannot safely do.

The most common reasons and times for restricting intercourse during pregnancy are:

• *At any time if there is any sign of bleeding. The bleeding may well be quite harmless, but you should consult your doctor without delay*

• *If you have a history of miscarriages in the first trimester or if you are showing signs that you might miscarry early in pregnancy*

• *If placenta previa is suspected or confirmed (see p.202)*

• *In the last trimester if you have a multiple pregnancy*

• *In the last 12 weeks if you have a history of premature labor or if you are showing signs that you might go into premature labor*

• *If your water has broken*

SEXUAL PROBLEMS

During pregnancy, there are numerous physical and emotional factors that can diminish your enjoyment of sex. Fortunately, the few that actually prevent you from having intercourse are relatively uncommon.

Probably the most common reason for a drop in sexual enjoyment is that you believe your body is becoming less and less attractive to your partner as pregnancy proceeds. In addition to a swelling abdomen with its growing baby, you may view with some alarm the loss of your waistline, your spreading hips, your swelling breasts, and your widening thighs and upper arms. When heavily pregnant, women sometimes become shy and defensive about their appearance and believe that all femininity has gone. This, too, can lead to a reticence about being seen naked.

The best thing to do if this happens is to seek reassurance from your partner, who will allay your fears and probably be astonished that you feel unsure of your attractiveness.

LOSS OF LIBIDO

While you may experience an increased libido (sex drive) in pregnancy, it has to be said that some women feel a loss of sex drive during the first trimester. This is largely the result of morning sickness, which makes you feel thoroughly wretched and unattractive in every way. Fatigue is another enemy of the libido, and because pregnancy is exhausting, you sometimes have little energy left over to devote to enjoying sex. Like morning sickness, fatigue is a common problem of the first trimester and usually diminishes or disappears in the second.

In the second trimester, once free of the distractions of morning sickness and fatigue, most women find that their interest and pleasure in sex increase. Toward the latter end of pregnancy, though, libido may wane again, largely due once more to fatigue. It is sad that so many women feel like beached whales at this time and do not enjoy their rounded beauty. In addition, some may feel too embarrassed to want to strip bare and make love.

Hormone levels can swing quite violently during pregnancy and a woman may find that she's emotionally volatile, switching from contentment to sadness and tearfulness, and then to great elation. This is perfectly normal but, of course, it can have an adverse effect on your sexual relationship with your partner. At times like this, you must be open with your partner and honest about your feelings. If you don't want to make love because you feel physically ill or excessively tired, tell him so; otherwise he may feel rejected.

DISCOMFORT

The hormone-controlled changes in your breasts and genitals make them more sensitive and responsive to touch. This usually has the effect of heightening your sexuality, but sometimes the increased sensitivity causes discomfort. This is especially true of the breasts in early pregnancy, and you may find that for the first few months they are very tender. Tell your partner about this discomfort, so that he will avoid touching them during love play.

The engorgement of your genitals may also cause some discomfort, particularly later on in pregnancy, because they remain swollen and aching after orgasm. This can create a feeling of unrelieved fullness, which may make sex less satisfying. Some women find they can overcome this lack of satisfaction by masturbation, especially if they often have better orgasms through masturbation (by themselves or by their partners) than via intercourse.

A common source of discomfort comes when the baby enlarges. Eventually, your abdomen becomes so swollen that it is increasingly difficult for you to engage in sex in the usual missionary position. When you reach that stage, you could try one or more of the alternative lovemaking positions discussed on page 214.

WHEN TO STOP

Refrain from sex if bleeding occurs at any time, and consult your doctor as soon as possible as to the possible cause. The likelihood is that the bleeding is not serious at all, and is the result of changes in the cervix that make it soft and easily damaged by deep penetration, but medical advice is essential. If the bleeding is confirmed as being due to the sensitivity of the cervix, you should avoid deep penetration when you subsequently have intercourse.

It is inadvisable to have sex if the mucus plug that seals the cervix has become dislodged, and you should also abstain after your water has broken. So if you have a show (the blood-stained vaginal discharge – see p.251) or the water breaks, do not have intercourse.

A history of previous miscarriages may mean that you should abstain from sex in the early weeks of pregnancy until the fetus becomes well established, so you should always consult your doctor.

ANXIETIES

In any relationship, relaxed and happy lovemaking can be difficult to achieve if either, or both, of the partners is feeling anxious, tense, or nervous. During pregnancy there are many potential sources of anxiety, including fears about the safety of having sex, and the difficulty some couples or individuals have in adjusting to the idea of imminent parenthood.

Worries about the safety of sex during pregnancy are usually unfounded, and you and your partner should openly and fully discuss your feelings about the growth and extension of your relationship from partnership into parenthood.

If your sex life is causing you concern, and you and your partner cannot resolve it between you, do not hesitate to seek professional advice and counseling.

SEX WITHOUT INTERCOURSE

When intercourse is unwanted or unwise, there are alternative routes to sexual pleasure.

Extended foreplay Sensual massage and passionate kissing and caressing can stop short of or lead to orgasm, as desired.

Mutual masturbation This enables you and your partner to give each other sexual pleasure, and bring each other to orgasm, without having intercourse. To make the experience more sensual and also to avoid harming the delicate skin of your genitals, have your partner smear his hands and fingers with a suitable lubricant such as saliva or K-Y Jelly.

Oral sex Fellatio and cunnilingus, as well as or instead of mutual masturbation, are perfectly safe throughout pregnancy. However, throughout pregnancy the vaginal secretions generally have a much stronger odor than at other times, and some men find this off-putting.

11

Getting

READY

for your baby

From the 36th week, nesting begins in earnest. There's plenty to do in terms of getting the baby's room ready, choosing nursery equipment and baby clothes, making a final choice of names, deciding on the kind of care, if any, you will seek for your child, and making preparations for the birth you wish to have.

PREPARING FOR YOUR BABY

POINTERS FOR MOTHER

When arranging your baby's nursery, remember to think of your own needs; equipment and accessories should be easy and convenient to reach without creating hazards.

• *Put up shelves so that you are able to see everything at a glance and withdraw items with ease*

• *Keep powders and creams on shelves close to the changing mat but out of your baby's reach*

• *Make sure there are no obstructions between the changing table, bath, your chair, and her crib*

• *There should be no cords running across the floor. Set the lamp close to the wall outlet*

• *Put a comfortable, low chair in the nursery for night feedings – make sure it is easy to get out of*

Getting ready for your baby can be one of the most enjoyable aspects of your pregnancy – there is something indefinably thrilling about a finished nursery and tiny baby clothes. To avoid fatigue you should try to make your preparations in small bursts, rather than all at once, and get your partner to help you – it helps you both bond with your unborn child.

YOUR BABY'S ROOM

Over the past few months you may have had many ideas concerning the layout of your baby's room. It is a good idea to prepare the room before she arrives as once she is here your time and energy will be mainly taken up by her care. Safety and comfort for both of you should always be uppermost in your mind.

SLEEPING

During the first few weeks after delivery you may wish to have your baby sleeping in your own room. However, try to make sure there is a special place that can also be designated as your baby's nursery. This may be either a whole room, or an area in another child's room. Make sure you have enough space for sleeping, feeding, bathing, diaper changing, and dressing. The room doesn't have to be expensively decorated; a less elaborate treatment means fewer changes as she grows up. Much of the equipment can be obtained secondhand, or sometimes existing furniture can be easily adapted to your needs (see below).

Whether your baby has her own room or shares yours at first, the room needs to be kept warm. Try to maintain a constant temperature of around 60–70°F (16–20°C) and, if possible, install a thermostatically controlled heater.

FURNITURE AND STORAGE

A chest of drawers with a sturdy frame and legs is ideal both for storage and as a table for diaper changing. It should be high enough (about hip-height) to allow you or your partner to bend over without discomfort. Make sure the surface can be

Decorating baby's room
Choose colors and patterns that are bright and cheerful. Make sure that the decor and accessories will be suitable until your child is at least of school age.

cleaned easily and, if wooden, that there are no cracks or splinters. A plastic-covered changing mat with raised sides is hygienic and comfortable. Choose a chest with at least three spacious drawers or one that allows shelves to be inserted underneath. You can then store baby-changing supplies in the top drawer or along the back edge, where they are easily reached. A small trash can, lined with a plastic bag, should be placed nearby for the disposing of dirty diapers. Wall shelf units allow baby equipment to be stored neatly, and these can be used later for books and toys. A straight-backed chair will allow you or your partner to feed your baby in comfort. If possible, keep a small, sturdy table nearby for placing items on.

LIGHTING

You may want to check your baby while she is sleeping during the night. It is best to have lighting that will allow you to enter the room safely without disturbing her sleep. A dimmer switch fitted to the overhead lighting system will allow you to adjust the level of brightness so she is not suddenly awakened. A night light or shaded lamp may be used, but be very careful to avoid extended wires.

FLOORS AND WALLS

Your nursery floor should be non-slippery, warm, and easily cleaned. Don't use small rugs or mats as you may trip or slip on them. If possible, lay down linoleum or vinyl floor covering – these are hard-wearing and easy to clean. Carpeting provides warmth, but make sure it is stain-resistant. Walls should be painted with a non-toxic, washable emulsion paint, or if you are using wallpaper, make sure it can be wiped clean and doesn't stain.

WINDOWS AND CURTAINS

The nursery must be well ventilated, but make sure windows are draft proof, and above your baby's reach. Well-lined curtains, or blinds plus curtains will block out daylight when your baby is sleeping; take care to choose nonflammable materials.

SAFETY PRECAUTIONS

- *A safety lock should be installed on each window in the nursery, along with bars if the window is close to the floor*
- *Flameproof fabric must be used for bedding, upholstery, and curtains*
- *Place childproof covers over all electrical outlets*
- *Make sure the crib meets current safety standards*
- *Cover walls and furniture in non-toxic, lead-free paint or varnish*

WHAT'S GOOD FOR BABY

A very young baby will be stimulated by a brightly colored and noisy environment.

A bright musical crib mobile will provide her with many moments of pleasure if placed low down; hang another mobile above the changing table. Hang plastic-coated photographs or a small mirror in the crib; she likes looking at faces close up. Offer her rattles and other toys that make noise when thrown, batted, sucked, or shaken. Rubber duckies are good for sucking.

Toys for the newborn
Choose colorful light-weight toys that can't be swallowed or trap your baby's fingers.

MEETING YOUR NEEDS

Initially you need only a few pieces of equipment – something in which to transport your baby, somewhere for him to sleep, and something in which to bathe him.

Opt for a carriage or lie-back stroller that is easy to push with the handles at a comfortable height; you may strain your back if not. Good brakes are essential: you must be able to apply them without letting go of the handle.

Convertible transportation
Buying a carriage that will later convert to a stroller will save you money, and allows you to get full use from your equipment.

A baby will quickly outgrow a cradle, so it is better to choose a crib that later converts into a youth bed. Make sure its height can be adjusted so you don't have to bend low to lift out your baby.

CHOOSING EQUIPMENT

A baby grows quickly and certain items of equipment may prove to be poor investments. Try to choose equipment that has a long life – a crib that becomes a child's bed, for example. Baby equipment is rarely worn out, simply outgrown, and there is no need to overspend on expensive items – check for secondhand items in your local paper or on bulletin boards. Seek advice from friends and family; they may also be willing to loan or give you items.

TRAVEL

You will need some form of transportation for your baby as soon as he arrives. Before you buy, think carefully about how much space you have for storage and the kind of life you lead. You can take your baby anywhere if you use a sling; with both hands free.

Carriages and strollers Your newborn baby should be transported in a carriage, where he can lie flat. A stroller in which he can lie flat may also be suitable. Although a carriage is comfortable and sturdy, you may have difficulty when storing or transporting it, or if you have to use steps. Some carriages have removable bassinets; you may find this useful. You can use the bassinet for the baby's bed, and the accompanying frame can support his bath. Later, once your baby is able to sit upright, a stroller may be more manageable. Most of these have a reclining seat that can face backward or forward.

Car seats The law requires that your child be safely restrained in a car, so buy an appropriate safety seat before taking your baby home from the hospital and check that it is securely anchored. This should not be bought secondhand, and it must meet current safety regulations.

Portable baby chair This will allow your baby to see what's happening around him. A bouncing chair will provide enjoyment when he kicks his feet.

Baby carrier
Your baby will enjoy the warmth of your body and the sound of your heartbeat when carried next to your chest.

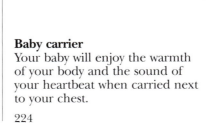

While these are easy to carry, always check that the base is wide and sturdy to prevent his tipping over, and always strap him in securely.

SLEEPING AND BATHING

At first your baby will fit snugly in a baby (Moses) basket, bassinet, or even a drawer! What you choose isn't really important as long as it is the right size and is comfortable. Choose a thin, close-fitting, waterproof mattress and cotton sheets. He should

His first bed
A baby (Moses) basket will make a snug first bed for your newborn.

not have a pillow. You can use bumpers around the insides of his bed, but make sure that there are no ribbons, ties, or fringes that your baby could put in his mouth (he may choke) or get his fingers caught in. Warm, light cotton thermal blankets are probably the best choice for bedding. Bear in mind that if your sleeping baby appears to be chilly, you shouldn't just add an extra covering as this will trap the cold air inside, making him colder. It is best to pick him up and cuddle him until he is warm, and then add an extra blanket to his bedding.

His crib Once your baby has outgrown his first bed, choose a new or secondhand crib. Make sure it is strong and sturdy and has non-toxic paint or varnish. The bars should be wide enough to allow your baby a good view but no wider than two and a half inches so he can't push his head through. Crib sides should be high enough to stop him from climbing over, and have safety catches on the drop side to prevent it from being accidentally released. As before, the mattress should be close-fitting and waterproof, with no gaps between the edges of the mattress and the frame. Bumpers will keep him from hitting the bars once he is able to roll over.

Changing There is no need to buy a baby changing table if you have a sturdy table or chest of drawers and a plastic changing mat. But if you do want to have a special changing area, opt for a changing unit that is stable with plenty of storage. Your baby can easily be bathed in a sink, but if you do choose a special bath with a stand, make sure that it is stable and at the right height.

Bathtime
Choose sturdy equipment for bathing your baby. Yellow ducks will be fun for you and visually stimulating for him.

MEETING YOUR BABY'S NEEDS

Safety should be the most important consideration when choosing equipment, as any number of items can take care of his basic needs.

• *Ties on bumpers shouldn't be too long as your baby may try to swallow them and choke. Tie them securely and trim off any excess*

• *Quilts, blankets, and bumpers should not have a fringe or anything that he can choke on*

• *Blankets must be closely woven to avoid trapping fingers and toes*

• *A baby carrier should have a neck support, and wide straps that will support your baby's weight*

• *Cribs, carriages, and strollers should not have any sharp edges or sharp screws*

• *If you buy a stroller, make sure there is adequate protection for his head*

• *There must be nothing on the stroller that will trap your baby's fingers or toes*

• *Covers should be brightly colored with vivid patterns to stimulate your baby*

ASSEMBLING A LAYETTE

Most of us over-prepare for a new baby, especially if it's our first. Babies, however, grow extremely fast, and very small garments will soon be outgrown. On the whole, it is always better to buy bigger, rather than smaller, as too close-fitting clothes will cause soreness and overheating. As babies have no idea what they are wearing, the golden rule is to keep all clothing simple and comfortable, creating fewer problems for both of you.

Choosing clothes and accessories Infant clothing is improving all the time in terms of fabric, design, and washability, so do shop around so that you can get a feel for what's available before making a final choice. You will probably never use many of the items sold, so don't waste your money. A friend or relative with a baby will be able to give advice, and maybe clothes and accessories their baby has outgrown. Don't be reluctant to accept such gifts.

You will need several sheets, stretchies, T-shirts, and receiving blankets so that you can have a few in the wash without running out. In order to prevent every stain showing, opt for patterned fabrics when choosing sheets and clothing, rather than solid pastels. Natural fibers are best as they allow sweat to evaporate, but do bear in mind that bedding or clothes with a high percentage of cotton may shrink once they are washed, so buy at least a size bigger than you think you will need. Choose T-shirts with wide necks, as babies hate having tight things pulled over their heads. Avoid any clothing with buttons or zippers that are close to the neck. Also, think what's convenient for you. Even if you prefer cloth diapers, keep a supply of disposable diapers on hand; they can be used when a quick change with minimum fuss is desired.

Don't wait until the last minute to purchase your layette; shop while you still feel comfortable enough to enjoy it.

- *Shop on more than one occasion, and ask your partner or a friend to help carry any heavy bags*

- *Color and style are irrelevant to your baby, so choose machine-washable garments with colors that will not run*

- *Don't buy too many clothes in advance, as you can't predict how fast your baby's going to grow or what the weather will be like*

- *Opt for medium-priced items from well-known stores. Cheap baby clothes fall apart at the seams, fabrics become rough and irritating, and the clothes may have to be discarded after only a few washings*

- *However, don't skimp on the number of essential items. You always need more of these than you think you do*

ESSENTIAL BABY ITEMS

1 hat: the type will depend on the season

6 cotton T-shirts with wrap fronts or envelope neck

2 plain knitted cardigans or loose sweaters

2 pairs cotton socks or slip-on booties

2 receiving blankets

6 stretchies

scratch mittens

6 pairs of plastic pants

1 box smallest-size disposable diapers or 2 dozen cloth diapers and 1 package diaper liners

2 diaper pails

2 soft new towels

8 bird's-eye diapers

small washcloths and cotton balls

baby lotion

1 package diaper pins

blunt-edged scissors

diaper cream

CHOOSING YOUR BABY'S CLOTHING

Choosing clothes for your baby can seem like a daunting task when entering a store for the first time as there are so many items to choose from. Just remember to be practical in your choices, taking into consideration some of the points that I have outlined below.

Garments should not have ribbons or lacy patterns that will catch fingers

Outdoor wear
When choosing clothing for outdoors your first priority is warmth. Don't be distracted by color or fashion. Be aware that his head, feet, and hands are vulnerable to the cold, and keep them covered.

Stretchies are ideal for keeping baby warm all over; snaps in the crotch and inside leg will make diaper changing easy

Nightie should be long enough for warmth, with a wide opening

Going to bed
Babies move around during their sleep – not as much as adults but it's something to consider. Choose clothing that will allow free movement and not entangle his limbs.

YOUR BABY'S NEEDS

Comfort and safety, rather than style, should be the main priorities when you choose your baby's clothing.

• *Fabrics should be soft and machine-washable. Cotton is ideal. Synthetics don't always absorb sweat, and wool can irritate a newborn baby's skin*

• *In warm weather 2 layers are usually ample. In winter add more layers, but do not overwrap him with tight clothes*

• *A baby's gestures are jerky and expansive so make sure garments are loose and easily stretched*

Envelope-neck T-shirt should be made of soft cotton or thermal material

Socks or booties should be soft and spacious

MOTHER'S
EXPERIENCE

Unless there are good reasons, breastfeeding is always preferable to bottlefeeding.

Breastfeeding *This ensures that your baby is getting the ideal food; breast milk is always available when needed, and doesn't require special equipment or preparation. Breastfeeding is also physically beneficial for you: for instance, it helps your uterus return quickly to its normal size – and like many women – you may find it a hugely enjoyable experience.*

While breastfeeding has a few drawbacks, these can be overcome easily. The quantity and quality of your milk depend on your overall health, so you must eat well and take care to remain in good condition. Breastfeeding can lead to sore nipples or breast infections (see p.334), which should be treated promptly. Also it can be quite tiring, so it is important to get sufficient rest.

Bottlefeeding *Infant formulas are very nourishing, but they are still only second-best to breast milk, they can prove expensive and, if you take your baby out for any length of time, you have to carry equipment and a supply of formula with you.*

BREAST OR BOTTLE?

Breastfeeding is better for your baby than bottlefeeding. However, the choice between breastfeeding or bottlefeeding may not be an easy one: both have many advantages.

The best possible preparation for breastfeeding is to acquaint yourself with the very real benefits that it offers (see below). Then, make sure that you are aware of what is involved, and that you are physically and mentally ready for it. The physical preparations that you can make are quite simple and straightforward and consist mainly of being well-nourished, avoiding hazards that could affect your milk supply, and making sure your breasts are properly looked after. Your midwife, doctor, obstetrician, or childbirth teacher can answer any questions you might have.

If you decide on bottlefeeding (see pp.308 & 310), you will have to buy supplies of formula, bottles and nipples, and sterilizing equipment in advance of the birth.

BREASTFEEDING

Breast milk is the perfect food for a baby. It contains all the essential nutrients (fat, protein, carbohydrate, vitamins, and iron) that the baby needs; it is never too rich or too watery; it is clean, readily available, and always at the right temperature; and, like the colostrum produced by your breasts before your milk comes in (see **Producing milk**, p.304), it contains antibodies that help protect the baby from common infections such as gastroenteritis.

Breastfeeding is a fulfilling and enjoyable experience that will enhance the loving relationship between you and your baby. Despite occasional snags, such as sore nipples or engorged breasts, it is physically beneficial. The extra calories you use up in producing breast milk help to deplete the fat reserves you accumulated during pregnancy, and so it is easier for you to get back to your pre-pregnant weight. When you breastfeed, the hormone oxytocin that makes your milk glands contract when your baby suckles (see p.304) also causes contractions in your uterus, enabling it to return to its normal size more quickly.

There is also some evidence that women who have breastfed are less prone to breast cancer and to osteoporosis (brittle bones). From a purely practical point of view, breastfeeding is quick, easy, and convenient, virtually free, and needs no special equipment.

However, breastfeeding does have some drawbacks: until you have a well-established milk supply that enables you to collect and store some for later feeding by bottle (see p.305), you are the only person who can feed your baby. If you prefer privacy when breastfeeding, it may not be easy to find away from home.

Breastfeeding can lead to sore or cracked nipples and other breast problems (see p.334); illness, tiredness, worry, and menstruation can reduce your milk supply; if you are taking any medication or drugs while breastfeeding, these can pass into your milk and possibly cause harm to your baby, while some foods that you eat, such as oranges, may upset your baby's stomach.

Most problems and difficulties you may have in getting your baby to breastfeed tend to occur in the first couple of weeks. So if you find breastfeeding trying at first, stick with it for a while – once the initial difficulties have passed, you will probably find that it is easy, immensely rewarding, and enjoyable.

BOTTLEFEEDING

Although modern infant formula provides adequate nourishment for the baby (as you can see from the chart below), it contains none of the protective antibodies found in colostrum and breast milk. It is also more difficult to digest than breast milk (but because of this, your baby will need feeding less frequently); gives more formed bowel movements with a stronger smell than those of a breastfed baby; may lay the foundation for a milk allergy later on; preparing it is time-consuming; and you may find it harder to lose weight because you are not using up calories in producing milk. You have to buy the equipment and the formula, and if you go out you have to take a supply of made-up formula with you.

COMPARISON OF MILKS AND FORMULAS

Nutrient (per 100 milliliters)	Human milk	Cow's milk formula	Soy-based formula
Energy (kcal)	68	66	65
Fat (g)	3.8	3.7	3.6
Protein (g)	1.25	1.45	1.8
Carbohydrate (g)	7.2	7.22	6.9
Vitamin A (mg)	60	80	60
Vitamin D (mg)	0.025	1.0	1.0
Vitamin C (mg)	3.7	6.8	5.5
Iron (mg)	0.07	0.58	0.67

BABY'S EXPERIENCE

Your baby will derive great pleasure from being breastfed and breast milk is specifically designed to give her the best start in life.

Breast milk *Nutritionally superior to formula, breast milk is easy to digest and, like colostrum, confers useful protection against many common infections, particularly those of the gastrointestinal and respiratory tracts. Even if you only breastfeed for the first few weeks, the antibodies in your colostrum and milk will be of great benefit to your baby, and the close contact between you will enhance your relationship.*

Formula *Should you be unable to breastfeed, your baby will, of course, thrive and grow on formula. Whenever you are bottlefeeding your baby, give her lots of skin and eye contact, and talk or sing to her to help intensify the bonding between you.*

Creating intimacy
As you bottlefeed your baby, keep your attention focused on her. Maintain eye contact, and smile and talk to her.

NAMING TRADITIONS

Around the world, the names given to children reflect the heritage and traditions of the country in which they are born. Parents from Eastern countries typically combine word elements to create meaningful names for their children or use nouns and adjectives for names.

Chinese *These children typically bear three names, the first being the family name, the second usually being a "generation name" that is shared by all the children in the family, the third being their individual name. The middle and last names are typically words with good connotations. Qiong or Chiang (strong), Tai (peace, healthy), and Wen (scholar) are common boys' names; Mei (beautiful), Shu (good), and Ying (flower) are popular choices for girls.*

Muslim *Their names are mainly descriptive words. Boys' names include Bakr (young camel), Ghayth (rain), and Salim (safe, secure). Girls' names are Fatin (charming), Nahla (a drink of water), and Sabah (morning). Names linked to the Prophet, Muhammed, such as the boys' names Abd-Allah (servant of Allah), Mahmud, and Ahmad (to praise), and for girls, Aisha (the Prophet's favorite wife) and Fatima (his favorite daughter) are popular. Pre-Islamic names such as Adnan for a boy and Lubna for a girl remain popular because of literary influences.*

Indian *Both Hindu and Sikh children often bear names that have religious meanings or connotations, such as the girls' name Gita (singing praises), or the boys' name Indra (the name of the Vedic deity of the sky and atmosphere). Combined word elements are also used.*

THE GIFT OF A NAME

Naming your baby can be surprisingly difficult. After all, there are so many things for you to consider – will the chosen name go with the family name, are the initials suitable, will the name you have chosen go out of fashion and therefore date your child? Many different associations and considerations may influence you, but you should always bear in mind that the name you choose is for your baby, and hopefully it will please him or her throughout the whole of his or her life.

FASHION

This is something that influences a great many parents, either consciously or unconsciously. You may worry that the name you choose will be too popular, which may mean that your child knows many others who share her name and always has to use her surname as well as her first name for identification purposes; or you may want to give her a remarkable name that will stand out.

Popularity A name that suddenly becomes highly popular, such as Tracy or Jason in recent times, is in danger of falling out of fashion equally suddenly, thus dating the child who bears it. It is very difficult to predict which names will become the "in" names in any given year, although some remain perennial favorites and many parents define what is fashionable or unfashionable by their own social set. Lists of names could be provided by the local government, your church, or synagogue. The *Guinness Book of Names* gives lists of the most popular names in America, Britain, and Australia over the past century. The book also refers to a central stock of 100 names from which are taken the vast majority (approximately 90 percent) of the names given to children born in any given year (see also p.234).

Traditional or modern? Whether you prefer old-fashioned or newly coined names will depend on the sort of person you are. Some people prefer names that are old, familiar, and somehow respectable and shrink from new, invented, or imported names; others see no reason to use fossilized names from the past, and choose names that are meaningful to them and part of the age in which they live. Both points of view are equally valid, although traditional names are often easier for people to spell and pronounce. Some parents look well beyond currently popular names to established names that are not much used today, and old-fashioned names, such as Henry, Arthur, Maisie, and Alice, are slowly making their reappearance.

ASSOCIATIONS

Given names are often the result of association, rather than being chosen because of their meaning. Meaning tends to play a much smaller role in the Western world than it does in other parts of the world (see column, left).

Personal associations These are usually private and can have a positive or negative influence. Family, friends, or someone you respect may provide a name; someone you dislike, a badly behaved child, or someone whose name is very much theirs is a name to reject. Relatives are sometimes honored, and some parents choose the names of public personalities such as TV characters (Krystle, Brenda, Michael, Brandon), pop singers (LaToya, Madonna, Harry), or film stars (Julia, Meg, Kevin, Ryan).

Fictional associations The characters in books and films are a primary source of inspiration for parents. The 1956 film *High Society* starred Grace Kelly as Tracy Samantha Lord, which led to a surge in popularity for Grace, and the use of Tracy, Samantha, and Kelly as first names for girls.

Another spectacular rise in usage was that of the name Jennifer, which came from nowhere to be the second-most popular girl's name in 1970, following the film success of Love Story earlier the same year. Hit songs, such as Michelle and Sweet Caroline, have also led to surges in popularity for these particular names.

Verbal associations Some names carry undesirable verbal associations, such as Dick and Willie, while the use of "the john" for the lavatory may be a factor in the decline of John's popularity as a first name, although it remains a popular choice for a middle name. Other names sound temptingly close to words (Sophia – sofa), which may then get used as nicknames.

Character associations Most people carry in their minds an individual idea or picture for every given name in their particular society. The name Fred, for example, probably conjures up a very different image from the name Barnabas, and people often, consciously or unconsciously, expect children to fit or suit their names. As this probably influences the way in which each child is treated, and therefore how each child responds, children may well grow into their names.

Other names, such as Patience or Grace, can reflect a desire for the child (usually female) to manifest a particular virtue and were first introduced by the Puritans (see column, right). They are often misnomers – Patience who hates to wait for anything, Grace who has a tendency to be clumsy.

Incidental associations Some first names are inspired by incidents that happen at conception, during pregnancy, or around the time of birth. These can include the place of conception or birth; the time of birth (Noël or Natalie for a Christmas baby; month names

NAMING FASHIONS

There are trends in name-giving just as there are in other things. Many of today's first names have been used for centuries.

Norman *After their conquest of Britain in 1066, the Normans introduced a fixed name system. Norman names included Alan, Henry, Hugh, Ralph, Roger, Richard, Oliver, William, Alice, Emma, Laura, Rosamund, and Yvonne. These names were given to the aristocracy; later they were copied by those lower on the social scale, so that Norman names rapidly replaced most Old English names. Of the latter, some, such as Edward and Edith, have survived.*

Biblical *During the 16th century, many names were used primarily by Catholics. These included Mary, and saints' names such as Sebastian, Benedict, and Agnes. The Protestants turned to the Bible for inspiration and Adam, Benjamin, David, Jonathan, Joshua, Michael, Samuel, Abigail, Dinah, Hannah, Rachel, Ruth, and Sarah became popular. The Puritans in the 17th century produced the "virtue" names – Faith, Charity, Grace, Hope, Patience, and Prudence.*

Victorian *At the end of the 19th century, there was a vogue for using gemstones or flowers as first names for girls. Thus Amber, Pearl, Ruby, Daisy, Poppy, and Rose, became popular. Sometimes, all the girls in a family would bear the name of a flower or gem.*

Contemporary *This century saw the rise of exotic spellings, such as Jayne, Nikki, Debra, and of combinations, such as Raelene and Charlene. Since the 1960s, many descriptive words, such as Sky, Free, Rainbow, and River, have been given as first names.*

NAMING
TWINS

There is a tradition of giving twins names that are related. The names may reflect an association; begin with the same initial (Paul, Patricia); sound alike (Suzanna, Hannah); or have a similar rhythm (Benjamin, Jonathan).

However, there are lots of reasons why your twins will not thank you if their names are too closely associated for comfort.

First, and most important, people will be much more likely to get them confused if there is a strong link between their names. Names are used as labels and twins, perhaps more than other children, need individual labels that belong solely to them.

Second, official forms, examination papers, and letters can easily become confused, especially if initials are shared.

Third, if the names are closely linked by association, they are likely to come in for a lot of name teasing or punning.

such as May, June, or occasionally Octavia for an October birth; Dawn or Eve for the actual time of birth); the weather (Gail, Storm); a favorite record played during pregnancy, at or after birth; the baby's appearance (Sophie – "wise one") or her type of arrival (Margaret is sometimes bestowed following a particularly difficult birth as St.Margaret is the patron saint of childbirth; Zoë – "life" – may be used under similar circumstances).

FAMILY TRADITIONS

Names that have passed down through a family from generation to generation have long been the automatic choice, especially for a first-born. If the traditional name was masculine, it was sometimes feminized for a girl (Thomas, Thomasina), especially if there was no male heir. In recent times, however, these customs have lapsed, with many traditional family names being dropped, although they are sometimes used as the middle name.

Maiden names Some families, particularly in the English aristocracy, Scotland, and the American South, used the mother's maiden name as the first-born son's given name. This appears to be dying out, although the maiden name is still used as a middle name. This tradition has resulted in the transferral of surnames (Russell, Howard, Cameron) to first-name usage, particularly for boys.

Siblings Many parents choose names for their children that work together, although few go as far as the Victorians (see **Naming fashions**, p.231). Some parents like all their children's names to start with the same initial, although this can cause confusion with letters and official documents.

INITIALS

Whether the initials of your child's name make up a viable word, or not, may be of special concern to you. In some cultures, parents like to make a meaningful word from their child's initials. However, if a word is created, it will often be used as, or as a starting point for, a nickname, which may or may not be desirable.

NATIONALITY

Many parents choose names that reflect their own nationality, as separate from their country of residence. This can lead to problems of spelling and pronunciation, so the usage may be restricted to middle names, or the spelling may be simplified – from Gaelic to English, for example (Síle – Sheila; Aodán – Aidan). In other cases, "national" first names may not be used in their country of origin. Colleen, for example, comes from the Celtic word *caitlín*, meaning "girl" or "wench." It is popular in the US and Australia, although it is not actually used as a given name in Ireland.

MEANINGS

The meaning or origin of a name tends to be a secondary factor for most modern Western parents. Many Western first names have had a more convoluted history than those of other cultures. This is because these names, along with other traditions and customs, have been transferred from one society to another, often by invasion followed by integration, migration, or intercultural contact. Consequently, many names, particularly those of dead or obscure languages, have become divorced from their original meanings. However, some Western parents do still choose names primarily because of their meanings.

FORM OF A NAME

The way our names are pronounced and spelled, and the shortened forms we prefer, are very important to us. It is extremely irritating if your name is constantly misspelled or mispronounced, and it can be very annoying if someone uses a short version you don't like, or the formal version that wasn't actually bestowed.

Diminutives The pet forms of names (Megan, Kate, Jamie) are often used, and sometimes given, in preference to the full versions (Margaret, Katherine, James). However, even if you intend always to use the diminutive, it is worth considering bestowing the formal name since there are likely to be occasions when the more dignified version is appropriate. On the other hand, if you intend always to use the full version of a name (Patricia, Edward) it is as well to consider the pet forms (Pat, Patty, Patsy, Trish, Tricia; Ed, Eddie, Ted, Ned) as your child's name will almost certainly be shortened by his or her friends. If you dislike all, or some, of the pet forms, you may consider avoiding the name altogether, or occasionally using your preference in order to influence your child's choice of a shortened form.

Sound You may be particularly attracted to a name because of its sound. Some names are inherently harmonious, while others appear particularly amusing to most people's ears. Another consideration is the sound of a first name alongside the middle and surnames. Most parents take particular care to select a happy partnership, with surnames balanced by given names. Indeed, some parents bestow names in the order they feel sounds best (Elizabeth Anne, Arthur James), but use the middle name (Anne, James) as the primary form of address.

Spelling and pronunciation A name that everyone can spell and pronounce is a good idea in order to avoid confusion and irritation for your child in later life. In the latter half of the 20th century, there has been a vogue for exotic spellings of ordinary first names (Jayne, Kathryn, Jonothon), which may confer no discernible advantage. Some names have more than one pronunciation (Helena), while others are confusing (Phoebe) and still others have more than one commonly used spelling (Clare, Claire; Jeffrey, Geoffrey).

YOUR CHILD'S NAME

Here are a few points that you should bear in mind when choosing a first name for your newborn baby.

- *Will the name be suitable for your child at all stages throughout his or her life?*

- *Is it obvious how the name is spelled and pronounced?*

- *Does the name sound right when put together with the middle name(s) and your surname?*

- *Will the initials of the full name make a word when they are put together?*

- *Are you happy with any associations that may be apparent?*

- *Is there any way in which your child might be teased as a result of the name that you have chosen?*

NAMES, NAMES, NAMES

Every year there appears to be a central stock of girls' and boys' names in each Western country from which the vast majority of given names are chosen. Although it is impossible to predict which

Many names are shared between countries, but their popularity varies. Girls' names are more likely than boys' to come from outside the central stock.

USA

1	Ashley	6	Megan
2	Jessica	7	Jennifer
3	Amanda	8	Nicole
4	Sarah	9	Stephanie
5	Brittany	10	Katherine

UK

1	Emma	6	Rebecca
2	Sarah	7	Gemma
3	Laura	8	Katherine
4	Charlotte	9	Lauren
5	Amy	10	Hayley

AUSTRALIA

1	Jessica	6	Ashleigh
2	Sarah	7	Amy
3	Emma	8	Emily
4	Lauren	9	Kate
5	Rebecca	10	Katherine

NAME	ORIGIN
Amanda	Latin, meaning "lovable"
Amy	Old French, meaning "beloved"; French original is Aimée
Ashley	Old English surname, meaning "ash wood clearing"
Charlotte	French feminine form of Charles – "a man" (Old German)
Cla(i)re	Latin, meaning "clear, bright"
Danielle	French feminine form of Daniel – "God has judged"
Elizabeth	Hebrew, meaning "God is my oath"
Emily	Latin, from the name of a noble Roman family, Aemilius
Emma	Old German, meaning "whole, entire, universal"
Gemma	Italian, meaning "gem." Sometimes spelled Jemma
Hannah	Hebrew, meaning "He has favored me"
Hayley	Old English surname meaning "hay meadow"
Helen(a)	Greek, meaning "the bright one"
Jennifer	Old Cornish, form of Guinevere – "white, soft" (Welsh)
Jessica	Hebrew, meaning "God beholds"
Katherine	Greek, meaning "pure." Catherine is the French form
Kelly	From the Irish surname, meaning "warlike"
Laura/en	Female forms of Lawrence – "laurel" (Latin)
Louise/a	Female forms of Louis – "famous warrior" (Old German)
Lucy	English form of Lucia – "light" (Latin)
Margaret	Greek, meaning "a pearl." Megan is a pet form (Welsh)
Michelle	Female form of Michael – "Who is like the Lord?" (Hebrew)
Natalie	From the Latin, particularly meaning "Christ's birthday"
Nicole/a	Female forms of Nicholas – "victory of the people" (Greek)
Rebecca	Hebrew, meaning "faithful wife"
Ruth	Hebrew, possibly meaning "vision of beauty"
Samantha	Female form of Samuel – "heard by God" (Hebrew)
Sara(h)	Hebrew, meaning "princess"
Sophie	Greek, meaning "wise one." Sophia is another form
Stephanie	French feminine form of Stephen – "crown" (Greek)
Victoria	Female form of Victor – "victory" (Latin)
Zoë	Greek, meaning "life"

names will be in the top one hundred, some names could be described as perennials, retaining their popularity year after year (Sarah, Thomas), while others are annuals, enjoying an intense period of popularity before lapsing into relative obscurity again (Sharon, Darren). Below we have a selection of some of the most popular names in English-speaking countries in 1990.

Name	Origin
Adam	*Hebrew, meaning "red earth"*
Adrian	*Latin, meaning "man from Adria"*
Alexander	*Greek, meaning "defender of men"*
Andrew	*Greek, meaning "manly"*
Ant(h)ony	*Latin, from the name of a Roman family, Antonius*
Benjamin	*Hebrew, meaning "son of the right hand"*
Christopher	*Greek, meaning "bearing Christ"*
Daniel	*Hebrew, meaning "God has judged"*
David	*Hebrew, meaning "beloved"*
Edward	*Old English, meaning "rich guardian"*
James	*Originally Hebrew. Unclear meaning. Jamie is a pet form*
Jason	*Greek, meaning "to heal"*
John/Jack	*Hebrew, meaning "God is gracious"*
Jonathan	*Hebrew, meaning "God has given"*
Joseph	*Hebrew, meaning "God shall add (another son)"*
Joshua	*Hebrew, meaning "God is generous/salutation"*
Luke	*Middle English, meaning "man from Lucania"*
Mark	*Latin, possibly from Mars, the Roman god of war*
Matthew	*Hebrew, meaning "gift of God"*
Michael	*Hebrew, meaning "Who is like the Lord?"*
Nathan	*Hebrew, meaning "gift"*
Nicholas	*Greek, meaning "victory of the people"*
Oliver	*From Olaf – "remains of his ancestors"*
Paul	*Latin, meaning "small"*
Richard	*Old German, meaning "strong ruler"*
Robert	*Old German, meaning "fame bright"*
Ryan	*Irish surname, possibly meaning "red" or "king"*
Samuel	*Hebrew, meaning "heard by God"*
Scott	*Old English surname meaning "a Scot"*
Stephen	*Greek, meaning "crown"*
Thomas	*Aramaic, meaning "twin"*
William	*Old German meaning "will/desire, helmet/protection"*

TOP TEN BOYS' NAMES IN 1990 *

The popularity of boys' names stays fairly constant from country to country. Boys are more often named from within the central stock than girls.

USA

1	Michael	6	Daniel
2	Christopher	7	Justin
3	Matthew	8	David
4	Joshua	9	Ryan
5	Andrew	10	John

UK

1	Daniel	6	Thomas
2	Matthew	7	David
3	James	8	Luke
4	Christopher	9	Jamie
5	Adam	10	Robert

AUSTRALIA

1	Matthew	6	James
2	Daniel	7	Samuel
3	Michael	8	Nicholas
4	Thomas	9	Joshua
5	Benjamin	10	Christopher

* Taken from the Guinness Book of Names by Leslie Dunkling.

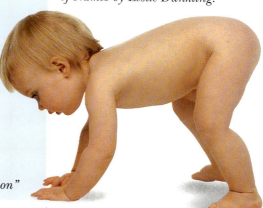

FATHER CARE

In many households, the father becomes the main helper when his partner arrives home with their new baby. Some men immediately involve themselves in caring for their partner and child, but others need to be prompted into action.

What you need from your partner more than anything else at this time is understanding, sympathy, and a readiness to let his routine relax and go along with you and the baby. This needs serious discussion, before the baby is born. Otherwise your partner may find it hard to adapt and could feel neglected, inadequate, and bereft of your affection and attention.

You may find it useful to divide up the work between you. For instance, your partner could take over the cleaning, shopping, and laundry, leaving you free to concentrate on looking after yourself and the baby. Or you could simply share all the house-hold and child care work.

Help at mealtimes
If you are breastfeeding, express milk into a bottle (see p.305) so that your partner can also enjoy the pleasure of feeding the baby.

ARRANGING CHILD CARE

During the last weeks of pregnancy, it's a good idea for you and your partner to spend some time discussing and planning how you are going to run your domestic routine once you settle down at home with your new child. If your partner is able and willing to play a full part, you should be able to cope without too much difficulty; if not, you should get someone in to help you, especially for the first few weeks.

The first few days of motherhood will be harder than you think. Labor and birth are physically and emotionally draining; you will feel you have very few reserves, and you will be very fatigued. You will realize, once you are home with your baby, that one job or activity succeeds another almost without respite, and in the middle of all this activity you are still learning about being a mother. Even if you read every baby book going, you will find that your baby conforms to no typical schedule or plan, and that you have to work out your life around your baby's routine. It is a mistake to try to impose a routine on your baby, and it will only cause you more work; you have to take your lead from him. As far as your sleep is concerned, you have to get it when you can – new babies don't know night from day and they require the same attention during the night as they do during the day.

SOURCES OF HELP

Unless you want to become extremely tired, even depressed and weepy, you will need some help to tide you over at least the first few days with your baby, and preferably the first week or two. Don't be too proud to ask for or accept help – if you are reticent, you may soon come to regret it. Having someone help out does not mean that you are in any way inadequate as a mother. The best possible solution is some live-in help, so that your day can be split into shifts. That way you can at least make sure you get sufficient rest and pay attention to your diet.

Family and friends Your mother and mother-in-law are probably the people you trust most in the world when it comes to child care. They have had children and are experienced at looking after babies, and they will give you lots of helpful support and advice. A good idea would be to get one of them, or a sister or other relative, or a good friend to come and live in your house around the time you go into labor. That way she can establish herself in your home with your family and partner, and be ready to receive you when you come home with the baby.

Such a helper is invaluable. You will feel confident that your household is running normally. She should take all the administration off your shoulders and see to meals, laundry, shopping, and so on. This can take some of the responsibility away from your partner, so you can devote more time to yourself and your baby. In addition, if your helper has had children of her own, she can be a fountain of information and advice.

Au pairs   Another option is to take in an au pair – a young woman (very occasionally a young man), often from another country, who works for room and board plus a small stipend. Although this option is less expensive than hiring a trained nanny, remember that most au pairs have no training in child care. Be sure to go through an established au pair program, and apply well in advance of your baby's birth. Most agencies will require a fee, and there may be a limit on how long the au pair can stay in the country.

Nannies   If you decide that you would like a nanny, try to arrange for her to be settled in with your family before the baby is born. Having a newborn baby in the house is quite a traumatic event, and it would be even more difficult to start out with a nanny who is irritating, unfriendly, or unprepared to follow your routine.

Again, use a reliable agency, and expect to pay a fee. (Word-of-mouth can also be a valuable resource, especially if you have a friend whose children are outgrowing their nanny.) Trained nannies are more expensive than au pairs, but they should be experienced in the care of infants and young children. Before hiring, interview applicants at least twice.

A good nanny will have strong views about raising children, but she must be prepared to bend her usual practices to fit in with yours. It would be pointless to hire someone who is a strict disciplinarian if you want your children to be brought up in a liberal manner. If that is what you want, there are some very flexible nannies who will be able to strike the right balance between discipline and freedom.

If you can, draw up some kind of employment contract in which the most important approaches, attitudes, and jobs that you require are carefully and clearly laid out; make it plain that dismissal may follow if your instructions are not adhered to.

Day care   An increasingly popular option, many day-care centers and home-based day-care providers will accept infants as young as six weeks old. Economic realities force more and more women back to work soon after the baby's birth; far-flung families mean a weaker support system for new parents. If you must find day care for an infant, try to make the best of the situation. There are many excellent facilities where your baby will be well cared for and nurtured. Word-of-mouth is by far the best recommendation for day care; also look for an open-door policy, trained caregivers, a good ratio of children to staff, and a clean, bright, cheerful atmosphere. Try to find a place where you would like to spend your days. Ask for references and check them.

BABY NURSES

If you want short-term, live-in help, you can hire a baby nurse. She will join your household just before or after the baby is born and will help you with all of the baby care.

As well as providing welcome help with the baby, baby nurses are invaluable teachers. They will show you how to see to your baby's daily care: how to change diapers; how to breast- or bottlefeed him, how to know when your baby's had enough, and how to take the baby carefully off your breast to avoid soreness and cracked nipples, for example.

However, it's up to you and your baby nurse to work out what kind of schedule you would like. You may decide, for instance, that you wish to have a night's sleep without any interruption; the nurse will be on duty all the way through the night but you will take over at, say, 7 a.m. so that she can get some rest. Later on in the day, she would be responsible for the baby's laundry, preparation of formula, keeping the nursery clean, and looking after all the baby's needs and some of yours.

As a rule, a baby nurse does not stay with you for more than 4 weeks, but you can arrange for her to stay longer if your finances allow it. Baby nurses are expensive but will get you off to a good start if there is no one else to help.

GETTING ENOUGH SLEEP

A good night's sleep is one of your top priorities in the late stages of pregnancy.

Aim to get 8 hours of sleep per night, but you may suffer from irritating insomnia because, although your metabolism slows down at night, your baby's does not. It keeps hammering away all through the night hours. If you cannot sleep, there are a number of ways in which you can alleviate the problem:

• A warm bath before going to bed is very relaxing and makes you sleepy and tranquil

• A hot milky drink at bedtime will help you drop off, and you can also induce sleep by reading a calming book, listening to music or the radio, or watching television

• Deep breathing and relaxation exercises are excellent treatments for insomnia, so find a bedtime routine that you can rely on

• Instead of worrying about your lack of sleep, get up in the middle of the night and do something – perhaps a job that you've been putting off for some time – or go into the nursery, look at things, touch them, rearrange them, and feel happy at the prospect of your soon-to-arrive baby

• If you have any worries that are stopping you from sleeping, visualize each one as being written on a piece of paper. Then mentally crumple it up and throw it away

THE LATE STAGES OF PREGNANCY

Very little goes wrong in the last few weeks of pregnancy. From week 32 onward, your doctor's main concern is the continued growth of the baby and the maintenance of your health. Threats to your well-being could occur with an increase in blood pressure, which might herald preeclampsia (see p.204), or cessation of weight gain, suggesting that your baby isn't growing. Your doctor or midwife will want to see you at two-week intervals between weeks 32 and 36, and then weekly between weeks 36 and 40.

One of the aspects of later pregnancy that you may be most concerned about is your comfort. As your abdomen gets larger, sitting or lying in your usual positions becomes uncomfortable. If you lie flat on your back, the weight of your growing baby will press down on the major blood vessels and nerves that lie against the spine, causing numbness and tingling pain, and even dizziness and shortness of breath. Pay attention to your sleeping position in bed and make sure that you can be comfortable. Sometimes you will need cushions or soft pillows to support your body (see below).

TENSE-AND-RELAX TECHNIQUE

Good relaxation techniques combine the release of tension in the mind and body with deep, regular breathing, and it is helpful to practice these techniques so that toward the end of pregnancy they are second nature.

A good way to relax your body is to use the tense-and-relax technique. This is a pleasant aid to relaxation during pregnancy, and good preparation for labor, when it is a great help to be able to relax most of the muscles in your body, so that your uterus contracts without the rest of your body tensing.

Resting on your back
If you can't rest lying on your side, prop yourself up with plenty of cushions or pillows.

The technique involves the tensing and relaxing of different parts of your body in sequence. Your partner can help by touching you where he can see you are tensing up: you respond to his touch by relaxing. It is best to practice this drill twice a day for 15–20 minutes if you can. Practice before meals or an hour or more after eating.

Sitting on the floor
This position, with your back straight, shoulders back, and legs apart, is good for your spine, inner thighs, and groin.

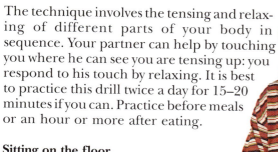

Find a comfortable position lying on your back or propped up with cushions. Close your eyes. Try to clear your mind of any stressful thoughts and anxieties by breathing in and out slowly and regularly and concentrating all your attention on your breathing actions. Let pleasant thoughts flow through your head, and if any worrying thought tries to recur, prevent it from doing so by saying "no" under your breath. Return to concentrating on your deep breathing. When your mind is relaxed and your breathing deep and regular, begin the tense-and-relax routine. Think about your right hand: tense it for a moment, palm upward, then relax it and tell it to feel heavy and warm. Work up through the right side of your body, tensing and relaxing your forearm, upper arm, and shoulder. Then repeat the process on the upper left side of your body. Roll your knees outward, and tense and relax your buttocks, thighs, calves, and feet. Press your lower back gently into the floor or cushions, then release and relax.

Finally, relax the muscles of your head and neck. Keep the muscles of your face, eyes, and forehead relaxed, and smooth away any frowns.

Sitting in a chair
When you sit in a chair, sitting up straight will help strengthen your back muscles. If you need extra support, put a cushion at the small of your back.

As a baby reaches full maturity at about 37 weeks, he becomes heavier and tips head-down. Some babies, however, remain breech (see p.281) until term.

If a baby is in the breech position at term, he may be delivered by Caesarean section (see p.284). If your baby is breech in the last weeks of pregnancy, though, you can be reassured that he will probably turn himself before labor actually begins:

- *30% of babies are breech at 30 weeks. More than half will turn around spontaneously during the next 2 weeks*

- *14% of babies are still breech at 32 weeks. There is a 60% chance that a baby that is bottom-down will turn of his own accord before labor starts*

- *Less than 5% of babies are still breech at 37 weeks. A quarter of these will turn on their own, although this is less likely if the legs are extended or there isn't much room in the uterus – for instance, because it is a multiple pregnancy, or the baby is large*

- *A few babies will kick themselves around once labor starts, as long as there is room*

*Although you can make most
of your preparations well in
advance, you will still have a
few things to take care of at the
last minute.*

*When you go into labor (see
p.250), you should:*

*• Call your birth attendant
(midwife or doctor)*

*• Make contact with your partner
or birth assistant*

*• Get in touch with whoever is
going to care for your other
children, if it is not your partner*

• Check that the room is ready

*• Check that your labor aids are
conveniently on hand*

• Make yourself a hot, sweet drink

PREPARING FOR A HOME BIRTH

*When you opt for a home birth, your midwife will give you
detailed advice on the preparations you need to make. Think
about what you will need for a home birth about four weeks in
advance of your due date so that you do not have to rush
around getting everything organized at the last minute, and
you are at least partly prepared if your baby comes early.*

ADVANCE PREPARATIONS

Your bedroom, or whichever room you intend to give birth in,
should be arranged so that it is convenient and comfortable for you.
Put the bed at right angles to the wall, with plenty of space on each
side so that the midwife or doctor has easy access.

Protection Whether you deliver your baby
onto the floor or the bed, the area below and
immediately around you will need to be protected during the birth. In order to do this,
make sure that you have some old clean sheets,
towels, and plastic sheeting to hand so that it
can be put down when the time comes.

Plastic sheeting is available from your local
hardware store, although an old shower
curtain or plastic tablecloth would be fine
to use instead.

Advance preparations
Try to prepare every-
thing you will need
well in advance.

Facilities for your midwife Ideally your attendant will have a small side table or a serving cart next to the bed on which to put her instruments and other equipment, although a couple of tea trays will do, and a bright, adjustable reading lamp so that she can direct light onto your perineum. A flashlight (with spare batteries and bulb) would be useful to have on hand in case of a power outage.

You should also make sure that you stock up on food and drink in the few days before you are due. When you do this, remember that you will need food not only for yourself, your partner, and your other children (if you have any), but also for your attendants and for any visitors you may be expecting.

WHEN LABOR STARTS

When your contractions are coming every 15 minutes, are about one minute long, and don't fade away when you move around, telephone your midwife according to your arrangements. It is common for first labors to take a while to get going so, although your midwife will want to know that labor has started, she is likely to advise you try and relax and get some rest until you are in full labor because it is important to conserve your energy.

Final preparations Make sure everything else that you and the midwife will need, for the birth and immediately afterward, is prepared and ready at hand – including your comfort aids (see p.244), bowls for washing, a bedpan (or a clean bucket), clean towels, and large plastic bags for the soiled sheets, sanitary pads, and used dressings. Then put out a clean nightgown or large T-shirt for yourself, air your baby's clothes, and prepare her crib.

Your midwife Her delivery equipment will include a sphygmomanometer to take blood pressure; Pinnard stethoscope or sonicaid (see column, p.161); urine-testing sticks; local anesthetic and syringes; scissors; suture material; mucus extractor; resuscitation equipment; intravenous equipment, in case of bleeding; medication. If you wish to have access to pain-relieving drugs she will give you a prescription in advance.

Unexpected hospitalization With the help of a skilled midwife or doctor, home birth is usually completely safe for both you and your baby. But, as is also the case with hospital births, there can be complications, and if a serious problem arises you might have to go to the hospital instead of giving birth at home. Should that happen, your midwife or doctor will accompany you, and your partner should quickly pack a bag with your labor aids and another with nightgowns and other items that will be needed in the hospital. Being unable to give birth at home, after all your preparation and anticipation, can be bitterly disappointing, but if you and your partner consider and discuss the possibility in advance it will be easier to cope with if it happens. It is better to tell yourself that you are going to start labor at home and see how it goes before deciding where your baby will actually be born.

WHEN NOT TO HAVE A HOME BIRTH

It is widely believed to be as safe to give birth at home as it is in a hospital, but in certain circumstances a hospital birth is your only option.

There are a number of factors that can make a hospital birth essential. Some, such as diabetes, will mean that you have to plan on a hospital delivery; others, such as abruptio placentae, will mean that you have to abandon your plans for a home birth and go immediately to a hospital. The factors that rule out a home birth include:

- *When you have had complications in previous pregnancies*

- *When your pelvis is too small for your baby's head to pass through it*

- *When your baby is presenting in a position other than the head-down (vertex) position*

- *When you have a medical problem that puts you, your baby, or both of you at risk, such as: high blood pressure; anemia; diabetes; excess amniotic fluid; active herpes; placenta previa; abruptio placentae; preeclampsia; eclampsia*

- *When you have a multiple pregnancy*

- *When your baby is premature*

- *When your pregnancy goes well beyond your EDD (see p.170)*

241

GOING TO THE HOSPITAL

By getting everything ready and packing the things you will need to take with you to the hospital, you won't have to worry about being caught unprepared.

WHAT TO TAKE

The items you will need in the hospital fall into three categories: clothes and other personal effects for yourself; clothes for your baby; and your comfort aids for labor (see p.244). Contact your hospital to find out what you should bring with you, and what it will provide, such as diapers and clothing, for your baby.

For yourself You will need two or three maternity bras and front opening cotton nightgowns, a supply of breast pads, a bathrobe and slippers, underpants, and a supply of super-absorbent, stick-on sanitary napkins (these may be supplied by the hospital). Pack an overnight bag with your hairbrush and shampoo, a couple of towels and washcloths, a small mirror, makeup, face cream, hand cream, and a box of tissues. If you have drawn up a birth plan (see p.106), remember to take it with you.

For your baby If the hospital does not provide diapers and baby clothing, you will need to do so. You will also need to take a nightshirt or stretchie, hat, and a blanket in which to wrap your baby when you leave the hospital and go home.

Getting ready
Make sure that you have everything ready and packed well in advance.

IS IT TIME?

As you approach your due date, your body will begin to give you signals that it is preparing for the birth. You may experience the symptoms of pre-labor (see p.250) and, in some cases, labor.

Although you don't have to rush to the hospital when any of the following occur, you should be prepared for them happening and make your final preparations. The show normally comes first, and either the water breaking or contractions will follow, although sometimes contractions precede the first two. A fuller explanation of each one will be found on page 250.

The show A plug of blood-tinged mucus that has been sealing your cervix prior to birth, becomes dislodged during the early first stage of labor, if not before. It is usually easily recognizable.

The water breaks Pressure due to contractions or the baby's head pressing on the membranes of the amniotic sac may cause it to rupture in advance of the start of labor. The amniotic fluid will then escape, either as a trickle or in a rush.

Regular contractions Whether or not you have been aware of any contractions previously, you start to experience them – in the form of severe cramp-like pains that come at regular intervals and last for longer and longer.

WHEN TO GO

If, over an hour, you notice that your contractions are coming every 15 minutes, are about one minute long, and don't fade away when you move around, call your doctor or midwife according to prior arrangement. At this time, your first level of breathing (see p.266) will probably no longer be adequate, and you will be getting ready for the second stage. Your cervix will be about four to six centimeters dilated. There is still more than enough time to go to the hospital; in fact it's early enough to complete all your last-minute checks without leaving you time to kill at the hospital.

There is absolutely no need to rush to the hospital. The first stage usually lasts about eight hours for the first baby. It is more comfortable at home anyway, particularly if you don't know whether your hospital is prepared to give you free rein to conduct your labor as you'd like. However, if you live a long way from the hospital or you are particularly worried about getting there in time, go as soon as you feel that you should.

Transportation You will probably travel to the hospital in a taxi or ambulance, or by car. If you call a taxi or ambulance, be sure to give your full address and, if necessary, a clear description of how to get to your house so that there is no unnecessary delay. If you plan to go by car, you or the driver should check beforehand that the battery is fully charged, the tires are in good condition and properly inflated, and there is a full tank of gas. Do not drive yourself unless there is absolutely no alternative.

YOUR TRIP TO THE HOSPITAL

If you are traveling to the hospital by car, try to ensure that your journey will be both safe and comfortable.

In the weeks leading up to the birth, both you and whoever is going to drive you to the hospital should be thoroughly familiar with the route you are going to take. Find out how long the journey is likely to take at different times of the day, and work out alternative routes in case, on the day, you encounter exceptionally heavy traffic or other delays. Check to see if you need to take any money for the parking garage, and make sure you have the right amount set aside. You should also check out the entrances to the hospital and find out how to get to the maternity ward from them – especially during the night.

The car *The bigger the car you travel in, the more comfortable you are likely to be. You will probably be more comfortable and safe in the backseat, and if it is large enough you can lie down rather than sit. If you have a station wagon, you might find it more comfortable to kneel in the back, holding on to the seat back for support.*

Sudden birth *If your baby starts to arrive while you are still on your way to the hospital, try to remain calm. If you are close to the hospital, you have a good chance of getting there before the baby is actually born, but if you are farther away, it is best to stop the car at the nearest telephone, call for an ambulance, and then prepare yourself for an emergency delivery (see also p.282).*

YOUR NOURISHMENT

Conserving your energy is important during the first stage, particularly in case you have a long and tiring labor.

Check whether the hospital's policy allows you to eat and drink during labor, and if so, pack a few small snacks such as chocolate bars, which will give you instant energy. Your partner will also need some sustenance and won't want to leave your side to get food. Make sure that there are sandwiches and fruit packed for him as well as for yourself.

Shortly before labor, the capacity of your stomach to absorb food decreases, so make sure what you choose can be easily digested.

On the other hand, you are likely to be ravenous after the birth and you'll want something to eat right away, so be prepared.

You will also need something to drink. A thermos bottle of diluted unsweetened fruit juice, or cold mineral water is ideal, although your partner might want some canned soft drinks.

COMFORT AIDS FOR LABOR

When organizing the things you will need for the birth, also get ready all the items that will make your labor a more comfortable experience. It's a good idea to prepare your comfort aids in advance so that you don't forget anything in the excitement when labor starts, and you won't be caught unprepared if your labor starts sooner than expected.

PROVISIONS FOR COMFORT

Your childbirth class teacher will give you advice about what comfort aids may be useful during labor. If you're having a home birth, keep all your aids together in the room where you intend to give birth. If you've opted for a hospital birth, pack them in a bag and put it next to your suitcase. Make sure your birth assistant knows where they are, and doesn't forget them in the excitement.

Distractions Many women find the discomfort of labor can be alleviated with massage (see p.267). Counterpressure can be provided by your partner using his hands or a spinal roll, or even a tennis ball or rolling pin! A small amount of talcum powder or vegetable-based massage oil will stop your skin from being dragged or pinched. A hot water bottle or a hot pad placed in the small of your back can act as a compress to soothe backache.

In the early stages of labor, before it is really established, it is likely that you will find that for quite a long period of time nothing much seems to be happening. It will probably help to distract your attention and pass the time if you and your partner have some books, magazines, playing cards, board games, and cassette tapes and a player available.

PAIN-RELIEVING COMFORT AIDS

Spinal roll

Powder *Tennis ball* *Massage oil* *Hot water bottle*

GENERAL COMFORT AIDS

Toothbrush

Toothpaste

Hair comb and barrettes

Tissues

Washcloth

Thick socks

Natural sponge

Lip balm

Keeping cool There will probably be times when you won't want anything to drink, but you really would like something wet and cool in your mouth. You may find it comforting to suck an ice cube or crushed ice, which is usually available at the hospital.

Alternatively, you may prefer moistening your lips and mouth by sucking on a small natural sponge that your birth partner has dipped in cold water.

Your face is likely to become very hot and sweaty, and you will probably find it refreshing to have it mopped with an absorbent washcloth. In addition, your birth assistant can create a slight breeze on your face by using a hand-held fan.

Keeping warm During the later stages of labor, and particularly immediately after the birth, some women begin to shake quite visibly with cold, so make sure that you have some leg warmers or thick socks in case this happens.

General comfort If your hair is long or falls in your face, a few hairpins, barrettes, combs, or a hair band will help stop it from irritating you. Your lips are likely to become very dry because of breathing through your mouth, so include lip balm that you can rub onto your lips to stop them from cracking.

If you feel nauseous and actually vomit, you will undoubtedly feel much better if you are able to clean your teeth, so don't forget to take your toothbrush and some toothpaste.

A box of tissues may come in handy, as may some scented wipes in single packs that can be opened when needed and used to cleanse the face, neck, and hands. For freshening up you may want to splash on some toilet water.

YOUR PARTNER'S COMFORT

Your birth partner may find your labor more pleasurable if he or she has certain items set aside for his or her own use. Here are a few suggestions:

• *A pack of wipes for freshening face and hands*

• *Snacks and drinks*

• *Distractions for your other children if they are present*

• *Change of clothing*

• *Camera and film, or video camera if permitted*

• *Coins and phone card with phone numbers of family and friends*

YOUR CHECKLIST

Use the following checklist when you assemble your aids:

• *Food and drink*

• *Spinal roll or tennis ball*

• *Massage oil or talcum powder*

• *Hot water bottle*

• *Magazines, board games, etc.*

• *Ice and storage if in hospital*

• *Small natural sponge*

• *Washcloth and hand-held fan*

• *Leg warmers or thick socks*

• *Hair combs, barrettes, or band*

• *Lip balm*

• *Toothbrush and toothpaste*

• *Box of tissues or wet wipes*

• *Toilet water*

NAME *Patrick Bade*

AGE *47 years*

PAST MEDICAL HISTORY *Nothing abnormal*

PARTNER'S OBSTETRIC HISTORY *This is his wife's first pregnancy. She is 35 years old and is 5 months pregnant*

Patrick is a somewhat reluctant father. He and his wife, Diane, have been married for 12 years and have a comfortable and enjoyable lifestyle. Patrick admits that he has become accustomed to being looked after by Diane and that he is probably a little bit "spoiled." Their relationship has already changed subtly – Diane felt the baby move for the first time a few weeks ago and they have both become increasingly aware of the baby's presence.

THE OLDER FATHER

Patrick is not terribly enthusiastic about impending fatherhood. He doesn't much like, or want, children and has confessed he agreed to try for a baby for Diane's sake. He is unsure about his feelings toward the baby and about how things will change, because he really likes them just the way they are.

A RATHER RELUCTANT FATHER

Diane is a music tutor who teaches the cello at a conservatory. She and Patrick are passionately fond of music and enjoy going out to concerts, musical recitals, and the opera, as well as going to the theater and out to dinner with their friends. Patrick is a director of a company that has offices in New York, Los Angeles, San Francisco, Chicago and in Europe, and Diane accompanies him on business trips and weekends as often as she can.

Patrick is unhappy at the thought that they will have to give up or curtail their social life and foreign trips, but doesn't see how they will be able to incorporate the baby into their lifestyle. He is rather old-fashioned in his attitudes and feels happier being the main breadwinner than he does about sharing the baby care. He has suggested to Diane that they get a nanny for the baby.

However, Diane intends to give up working in order to care for the baby and doesn't feel that a full-time helper will be necessary. She doesn't seem particularly bothered about the baby's effects on their social life, at least not for the first few months or so.

I suggested to Patrick that it would be a good idea if he were to discuss the situation fully with Diane, as it appeared to me that there were a few unresolved issues that could fester and cause trouble after the baby was born. I pointed out that he was going to feel very resentful if he felt that the new baby had, in effect, completely taken his place in Diane's affections and disrupted his lifestyle.

Making adjustments Patrick admitted that he was very afraid that the new baby would displace him. He is used to being pampered and fussed over by Diane and confessed to feeling slightly jealous at the prospect of having to share her attention.

I told him that he had to be realistic and realize that the baby's needs would have to take priority over his own, at least for a while, but that there was no reason why he and Diane couldn't manage to make time on their own together – although it would take more planning than before the baby was born.

BEING A GOOD SUPPORT

Patrick has ruled out attending any prenatal classes with Diane, although Diane has persuaded him to accompany her to the hospital for the actual delivery. This has caused him a degree of consternation as he has a great dislike, even fear, of hospitals. I told him that he really ought to try to come to terms with it, as negative feelings can interfere with both the personal and physical aspects of birth if they are not dealt with well beforehand.

I suggested that the best way of doing this would be to visit the hospital with Diane a number of times before her due date and, if they were to make the nursery their destination, this would help him to dissociate the fixed idea he has that hospitals equal sickness and fear. Patrick was skeptical at first, but I assured him that this system of familiarization really would work.

I asked Patrick what preferences Diane had about the birth, and whether she had thought about her birth plan (see p.106). He said that although Diane was thinking about a birth plan, he hadn't really talked to her about it. I told him that the most important aspects of being a birth partner are to be aware of what the mother actually wants, the situations that can occur, and to be aware of what the mother would prefer to happen under these circumstances. I suggested that he try to go to the prenatal classes with Diane so that he will be prepared – just as he would prepare himself for an important upcoming meeting. I assured him that couples usually attend prenatal classes together, rather than pregnant women going on their own, so he needn't feel self-conscious.

AFTER THE BIRTH

I told Patrick that it was almost inevitable that they would both be very tired for the first few months of the baby's life, so I suggested that they could make it a rule that they take a nap together at the end of the working day, while the baby is sleeping. This would give them a rewarding feeling of closeness and intimacy, while replenishing their energy levels. I also suggested that they set aside times that are their own, and ask a relative, baby-sitter, or friend to look after the baby. Perhaps they could use this time for going to the opera or to a concert, and I suggested that they could still see their friends on a fairly regular basis if they entertained at home. I also pointed out that small babies are extremely portable and they'd still be able to maintain much of their social life.

Patrick has not had much, if any, contact with babies and told me that he thought that he would get along much better with his child once it had grown up a bit and they could have a real conversation. I told him that a newborn baby is not a blank canvas, but a definite personality who has been able to hear and see, even in the uterus. She would recognize pieces of music that had been played to her before birth, as well as her father's voice as soon as she was born. Patrick was fascinated as he hadn't realized that the baby would be able to do that. He went away feeling quite intrigued and thought he might try to communicate with his baby at the earliest possible moment.

PATRICK'S BABY

Patrick's baby will start to bond with him before she is born – whether he is aware of it or not!

• *He will be an extremely important person in her life – she will recognize the sound of his voice as soon as she is born*

• *He may want peace and quiet, but she will take no account of that – particularly during her first few months*

• *She will enjoy being cuddled by him as they listen to classical music and opera. In fact, she will probably fall asleep if the piece is soothing, especially if it is something that she heard many times before she was born*

• *Her routine will take precedence over his routine*

• *When she is 10 years old, her father will be 57 and may not have the energy for active games*

• *Growing up with him, she will benefit from his maturity and experience of the world*

C H A P T E R

12

Managing your
LABOR

*Labor is the culmination of your pregnancy. Very few
labors are pain-free, but there are many methods and
types of pain relief available. The help and support of
your partner can be invaluable in making labor a
smoother, more comfortable experience.*

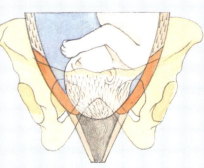

YOUR MOOD CHANGES

As you wait for indications that your baby is ready to be born, you may experience a number of differing emotions.

Contentment As your body changes in preparation for labor, you may respond to the ripening of your uterus in a sensual way. Particularly if this is your first pregnancy, you may feel a desire to enjoy these last days on your own, indulging your whims, sharing moments of intimacy with your partner, or spending the time just daydreaming. Pamper yourself, and allow your feelings to flow naturally and easily.

Elation You may experience a sense of jubilation when your body alerts you to the moment that you have been anticipating with such excitement. Don't try to quench this feeling; share it with others as it may help to release any pangs of nervous tension.

Anxiety The signals of pre-labor may also evoke apprehension. You might worry about the pain you may suffer during labor and its effect on the baby, or whether you will be able to cope. You may feel nervous about your water breaking in an embarrassing situation.

Impatience If your expected date of delivery comes and goes without any sign of impending delivery, don't be depressed. Remember the date is an approximation and most babies arrive either sooner or later than expected. This is particularly likely if you were born sooner or later than expected.

PRE-LABOR AND LABOR

Medical definitions of labor divide it into three separate stages. During the first stage, the cervix opens fully to allow the baby to pass through; in the second stage, the baby is born; in the third stage, the placenta is delivered. All these stages are discussed in detail over the following pages. But, in addition to these three stages, most women will experience pre-labor. Your experience of labor will be much more colorful and exciting than the above definition. Go into it believing that very little can go wrong, and very little will go wrong.

PRE-LABOR

Before real labor begins, hormones secreted by your uterus and the baby prepare your body for birth in a number of ways. During the last few weeks, you will probably notice a few signs of your impending labor. However, just as each woman's experience of labor and birth is unique, so these pre-labor symptoms affect each woman in varying degrees of intensity. They provide useful signals that indicate to you that labor is imminent.

Engagement To position himself for the journey through the birth canal, your baby will move lower down so that his presenting part, usually the head, will settle into your bony pelvis (see opposite). This is known as engagement and you will experience it as a feeling of lightening. If this is your first pregnancy, engagement will probably occur about two to three weeks before the onset of labor. If you've had previous babies, the baby's head may remain higher until just before labor starts, as your uterine muscles may have stretched and so will exert less pressure on your baby. You will know when engagement takes place because pressure on your diaphragm eases and breathing becomes easier. On the other hand, you will probably have to pass urine more frequently, as your baby will now be pressing down on your bladder.

Braxton Hicks contractions Your uterus practices for the strong contractions needed during labor with weak, irregular contractions. Named after the doctor who first described them, most women feel them throughout the last few months of pregnancy. If you place your hand on your abdomen, you may be able to feel a hardening and tightening of your uterus that lasts about 25 seconds. Unlike real labor contractions, these are usually painless, although a few women find them uncomfortable. If you feel any discomfort, sitting down quietly should help ease them.

Runs of Braxton Hicks contractions may become more frequent and intense as real labor approaches, helping to prepare the cervix for dilation, and to increase the circulation of blood to the placenta. When you feel a run of Braxton Hicks, practice the relaxation techniques you intend to use during labor; the tightening and relaxing of your uterus will give you a good idea of how a contraction feels as it waxes, and then wanes.

Some mothers misinterpret Braxton Hicks contractions for real labor, arriving at the hospital only to be told they can go home again (see **A false labor?** p.254).

"Nesting instinct" You may feel a surge of energy to make final preparations for the arrival of your baby. If you feel the urge to rush around cleaning or decorating the house, or cooking large meals, try to restrain yourself. You will need all this extra energy for coping with labor and delivery.

The show An obvious sign that labor is imminent is the appearance of the show – the plug of mucus that seals your cervix during pregnancy, providing protection against infection. Although the show often does not appear until labor is underway, the cervix may widen enough for the mucus plug to be dislodged up to 12 days before labor begins. This sticky substance may be slightly brown, pink, or blood-tinged from the blood vessels that attached it to the cervix. The show signals dilation of the cervix.

Premenstrual feelings Physical and emotional changes similar to those you experience premenstrually may occur. You may also feel crampy, with pressure in your rectum, and feel the need to empty your bowels and pass urine frequently.

YOUR BABY'S DESCENT

Your birth attendant will check the descent of your baby with an internal examination. This is described as "stations." These are imaginary lines measured in centimeters from –5 to +5 in relation to the level of your ischial spines and your baby's head. When his head first enters your pelvis, it is at station –5. When the top of his head is level with your ischial spines, it is at station 0 (engaged). The lower stations describe his head's position as it passes through the birth canal to the vaginal opening, station +5.

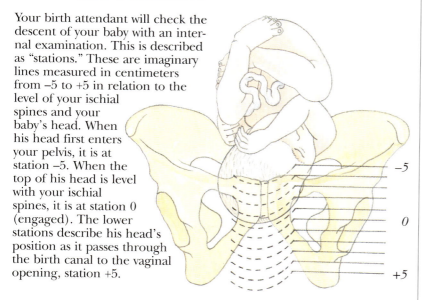

-5

0

+5

WHAT YOUR BABY IS DOING

While no one actually knows for certain why labor starts, there is increasing evidence to show that the baby plays a major role.

Secreting hormones *The onset of labor is triggered by the secretion of hormones; some pregnancy hormone levels drop, others rise. New hormones are secreted, one of which is produced by your baby.*

Engagement *Throughout your pregnancy, your baby will be floating in his amniotic sac above the pelvic brim. Then, as his birth approaches, his head, or his bottom if he is in a breech presentation, will descend lower down into your pelvis and become engaged.*

Kicking less *You may notice that he is quieter than in previous months. From time to time you may feel a slight flurry of movement, although if his actions appear to have ceased completely, contact your doctor or midwife.*

THE OLDER MOTHER

Toward the end of pregnancy obstetricians are always on the lookout for signs of placental insufficiency as the baby outgrows its food supply. Older mothers receive especially careful scrutiny.

Some doctors will state at the first prenatal visit that they intend to induce labor in an older mother on or around the expected date of delivery without waiting for spontaneous labor to begin. It should be one of the questions you ask if the subject doesn't come up for discussion. Of course induction is not always necessary. A mother who reaches her estimated date of delivery, given that she and the baby are perfectly normal, should be allowed to go into spontaneous labor. I would very much advocate, however, that you cooperate with the frequent monitoring of your condition and that of the baby once the EDD has been passed and, if there is any fetal distress, agree to have the appropriate medical intervention.

REASONS FOR INDUCTION

Anything that makes the uterine environment unhealthy for the baby is a reason for induction. Your labor is likely to be induced if:

• *You are suffering from hypertension, preeclampsia, heart disease, diabetes, or have any prepartum bleeding*

• *There are signs of placental insufficiency (so that the baby is in danger of not getting enough nutrients and oxygen from the placenta)*

• *Your pregnancy is prolonged beyond 42 weeks*

INDUCTION OF LABOR

Induction triggers labor artificially with rupture of the membranes and oxytocin or prostaglandins being given to stimulate uterine contractions. The same techniques are used to accelerate labor if the contractions are weak and progress slow.

If your induction is not being done for the medical reasons set out below (see box) or as an emergency, you will have an elective induction. An appointment will be made for you to be admitted to hospital at a certain time. Your partner will be able to be with you at all times. If you are in any doubt about why your doctor is suggesting induction of labor, ask for a detailed explanation – this should cover all of the alternatives. The ultimate decision rests, of course, with yourself.

THE HISTORY OF INDUCTION

Sixty years ago, when drugs first became available, the induction of labor was frequently used for hospital or social convenience. Induction was sometimes planned to suit working hours or changes in shifts. A woman would occasionally ask to be induced so that the birth could fall on her husband's birthday, or inside the tax year, or so that the child would be the right age for the school year! Such reasons are no longer accepted as valid.

When induction first became fashionable, there was not today's technological backup, such as ultrasound and amniocentesis, for doctors to establish fetal maturity, and babies might be born too early with respiratory problems. The rate of Caesarean section also rose. Nowadays, fewer than one in five labors are induced.

However, only 5 percent of babies actually arrive on the due date, and it can be hard for some doctors and quite a lot of mothers to remain philosophical when that magic date passes. There may be concern that the placenta may be becoming inadequate to support the baby and that the baby is outgrowing its environment.

If you feel anxious when you learn that your labor is to be induced, I'd like to reassure you that induction is a great asset provided it is done strictly for medical reasons. You shouldn't worry unduly, as it's being done either for your well-being or the baby's. Don't be angry with yourself if your birth does not turn out the way that you had planned or imagined it to be.

HOW IT IS DONE

Most obstetricians will normally use a combination of three different methods to induce labor.

Prostaglandin pessaries One of the more modern methods of induction is by use of prostaglandin pessaries, which affect the pregnant uterus, causing it to go into labor. Pessaries are inserted into the vagina during the evening and you may be lucky enough to be in labor by morning. This is a very satisfactory method of induction as you can move freely around the labor room.

Artificial rupture of the membranes (ARM) Also known as amniotomy, this method of induction, often accompanied by an oxytocin drip (see below), involves insertion of a tool, not unlike a crochet hook, into the uterus to make a small opening in the membrane so that the water escapes. For most women this is a painless procedure because the amniotic membranes are entirely insensitive. Labor usually reaches full intensity quickly after ARM because the baby's head is no longer cushioned; it presses down hard against the cervix, encouraging the uterus to contract and the cervix to dilate. Amniotomy is now almost routine during the preparation for any labor; if left alone, the water does not usually break until late in the first stage. Once the water has broken, labor becomes faster and more intense.

Amniotomy is not just a method of induction. It will be performed if an electrode must be attached to the baby's scalp to monitor its heartbeat (see p.263). It will also be performed if the baby's heart rate goes down because of fetal distress. In this case, traces of meconium, the baby's first bowel movements, may be seen in the amniotic fluid. (This is one reason why you must call your doctor or midwife immediately when your water breaks. The call is especially important if the amniotic fluid is tinged brown or green, or if it smells unpleasant.)

Oxytocin-induced labor The natural hormone from the posterior pituitary gland in the brain, oxytocin, will stimulate labor and the synthetic form is used for inducing and stimulating labor. Because oxytocin is given in a drip, ask for it to be inserted in the arm you use least, and check that you can have a long tube connecting you to the drip. You should then have more room to move around, even if you are lying on the bed.

The drip can be turned down if you go into strong labor quickly and the cervix becomes half dilated. The needle won't be removed from your arm until after the baby is born because the uterine contractions help to expel the placenta.

The contractions caused by an oxytocin drip are often stronger, longer, and more painful than normal, with shorter periods of relaxation between them, resulting in an increased need for pain medication. As the blood supply to the uterus is temporarily shut off during each strong contraction, it's thought that this may be detrimental to the fetus. Today, obstetricians believe that only a small percentage of deliveries need oxytocin-induced labor.

EXPECTATIONS OF INDUCED LABOR

If properly handled, induced labor need not be more painful or difficult than natural labor and, using oxytocin, your doctor should be able to get you to the stage where you will have a *normal* labor. You can still do all your breathing exercises and push the baby out at your own pace if you prefer to have a completely natural childbirth. If the induced labor does become too painful, which it may, you can always request an epidural anesthetic or some other form of pain relief (see p.264).

AMNIOTOMY AND YOUR BABY

The membranes usually rupture naturally toward the end of the first stage of labor.

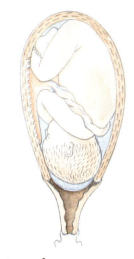

Intact membranes
The bag of water provides a cushion for the baby's head as it presses against the cervix.

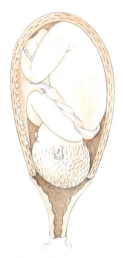

Ruptured membranes
Contractions increase in intensity pressing the baby's head against the cervix and helping it open.

A FALSE LABOR?

It's not always easy to distinguish false from real labor if it's your first pregnancy. As a general rule, if you're in doubt, you're not in real labor.

Although false labor is only a rehearsal, it is not a reason to be disappointed; false labor heralds real labor, and you won't have very much longer to wait.

There are some simple distinctions between the contractions of false and real labor.

Regularity *False contractions never really settle down; they never become truly regular.*

Frequency *Contractions are sporadic. The time between them may vary from 15 minutes to 20 minutes to 10 minutes, etc., with no steady pattern.*

Effect of movement *False contractions usually weaken or subside altogether if you move around. Real contractions increase.*

Strength *False contractions do not get progressively stronger. They may even weaken from time to time and completely disappear.*

Some women, especially if they are working, get overly tired or overly excited, and slip in and out of false labor for a few days before real labor begins.

Inform your doctor or midwife about the contractions. Go to the hospital if you want to. If you stay at home, keep moving and stay upright to help labor progress.

THE FIRST STAGE

The months of preparing for your baby's birth have now reached their climax as you start to experience labor. In medical terms, the first stage begins when your contractions bring about dilation and thinning of the cervix and ends when effacement (thinning) and dilation (opening) are complete. At this point your midwife, nurse, or doctor will confirm that you are fully dilated.

WHAT HAPPENS IN LABOR

It is difficult to be sure about the onset of labor as it is different for each woman. However, certain classic signs – intense, uterine contractions, dilation and thinning of the cervix, rupturing of the membranes – are taken to mean that labor is under way.

Contractions When true labor starts, the nature of contractions changes. They become more rhythmical, more painful, and occur at regular intervals. These contractions are not within your control and, once they have begun, will not stop until your baby is born.

You can time your contractions from the beginning of one contraction to the beginning of the next. In early labor, contractions are usually about 30–60 seconds long, at intervals of about 5–20 minutes. This can vary as some women may not notice their first contractions until they are closer together, say every five minutes. In the *active phase*, contractions usually last 60–90 seconds, at intervals of 2–4 minutes.

As the muscles of your uterus tighten, you may feel a sensation of pain similar to menstrual cramps, spreading around your lower abdomen like a tight band. This is because the uterine muscle becomes short of oxygen as the blood vessels of the wall are compressed. The uterus is a huge muscle and needs a lot of energy during contractions.

Every woman feels contraction pains differently, but in early labor they may have the same character as dysmenorrhea (menstrual cramps) or pain may be confined to mild backache. Some women experience persistent and severe backache (see p. 256). Very often a contraction feels like a wave of discomfort right across your abdomen that reaches a peak for a few seconds and then diminishes. At the same time you can feel a hardening and tightening of the uterine muscle, which is held at the peak of its intensity for a few seconds before the muscle begins to relax.

Women assume that contractions will get steadily longer, more frequent, and stronger. This is not so; don't be disturbed if your contractions seem to vary. It is as normal for a strong contraction to be followed by a weaker one that doesn't last quite as long, as it is for contractions to follow one another relentlessly.

The cervix dilates and thins The cervix is usually a thick-walled canal about three-quarters of an inch (two centimeters) long, and firmly closed. During the last few weeks, pregnancy hormones may help to soften your cervix, but the intense contractions of first-stage labor are needed to dilate and thin it. Dilation is measured in centimeters from 0–10 (about four inches). Your cervix will dilate only about four centimeters (one and a half inches) during the *latent phase*, then progress to eight centimeters (about three inches) during the *active phase* (see below). The pain increases as it becomes fully dilated during transition. Eventually, the whole cervix opens up and is made one with the body of the uterus, thus creating a continuous channel through which your baby can emerge.

The water breaks The membranes of the amniotic sac may rupture painlessly at any time during labor, although this usually occurs toward the end of the first stage. Fluid may leak or gush out; the flow depends on the size and site of the break and whether or not the baby's head is plugging the hole.

Usually when the membranes rupture spontaneously near term, labor occurs within a short time, although in a few instances it is delayed – if the baby's presenting part is not engaged, or if the baby is presenting abnormally. Delay also occurs in many normal cases.

HOW LONG DOES LABOR LAST?

Every woman's experience of labor varies greatly, and the time span of each cannot be predicted. An average labor lasts about 12–14 hours for first-time mothers, and about seven hours for subsequent labors. If your labor lasts longer than 12 hours the first time, or nine hours in subsequent labors, your doctor will look for the cause of slow progress, and may intervene.

The first stage of labor can be further divided into three separate phases. The *latent phase* is the longest of these, lasting about eight hours for first babies, and you will feel contractions occurring with increasing frequency and length, but they won't be too distressing. Try to conserve your energy during this time as your body will be warming up for the more demanding phases to follow. The next, *active phase,* will be shorter, lasting about three to five hours, but this is when contractions become more painful, and you may seek pain relief (see p.264). The final, *transitional phase,* is the shortest and most intense, usually lasting under an hour, and comes just before the delivery.

Transition This is the most intense phase of the first stage. Your contractions will now be lasting about 60–90 seconds, with intervals of only 30–90 seconds. As the contractions become more forceful, you may find it difficult to relax. This is the time you may feel the most discomfort. You may also feel a very strong urge to push, but should not do so unless told you are fully dilated. The intense pain may make you feel extremely irritable, to the point of being ill-tempered with your birth partner. This is natural, and you must not feel that you are failing if you think you haven't the energy to go on anymore; you will find hidden resources of energy to help you cope. Try to bear in mind that this phase means your baby's birth is now just minutes away.

YOUR CERVIX DILATES

The normally tough cervix must be stretched thin and opened wide before your baby's head can pass through.

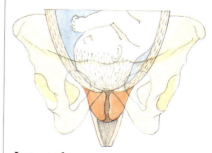

Latent phase
Your cervix remains about 2cm (³/₄in) long until contractions start thinning it out (effacing).

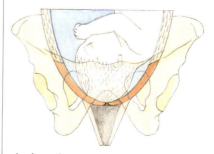

Active phase
When the cervical canal is fully effaced, further contractions will widen (dilate) your cervix.

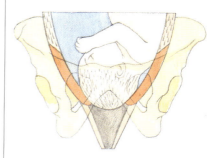

Transitional phase
At full dilation the last part of your cervix at the front has opened to 10cm (4in).

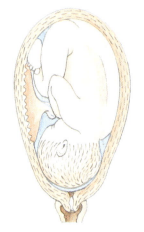

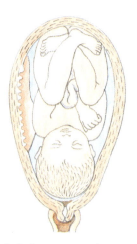

Your baby's presentation
The way your baby is presenting can affect your labor and birth. The usual presentation is when your baby's spine faces outward (top), but if your baby's head is facing outward (bottom), labor might possibly be delayed. Most babies, however, rotate to the correct position before passing down the birth canal.

SPECIAL TYPES OF LABOR

Most labors are quite straightforward, but occasionally a complication may arise that necessitates the use of special treatment. With vigilant prenatal care, potential problems should be anticipated and easily treated, but sometimes the first stage may be under way before a particular problem is identified.

BACKACHE LABOR

Occasionally, the discomfort of uterine contractions will be experienced primarily as low back pain. This is usually due to stretching of the cervix as it dilates. It may also occur if your baby lies in the posterior position with the back of his head up against your spine (one in ten babies lie in this position; it is not abnormal). In this position, your baby's neck may not be properly flexed and a larger proportion of the head than normal presents, which may prolong labor. Most of the time, your baby will rotate the 180 degrees into the anterior position and labor will proceed smoothly. If, as occasionally happens, the baby fails to rotate to the anterior position, this is no cause for alarm, although your doctor may deliver him using forceps or, more rarely, vacuum extraction.

This kind of labor may start slowly and be protracted, so it can be very tiring. There are various ways in which you and your birth assistant can relieve your backache:

Counterpressure This is the most effective way of relieving backache (see p.267). However, if being touched by someone else is irritating, for example, during transition, you may prefer to use your own knuckles by placing a hand underneath each buttock.

Change in position When you are lying flat on your back, your baby is pressing down hardest on your spine and its nerves. Try to stay upright and walk around as much as possible.

You can also relieve the pressure of your baby on your spine by sitting tailor-fashion (see p.132), leaning forward, or by rocking your pelvis. If you feel more comfortable lying down, lie on the side that your baby is turning toward (your birth attendant will advise you which side that is).

Application of heat You may find it helpful if, during or between contractions, your birth assistant places a heating pad or hot water bottle against the lower part of your back. A hot shower, if directed particularly onto your back, may also provide some relief.

PROLONGED LABOR

Labor is said to be prolonged when strong uterine contractions fail to bring about the expected delivery. This may be due to the inability of the cervix to dilate, or failure of the baby to descend through the birth canal. Doctors keep a very careful eye on the length of each stage of labor. When labor appears to be progressing more slowly than normal, your obstetrician may suspect obstruction and make an early decision to intervene – with a forceps delivery if it's suitable, or a Caesarean section.

No woman is allowed to go on with a difficult birth for much over the accepted times (see p.255) as this may lead to maternal exhaustion and fetal distress.

Obstruction can be more quickly detected in a mother who has had several children. However, your doctor or midwife will be monitoring your general condition throughout labor, and will be alerted to possible obstruction if your condition appears to deteriorate and you look tired and anxious.

With a very long labor, when you are forgoing food and rest, you might become too tired or distressed to push adequately. Your doctor or midwife will not allow this to happen.

Failure to dilate   When contractions are weak and infrequent with the cervix dilating slowly, the uterus may be failing to coordinate muscular activity. One way in which your doctor or midwife will be able to see exactly how your labor is progressing is by plotting a partogram (see below).

If the failure of the uterus to contract efficiently is the only reason for the lack of progress, your doctor may begin special procedures to speed up effacement and dilation. The membranes may be artificially ruptured and then, if necessary, oxytocin may be administered. The dosage will then be carefully increased until strong

CAUSES OF FETAL OBSTRUCTION

Certain fetal conditions may exist that cause you to have an obstructed labor. Fortunately, most problems can usually be detected beforehand so everybody is well prepared.

- *Your baby is large in relation to your pelvis*

- *Your baby is lying in a transverse or oblique position*

- *Your baby is in a breech, face, or brow presentation*

- *Your baby is lying in the posterior position*

- *Your twin babies are entwined*

- *Your baby has a congenital abnormality such as hydrocephalus*

YOUR LABOR'S PROGRESS

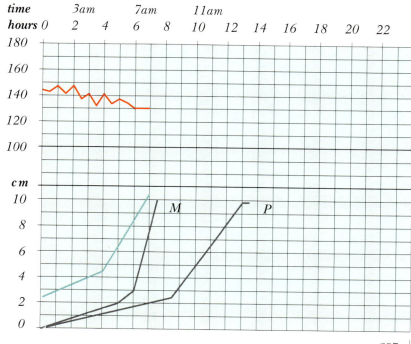

Plotting your partogram
The partogram records the baby's heart rate and the mother's cervical dilation. The other lines on the graph depict the expected dilation of a multiparous (more than one pregnancy) woman (M) and a primiparous (first pregnancy) woman (P), which are compared with the mother's actual progress. This chart represents a multiparous mother who got off to a slow start, although labor eventually became normal.

——— *fetal heart rate beats/minute*

——— *mother's cervical dilation*

——— *expected cervical dilation*

MATERNAL CAUSES OF OBSTRUCTION

If your labor is failing to progress normally, there may be reasons why your pelvis or uterus is obstructing the descent of your baby.

- *Deformity or disproportion of the bony pelvis*

- *Pelvic tumors such as fibroids or an ovarian cyst*

- *Abnormalities of the uterus, cervix, or vagina*

- *A contraction ring of the uterus, which is when the uterus pulls in excessively and a band of tight muscle occurs. This can stop contractions from passing all the way down and may result in constriction of the uterus or cervix. Fortunately, it is very rare unless the uterus has been overstimulated by oxytocin or prostaglandin, such as during induction (see p.252). A Caesarean section is almost always required*

contractions are occurring about every three minutes. Your doctor will pay close attention to ensure there are no dangerous increases in the strength or frequency of your contractions.

Failure to descend I have already mentioned breech and posterior presentation as causes of obstruction. One other reason for an obstructed labor is disproportion. Disproportion is a result of the size of your baby's head and the size of your pelvis failing to match up. If your pelvis is too small relative to your baby's head, disproportion results. It is easy to understand how your baby might fail to descend in such circumstances (see also p.158).

If you're a first-time mother and your baby is still high and non-engaged during the last few weeks of your pregnancy (see column, p.171), your doctor may suspect disproportion. This will also be taken into account if the baby's head remains high during labor despite strong contractions.

If the disproportion is quite slight, your doctor may let you try to have a trial of labor (bear in mind that your uterus is on trial, not you), provided there are no other irregularities, and the baby's head is felt to be descending. Once the baby's head has entered the pelvic cavity, a vaginal delivery usually occurs. If the disproportion is major, doctors will perform a Caesarean section.

Rest assured that most of the abnormalities that cause obstruction and a prolonged labor (see column, left, and p.256) will be picked up during your pregnancy so that early treatment is possible and a plan of action can be made before labor begins.

PREMATURE LABOR

A premature labor is one that occurs at less than 37 weeks of gestation. In about 40 percent of cases the cause is a mystery. It is, however, known to occur in the following instances: premature rupture of the membranes; multiple pregnancy; preeclampsia; cervical incompetence; and uterine abnormalities. Overwork, stress, and some maternal diseases, such as anemia or malnutrition, may also have an effect.

Knowing whether you've actually gone into premature labor is almost as difficult for your doctors as it is for you (see column, right). The diagnosis is not easy, and criteria differ at different hospitals – showing that often it's quite arbitrary. As a general rule, a premature labor begins without any warning; the first sign may be rupture of the membranes, the beginning of uterine contractions, or some vaginal bleeding. There is no stopping labor if your membranes have ruptured and labor has begun, but you or your doctor can take certain precautions while the membranes are intact or before labor really gets going.

What you can do If your membranes have ruptured, notify your doctor (see p.255). If labor hasn't started within 48 hours, you must rest for most of the day, whether you are at home or in the hospital. Do not have sexual intercourse. Contact your doctor if anything untoward occurs. Apart from these precautions, it is inadvisable to try to suppress labor once the membranes have ruptured spontaneously because of the risk of infection. In fact, if contractions do not begin on their own within a day or so, oxytocin will usually be given in order to encourage them to start.

What the hospital will do   If you are in premature labor, the main aim of hospitalization is to give you treatment that may delay or suppress the onset of labor so that your child can remain in your uterus for as long as possible, thereby continuing to be nourished by you. The reason for trying to curtail your premature labor is that a premature baby (see also pp.320 & 321) has an increased risk of developing respiratory distress syndrome, and the shorter the gestation period, the greater the risk.

If your pregnancy is less than 34 weeks gestation or your baby weighs less than 1.5 kilograms (3lb), and your cervix is less than five centimeters (two inches) dilated with the membranes intact, bed rest to improve uterine blood supply and, more rarely, drugs to suppress labor are what a hospital can offer.

Additionally, being in the hospital allows your doctor to check for evidence of infection in cases of premature rupture of the membranes and to monitor your baby's condition. It also ensures that your premature baby can be looked after in intensive care immediately after delivery.

All of the drugs used cause some side effects, and for that reason only certain cases of premature labor are suitable for receiving them. The main criteria for drug treatment are that you are healthy, you have no heart disease, diabetes, high blood pressure, or an abnormally placed placenta and of course, that your baby is alive, with no evidence of a congenital defect.

If you are very nervous and anxious, a mild sedative may be given to you, but pain medication will not be administered unless your pain is extremely severe. These drugs may make your uterine muscles more irritable rather than calming them down.

Managing labor   Once the membranes have ruptured, labor will proceed as normal (see p.250). As a general rule, premature labor tends to be shorter and easier than full-term, mainly because the baby's head is smaller and softer. However, an episiotomy is usually given to protect the baby's head from pressure changes within the birth canal. Certain precautions will be taken, such as injecting you with vitamin K at six-hour intervals during labor as the premature fetus only has a primitive blood-clotting mechanism. You will probably be offered an epidural anesthetic instead of analgesic drugs, which can depress the fetal respiratory system. Doctors will take special care to avoid hypoxia (lack of oxygen to the tissues) throughout labor and delivery.

Once your membranes have ruptured, doctors worry mainly about an infection of the uterus and, although antibiotics are not given as a precaution, they are given immediately if you develop any sign of infection such as fever. Caesarean delivery in premature labor is used in some situations, particularly if fetal distress occurs.

ARE YOU IN PREMATURE LABOR?

Here are some useful pointers for deciding whether or not you're in premature labor.

- *You are less than 37 weeks into your pregnancy*

- *You've observed uterine contractions for at least an hour*

- *Contractions are occurring every 5–10 minutes*

- *The contractions last for 30 seconds and persist over a period of an hour*

- *A vaginal examination by your doctor or midwife shows that your cervix is more than 2.5cm (1in) dilated and therefore more than three-quarters effaced*

According to these criteria, two-thirds of all patients who are thought to be in premature labor will actually be found not to be in real labor, and no treatment will be required. This will be quickly confirmed if you go straight to the hospital so that its staff can observe uterine activity carefully.

NAME *Joanna Rolfe*

AGE *33 years*

PAST MEDICAL
HISTORY *Nothing abnormal*

OBSTETRIC
HISTORY *2 children aged 7 and 4, both normal pregnancies, normal deliveries in the cephalic (head-down) position*

Joanna is American, married to an Englishman, David, and living in Great Britain. When her baby was found to be breech, Joanna was glad she had decided to have her baby in the UK; British and European obstetricians do not favor delivering breech babies by Caesarean section to the extent that US obstetricians do. There is evidence that most mothers have breech babies by vaginal delivery without very much difficulty; however, babies born by Caesarean section do appear to have a slightly higher survival rate.

BREECH BABY

Joanna was a firm believer in home delivery, but when her baby was diagnosed as being breech, I advised her to have the baby in the hospital. While most breech labors proceed smoothly, she would want to have her obstetrician, as well as an anesthesiologist and pediatrician, present at the delivery, in case there were any complications.

EXPECTATIONS OF THE BIRTH

Most babies are in the breech position until around the 32nd week of pregnancy, when they usually turn upside down of their own accord, but Joanna's baby was still breech at 36 weeks.

I advised her of recent findings that show a slightly lower mortality rate with Caesarean section (see p.284), but Joanna wanted to have a vaginal delivery and her obstetrician was willing to comply with her wishes. Even so, I advised her to expect special measures. Since her baby's bottom would be smaller, softer, and more squashable than the head, Joanna's vaginal and pelvic tissues might not be stretched enough to allow the head, the largest part of her baby, through the birth canal. Forceps would then be necessary to protect the head in the narrowed birth canal, and an episiotomy would make the application of forceps easier. I also told her the obstetrician would be most concerned about the position of the cord, as this may appear before the baby and become compressed. External fetal monitoring would be carried out at the beginning of labor, and this would be continued via a fetal scalp monitor (see p.263) as soon as the membranes ruptured.

I also warned her that the first stage of labor could be somewhat prolonged because the buttocks aren't as efficient as the head at dilating the cervix. However, Joanna made excellent progress.

A GOOD START

Joanna's labor started with simple backache, which went on for four hours until her contractions began. On arriving at the hospital she was examined by a midwife, who found the baby's buttocks pressed against the cervix with five centimeters (two inches) of dilation. Shortly afterward, Joanna's backache became very severe, but she was able to get some relief by kneeling on all fours. However, when the contractions became more painful than she felt able to cope with, she requested an epidural anesthetic.

Because a baby's bottom is smaller than its head, the second stage of labor may be shorter in a breech delivery, and Joanna's doctors expected an imminent birth once she entered the transition stage. For the birth, Joanna propped herself up in a sitting position. Just prior to delivery, the obstetrician rapidly gave Joanna a local anesthetic in the perineum (rather than topping off her epidural, which was wearing off) and then performed a large episiotomy in order to assist the birth of the baby's head. After examining her again, the obstetrician told Joanna that there was a foot presenting ahead of the buttocks, and he could feel the projection of the heel. With the next contraction both feet and legs presented, and the doctor gradually eased them out. The buttocks started to appear soon after: first the uppermost buttock and then the one lying behind. Joanna's obstetrician advised her not to push, but to allow the power of the uterine contractions to ease out the baby's buttocks very gently. He was particularly good in reassuring her that they had plenty of time available and she was going to be able to deliver the baby quite easily. And, with the next uterine contraction, the baby was born up to the level of the shoulders.

To help deliver the shoulders, the obstetrician rotated the baby's body very gently through 180 degrees, keeping her back upward. An arm appeared underneath Joanna's pubic arch and was easily delivered, as was the second arm after rotation back through 180 degrees in the opposite direction.

A PROBLEM

Delivering the head was not so easy. It was rather slow, too slow for the obstetrician, especially when he saw that the baby's heart rate was slowing, a sign of mild fetal distress. The baby's chest was free and she was making attempts to take her first breath.

Joanna's obstetrician reached his hand into her vagina and over the baby's face. Putting a finger on either side of her nose, he attempted to flex her head and bring her out over the perineum. This maneuver proved unsuccessful and forceps had to be applied. An assistant held the baby's feet up out of the way while the doctor applied the forceps blades around the sides of her head just in front of her ears. Her head was delivered within seconds, and she immediately gave a loud, healthy cry.

Forceps delivery
Forceps are slipped into the vagina, one on either side of the baby's head. This guards the head as it is carefully drawn through the pelvis and delivered. Once the nose and mouth are free, they are usually suctioned to clear them of mucus, since a breech baby often attempts to breathe while the head is still in the birth canal.

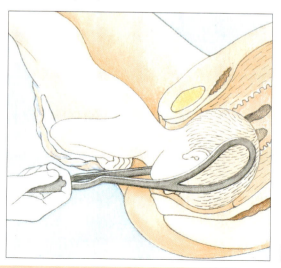

There are 3 main breech presentations. Joanna's baby, Grace, was diagnosed as being complete – her buttocks were presenting and her feet were low in Joanna's pelvis.

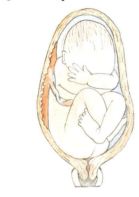

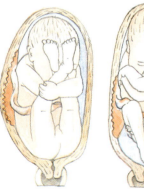

Breech positions
In flexed or complete breech (top), the thighs are flexed against the body and the knees are bent. This was the position that Joanna's baby was in. In frank breech (bottom, left), the thighs are flexed but the legs are extended upward. The arms are often wrapped around the legs. In a footling breech (bottom, right), the thighs are poorly flexed and the feet are above the cervix – they drop down after the rupture of the membranes.

HOSPITAL PROCEDURES

When you arrive at the hospital, the staff will prepare you for the birth. There are certain routine examinations that you will need to undergo.

• *While consulting your notes the midwife or doctor will ask you questions about your labor's progress – whether your water has broken and how frequently your contractions are coming*

• *You will be asked to undress and put on a hospital gown*

• *You will then be examined; the attendant will palpate your abdomen to feel the baby's position; she will listen to the fetal heartbeat, take your blood pressure, pulse, and temperature, and give you an internal examination to see how far your cervix has dilated*

• *You will be asked to give a urine sample to test for the presence of protein and sugar*

• *You'll be asked when you last moved your bowels and it may be suggested that you have an enema or a suppository. Be prepared for this, and say whether you do or do not want this*

• *You will be shown to the first stage labor room. (You may get to take a shower or bath first.) If you have any questions or you want to make your feelings known to the staff, now is the time to remind them of your preferences*

Each hospital has its own set of routine procedures for labor. You will probably have a good idea what regulations your hospital staff follow if you have visited the hospital beforehand, met the staff members who will be looking after you, looked at the labor and delivery rooms, and had some idea of what the routine is like. Hospitals can be intimidating, but they are much less so when you get to know them.

Admission to hospital   Once you've arrived in the hospital you may be put in a wheelchair to transport you from the hospital entrance to the labor suite. If your labor is well advanced, you'll welcome a wheelchair, but if not, you will be able to walk comfortably and you should make sure you are allowed to do so.

You should have outlined in your birth plan (see p.106) how you wish your labor to go, and once you have met your midwife or doctor, this is the time to make sure they have a copy that you can look over with them. They will also make some checks and ask you various questions about your labor (see column, left, and p.98).

If you aren't happy with any procedure, if equipment, lights, and needles frighten you, or if you are upset by a staff member, act at the time. Don't wait so that your fears and anxieties fester and grow. Your birth assistant can voice your feelings if you aren't feeling strong enough to be assertive.

Examinations   Your baby's heart will be regularly monitored by fetoscope, sonicaid, or an electronic fetal monitor (see right). You will probably have an internal examination every two to four hours during the first stage to check the dilation of your cervix but there's no hard and fast rule. This examination is usually done while you are lying flat on your back.

Each time you have an internal examination, ask how you are progressing. It is very comforting to know how far your cervix has dilated between examinations.

If you're asked a question while you are having a contraction, concentrate on your relaxation techniques and answer the question when the contraction is over.

Pain relief   After the admission procedures, the anesthesiologist will visit you if you have opted for some form of medical pain relief (see p.264). If you are having epidural anesthesia, the procedure will be set up now. This usually takes 10–20 minutes. The anesthesiologist may then leave you with your birth assistant and midwife, but will return later to check whether the anesthetic needs topping off. If you have decided not to have medical pain relief, you will be left with your birth assistant and a midwife or nurse who will stay with you throughout your labor.

ELECTRONIC FETAL MONITORING

This high-tech replacement for the ear trumpet is used to track the baby's heartbeat. Electronic fetal monitoring (EFM) will be used routinely in all cases of high-risk pregnancies, but most mothers and babies don't require it. You will have EFM if you are being induced or your labor is being stimulated for any reason, or if you have opted for epidural anesthesia. Its main function is that it gives warning of fetal distress.

What it is There are two kinds of electronic monitors: external and internal. An external monitor can be used early in labor and is sometimes used during pregnancy to check the baby's well-being (see p.166). The internal monitor is slightly more accurate. You'll have belts strapped around your body, and a tiny electrode will be clipped onto your baby's head. Your contractions and the baby's heartbeat are then recorded on a paper printout. There is also a video screen that records the contractions and heartbeats as visible waves, punctuated by flashing lights. During a contraction, blood flow to the placenta is reduced very briefly, and during this time your baby's heart rate will dip. This is quite normal and the heart rate returns to baseline when the contraction passes (see p.167). If the return to baseline is delayed, your baby may be distressed and action can be taken early to protect him. The latest type of EFM, known as telemetry, uses radio waves and allows you to walk around as the baby's monitor is attached to a transmitter strapped to your thigh. The older equipment confines you to a bed or chair.

How it is done Your water is broken when the cervix is at least two to three centimeters (two to two and a half inches) dilated and the electrode is applied to your baby's head. In addition to the baby's monitor, which picks up his heartbeat, a second monitor is placed between your baby and the wall of the uterus to measure the pressure and rate of uterine contractions.

How it helps doctors EFM provides medical staff with a second-by-second report on the condition of your baby. It will warn the doctors if your baby is in distress so they can intervene before anything untoward has happened. If your doctors decide that you and your baby would be better off with EFM, try to see it as something that gives reassurance that your baby is doing fine.

Disadvantages EFM increases the amount of electronic equipment in the delivery room, making the atmosphere very clinical, and the staff may concentrate more on the machine than on you. Because attendants are aware of any tiny changes that may occur, they are more likely to intervene rather than letting labor take its natural course over time.

Monitoring in labor
Contractions are recorded by an external monitor strapped to your abdomen. An internal monitor is attached to your baby.

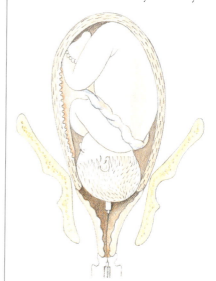

Monitoring your baby
The electrode is attached to his presenting part, usually his head, by piercing the skin and provides an electrical contact that picks up his heartbeat. Some babies' heads will be bruised or have a rash where the electrode was attached. However, many mothers find EFM reassuring as they can watch their baby's heartbeat throughout labor.

PAIN RELIEF

Apart from offering pain relief, drugs can affect your experience of childbirth in other ways. Make sure you opt for the type that will help to enhance, rather than detract from, the pleasure of your baby's birth.

Drowsiness *This is a common side effect of anesthetic gases, tranquilizers, and narcotics. Some women enjoy the sensation of drifting, but sometimes the sleepiness can make mothers feel they lack control. After using narcotics, a few women have become so lightheaded they were unaware of what was happening around them, and gave birth without realizing it had happened.*

Dizziness *Demerol and other narcotics can sometimes induce a feeling of confusion, or disorientation, and some mothers have even had hallucinations.*

Nausea *The sensation of nausea is usually quite slight with gas and oxygen, but is quite common after using Demerol and other narcotics, and a few mothers may even suffer attacks of vomiting.*

Your state of mind can have a major effect on the intensity of pain experienced during labor. So if the use of drugs will make you less anxious, there is no point in depriving yourself. Excessive tension may affect the uterus, slow down labor, and adversely affect your baby (see column, opposite).

For many women, particularly first-time mothers, anticipation of their baby's birth may be overshadowed by worry about pain during labor. Labor invariably involves pain, but you can build up your confidence by preparing for the intensity of contractions, by understanding your own limits of pain tolerance, and by learning about different methods of pain relief. If possible, try to view the pain as a positive element of labor — each contraction brings the birth of your baby nearer.

COPING WITH PAIN

The kind of pain you'll experience during contractions can vary. Very often, it feels like a thick band being squeezed around your abdomen as the uterine muscles harden and tighten for several seconds before relaxing. Some women describe it as being like severe menstrual cramps, others experience backache, but there may be a combination of sensations as the contraction reaches its peak, culminating in a wave of discomfort, which then subsides.

Individual response You may prefer not to use drugs during your labor as they can dim your awareness of what is happening and deprive you of the sensation of giving birth. However, it is very difficult to know the level of pain you can manage without relief, particularly if this is your first baby. Some women are surprised by the overpowering intensity of their contractions; others may worsen their pain through fear and anxiety. Analgesia in childbirth can offer complete relief of pain as in epidural anesthesia or reduction of pain to bearable levels as with gas combined with oxygen, and narcotics. Many people opt for no drugs in the early part of the first stage, then have a low dose of gas and oxygen toward transition. Don't be self-critical if you do opt for pain relief with drugs; it isn't a sign of cowardice. Remember your labor isn't a test, and the use of drugs may even be essential for you to deliver your baby.

If you haven't made up your mind about the use of pain medication, you may try to do without drugs for as long as possible. If so, a useful tip is to wait 15 minutes after you feel you want pain relief before having it. During that time your labor may progress well, and it gives you and your birth assistant time to discuss whether or not you can get by with encouragement, or whether you really do feel the pain is increasing to the point where relief is necessary.

If you wish to have full participation in your baby's birth without dimming your consciousness of the physical and emotional sensations, there are alternatives to drugs for pain relief. Also, your body can provide its own brand of painkiller and relaxant, endorphins (see column, p.89). The more natural your labor, the more quickly your own endorphins will be produced, not earlier than a half-hour into the transition stage.

A clear choice Find out as much as possible about the types of pain relief that will be available. Have a discussion with your doctor, midwife, and hospital attendants, and then outline your choices in your birth plan (see p.106) with an alternative version available in case any complications arise.

Many doctors and midwives seek to make labor and delivery as pain-free as possible with the aid of drugs. Unless you state your preferences very clearly, you may find certain analgesics are used automatically whether you want them or not. Don't hesitate to question their use, or to request a smaller dosage.

PAIN-RELIEVING DRUGS

Some types of pain relief will be available only in large or teaching hospitals, but most are widely available in all hospitals. Your midwife will also be able to offer certain types for a home delivery.

Regional anesthetics These remove sensation from part of your body by blocking the transmission of pain from nerve fibers. Caudal anesthesia is administered by an injection into your spinal area around the sacrum, and numbs your vagina and perineum. This may be used for short-term relief if the birth involves a vacuum extraction, or forceps delivery.

To administer a pudendal block, anesthesia is injected straight into your vagina near the pelvic region, blocking the pudendal nerve. This numbs the lower part of your vagina and may be used if you have an episiotomy, although it is used infrequently. The most widely used form of this type of anesthesia is the epidural block. This prevents pain spreading from your uterus by acting as a "nerve block" in your spine. A well-managed epidural removes all sensation from your waist to your knees, but you remain alert. It may be particularly recommended if you have a difficult

HOW DRUGS AFFECT YOUR BABY

Most drugs will cross the placenta to affect your baby once they are in your bloodstream. There will be a higher concentration in your baby's blood than in your own.

Drowsiness *Large doses of sedatives and tranquilizers will have a sedating effect on your baby. This may affect his ability to suckle, and to respond to you for a while after he is born.*

Breathing and sucking difficulties *Narcotics can depress your baby's respiration and make sucking inefficient. If you take one late in your labor it will remain longer in your baby's bloodstream. Drugs used in epidural anesthesia cannot enter your baby's blood. A baby born after epidural anesthesia therefore stands a very good chance of being alert and breathing well.*

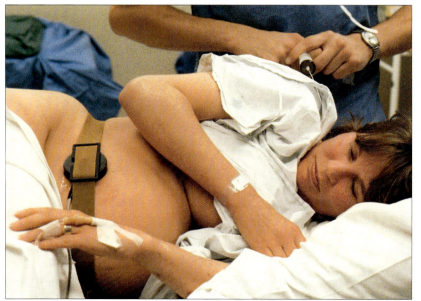

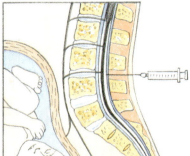

Epidural anesthetic
Once you have had an injection of local anesthetic in your back, (to numb it), the anesthesiologist will insert a fine, hollow needle into the epidural space – the region around the spinal cord inside the spinal column (see picture above).

WAYS YOU CAN BREATHE

Relaxing your body and focusing on your breathing will help alleviate your anxiety and let you ride out your contractions. Practice breathing patterns beforehand with your birth assistant so he or she can guide you during labor, if necessary.

Slow breathing *During the early stages, calmly and deliberately breathe out through your mouth as the contraction begins. Then slowly breathe in through your nose. Sustain the same steady pattern throughout the contraction, which may last about 45–60 seconds.*

Light breathing *As your contractions become more intense and frequent, you may find it easier to breathe above them. Take light, short breaths that seem to involve only the upper part of your body, and not your abdomen where the contraction is taking place.*

You will probably find that you will use different breathing techniques at different stages of your labor.

labor, preeclampsia, or severe asthma, or if you have a forceps delivery. Most mothers who have a Caesarean have an epidural instead of a general anesthetic, which means they are able to stay awake during the birth. First of all a local anesthetic will be given in your back in order to numb the area for the injection. A fine, hollow needle is then carefully inserted into the epidural space (see previous page) and a thin tube known as a catheter is threaded down inside the hollow needle. The needle is removed leaving the catheter in position and the catheter is taped in place against your skin. Anesthetic is syringed down the catheter, which is then sealed, although it can be topped off at any time if necessary.

You need to let the nurses or other attendants know in advance that you wish to have an epidural as it has to be given by a skilled anesthesiologist, and it usually takes 10–20 minutes for the procedure to be set up. Once it has been adminstered, the anesthetic will take effect within a few minutes.

Inhalation analgesics This is a mixture of gas and oxygen that you administer yourself, using a face mask. You inhale deeply as the contraction starts, and keep breathing until the contraction peaks or you have had enough. You then put the mask aside and breathe normally. Gas works by numbing the pain center in the brain, and can make you feel as though you're floating. You may be able to practice this in a prenatal class.

Narcotics The most commonly used narcotic is meperidine (Demerol), which is derived from morphine, and is given by injection in the thigh or buttock in varying dosages during the first stage. Demerol and other narcotics dull the sensation of pain by acting on the nerve cells in the brain and spine. If you choose to take a narcotic, it is probably wise to ask for a small dose to see how you are affected. Narcotics take about 20 minutes to work.

Sedatives and tranquilizers These help to make you calm and sleepy. Small doses will help to reduce anxiety, and encourage you to rest between contractions. Tranquilizers will also help to control nausea and to lower blood pressure.

RELIEF WITHOUT DRUGS

It's important that you have mastered your chosen pain-relief method, and familiarized your birth assistant with the technique, some time before you go into labor. If special equipment is needed to help you along, make sure it will be available when you go into labor, either at home or in the hospital. You may find that one method on its own may not be enough – you may need a combination for more complete relief.

Positions Walking, leaning against your partner or the wall, and rocking your pelvis will probably feel much more comfortable than lying on your back in bed. There are certain positions that will take the pressure off your back (see p.270).

Massage This is a wonderful way of getting reassurance from your partner while relieving discomfort, whether you're lying, standing, or squatting. It can be particularly effective if you have backache during labor, as approximately 90 percent of women do (see column, right), or if you suffer from back labor (see p.256).

Water Lying in warm water can be very relaxing and soothing. Immersion in water renders you virtually weightless, and this brings relief between contractions. For these reasons birthing pools are used by some mothers, under supervision (see p.88).

Visualizing Creating images in your mind can be a very effective way of calming fear and reducing pain. As your contraction begins, imagine something that you find particularly soothing – for example, warm, bright sunshine. Contractions in the first stage are opening the cervix and you may find it helpful to imagine the bud of your favorite flower opening very slowly, petal by petal. Many women find thoughts of waves very comforting, matching the flow of the waves with their own contractions.

Sounds You can help to diffuse the pain and anxiety of labor by vocalizing in the way you feel most helpful. Sighing, moaning, groaning, and grunting – all are ways of releasing tension, and you shouldn't be inhibited or worry about disturbing others.

Many women find that listening to music is very effective. Your birth assistant can play different pieces on a tape recorder, according to how you are feeling. A light, uplifting piece of music may help you rise above your contraction. When your contractions intensify, more dramatic pieces of music, building up to a crescendo, may help you to cope with them.

Hypnosis This isn't something that you should try on a whim as you need to respond to hypnosis very easily. Women who go into a deep trance have been able to have a forceps delivery, stitches, or Caesarean without feeling pain. A period of practice sessions is advisable, and both you and your hypnotist should be completely familiar with what you will have to do during labor and delivery.

Acupuncture You should opt for this method only if you have already found that it can relieve pain in other situations. In addition, your acupuncturist must be familiar with labor and delivery. This may not stop you from feeling any pain at all, but it will certainly reduce it, and it can also help stop nausea.

TENS (Trans-cutaneous Electrical Nerve Stimulation) Pain impulses conducted by nerves are blocked by an electric current that also stimulates the production of endorphins. A battery-powered stimulator is connected by wires to electrodes placed on either side of the spine. You are then able to use a handset that regulates the amount of stimulation, enabling you to control the amount of pain relief that you require.

RELIEVING BACKACHE

Many women suffer from backache during labor, sometimes because of the baby's head pressing against the sacrum. Massage by your birth assistant can help relieve this.

Rubbing the sacrum
Using the heel of your hand, rub all around the mother's sacrum and lower back.

Circular pressure
Press your thumbs over the sacrum and move them gently in a circle. Rest your hands on the mother's hips for support.

Deep pressure
Press your thumbs into the middle of each buttock. Make sure she is focusing on her breathing to help her relax.

PARTNER'S ROLE IN LABOR

The more comfortable and relaxed a mother feels during labor, the better her ability to cope with pain. She can find this security with loving support from a birth assistant. A partner is the natural choice, as he will probably be closely involved throughout the pregnancy and eager to share the experience of his child's birth. Most hospitals now welcome fathers, friends, or relatives to support the mother during labor.

UNDERSTANDING YOUR ROLE

Like many partners, you may be nervous. You may worry about feeling squeamish, or being inadequate at offering sufficient support. You can help to combat this by preparing yourself in advance. It's important you know as much as possible so you can effectively help the mother meet the physical and emotional demands of labor. At the prenatal classes there will be demonstrations to describe the onset of labor and the effect of contractions, and you will be taught techniques for helping her relax.

If it's going to be a hospital birth, visit the hospital's labor and delivery rooms and introduce yourself to her hospital attendants so you won't feel like an outsider when the time comes. If the birth is to be at home, make sure you know the route to the hospital in case of an emergency, and find out what will be expected of you; trust will create a calmer atmosphere.

HOW TO HELP DURING LABOR

You may have a very active role throughout the labor and birth, but sometimes your presence is all the mother needs. Make sure you are familiar with her birth plan and the alternative version (see p.106). You need to be aware of her wishes in order to provide her with the best care and attention during labor.

Use your intuition You need to judge the situation, observing the mother's moods and fitting in. She may want to stay quiet, going through contractions alone without being touched. Alternatively, she may need much verbal or physical encouragement, or to be distracted.

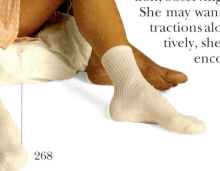

Supporting your partner
If your partner leans back against you, you can support her weight and hug her at the same time.

Provide emotional support   Remain as intimate as possible, using loving words, and keep your movements slow, quiet, and steady. Always be positive: offer praise, never criticism. If she wants to hear your voice, constantly tell her how well she is doing (how far dilated), how she can relax herself, what others such as the midwife or nurse are doing to help her, and what will soon happen. Also, help her to see how much she has achieved already – it's easy for her to be overwhelmed by how far she thinks she has to go. Massage and stroke her slowly, but if she just wants to hold your hand, you can offer encouragement by using facial expressions and lots of eye contact. Sometimes just the expression of love in her partner's eyes can help a woman bear the pain of contractions.

Combat fatigue   Before labor, advise her to rest as much as possible, particularly if she seems to spend a lot of energy cleaning during the nesting period. If she has a long, tiring labor, try to help her relax between contractions to conserve her energy for the second stage. If she's not feeling nauseous, provide her with as much nourishment as she wants (see also p.244).

Help her cope with pain   It's hard to see someone you care about in pain, but try not to reveal your anxiety, as she will become discouraged. On the other hand, don't discredit her suffering. Acknowledge it positively, telling her each contraction is bringing your baby's birth nearer, and offer different suggestions for relief. Don't let her feel embarrassed about expressing her discomfort – encourage her to be as uninhibited as possible.

   If she feels particularly anxious during a contraction, try to calm her fears by discussing how she felt before the next one starts. Try not to be upset if she becomes critical or aggressive because this often happens when the pain is very intense.

Assist with breathing   You will probably have practiced the mother's preferred method during prenatal classes, but allow her to follow her own rhythm. If she seems to lose control, remain close to her and slowly guide her through the pattern until she has enough reassurance to carry on alone. Be prepared to adapt – very few people follow exactly what they practiced at prenatal classes.

Offer comfort   You can be a great help in relieving her discomfort. Suggest different positions (see p.270) and support her with cushions or blankets, or let her lean her weight against you while you cuddle and rock together. Look out for any signs of tension in her neck, shoulders, or forehead, and gently stroke these areas. Massage will also offer some relief, and if she's using visualization techniques, you can help by talking her through them with a soft, gentle voice. She may find that having her face and hands wiped will be very soothing. Offer her ice chips to suck. If she feels cold, help her put on socks or leg warmers. As labor progresses she may want to talk less, but you can communicate by touching or caressing, or by using eye contact.

A birth partner can do a lot to help during labor, not only providing you with comfort and reassurance, but also dealing with staff on your behalf. Bear in mind that although the hospital uniforms and equipment may appear daunting, the medical team is there to support both of you.

Your birth partner can:

• *Answer questions for you (if allowed to by the staff), which saves you from having your concentration disturbed*

• *Support you in the positions you choose for pain relief and/or to give birth*

• *Stroke and massage you if you find it comforting*

• *Change the atmosphere (dim the lights, change the music) for you*

• *Ask people to leave if too many build up in your personal space during a home birth*

• *Be the one you can really rely on to interact with the staff on your behalf and to stand by your decisions regarding pain relief – whether to accept it or not, and if so, when and how much. If you do decide to ask for relief, he should encourage you to have a breathing space of about 15 minutes before it is administered, as things can change very quickly and you may find you don't need it after all*

FIRST STAGE POSITIONS

There are many different positions that you can adopt to ease your discomfort. Some women prefer to stand up and move around, as this helps to strengthen contractions, which then accelerates labor. As the contractions proceed, you may instinctively choose a sitting or kneeling position, but if not, try using cushions, chairs, or your partner for support.

YOUR POSITIONS FOR LABOR

Massage your partner's back as she rests against you. You may also find rocking together helps

Standing
Lean forward and rest against your birth assist-ant, or a wall. The weight of your baby will be taken off your spine and the contractions will be more efficient. Rotate your hips. Your birth assistant will be able to help you breathe correctly.

Let your shoulders drop. You can rest against a cushion during contractions

Make sure your back is straight

Sitting
If you find it more comfortable to sit down, try leaning forward with your legs wide apart. You can sit facing the chair back, resting on a pillow or cushion. Alterna-tively, to keep your body sup-ported, you may prefer to lean against your birth assistant, who can also rub your back.

Rock your pelvis backward and forward during contractions to relieve backache

Kneeling
As the contractions strengthen you may find it less tiring to go down onto your hands and knees. This helps to alleviate backache. Keep your legs wide apart, and rock your pelvis. Make sure your back is straight; don't allow it to arch. Between contractions, lean forward onto your folded arms or sit back on your heels.

During transition
If your cervix is not fully dilated toward the end of the first stage just before giving birth, use gravity to slow down the baby while the cervix continues to dilate. Lean onto a pile of cushions with your legs wide apart, or kneel with your head down and your bottom raised.

Take the pressure off your lower back by leaning forward with your head on a pillow

Kneeling on the floor with your bottom raised and your head on the floor may relieve backache

Lying down
During labor, you may find it comfortable to lie down. If so, try lying on your side, and place cushions under your head and upper thigh. Keep your legs wide apart.

Relax your shoulders, and concentrate on your breathing with your eyes closed

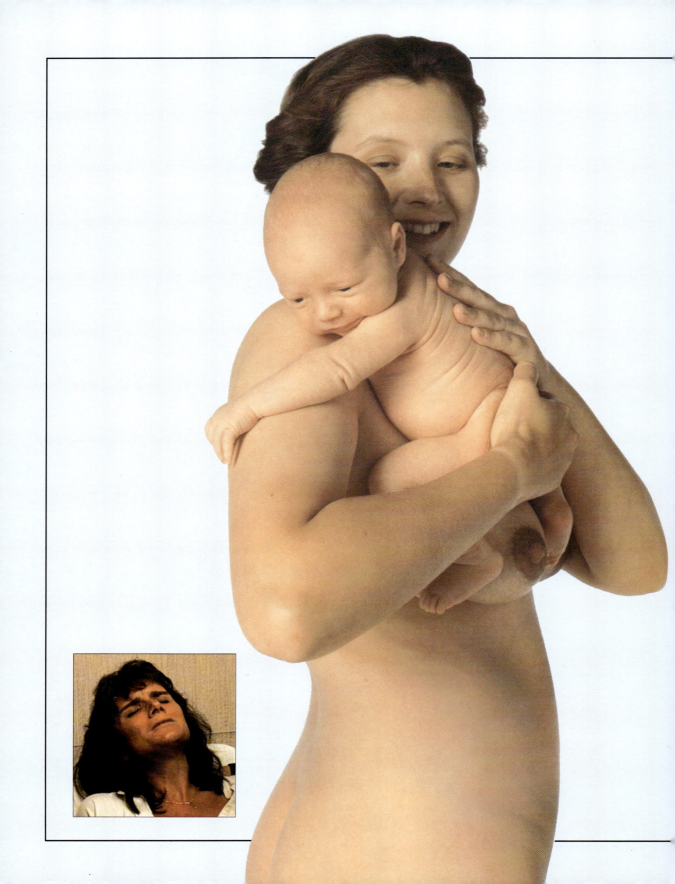

13

Your baby is
BORN

*During the second stage of labor, you are overcome by the
instinctive urge to bear down, which is caused by the
pressure of your baby's head on the pelvic floor and the
rectum. Your feeling of release as your baby's body finally
emerges will be swiftly followed by a feeling of wonder and
exhilaration as you greet your baby for the first time.*

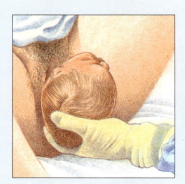

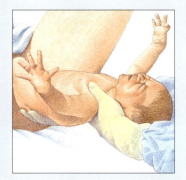

BREATHING IN THE SECOND STAGE

You will be taught breathing exercises in prenatal classes. The importance of good breathing techniques during the second stage of labor cannot be over-estimated. It gives you the sensation of being in control of your own body, and this is very empowering.

As you begin the second stage, you may want to accelerate your breathing. This is the most shallow form of breathing you should use in labor. Instead of using your chest and throat, focus on breathing only through your mouth. Breathe lightly in and out through your lips, starting slowly and gradually quickening. Be careful not to breathe out too deeply or you will start to hyperventilate. If you feel dizzy, place your hands lightly over your nose and mouth while you are breathing.

Into the second stage
Full dilation occurs at the end of the transition stage. The first indication that this has happened is a tremendous urge to push. Always ask an attendant to check your cervix – don't hang on and fight the urge, even if it isn't long since you were checked, because the final few centimeters of dilation can be reached in seconds. Once full dilation is confirmed you are able to push with force. Your mood will change and you will probably feel re-energized and positive as you work hard toward the birth of your baby, which is now only a short time away.

DELIVERY: THE SECOND STAGE

Delivery is the main event: it's what you've been preparing for over the past nine months. Your expectations are realistic – a manageable labor, not necessarily painless, but happy and relaxed with a birth assistant of your choosing, with medical attendants whom you know well, and with equipment and surroundings that are familiar. The most important factor in relaxing you is that everyone around you is a friend.

CONTRACTIONS AND PUSHING

The second stage is the expulsive stage when you push your baby out through the birth canal. It lasts from full dilation of the cervix until the baby is born and, for a first baby, it generally doesn't take longer than two hours (the average is about one hour). It may be as little as 15–20 minutes for subsequent babies. The uterine contractions are at this time 60–90 seconds long and occur at two- to four-minute intervals.

You will almost certainly feel the urge to push down, known as bearing down, which is caused by your baby's head pressing down on your pelvic floor and rectum, and which is quite involuntary. Your pushing should be smooth and continuous; all the muscular effort should be smooth and slow so that the vaginal and perineal tissues and muscles are given enough time to stretch so they will be able to accommodate your baby's head.

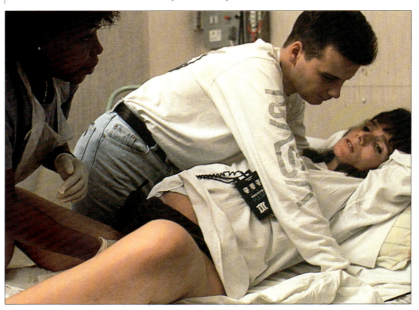

Upright is the most efficient position to be in when you're pushing, whether you are seated on a birthing stool, standing with your arms around your partner's neck, or in a squatting position. This means that the downward muscular force of your body and the downward force of gravity are working in unison to expel your baby.

Avoid being delivered while lying on your back because in this position you are pushing your baby out uphill, *against* the force of gravity. This requires much harder work, and therefore the delivery will be slower (see p.90).

During pushing, the pelvic floor and the anal area should be fully relaxed, so make a conscious effort to let go of this part of your body. You may lose a little stool or urinate, but don't be embarrassed; it is very common and your attendants have seen it all before. When you've finished a push, you will find two slow, deep breaths helpful, but don't relax too quickly at the end of each contraction. The baby will continue to maintain its forward progress if you relax slowly. If your second stage is considered to be prolonged, the delivery of your baby could be assisted by forceps (see p.280).

NORMAL DELIVERY

The first sign that the baby is coming is the bulging of your anus and perineum. With each contraction, more and more of the baby's head appears at your vaginal opening, until it doesn't slip back at all between contractions. This is known as crowning.

You will probably feel a stinging or burning sensation as the baby stretches the outlet of your vagina. As soon as you feel it, try to stop bearing down, pant, and allow the contractions of your uterus to push the baby out. This may be difficult as you may still be feeling like pushing, but if you continue to push you increase the risk that you will tear or need an episiotomy. As you stop pushing, lean back and try to go limp. Make a conscious effort to relax the muscles of the perineal floor. The stinging or burning sensation lasts only for a short time and is followed by a numb feeling as the baby's head stretches your vaginal tissues so thin that the nerves are blocked, having a naturally anesthetic effect.

If the medical staff feel you are going to tear, this is the moment they may do an episiotomy (see p.92). They will also check that the umbilical cord is not around the baby's neck – if it is, they will gently lift it over her head, make a loop through which she can be delivered or, if it is very tight, they may clamp and cut it.

When her head has been delivered, your baby will be face down, but almost immediately she will twist her head so that she is facing your left or right thigh. The midwife, nurse, or other attendant will then wipe your baby's eyes, nose, and mouth, and clear any fluid from her nose and upper air passages.

After delivery of the head, your uterine contractions will stop for a minute or so. When they restart, the first contraction will usually deliver one shoulder and the next will deliver the other. Once both shoulders are delivered, the rest of your baby will slide out quickly and easily. Your attendants will hold her firmly as she will be very slippery with blood, amniotic fluid, and *vernix caseosa*.

WHAT YOUR BABY DOES

Her body goes through several twists and turns as she descends through the birth canal, all of which are aimed toward achieving a smooth, safe birth.

Your baby has a pliable body but a fairly firm, oval head. Both these parts have to adapt themselves to a curved lower birth canal made up of the lower part of the uterus inside the pelvis, dilated cervix, and stretched vagina. There are various adjustments that your baby makes as labor progresses.

• *She will bring her chin down onto her chest as she descends through the pelvis*

• *She will rotate her head*

• *She will extend her head backward so that the back of her head touches her back as she emerges from the birth canal and vagina*

• *She will make a little sideways wriggle so that her head turns to one side or the other; the shoulder of that side can then be delivered through the vagina*

• *She will make another little wriggle to swing her head all the way around so that the other shoulder is delivered. (If you imagine this in quick succession, it's like a shrug of one shoulder after the other: during delivery this is so fast that you hardly perceive it)*

• *Her trunk, buttocks, and legs follow her head out through the birth canal*

GIVING BIRTH

The urge to push out your baby is usually an overwhelming and irresistible feeling

Your baby's journey down the birth canal lasts about an hour on average, if this is your first birth. You will probably feel swept along by an unbelievably strong, fundamental urge to bear down and push your baby out of the uterus, although a few women, especially if they have already had a baby, do not really experience the urge to push.

Your caregivers will be on hand at all times to offer you support and encouragement. They will also be ready to act very promptly if any complications should arise

Pushing
As each contraction builds until it reaches its peak, you will experience powerful urges to bear down and push out your baby as she descends. Bearing down is not something that you *decide* to do; it is an instinctive reaction, which you will be powerless to resist.

The head crowns
There comes a point when your baby's head does not slip back between contractions, but remains visible at the vaginal outlet. This is when the head is said to crown, and you will feel a burning or stinging sensation as her head stretches your vagina. It is important that you stop pushing at this point so that you give the tissues of your perineum a chance to thin and stretch. This may be difficult as you may still be experiencing the urge to bear down, but you must try to resist. If you continue to push you will put undue stress on the perineal area, which is likely to result in a tear or necessitate an episiotomy. Panting is a good way to try and control your desire to bear down.

The head emerges

As her head is born, she will immediately turn her head sideways. Your contractions will probably pause for a few moments at this point, and your caregivers will feel around your baby's neck to make sure that the cord is not present. If it is, they will either lift it up over her head or make a loop through which she can be born. Her shoulders will be born within minutes.

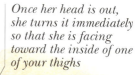

Once her head is out, she turns it immediately so that she is facing toward the inside of one of your thighs

With a couple of almost imperceivable shrugs, her shoulders are born and she slithers out into the hands that are waiting to catch her

The baby is born

As soon as her shoulders are free, the rest of her body will be born immediately. As she slithers out of your vagina she will probably be followed by a great gush of amniotic fluid. Your caregivers will hold her carefully as she will be slippery. She may be breathing and crying already.

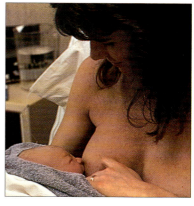

The first cuddle

Your caregivers will usually wrap or cover her in a blanket to keep her warm and then give her to you to hold in the first few minutes after her birth. She may start to suckle spontaneously.

RECORDING THE BIRTH

Photographs of the baby's birth can provide great joy for all involved, including family and friends. However, it's important to bear a few things in mind.

• Remember to seek special permission from the doctor, nurse, and midwife before labor begins

• If you intend to take more than a few photographs, or if you want to videotape the event, it would be better for a friend or relative to do this. The mother will need you to be sensitive to her every need, not rushing around clicking the camera or focusing on the best image. You may alienate yourself from her, not to mention the doctor or midwife, if you are constantly behind a piece of equipment

• The room's atmosphere will have a great effect on the mother's labor. The lighting should be dim enough for her to feel relaxed, so use high-speed film (400 ASA) instead of brightening the room. Many hospitals will not allow direct flash to be used, as it can be irritating for the mother and may damage the baby's eyes

PARTNER'S ROLE AT BIRTH

By this second stage of labor, your role in providing loving support for the mother will be well established. You have now passed through the most painful phase and have reached the climactic stage of delivery.

SECOND STAGE JOBS

Many of the jobs you performed during the first stage – making her comfortable, supporting different positions, providing refreshment, giving moral support – may also be needed at this stage. However, this is when you will also have to encourage her to push. All this will make the mother's job very much easier and help her feel emotionally secure and relaxed.

If you are in a hospital and are asked to leave the delivery room, do so without question. There may be a medical emergency, and the staff will have to move quickly. You cannot guarantee that you will not be in the way, so leave the delivery room but stay nearby.

Helping with the delivery position Your partner, having been through the first stage of labor, will probably know by now which position she finds the most comfortable. You can offer valuable support to help her through the pushing stage, but don't hesitate

Semi-upright position
If she's happy for you to be as near as possible, she can lean back against you for support. You will be able to guide her through the contractions. The closeness of your body next to her may help make her feel more relaxed during the delivery.

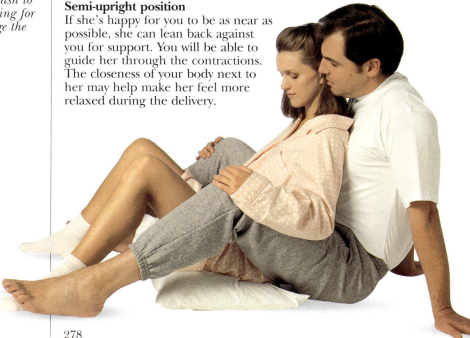

to ask for advice if you're not certain what to do. If she doesn't want to be held, you can offer suggestions for other positions that she may find comfortable, and place pillows or cushions underneath and behind her for support.

Try to practice different ways of sitting or squatting before labor so that you are both familiar with them; if you are feeling uncomfortable this may make your partner nervous. If your partner is happy sitting in bed or on the floor, suggest that she try the knee-chest position, which many women find comfortable during the second stage. She should drop her chin onto her chest while holding on to her knees. Between contractions, suggest that she relax against the pillow to conserve her energy.

Helping her with breathing and pushing To help her through these last few contractions, tap out a rhythm for the different kinds of breathing, using words like: breathe, breathe, pant, pant, blow. As she's pushing, gently remind her to relax her pelvic floor.

At the peak of contractions suggest that she take two or three deep breaths and push as hard as she can. She should push in a strong and steady way, and you can remind her that each push brings the birth of your baby nearer.

Encouraging her to relax Between contractions, make sure she relaxes fully because she needs to conserve her strength for pushing her baby through the birth canal.

Standing by Once the baby's head has crowned, you may then have a more passive role and become an observer. The midwife, doctor, or nurse will guide your partner through this pushing stage. Don't be disappointed if the mother doesn't communicate with you during the birth and seems to rely more on the caregiver. She will be fully preoccupied and may not notice you for some time.

Showing her the baby When the baby's head is emerging, hold a mirror nearby so that she can see his head crowning and then his whole body being pushed out.

Many hospitals have large mirrors mounted over the delivery table or bed so that laboring mothers can see what is going on. If your room doesn't have a suitable mirror, the birth attendant can ask for a large mirror on a stand to be wheeled in. It's best to ask for this as early in labor as possible – don't wait for the last minute.

Loving reception With the assistance of the doctor or midwife, you may be able to catch your baby as his body emerges. After you have greeted him for the first time, place him on your partner's stomach. You can then cuddle them both to help keep them warm and to let them know that you're there.

Be prepared for your own and the mother's reactions – tears, silence, whoops of joy. You may even feel squeamish at the sight of his tiny, greasy body. It's all perfectly understandable.

Supported squat
If your partner wants to deliver standing up, you can help support her by taking her weight on your arms. When she is supported in this position, her pelvis will be completely open and she will be able to take full advantage of gravity. Her legs should be wide apart.

FORCEPS-ASSISTED DELIVERY

"SPECIAL" DELIVERIES

Forceps look like large sugar tongs and are designed so that they will fit snugly over the sides of the baby's head, covering the ears. They're rather like a cage that protects the head from any pressure within the birth canal.

The decision to use forceps is a medical judgement on the part of your obstetrician. Forceps are only applied when the first stage is complete, the cervix is fully dilated, and the head is in the birth canal.

Why it is done *Forceps are applied when the baby's head has descended into the mother's pelvis but fails to descend further; when the baby is presenting in a posterior position; in a breech delivery (see main text); when the uterus fails to maintain contractions; and when the mother lacks the strength to push out her baby. Nowadays, most premature babies are delivered by forceps to protect their skull bones from being compressed in the birth canal.*

How it is done *If you're going to have a forceps delivery, you will be asked to lie on your back and your legs will be put up in stirrups. A local anesthetic will be injected into your perineum and an episiotomy (see p.92) performed. Then the forceps will be inserted into your vagina one at a time. A few gentle pulls on the forceps, 30–40 seconds at a time, will bring your baby's head down on to the perineum. You should feel no pain. Once his head is delivered, the forceps are removed, and the rest of his body will then be delivered as normal.*

The usual course of delivery is explained on the previous pages. Certain factors, however, may complicate a delivery and special procedures may be required. Sometimes a delivery is special because the complicating factor may not have been anticipated and forceps or a vacuum extractor will have to be used. On the other hand, multiple and breech births are special but are usually diagnosed well in advance.

ASSISTED DELIVERY

Occasionally, labor and delivery do not proceed as smoothly as expected, so your obstetrician will require assistance to complete a vaginal delivery. Forceps (see column, left) can be used to protect the baby's head or, along with vacuum extraction, may be used to accelerate the baby's progress through the birth canal.

Vacuum extraction The vacuum extractor is a gentler alternative to forceps. It consists of a metal plate or cone-shaped cup of synthetic material. This plate or cup is placed over the baby's scalp and, using an attached pump, a vacuum is created that makes the plate or cup adhere. This instrument then becomes a "handle" with which the obstetrician can both rotate the head and apply traction. Although it leaves a conspicuous (but temporary) bruise on the baby's head, it has many advantages (see column, right).

MULTIPLE DELIVERIES

The delivery of twins is always approached as if there were two single babies; because one baby has a vaginal delivery, it does not follow that the other one will too. Almost certainly you will be advised to have the babies in a hospital, in case they are not presenting properly. However, the most common way for twin babies to present at birth is for them both to be head-down. The second one usually arrives eight to ten minutes after the first.

Your obstetrician will probably recommend an epidural anesthetic (see p.265), as twin labors can be prolonged, or the second baby may have to be turned. This is done by rupturing the second baby's membrane, if necessary, and manually moving the baby into the correct position for birth.

Twin deliveries have become much safer in the past few years because the exact position of the second baby and its condition can be confirmed by ultrasound and fetal monitors. If there should be three or more babies, it is more likely that you will have a Caesarean section, although some doctors will deliver triplets vaginally if they have great experience in this procedure.

BREECH BIRTH

If your baby is in a breech position, and your obstetrician decides that he can most likely be delivered safely without a Caesarean section, he will be born buttocks first. The breech birth should not be thought of as an abnormal birth – it is better to think of it as a variation of normal, because four out of every 100 babies come out breech and most of them do so smoothly and are healthy.

In a breech birth, the buttocks are delivered first, then the legs. Before the head is delivered, you will almost certainly have to have an episiotomy because the head is the widest part and your baby's rump will not have stretched your birth canal sufficiently for his head to pass through it unpressurized (see **Case study**, p.260).

Once the baby's body is born, his weight pulls the head down to the vagina. His body is then lifted upward and slightly backward by the midwife, and one push is usually enough to deliver him. Forceps may be used to protect the baby's head. It is now fairly common practice for you to be given an epidural if you are having a breech birth. This is so that if you need a Caesarean section it can be done quickly and simply without further anesthesia, and you will be able to hold your baby as soon as he is born.

VACUUM EXTRACTOR

Because the device takes up less room in the vagina and is easier to apply, it offers certain advantages over forceps.

- *It can be applied before the cervix is fully dilated, and with less discomfort than forceps*

- *It can be applied to the lowest part of the baby's head.*

- *The shape of the baby's head is unaffected*

- *An episiotomy is not always necessary*

DELIVERING A BREECH BABY VAGINALLY

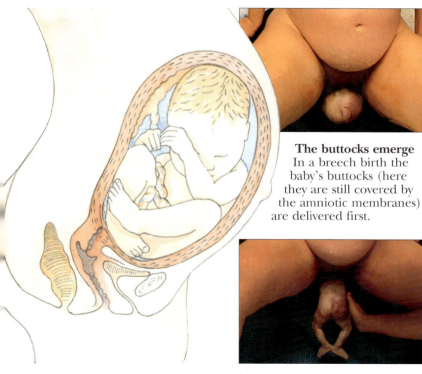

The buttocks emerge
In a breech birth the baby's buttocks (here they are still covered by the amniotic membranes) are delivered first.

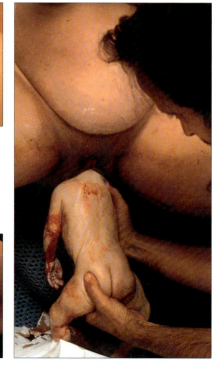

Breech position
Before labor begins, the baby's breech (buttocks) has not engaged in his mother's pelvis and her cervix is uneffaced.

Legs and body
Once the buttocks are clear of the birth opening, the membranes rupture and the baby's legs and body are delivered.

Arms and head
In the final stages of a breech delivery, the baby's arms emerge and then he is gently supported as his head is guided out.

SUDDEN BIRTH

Sometimes labor progresses so quickly that the birth happens away from medical assistance, whether at home or on the way to the hospital. If this happens, the following information will help you and your partner deliver your baby safely. This is not intended to be used as a guide for an out-of-hospital birth without a professional attendant being present, as this can be very risky indeed. However, it is reassuring that the majority of emergency births that happen at home rarely suffer any complications.

If the urge to bear down comes as you are driving to the hospital, use your breathing techniques to avoid pushing; try to remain calm.

Assess the situation with your partner. If the urge is too strong for you to control, your partner should pull the car over and stop. If possible, cover the backseat and car floor with a thick layer of newspapers or towels. You can then lie down and deliver the baby on the backseat into his hands.

Follow the procedure for the birth in the main text. Once the baby is born, it is essential that he be kept warm, so wrap him in a blanket or towel (or in your partner's shirt, sweater, or coat, if no other covering is available) and hold him close against your skin. If the placenta arrives before you reach the hospital, wrap it up with the baby, as this provides him with much-needed extra warmth. Do not cut the umbilical cord.

WHAT YOU SHOULD DO

As you get the urge to push, try to pant or blow for as long as you can in order to delay your baby's birth. However, the contractions alone are usually enough to expel the baby when he is coming this fast, so this will not delay things for long, although it may be long enough for your attendant or the ambulance to arrive. Never try to hold your legs together to delay delivery, or allow anyone else to do so, as it may result in your baby having brain damage. If you cannot comfortably delay your baby's birth, don't try to interfere. Deliver the head slowly. There is a greater chance that your vagina and perineum will tear if you push along with the force of your uterus, so pant lightly with each contraction.

Prolapsed cord If a loop of the umbilical cord washes out when the membranes rupture and your partner can see a piece of gray-blue shiny cord bulging out of your vagina, this means that you have a prolapsed cord and you must get help as soon as possible because your baby's oxygen supply is in danger of being cut off. Don't panic; you have time. Get onto the floor on your knees, with your chest to your knees, your head on the floor, and your buttocks in the air. This will help take the pressure of the baby's head off your cervix. If the cord is still protruding, your partner should cover it with a wet, warm, very clean towel while he calls the hospital or goes for help. Do not touch or put any pressure on the cord; stay in the knee-chest position even on the way to the hospital, because it reduces pressure on the cord. A prolapsed cord always necessitates a Caesarean delivery.

WHAT THE BIRTH ASSISTANT SHOULD DO

If it looks as if your baby will be born at home without medical assistance, you should telephone your doctor or midwife if you haven't done so already. If you haven't got a telephone, on no account should you leave the mother alone. However anxious and overwhelmed you feel, you must stay calm and reassure your partner – she needs to feel confident and relaxed. Bear in mind that the vast majority of sudden births are entirely uncomplicated. Encourage your partner to take up any positions in which she feels most comfortable (see p.270). Speak quietly and keep onlookers away to reduce stress.

Between contractions Turn up the heat in the room if at all possible. Wash your hands thoroughly with soap and water, and then fetch as many clean towels and sheets as you have and place them conveniently at hand. Fold one and put it on the floor so that you have something soft on which the baby can be laid.

Fill several bowls with lukewarm water, and then collect as many clean hand towels, washcloths, and soft rags as you have, to be immersed in the water and used as wipes for the baby and mother during and after delivery.

The birth Your partner will know when the baby is coming because she'll feel a stinging or burning sensation as the baby stretches her vagina. After washing your hands thoroughly again, look to see if you can see the top of the baby's head in the vaginal outlet (known as crowning – see p.275). Remind your partner to pant or blow, so that her vagina and perineum have time to thin and stretch, which may mean she will be able to avoid tearing.

The baby's head will probably be born in one contraction and the rest of his body in the contraction after. When the head is born, wipe each of the baby's eyes from inside to outside with separate pieces of moist soft cloth, and then feel around his neck to see if the cord is present. If it is, crook your little finger underneath it and pull it very gently over the his head, or lift it so that his body can be born through the loop.

Under no other circumstances should you interfere with the cord because it may go into a spasm and deprive your baby of oxygen. If the membranes are still present over the baby's face (traditionally known as the caul), you must tear this off very gently with your fingernail so that your baby can breathe.

Be careful to hold him firmly as he is born; he will be slippery with blood, mucus, and *vernix caseosa*. Never pull on his head, his body, or his cord. Once he is born, he will probably give a couple of gasps, a cry, and then start to cry for real.

If he doesn't start to cry immediately, place him across your partner's thigh or abdomen, with his head lower than his feet, and then gently rub his back. This helps any remaining mucus to drain away and usually causes a change in blood pressure, which will bring about his first breath. Talking to him lovingly will also help.

After the birth Once he is breathing, pass him to your partner so she can put him to her breast and keep him warm against her skin. He may not be interested in feeding but, if he is, the nipple stimulation will release oxytocin, which will encourage your partner's uterus to contract and expel the placenta.

Place blankets or towels over your partner (who may well be shivering by this time) so that she and the baby are well covered, especially the baby's head, as most of the heat is lost from here. Bear in mind that the normal color of a baby at birth is a bluish-white. He will gradually become pink in the first minutes as oxygen enters his body; his hands and feet will take somewhat longer. Do not try to wash off the baby's *vernix*, and never cut the umbilical cord.

THE DELIVERY OF THE PLACENTA

If the placenta is born before an attendant arrives:

- *Never pull on the cord*

- *Do not cut the cord*

- *After the placenta is born, massage the mother's uterus firmly, with a deep circular motion, pushing gently downward 2–3in (5–7cm) below the navel and rubbing. This is important to make sure the uterus contracts and stays hard after the birth so that there is no hemorrhage*

- *It's normal for a couple of cups of blood to be delivered when the placenta comes out*

- *Getting the baby to nurse immediately will help contract the uterus and minimize blood loss*

- *If your baby won't suck, the mother should gently massage her nipples as a substitute way of releasing oxytocin into her system*

CAESAREAN SECTION

WHAT HAPPENS TO YOU

A Caesarean section usually takes 45–60 minutes, but the baby is delivered within the first 5–10 minutes; the rest is spent stitching you up.

Preparation *Before the operation begins, your pubic hair is shaved, you are given the epidural, and an intravenous drip is set up to supply you with fluids during the operation. Then a catheter (a thin, flexible tube) is inserted up your urethra and into your bladder to drain it of urine. A small screen is placed in front of your face so you don't have to watch the operation. Your abdomen is swabbed to prevent any infection.*

The operation *The obstetrician makes a short, horizontal incision along the "bikini line" at the base of your abdomen, then makes a similar incision in the lower segment of your uterus. The amniotic fluid is drained off by suction, and the baby is gently lifted out. Then the cord is cut, the placenta is removed, and your uterus and abdomen are stitched.*

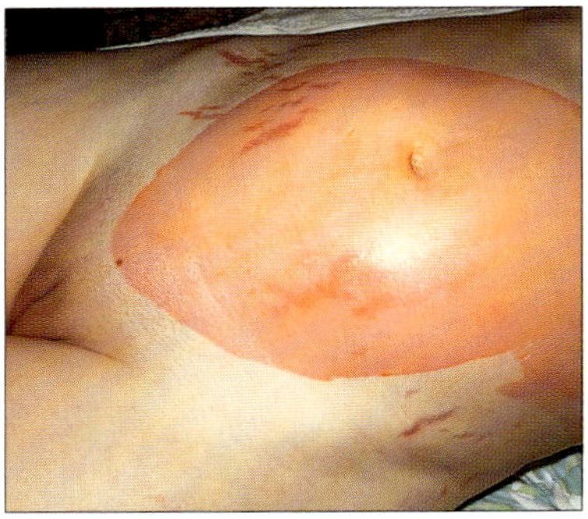

Surgical hygiene
This woman's abdomen has been swabbed with antiseptic. This kills any bacteria on her skin that could enter her body via the incision. The colored antiseptic in the above picture shows the area that has been treated.

When a normal vaginal delivery is considered dangerous or even impossible, your baby will be delivered by Caesarean section: small horizontal incisions are made in your abdomen and uterus, and your baby is delivered through them.

The percentage of babies delivered by Caesarean section has increased rapidly and is currently around 15–20 percent in the United States. This is partly because doctors are worried about being sued if a difficult birth causes complications that could have been avoided by Caesarean section, and partly because the operation is now so safe that it can be less risky than some other forms of delivery, such as breech or difficult forceps deliveries.

Very often, when a Caesarean section is necessary, the need for it will be apparent before labor begins, which means that you, your partner, and the obstetrician have time to discuss and plan for it. This type of planned Caesarean, known as elective, is in contrast to an emergency Caesarean, where the necessity for the operation may only become evident once labor is under way.

ELECTIVE CAESAREAN SECTION

Common reasons for electing to have a Caesarean section include the baby's head being too large to pass through your pelvis, the baby being in a breech position (see p.281) or lying across your pelvis; placenta previa (see p.202); and certain medical conditions such as diabetes or active herpes type II infection. It may also be necessary if you have previously had a Caesarean. This was once thought essential, because it was feared that the scar of the previous Caesarean section would open up during labor. But experience has shown that this does not happen with the horizontal or "bikini" cut, and so hospitals often allow a vaginal delivery to begin and, if there are no problems, to proceed as normal – a "trial of labor."

Elective Caesareans are often carried out under an epidural anesthetic (see p.265). This has several advantages over a general anesthetic: it is safer for your baby; you have no post-operative nausea or vomiting; and because you are conscious, you can hold your baby as soon as he is born. In addition, it may be possible for your partner to be with you during the operation, just as he could be if you were having a vaginal delivery. Usually your partner will be encouraged to sit on "your side" of the screen, near your head. He will have a slightly better view of the birth than you do,

When you have had a Caesarean, you may feel disappointed or even cheated that you did not have a vaginal delivery. Such feelings are perfectly natural, and the best thing you can do is talk about them with your partner. It will probably help if he can describe the birth to you in detail – this will help you to visualize and accept it.

It also helps, of course, to prepare yourself in advance for this type of birth. With your partner present, find out from the obstetrician what the operation entails, the procedures that will be used, and whether your partner is allowed to be present. Ask if you can see a film or video so you will know what is going to happen to you. If at all possible, talk to other women who have had Caesarean sections. They will not only provide you with useful information but emotional and moral support.

EMERGENCY CAESAREAN SECTION

This is needed when something goes wrong during labor, such as a prolapsed umbilical cord or hemorrhage from placenta previa, or if there is evidence of fetal distress. Emergency Caesareans may be carried out under epidural anesthesia and the hospital may not allow your partner to be present at the operation.

AFTER A CAESAREAN SECTION

As is the case with any major surgery, it takes time to recover from a Caesarean, but even so you will be encouraged to get up and walk around a few hours afterward to stimulate your circulation. You will be given pain medication if needed, and the dressings will be removed after three or four days. Your internal stitches will be made with absorbable sutures, which will dissolve away naturally, and your external stitches will be removed within about a week.

CAESAREAN SECTION WITH EPIDURAL

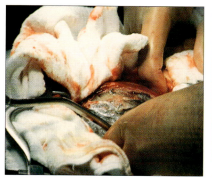
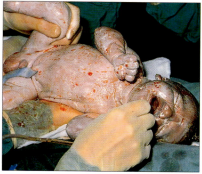

The operation
When the incisions have been made, the obstetrician begins to ease the baby out (above), sometimes with the aid of forceps. Within 5–10 minutes of the incisions being made, the baby has been delivered (above right) and the umbilical cord is clamped and cut. While the placenta is being delivered and the incisions stitched up, you will be able to hold your baby.

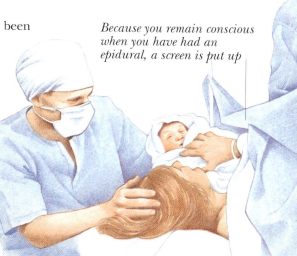

Because you remain conscious when you have had an epidural, a screen is put up

THE EFFECTS ON YOUR BABY

Not having to pass through the birth canal is both a benefit and a drawback for the baby born by Caesarean section.

Unlike a baby born by vaginal delivery, who initially has a rather squashed appearance after being squeezed through the birth canal, a Caesarean baby has smooth features and a rounded head. But often the Caesarean baby needs more time to adjust to the outside world because of his sudden entry into it, and because he has missed the journey through the birth canal that helps to clear amniotic fluid from a baby's lungs and stimulates his circulation.

After the obstetrician has delivered the placenta, he will sew up your incisions

AN EMERGENCY DELIVERY

About 15–20 percent of births in the United States are by Caesarean section, either planned or due to an emergency. Fran was glad she'd taken the trouble to find out about it.

NAME *Frances Ward*

AGE *27 years*

PAST MEDICAL HISTORY *Nothing abnormal*

OBSTETRIC HISTORY *1 child aged 3, pregnancy and delivery normal*

Fran's second pregnancy was uneventful. She and the baby were both doing well. Just 3 days before her expected date of delivery, she went into labor, which proceeded normally until the end of the first stage, when Fran was suddenly told she would have to have a Caesarean section.

WELL-INFORMED PARENTS

Fran had been surprised when I told her how frequently Caesarean sections are performed. Her prenatal classes did not cover the subject so she and her husband, Jonathan, decided to find out about it for themselves. They like to be well informed about anything they plan to do, whether it's visiting a foreign country or having a baby. They questioned birth attendants, read books, and watched videos on all types of birth, including Caesarean deliveries.

AN UNEXPECTED EMERGENCY

Fran's water broke halfway through the first stage, when her cervix was only four centimeters dilated. Following the rule that every mother must have an examination as soon as her membranes have ruptured, the midwife examined Fran at once. She discovered a prolapsed cord – a loop of the umbilical cord coming through the cervix into the vagina in advance of the baby. This is an extremely dangerous situation. As the baby's head presses down on the undilated cervix, the prolapsed section of the cord is squeezed tighter and tighter, cutting off the baby's blood and oxygen supply.

The midwife could feel the cord pulsating, meaning that the baby was still receiving an adequate blood supply. Within two minutes, though, the sonicaid picked up that the baby's heartbeat was dipping and showing signs of considerable fetal distress. Fran's obstetrician told her it was essential for the baby that it be delivered by Caesarean section.

HEADING OFF DISASTER

While the operating room was prepared, Fran was asked to lie with her legs up in stirrups so that the baby would slip backward, up into the pelvis, relieving the pressure on the cord. Meanwhile, the nurse inserted three fingers into Fran's vagina in order to keep the baby's head pushed up away from the cervix.

Fortunately, Fran had elected to have an epidural anesthetic early in labor, so she didn't need to have a general anesthetic or intragastric suction to prevent inhalation of vomit. There was the added bonus that she would be alert during the whole procedure.

THE OPERATION

Fran had chosen her particular hospital because it encouraged fathers to participate in their baby's births. She was pleased that Jonathan was allowed to gown up and watch the operation, because it meant that, even if she couldn't see the baby being born, at least Jonathan would see their child's entrance into the world.

The surgeon made a standard transverse incision (see column, p.284) through which Fran's baby was gently lifted out. As soon as the baby's head was delivered, the anesthesiologist gave Fran an injection of oxytocin. This stimulates uterine contractions, making it easier for the placenta to separate from the uterine wall and follow the baby out through the incision.

While Fran was being sewn up, the baby was handed to Jonathan so that he could hold her before taking her for her mother to see for the first time. Although she was disappointed about not having a normal vaginal delivery, Fran and Jonathan had still shared the experience of Ella's birth and she was able to hold and bond with Ella in the first few minutes after her birth.

RECOVERING FROM THE CAESAREAN

Fran found getting back to normal was almost the hardest part. I suggested she could join a self-help group for post-Caesarean mothers, where she would get useful advice on how to handle the postpartum period. Fran also worried that her next baby would have to be delivered by Caesarean, too. I reassured her that most mothers have vaginal deliveries following Caesareans, although there may be clear-cut reasons for having another one.

Rest and healing Fran had undergone abdominal surgery, so she needed plenty of rest and time for her scar to heal. When her stitches were removed, a week after the operation, she was told that the scar would be completely healed in three weeks and would fade after six months. Fran was surprised to find herself losing blood from her vagina, just as she did after her first child, which was a vaginal delivery, but I reassured her that this is quite normal.

Breastfeeding I told Fran that if she was going to breastfeed while sitting up, it was important for her to sit up straight. Her abdominal wall was tender so she used pillows to prop up Ella level with her breasts. She also found it comfortable to breastfeed lying on her side, resting on one elbow, with Ella on a pillow next to her.

Moving about Fran found standing up difficult because her stomach hurt, but I advised her to try and stand up perfectly straight as soon as she got out of bed, and to place her hands over her wound, supporting it, whenever she wanted to laugh or cough. The more she moved around, the speedier her recovery would be. After her stitches were removed, she was allowed home but was advised to rest and to be very careful when lifting, including picking up her children for cuddles or carrying heavy objects. She also had to refrain from strenuous exercise for at least six weeks.

FRAN'S BABY

Ella's birth was very different from that of a baby who is pushed down the birth canal.

- *Once the incision was made, the surgeon slipped a hand under her head and applied forceps*

- *Her head was gently pulled out with the forceps*

- *Her shoulders were maneuvered carefully through the incision*

- *Her body was gently pulled out – she was now delivered*

- *She was held with her head downward while her mouth and pharynx were cleansed of fluid with a soft catheter attached to suction apparatus*

- *She took her first breath*

- *Her cord was clamped and cut*

- *She was checked to make sure that all her systems were functioning (see **Apgar score**, p.290)*

- *As soon as she was breathing normally, she was handed to her father for a cuddle*

WHAT THE PLACENTA LOOKS LIKE

The majority of first-time mothers are very interested in seeing their baby's placenta.

The placenta measures about 8–10in (20–25cm) in diameter and weighs about 1lb (0.5kg). It is disk-shaped and its surfaces are very different in apppearance.

The fetal side was continuous with the wall of your uterus and covered by membranes. It is flat and smooth, and blue-gray in color with blood vessels radiating out from the umbilical cord. The maternal side was embedded in the wall of your uterus, and is made up of wedges (cotyledons) so that the surface area is increased for gaseous exchange. This side is dark red and looks like several pieces of raw liver joined together.

The fetal side
The side of the placenta that was facing toward your baby is flat and smooth. Note the umbilical cord emerging from its center and the prominent blood vessels.

THE THIRD STAGE

Once your baby has been born, your uterus will rest for about 15 minutes. It will then start to contract again in order to expel the placenta. This is the third stage of labor and is comparatively painless – you will probably hardly notice it.

THE THIRD STAGE

During the third stage of labor the placenta becomes detached from the uterine wall and is delivered by expulsion down the birth canal. The large blood vessels, which are about the thickness of a pencil, and which run to and from the placenta, are simply torn across. However, bleeding is rare because the muscle fibers of the uterus are arranged in a criss-cross fashion, which means that when the uterus contracts down, the muscles tighten around the blood vessels and prevent them from bleeding. This is why it is essential that the uterus contract down into a hard ball once the placenta has been expelled. The uterus can be kept tightly contracted by massaging it intermittently for an hour or so after the third stage is complete. Normally the third stage lasts about 10–20 minutes, but with active management this can be much shorter.

THE PLACENTA IS DELIVERED

Traditionally no attempt is made to deliver the placenta until there are clear signs that it is separating from the uterine wall and moving down into the vagina. The signs that your attendants will look out for are the resumption of contractions a few minutes after the birth of your baby, which indicates that the placenta is about to separate, and a desire to bear down on your part, which indicates that the placenta has separated from the uterine wall and is pressing down on your pelvic floor.

When these signs have appeared, delivery of the placenta is encouraged by holding the cord gently while pressing above the rim of the pelvis to control descent. The placenta is expelled from the vagina, followed by the membranes and what is called a retro-placental blood clot.

Delivery There are two ways in which the placenta may pass through the vulva. The first is when the center of the placenta comes out first, dragging the membranes behind it. In the second way, the placenta presents by an edge and slips out of the vulva sideways. Most women want to see the placenta – this is very understandable as it is an amazing organ that has been the life-support system for your baby for nine months (see column, left).

After delivery Once the placenta is delivered, medical staff carefully examine it to make sure that it's complete and that none of it has been left behind. If any of the placenta has been retained by the uterus, it can be a cause of hemorrhage later on, so it should be removed as soon as the diagnosis is made. In cases of doubt, an ultrasound scan will show whether the uterus is completely empty. The membranes should form a complete bag except for the hole through which the fetus has passed. The cut end of the cord will be examined to check that the umbilical blood vessels are normal. After the placenta is delivered, the whole of the vulva will be examined carefully for tears, and anything other than a minute one must be stitched immediately.

ACTIVE MANAGEMENT OF THE THIRD STAGE

Using a hormonal drug known as ergonovine maleate, many hospitals and obstetricians now actively manage the third stage of labor. Given at the time of birth or immediately afterward, this drug can reduce the number of cases of excessive bleeding (more than one pint of blood lost during childbirth).

This drug causes prolonged contraction of the uterus without a period of relaxation, and while the uterus is contracted there is not likely to be any bleeding.

The placenta will separate very quickly from the uterine wall once the uterus starts to contract, thereby shortening the third stage of labor. Nowadays, most attendants use a combination of oxytocin and ergonovine. This is because ergonovine may induce nausea, so using it with oxytocin, which acts quickly to stimulate uterine contractions, gives a better result.

These drugs are given by intramuscular injection just when the head is crowning or with delivery of the first shoulder. The hormone oxytocin is naturally produced by your body in response to seeing and touching your baby, and by putting her to your breast. It does the same job as ergonovine, but is less reliable.

HOW YOU WILL FEEL

Shivering and shaking can be quite profound after delivery of the placenta. After the delivery of my second child I was shivering so much and my teeth were chattering so much that I couldn't speak or breathe properly.

My own explanation for this reaction is that for nine months I had a little furnace inside me, producing quite a lot of heat, and my body had adjusted to take account of that heat production by turning my own thermostat down slightly. When my baby left my body, I was deprived of that heat and my body temperature probably dropped a few degrees – a significant drop, especially when you have been feeling generally overheated for several months! The only way the body can raise its temperature is to generate heat through muscular work. That's exactly what shivering does; by rapid contraction and relaxation of muscles, body heat is produced. Fortunately for new mothers, the shivering usually passes in about half an hour, during which time the body temperature has been brought back up to normal and your own thermostat reset. Then you are free to enjoy your new baby without the distractions of shivering, shaking, and chills.

POSTPARTUM HEMORRHAGE

This is rare, largely because the uterus has a self-protecting device to stop it from bleeding.

Once the uterus is completely empty, it contracts down to about the size of a tennis ball. The contraction of the uterine muscles nips the uterine arteries so that they cannot bleed. Under normal circumstances, therefore, little bleeding occurs after the delivery. What little bleeding there is appears as the lochia – the usual postpartum vaginal discharge, which is red for 2–3 days, then turns brown, and disappears within 2 weeks.

A uterus in which remnants of the placenta are retained will bleed, and this bleeding is called postpartum hemorrhage. If a small fragment of placenta is left in the uterus, it is usually diagnosed by examining the placenta and finding that a portion is missing. The mother is given a general anesthetic and the placenta is gently scraped away from inside the uterus.

If bleeding occurs more than 24 hours after delivery, the lochia may become bright red again. This can occur as a result of being too energetic. Consult your doctor, who will probably advise you to rest for several days. If the bleeding recurs or becomes heavy, it can signal infection or the retention of a small piece of placenta. Contact your doctor immediately.

THE APGAR SCORE

When your baby is born, she is checked to see whether she is fit and healthy. Within a minute of her birth, 5 simple tests are carried out. These are scored on the Apgar scale (named after Dr. Virginia Apgar, who devised it). The Apgar score includes the following checks:

Pulse/heart rate *This measures the strength and regularity of the heartbeat. 100 beats per minute scores 2; below 100 scores 1; no pulse scores 0.*

Breathing *This reveals the maturity and health of the baby's lungs. Regular breathing scores 2; irregular 1; none 0.*

Movements *An indication of the baby's muscle tone. Active movements score 2; some movements 1; limp scores 0.*

Skin color *This shows how well the lungs are working to oxygenate the blood. Pink skin scores 2; bluish extremities 1; totally blue skin scores 0.*

Reflexes *Crying and grimacing can reveal that the baby responds to stimuli. Crying scores 2; whimpering 1; silence 0.*

Most babies score between 7 and 10. A second test is done about 5 minutes later.

Your brand new baby
As you hold her you will experience the glow of motherhood – a mixture of love, pride, awe, and wonder, mixed with the all-encompassing tiredness that comes with a hard job well done.

BABY'S FIRST HOURS

Once your baby is delivered, most of the attention will be given to her, not to you, and rightly so. She may cry when delivered and will be crying lustily a few seconds after birth. She will probably be a bluish-white color at first and may be covered with vernix caseosa. *She will have streaks of blood on her head and body and, depending on your delivery, her head may look slightly pointed after her journey down the birth canal.*

HER FIRST MOMENTS

If her breathing is normal, there's absolutely no reason why you should not hold her immediately. If there's a danger of her being cold, you can be covered with a large towel or blanket. Your gentle stroking movements and the sound of your heartbeat and voice will be reassuring for your baby. Her eyes will almost certainly be fastened on your face and she may make movements as if she is trying to swim toward you.

Cutting the cord   The first procedure is the clamping of the cord. It is now generally believed that the baby benefits from the return of placental blood through the umbilical cord, and that the cord

should not be clamped until it stops pulsating. Blood can flow from the placenta to the baby only if the baby is at a lower level than the uterus. At the appropriate time, two clamps are applied to the cord, one a short distance from the navel, the other about an inch away. These clamps prevent the cord from bleeding; the one closest to the baby being the most important. The cord is then cut between the clamps. It may have been clamped and cut during delivery if it was looped tightly around the baby's neck. This is quite common.

Her general condition The midwife, nurse, or doctor will check your baby's general condition. This attendant will remove any remaining fluid in the baby's mouth, nose, or air passages by sucking it out with a rubber bulb. If the baby doesn't start to breathe immediately, she will be given oxygen.

WELCOMING YOUR BABY

Once the well-being of your baby is established, by all means ask the nursing and medical staff to leave if you wish to be left alone in the warmth of your house or hospital birthing room with your partner and your baby. You can relax after your hard work and mutually enjoy this amazing new experience. It's a good idea to put your baby to the breast immediately because it stimulates the delivery of the placenta, even if your baby isn't hungry at first.

These initial few moments should be spent in concentrating on your baby, getting to know her, learning to recognize her face, cooing at her so that she can hear the sound of your voice. You should hold her about 8–10 inches away from your face because at this distance she can make out your face quite clearly. Smile and talk gently in a sing-song voice, because newborn babies are attuned to high vocal pitches.

Within half an hour of birth your partner should be given his baby to hold for the first time. Men have the potential to bond as deeply and as quickly with their newborn children as women do.

After this initial bonding process, you will be washed down, stitched if necessary, and asked to pass urine to make sure that everything is in working order. You can then change and the birth attendants will give your baby a thorough check over.

CHECKING HER THOROUGHLY

Shortly after birth (in addition to the Apgar score, see column, left), your baby will be examined by the doctor or midwife so that specific checks can be made. The doctor will check to make sure her facial features and body proportions are normal. She will be turned over so the doctor can see that the back is normal and there are no indications of spina bifida. Her anus is checked to make sure it is perforated, and her fingers and toes are checked. The number of blood vessels in the umbilical cord is recorded; there are usually two arteries and one vein. She will then be weighed, and her head circumference and body length will be measured. This preliminary examination takes only a few seconds in the hands of an experienced doctor or midwife.

YOUR BABY'S IDENTIFICATION

Before your baby leaves the delivery room, she will have some form of identification fastened to her, so that all the hospital staff will know that she is yours.

Plastic bracelets will usually be sealed around both your baby's wrist and her ankle. The identifying bracelets must remain on your baby at all times while she is in the hospital. These bracelets are usually marked with:

• *Your surname (she will be referred to by the staff as "baby Brown," for example)*

• *Her date of birth*

• *An identification number (an identification number is used by most hospitals for both you and your baby)*

In addition to the above:

• *Her footprints may be taken*

• *Her bassinet may be marked with her name and number*

Keeping her bracelets
Like many mothers, you may want to keep your baby's identity bracelets as souvenirs. As your baby grows day by day, it will soon seem astonishing that her wrists and ankles could ever have been quite so tiny.

IF A BABY DIES

A PARTNER'S REACTION

The death of a baby will be as painful for the father as it is for you. However, he may express his grief very differently, and this can lead to tension in the relationship.

If a father grieves in a different way than his partner, it does not mean his grief is any less intense. Some men feel they should hide their grief and throw themselves into work in order to find some relief from the pain they are feeling. Fortunately, all of us are learning that it is more healthy to express feelings than to suppress them, and men should be encouraged to let their true feelings show, especially to their partners.

Support groups for bereaved parents can put fathers in contact with other men who have lost their babies. By being with such other men, a father may learn to express his grief, anger, and all the other emotions he may feel, in whatever way is appropriate. What is essential is that he be able to express his grief in his own way.

The death of any child is always a tragic event, but the death of a baby before, during, or very soon after birth can be especially distressing. Today, the number of babies who are stillborn after 28 weeks or who die within the first few weeks of life has fallen to about 1 percent in the Western world, largely owing to improved obstetric and pediatric care.

WHY BABIES DIE

Perinatal deaths can be divided into three main groups: stillbirths (babies who die after 28 weeks' gestation but before labor begins), intrapartum deaths (babies who die during labor), and neonatal deaths (babies who die within four weeks of their birth).

Stillbirth Approximately 45 percent of perinatal deaths are stillbirths, and in about a third of these cases the precise cause is not known. Of the rest, the most important causes are severe fetal defects (see also p.178) and a placenta that is not entirely healthy. It could be that the placenta failed to develop adequately, became diseased in some way, or became unable to continue to support the baby (see p.170). Whatever the cause of death, the placenta was unable to provide adequate nutrition for the baby. It might even have begun to separate from the wall of the uterus before labor started. Other, less common, causes of stillbirth include Rhesus incompatibility (see p.184), and maternal diabetes that is not carefully controlled.

The first thing that happens when a baby dies in the uterus is the almost complete disappearance from your blood of pregnancy hormones, estrogen and progesterone. As a result, many of the signs and sensations of being pregnant fade quite quickly, and the uterus may even diminish in size due to absorption of the amniotic fluid. This could result in rapid weight loss, which is why loss of weight or a lack of weight gain is taken seriously throughout your pregnancy. If your doctors or midwives suspect that your baby has died, a sonogram will be done in order to detect your baby's heartbeat. Labor usually starts within two to three days of a baby's death, although many women want to have their baby removed as soon as they find out that it has died. If you find yourself in this unhappy situation, your wishes should be respected. You can decide to have a Caesarean section (see p.284) if you wish to avoid labor, and ask for the operation to be done as soon as possible.

If you opt to go into labor naturally, there will be no physical difference between this labor and a normal one. You will require a great deal of sympathy and support, and may need more analgesics as you will probably feel pain more acutely. Everybody involved will recognize that your attitude to this labor will be severely affected by the fact that you are not giving birth to a live baby.

Intrapartum death   This is exceptionally rare, but the death of a baby during labor is usually due to a lack of oxygen, as happens in arrested labor. Another possible cause is injury to the baby during labor and delivery, although this is far less common than it was in the past, thanks to high levels of modern obstetric care.

Neonatal death   Death of the newborn is often due to breathing difficulties, especially in babies born preterm (see pp.320 & 322), who are postmature, or who are suffering from severe fetal defects. Fatal neonatal infections, once a significant cause of the deaths of newborn babies, are now very rare because of improved hygiene standards and antibiotics.

COPING WITH A DEATH

It is very important for both partners to come to terms with their grief, to be open about the death of their baby, to accept it, and to go through the grieving process.

It is common for bereaved parents to feel isolated, angry with themselves, each other, the staff, or the unfairness of life, and often guilty about something they did or didn't do. These emotions are absolutely normal. However, accepting that everyone involved did everything possible and that nobody was to blame, while acknowledging how you feel, will help to speed the healing process.

Having a photograph of the baby can also help, and holding him after he is born is often a consolation. It is also a good idea to give the baby a name, to bury the baby formally, and to be present at the burial. Another important form of solace is to get in touch with other parents who have had stillbirths. Details of local support groups are usually available at the hospital. Don't be afraid to ask for help from a counselor if you need it.

Emotional effects   The emotional and physical effects on the mother are due not only to the shock and grief of losing her baby but also to the sudden withdrawal of pregnancy hormones. This can greatly affect her mood, bringing on tearfulness, depression, insomnia, loss of appetite, and withdrawal. The comfort and generosity of her partner, family, and friends will be absolutely vital.

It is also important that both partners try to be open with each other and share their grief so that they can offer each other support and comfort. In addition, the hospital should be able to provide a counseling service for both parents.

GETTING PREGNANT AGAIN

Grief over the death of a baby should have subsided before another pregnancy is contemplated. This usually takes at least six months and sometimes a year or more. Many women, however, find the key to normality and a return to happiness is through conceiving again. Once partners have decided to try for another baby, they may find that worry about losing this baby will be hard to shake off, but the risk of a recurrence is very slight. Where a predisposing cause is determined, subsequent pregnancies are carefully managed.

LOSING A TWIN

The death of a twin or triplet is just as tragic to the parents as the death of a singleton, and carries additional problems.

The loss of a twin or triplet results in a complex psychological situation: the parents have to mourn the death of one baby, while celebrating the life of another. Faced with this impossible combination of emotions, many parents postpone their mourning, although some find they cannot attend to the needs of their living baby properly because of the intensity of grief for the dead one.

The loss of a twin may also cast a shadow over the life of the surviving twin, and birthdays may be particularly difficult at first.

It must be stressed that a mother who's had a multiple pregnancy continues to think of herself as the mother of more than a single baby regardless of whether one or more has died.

14

Getting to know your

NEWBORN

baby

Establishing a relationship with your baby begins at the moment of birth. As you both learn how to care for a child, your relationship will deepen and grow, and what your child can do will amaze you.

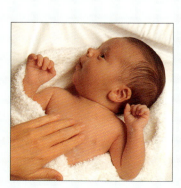

YOUR FIRST REACTION

Your newborn baby's appearance may startle you at first glance. With his wrinkly skin, he may look more like an old man than a baby.

A few parents are worried about their feelings when their baby actually arrives: he doesn't seem to be quite what they'd expected.

Unless you've had a Caesarean, his head may be slightly squashed with some bruising; his eyelids may be puffy, because of the pressure of passing through the birth canal.

He may seem quite messy as he will be coated in a greasy substance (see right), possibly mixed with some of your blood, and have patches of body hair. His limbs may also have a slightly bluish tint, and his genitals will seem huge.

Don't be disappointed if his initial appearance doesn't immediately or automatically inspire feelings of love and tenderness. These will develop the more you get to know each other.

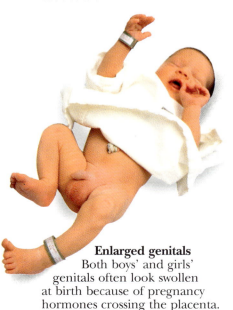

Enlarged genitals
Both boys' and girls' genitals often look swollen at birth because of pregnancy hormones crossing the placenta.

YOUR NEW BABY

Hold your baby soon after birth so that you can establish a strong emotional bond. Your baby will start to learn about you, and how much you love him, by hearing your voice, smelling and feeling your skin, and being cuddled and suckled.

A newborn baby's tiny, vulnerable body and complete dependence on you will arouse many new emotions. Your initial responses and behavior are probably the most important interactions that will ever occur between you and your child. Research has shown that parents who are given unrestricted contact with their babies immediately after delivery later tend to be more sympathetic to their children's needs than are parents whose babies are taken away at birth. Lack of initial contact can make some mothers feel alienated from their new babies, and so less attentive.

WHAT YOUR BABY LOOKS LIKE

There are huge variations in what is considered normal for the weight and length of a newborn baby. Average weights are between 5 pounds 8 ounces to 9 pounds 12 ounces, and average lengths vary from 19 to 20 inches.

Head This is still large in comparison with the rest of his body. It usually has a somewhat strange shape because it has been molded as it came through the birth canal. Molding is caused by the skull bones overriding each other. Sometimes this pressure also causes swelling on one or both sides of the head. This swelling leaves the brain unaffected and it subsides in a few weeks. There may be slight bruising if your baby was delivered by forceps. You will feel a soft spot on the top, called a fontanelle, where the skull bones have not yet joined together and won't until your baby is 18 months. Almost all babies are born with blue eyes, and their adult eye color may not develop until about six months.

Skin Some babies are born completely covered in a greasy white substance called *vernix caseosa,* others only on their face and hands. *Vernix* eases the baby's delivery and offers protection against minor skin infections. In some hospitals it is cleaned off immediately, whereas in others it is left to be naturally rubbed off the skin, which happens within two or three days.

Your baby's circulation takes some time to stabilize. This may cause the top half of his body to look paler than the bottom half. There is nothing to worry about

You may notice downy hair on his body known as lanugo hair; it covered your baby's body while he was in your uterus (see p.62). Some babies only have it on the head, while on others it covers the shoulders. Both are quite normal and the hair usually rubs off

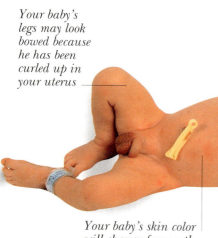

Your baby's legs may look bowed because he has been curled up in your uterus

A beating pulse can often be seen under the fontanelle. It's quite tough but should never be pressed hard

Your baby's skin color will change frequently and look blotchy

Your baby's fingers will be curled in a clenched fist, and may have a bluish tint

in a couple of weeks. More permanent hair will appear later. However, the hair on your baby's head when he's born may not be the color he eventually gets.

Hands and feet   These are always slightly more bluish than the rest of his body because of his primitive circulation. There may be dry patches with peeling skin, which will disappear in a few days. His fingernails may be long and sharp; you can gently nibble off the tips if he's getting scratched, but don't cut them.

Umbilicus   The clamped umbilical cord doesn't separate from the navel until about ten days after birth. Some babies have umbilical hernias (small swellings near the navel) but these usually clear up within a year. If it persists or enlarges consult your doctor.

Breasts   In both boy and girl babies, the breasts may be slightly enlarged and leak a little milk, owing to pregnancy hormones. This is quite normal, and will subside in a couple of days.

YOUR BABY'S BIRTHMARKS

A group of small blood vessels under the surface of the skin may appear as a small blemish on your baby's body, but won't usually need any treatment.

Stork bites   *These are mild pink patches; they are very common and usually appear on the nose, eyelids, and neck under the hairline. They take about a year to disappear.*

Strawberry birthmarks   *These first appear as tiny red dots and may increase in size up to the end of the first year. They almost always disappear by 5 years of age.*

Mongolian spots   *These are blue and are found on the lower backs of babies with dark skin tones (nearly all black and Asian babies, and some Mediterranean babies, have them). The spots look like bruises, but they are harmless and fade away naturally.*

Port-wine stains   *These are large, flat red or purple marks on the baby's skin. They are often found on the face and neck. These marks are permanent, so if you are worried consult your doctor.*

Puffy eyelids
Your baby's eyelids may be quite puffy because of the constriction of the birth canal, but this swelling will subside in a couple of days.

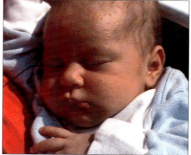

Spotty skin
Small white spots, called milia, are caused by blocked sebaceous glands that lubricate the skin. They will soon disappear.

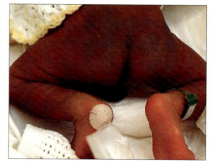

Blotchy skin tone
His circulation hasn't yet stabilized. You may see red and white blotches on his body, and his legs may be a different color.

WHAT YOUR BABY CAN DO

Make time to play with your baby, as this is vital to her development.

Try to recognize her needs *She will have many expressions that you will soon find easy to interpret. When she's content she will appear tranquil and quiet, and she will look red and flustered when she's feeling miserable or uncomfortable.*

Playing together *Don't be self-conscious; when cuddling her, make silly faces and use funny, high-pitched tones to tell her how much you love her. She will respond by nodding, moving her mouth, maybe sticking out her tongue, and jerking her body.*

Your newborn baby has her own distinctive personality and may surprise you with her behavior. Spend as much time as you can studying her, and you will discover, and grow to understand, her unique expressions and responses.

POSTURE AND SENSES

Your baby's head is too heavy for her back and neck muscles to support, so all her postures when not lying down are governed by her gradual ability to control her head. If your baby is placed on her back, she will probably turn her head to one side, extend the arm on that side, and flex the opposite arm in toward her chest. By the time she is a week old, she will raise her head in small jerks when supported on your shoulder, and at six weeks she will probably be able to hold up her head for more than a minute.

At birth, her senses of sound, smell, and taste are fairly acute. She will soon recognize you by smell, and within two weeks by sight. At first, her mouth is her main instrument for touching. When you hold your baby close to you for the first time, she will focus on your face and look into your eyes. Babies like looking at faces more than anything else. Hearing high-pitched human voices gives her great pleasure, and she will prefer yours, and your partner's deeper one, to all others. She'll also respond to sounds with a change in her breathing, and be startled by loud noises.

REFLEX ACTIONS

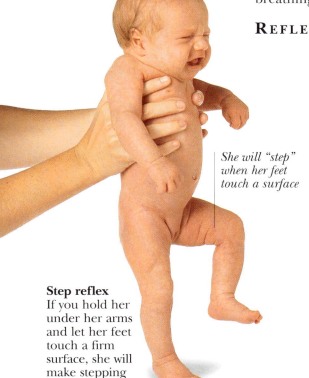

She will "step" when her feet touch a surface

Step reflex
If you hold her under her arms and let her feet touch a firm surface, she will make stepping movements.

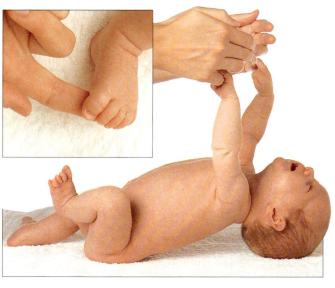

Grasp reflex
Your baby's fingers will tightly grasp anything placed in her palm. The grasp is so strong that her whole weight can be supported if she grabs your fingers with both hands. The soles of her feet will also curl up if touched.

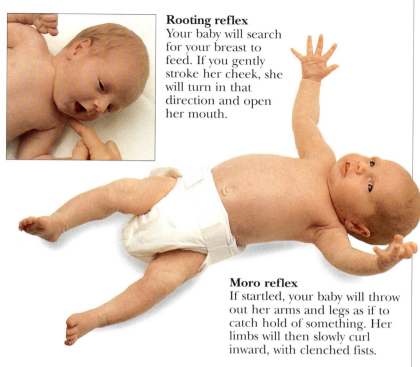

Rooting reflex
Your baby will search for your breast to feed. If you gently stroke her cheek, she will turn in that direction and open her mouth.

Moro reflex
If startled, your baby will throw out her arms and legs as if to catch hold of something. Her limbs will then slowly curl inward, with clenched fists.

All babies use certain reflexive movements to protect themselves. These reflexes usually last about three months, after which time your baby will gradually lose them. Your baby will close her eyes reflexively if you touch her eyelids. All babies have a sucking reflex when pressure is put on the palate in the baby's mouth. The sucking is more like chomping, is very strong, and lasts for some time. The swallowing reflex is inherent in all babies at birth as they will have used it when swallowing fluids in the uterus. This enables them to swallow colostrum or milk the instant they are born. If she swallows too much liquid, her gagging reflex will immediately take over in order to clear her breathing passages.

WHY YOUR BABY CRIES

Crying is her only way of signaling to you. You'll soon learn to recognize all the different kinds of cries and how to respond to them.

• *Your baby's first cry may sound more like a whimper or a splutter, before escalating to a full-blown normal cry. Before bellowing, she will take a deep breath, her body will tense, her face will grimace and become bright red, and she will then open her mouth wide and literally scream. Distressing as this is to you, it does show she's perfectly healthy*

• *She will cry when she's hungry and usually won't stop until she's put to your nipple or given a bottle. Some babies will cry sooner than others when hungry*

• *Tiredness, uncomfortable clothing, being too hot or too cold, or being undressed are all reasons why she may cry*

• *One of the main causes for distress is loneliness. Babies thrive on physical contact, and if they feel abandoned they will cry until picked up and cuddled*

SOUNDS YOUR BABY WILL MAKE

BREATHING
Your baby's breathing will seem very light in comparison to your own. At times it may be fast and noisy, or it may be irregular. She may snuffle as air passes through her small nasal passages. Don't be alarmed if at first you cannot detect her breathing; it will get stronger every day.

SNEEZES
Your baby's sensitivity to bright lights makes her sneeze because light stimulates the nerves to her nose as well as her eyes. A sneeze will clear out her nasal passages, preventing dust from getting into her lungs. Sneezing is quite common – it doesn't mean she has a cold.

HICCUPS
Your baby will often hiccup, and this is normal. The hiccups are often caused by sudden, irregular contractions of the diaphragm. They signal that the muscles involved in breathing are getting stronger and trying to work in harmony.

A cry for attention
Sudden movements, very bright lights, loud noises, or feeling too hot or too cold may make your baby start to cry.

GOING HOME

Make sure the hospital is informed of how long you intend to stay. The routine for checking out will vary from hospital to hospital. Some women leave quite soon after the birth; others are in for over a week. The usual stay is 1–2 days. Before you are discharged:

• A doctor will examine you, and this will include checking to see that your uterus is returning to its pre-pregnant size, that your stitches (if any) are healing, and that your breasts are okay. The flow of lochia will be checked for color and amount, and to see if you have passed any clots. Clotting accompanied by persistent bleeding may indicate that some placental tissue has been retained

• If you have had a Caesarean, your incision will be checked and nonabsorbable sutures removed

• You will be asked about contraception and given a prescription for the pill if necessary

• If you weren't immune to rubella (German measles) during your pregnancy, you will be immunized

• A nurse or midwife will show you how to clean your baby's umbilical cord

• You will be given a date for your postpartum checkup, and advised to take your baby to a pediatrician for a checkup

• When you leave, dress your baby warmly; she will not be efficient at regulating her temperature. You will need some loose clothing, as your breasts will enlarge when your milk comes in and your abdomen will not return to its pre-pregnancy flatness until some months after the birth

YOUR STAY IN THE HOSPITAL

Your hospital care routine will vary, depending on whether you had a vaginal or Caesarean delivery (see p.280), the hospital you are in, how long you stay and the condition of both you and your newborn baby.

YOUR BABY'S CARE

Whether you leave the hospital after 12 hours or a few days, your baby will have been thoroughly examined by a pediatrician to make sure that everything is going well and that there are no problems. Your doctor or midwife will also want to check that your baby is feeding and that her stools are normal. She will be given a blood test to check for phenylketonuria (PKU), a rare metabolic disease, and for thyroid gland underactivity.

YOUR CARE

Immediately after delivery, your temperature will be taken and your pulse rate and blood pressure recorded. They will continue to be recorded every four hours for the first day or so, then twice daily during the rest of your stay in the hospital, or your first week to ten days at home. There may be slight shifts in the rate but these are normal, so there is no need for you to worry.

Medical staff will also check that any stitches or tears are healing properly and that there is no infection. They may also advise you about applying ice packs to the area to prevent swelling and prescribe pain medication during the first few days for afterpains.

The amount and appearance of lochia will be regularly monitored by staff. They will want to make sure that there are no abnormal blood clots or excessive bleeding. The condition of your uterus and cervix will be checked, to ensure that they are starting to return to their pre-pregnant condition. Your doctor will also examine your legs for signs of thrombosis and check your general emotional state.

Regaining mobility New mothers should move about as much as possible soon after delivery. Early mobility will help you regain your strength more quickly and facilitate bowel and bladder function (see also p.332).

You will probably remain in bed for the first six hours and then be allowed up to go to the toilet, shower, or walk about. It is wise to ask for assistance the first time you get out of bed, as you could feel a little faint or weak. Blood tests are often routinely taken before your discharge from the hospital to ensure that your hemoglobin is returning to normal.

Caesarean births About 15–20 percent of women have Caesarean births in the United States; if you have had a general anesthetic, you will probably feel sick and shaky. The incision will be painful and the stitches will be covered by a soft dressing. You will probably have an intravenous drip in your arm, and you will be given some analgesics to help you sleep. If your baby is in good condition there is no reason why she can't be with you all the time.

If your stitches are not self-absorbing, they will be removed about five or six days after delivery. This will cause you only mild discomfort. After a Caesarean, you will usually stay in the hospital for about a week to ten days (see also pp.280 & 284).

HOSPITAL PROCEDURES

It may appear that the maternity unit is being run for the convenience of the staff rather than for the mothers and babies – and to a degree this is true. Don't let any negative attitudes of hospital personnel get to you, particularly where breastfeeding is concerned. Insist that you are given sufficient time to feed your baby without having to fit into the hospital routine. Routines vary from hospital to hospital, but the baby is usually put to the breast four times on the first day and five to six times on the second day. Everyone should start slowly with only short periods of two to three minutes on each breast so that the nipples have a chance to harden up, which will prevent soreness and cracking.

It may also seem as if routines are timed specifically to interrupt your naps. It is frustrating to find that you have to take a hot drink just as you have dropped off to sleep! Hospital food can be bland and unappetizing, as well as being nutritionally inadequate and low in fiber, so have special packages brought in by your visitors, or ask a friend to visit you around mealtime and bring food of your choice. Most visitors will be delighted to bring something you really need.

Visitors Welcome though they undoubtedly will be, bear in mind that visitors will tire you out more than you will imagine, so try to limit each visit to a maximum of half an hour. Check with the hospital on the number of visitors you can have at any one time, and make sure that they come during visiting hours.

Social contact There is also a lot to enjoy while you are in the hospital. You will have company and can share your experiences, observations, and worries with other mothers. A pleasant social life can develop between mothers with new babies. Sharing your learning experiences and working out plans together, you may form lasting friendships.

Feeling unhappy If you find that hospital routine doesn't suit you, there are nurses and Social Service workers who take an enlightened and flexible view and will do their best to accommodate you. If this isn't possible, it would probably be best if you asked for a discharge from the hospital. It would be very sad if your first few days with your baby were marred by the frustrations of hospital life.

YOUR BABY'S BIRTH CERTIFICATE

By law, all births must be registered by means of a birth certificate.

After your delivery, the hospital staff will compile such information as: the baby's surname, sex, date and time of birth, birth weight, type of delivery, birth attendants' names, mother's and father's names and occupations, date of marriage to the father (if applicable), and the number of babies born to you prior to this one.

You will be given a copy of this record. Although individual state laws and procedures vary, you will probably receive in the mail a copy of the baby's birth certificate within the next few weeks.

BENEFITS FOR YOU

From the moment your baby is born you can develop a special feeling of intimacy by holding him close to your bare skin.

Skin-to-skin contact enables you to become intimate with your baby. You will enjoy "skin bathing" with your baby – the feel of his soft, warm skin against yours, and the wonderful smell of newborn baby.

When you are feeding, whether by breast or by bottle, don't let a barrier of clothing always come between you. You will both benefit from him being held close against your bare skin (see column, right) – not least because he will begin to recognize your smell (an important step in the bonding process), especially if you are not breastfeeding.

HOLDING AND HANDLING

A newborn baby can appear very fragile and, at first, many parents are quite scared to pick up and handle their baby because of the feeling that he is so breakable. However, your baby is actually very resilient and, as long as you support him firmly, there's no need to be afraid.

FIRM SUPPORT

Even if he's crying to be picked up, don't use jerky or quick movements when lifting him – do it as slowly, as gently, and as quietly as you can. Most babies like to be handled in a firm way; it makes them feel more secure. He won't be able to support his head for several weeks so you will have to support it so that it doesn't loll. Always hold your baby close to you, keeping your arms close to your body, and bending over the place you are lifting from or putting down. You will gain confidence very quickly.

To put him down you simply reverse the process of picking him up, making sure to support his neck. When you lay your baby down, it's safest to put him on his back, or his side, if propped.

PICKING UP YOUR BABY

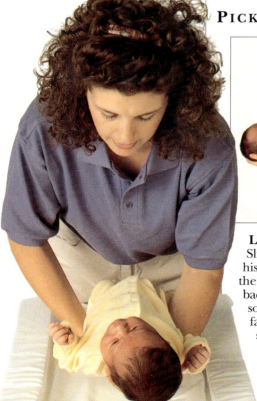

Lifting your baby
Slide one hand underneath his neck and head, and slide the other behind his lower back (left). Lift him gently so that his head doesn't fall back. Remember to support his head in the crook of your arm (above) so that it does not loll around.

Cradle him in your arms
Your baby will feel secure cradled in the crook of your elbow, his head and limbs well supported.

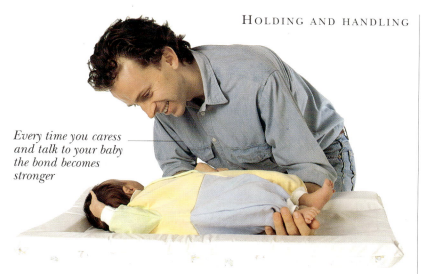

Every time you caress and talk to your baby the bond becomes stronger

Recent research has shown that the more physical contact babies have, the healthier and happier they become.

You can appeal to your baby's sense of rhythm by rocking and swaying him. Skin-to-skin contact stimulates his senses of touch and smell, and even helps him to grow. Human skin sends and receives warmth that has a positive effect on other human skin. Snuggling together will evoke a feeling of contentment.

Loving support A mother often feels prime responsibility for her newborn baby, but most partners are eager to be fully involved as early as possible. Both your baby and his father will develop a better understanding of each other through cuddling, handling, and carrying, and the more tactile their relationship, the more loving it will be.

All through the day, especially when changing him, you can discover ways to gently explore and caress his body. The best way to cuddle together is by snuggling in bed. In this way he can smell your skin, feel its touch and warmth, and hear your heart beating clearly.

Hold him face down
Your baby may like being held face down in your arms, his cheek resting on your forearm.

Your baby will be comforted by the familiar beat of your heart

Hold him against your shoulder
Held upright like this, your baby feels secure. Take his weight with a hand under his bottom, and support his head with the other hand.

PRODUCING MILK

The changes to your breasts during pregnancy prepare them for the production of milk, which begins a few days after you have given birth.

Each female breast contains 15–20 groups of milk-secreting glands, connected to the nipple by the milk ducts. During pregnancy, the placenta and ovaries secrete high levels of the hormones estrogen and progesterone, which stimulate the glands to produce colostrum. Colostrum provides your baby with water, protein, sugar, vitamins, minerals, and antibodies to protect him against infection. The production of colostrum ceases, and that of milk begins, about 3–5 days after the baby is born.

Stimulating milk
Your baby's sucking stimulates nerve endings in the areolae, which send messages to the brain to produce prolactin and oxytocin.

Pituitary gland

Hypothalamus

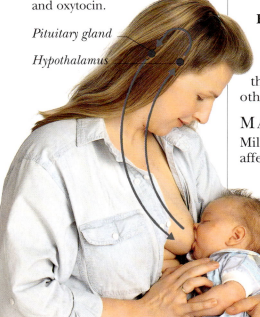

BEGINNING TO BREASTFEED

Pregnant women who are planning to breastfeed for the first time often worry that they will not produce enough milk, or that their milk will not be sufficiently nourishing. These understandable fears are usually groundless. Bear in mind that every woman is equipped to feed her baby. No breast is too small and, in most cases, supply automatically meets demand.

FEEDING ON DEMAND

A baby can digest a full feeding of breast milk in about an hour and a half to two hours (half the time it takes for a bottlefed baby to digest a full feeding of infant formula). Breastfeeding on demand thus means frequent feeding, but this will not deplete your milk resources – research has shown that mothers who breastfeed their babies on demand produce more milk than those who feed their babies at regular but less frequent intervals.

One study compared babies breastfed on demand with those fed only every three or four hours. The babies fed on demand got an average of nearly ten feedings a day, compared to an average for the others of just over seven. However, the more frequent feeding didn't mean that a daily amount of milk was being divided into more but smaller feeds – quite the contrary, in fact.

Better fed The fed-on-demand babies got an average of just over 2.5 fluid ounces per feeding (24.5 fluid ounces per day), while those fed at fixed intervals got only 2.3 fluid ounces per feeding (17 fluid ounces per day). As a result, after two weeks the fed-on-demand babies had gained more weight than the others, an average of 1.2 pounds compared to 0.8 pounds.

MAINTAINING YOUR MILK SUPPLY

Milk production is quite a complex affair and many factors can affect it, including your emotions, health, and diet.

Producing milk The change from colostrum to milk is initially triggered by hormonal changes following the birth, but the continuation of milk production depends on the sucking action of the breastfed baby. When he sucks, this stimulates nerve endings in the breast, and the signals from these nerves go to a part of the brain called the hypothalamus. When the hypothalamus receives these signals, it in turn sends out signals to the pituitary gland instructing it to release a hormone, prolactin, that stimulates milk production. Consequently, this response to the baby's sucking is known as the prolactin reflex. The pituitary gland also releases oxytocin, a hormone that causes the muscle fibers around the milk glands to contract, squeezing the milk from the glands into the milk ducts. This is called the milk ejection or let down reflex and, when your breasts are full, it can be triggered not only by sucking but also by your baby's hunger cries or even simply his proximity to you.

A good milk supply By far the most important factor in maintaining your milk supply is frequent feeding, so that the prolactin reflex and the milk ejection reflex are initiated frequently and engorgement (swelling of the milk-producing glands by milk) is prevented.

If the glands do swell, they are unable to make milk efficiently. At the same time, you will tend to avoid feeding because it is painful, and for these reasons the reflex that promotes the release of prolactin diminishes and so milk production slows down. You can relieve the engorgement by expressing milk (see column, right), and prevent recurrence by regular and frequent feeding.

As well as regular feeding, at each feeding wait until your baby empties the first breast before switching him to the other. This will ensure that he gets not only the thirst-quenching, low-fat foremilk that is delivered from the breast first, but also the highly nourishing, fat-rich hindmilk that follows.

It is important to eat a nutritious diet at this time, as your body will be under even more nutritional stress than during pregnancy. You don't need any special foods for breastfeeding, but try to maintain a balanced diet with plenty of protein, iron, and calcium, and lots of fluids, fresh fruit, and vegetables. Three good meals, and light snacks of fruit, cheese, or milky drinks in-between, will keep your energy levels high and help you avoid fatigue. It is a good idea to continue taking an iron supplement daily. Taking care of an infant can be exhausting, so as well as eating properly you should take every opportunity to rest, or even sleep, during the day. If you are diabetic, your doctor will carefully monitor your diet, and your glucose and insulin levels. When you resume lovemaking, don't use oral contraceptives until you stop breastfeeding (see p.338).

REFUSAL TO FEED

Occasionally, a baby will refuse to breastfeed. This happens most often during the early days, when he may be too sleepy to be interested in feeding. If this happens, don't give up; simply express the milk your baby would have suckled and wait for him to want food – babies feed much better when they are hungry. However, should he tend to fall asleep soon after you have started to feed him, try lying on your side with your baby lying beside you so that he finds feeding a less tiring activity.

A refusal to feed may also be due to difficulty with latching on (see p.306). This usually happens because your breasts are engorged – the swelling this causes makes it difficult, even impossible, for your baby to latch on. If you express some milk from your swollen breasts he will be able to latch on more easily.

EXPRESSING YOUR MILK

Occasionally you may want to remove milk from your breasts without feeding – perhaps so that your baby can be fed using a bottle if you go out for the evening, or if your breasts become engorged (see p.334). Milk can be expressed by hand, but it is quicker to use a pump.

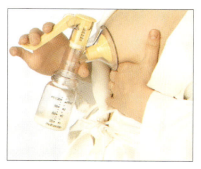

Using a manual pump
Fit the funnel of the pump over your areola to form an airtight seal then operate the lever or plunger to express the milk.

Storing your milk
When your milk has been expressed, put the cap tightly on the bottle. Refrigerate the milk until needed; it will keep for up to 48 hours in a refrigerator, or can be stored for up to 6 months in the freezer. Whenever you express milk, wash your hands and ensure that all equipment is sterilized beforehand.

LATCHING ON

The key to happy, trouble-free breastfeeding is knowing how to get your baby's mouth correctly fixed or latched on to your breast. Proper latching on ensures that baby gets enough milk and helps you to avoid breast and lactation problems.

When your baby is properly latched on, his jaws will be clamped on your breast tissue rather than on your nipple, which will be completely inside his mouth.

Correct latching on is important to both you and your baby for 2 principal reasons. First, it prevents your baby from sucking on the nipple itself, which would cause soreness and cracking. Second, it enables him to stimulate a good flow of milk, ensuring that he gets the rich hindmilk as well as the less nourishing but thirst-quenching foremilk (see p.305). A good flow of milk also prevents your breast from becoming engorged (see p.334) because it has been inadequately emptied.

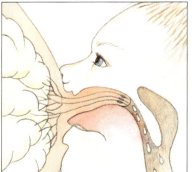

The sucking effect
A baby first stimulates milk to flow into the nipple by pressing the tip of his tongue against the areola at the base of your nipple. Then he presses the back of his tongue up toward his palate to squeeze the milk from the nipple into his throat.

BREASTFEEDING YOUR BABY

Breastfeeding your baby is a loving, nurturing experience that strengthens the bond between you. It is a continuation of the physiological relationship that began when your baby was in your uterus. As your baby can trust your milk to be there when he needs it, and to be pure and good, it has been said that breastfeeding is the first way to tell the truth to a baby and to keep a promise.

Talk, sing, or hum to him while he feeds

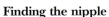

Finding the nipple
Until your baby learns to seek out or "root" for the nipple, stimulate his rooting reflex by gently touching the cheek nearest you. He will then instinctively turn his head toward the touch, and so toward your nipple.

Feeding positions
Hold your baby so that his stomach is facing yours. Hold him with his head higher than his body and, if sitting, keep your back straight. It will be more comfortable to place him on a pillow on your lap so that you are not holding his weight.

Proper feeding

When he is feeding correctly, his mouth will be wide open and, as his tongue and jaw muscles work to suck milk from your breast, you will see his ears and temples moving.

Releasing the breast

When he has finished feeding, or when all the milk is gone from the breast and you want to put him to the other, slip your finger gently in-between his jaws.

BREAST CARE

Replace your breast pads after every feeding

Breast pads

Leaking breasts can be embarrassing and uncomfortable, can cause cracked nipples, and stain your clothes. Breast pads tucked in the cups of your bra will soak up the leaking milk and are easy to wear. Washable and disposable ones are available.

Sore nipples

Use lotion to relieve cracked or sore nipples. Apply often, and especially after each feeding.

BREASTFEEDING TIPS

Breastfeeding is simple – if it weren't, so many millions of infants and mothers wouldn't have managed it successfully. However, it can be challenging, so ask for help from friends, nurses, midwives, or the La Lêche League, if needed.

- *Establishing breastfeeding is always easier if you put your baby to the breast within a few minutes of delivery. Once you've achieved successful suckling in the celebratory atmosphere that surrounds birth, you'll feel confident about future feeding*

- *If your baby has trouble locating your nipple because it is soft and small, put a cold, wet cloth on it momentarily and it will protrude and firm up*

- *Milk flows in both breasts at every nursing and it is better to use both at each feeding. Start with the heavier of them*

- *Let your baby suck for as long as he likes on the first side, so he gets both the fore- and the hindmilk. (Foremilk is the dilute, thirst-quenching part; the hindmilk is the richer, creamier part.) Then switch to the other breast. He can stay there as long as he likes*

BOTTLEFEEDING

Bottlefeeding your baby with an infant formula, instead of breastfeeding, is perfectly safe and healthy provided you follow the manufacturer's instructions carefully. Give your baby plenty of warm, loving attention and eye contact.

PREPARING FORMULAS

Infant formula products range from relatively inexpensive dried-milk-based powders to ready-to-use but expensive liquid milk products. Infant formulas are vitamin- and iron-enriched, and are carefully formulated to make them as close as possible to human milk. They are usually based on cow's milk, but soy-based formulas are available for babies who cannot digest, or who have an allergy to, ordinary milk. If you are unsure which product to choose, ask your doctor recommend one.

Whichever formula you use, absolute cleanliness of the bottles, spoons, mixing jugs, and nipples is essential, because a newborn baby is very vulnerable to infection. In addition, you must always wash your hands thoroughly before a feeding.

BOTTLEFEEDING EQUIPMENT

Bottle brush

Plastic knife

Scissors

Cap

Ring

Nipple

Bottle

Plastic spoon

Measuring jug

Sterilizing liquid or tablets

Sterilizer

Plastic funnel

Household salt

KEEPING EVERYTHING CLEAN

You will soon develop your own routine for washing and sterilizing bottles, but it will probably be easiest to keep your sterilizing equipment in the kitchen.

Some pediatricians feel sterilizing is not necessary, especially if you run all equipment through the dishwasher. Others recommend sterilizing for the first few months.

Washing and rinsing
Put all the equipment into hot, soapy water. Scrub the insides of the bottles with a bottle brush, and rub salt inside the nipples to remove any traces of milk. Rinse the bottles and nipples thoroughly under warm, running water.

If you have a dishwasher, you can put the bottles, jug, and knife into the dishwasher on the normal cycle. However, nipples must be cleaned separately.

Sterilizing in a tank
Half-fill your sterilizing tank with cold water. Add a sterilizing tablet, if your doctor recommends them, and let it dissolve. Put in the equipment, filling the bottles with water so that they stay submerged. Fill the tank with cold water.

Use the float of the sterilizer to keep everything below the surface of the water

MEASURING AND MIXING

The can or package will give instructions on preparing the formula, and you should follow them as closely as possible. Never make the formula "more nourishing" by adding more powder than specified – your baby will get too much protein and fat and not enough water. If you habitually add too little powder to the water, because you want to make the formula more thirst-quenching, you risk under-nourishing your baby.

Measuring out
Using the scoop provided, measure out the quantities accurately. Use a sterilized knife blade to level off the powder in the scoop; don't heap up the powder in the scoop, or pack it down tightly.

Mixing
Use only freshly boiled water that has been allowed to cool down slightly, and measure it out after it has cooled; if you measure it out before you boil it, the made-up formula will be too strong because of the water lost by evaporation.

BREAST TO BOTTLE

If you have been breastfeeding your baby and for any reason you want to change over to bottlefeeding with formula, you should do it gradually.

Switching from breast to bottle must be done very slowly so that your baby gets used to bottlefeeding and to the taste of formula. Your supply of milk can then slowly decline in keeping with the reduced demand for it.

Before beginning the change to bottlefeeding, it is important that you consult your pediatrician for detailed advice on the best way to make the change.

GIVING THE BOTTLE

When you feed your baby by bottle, whether with formula or with expressed breast milk, you should be just as patient and loving as you would be if you were breastfeeding. Don't hurry her. Allow her to take a break if she feels like it and to decide when she has had enough. During feeding, cuddle her close against you (especially against your bare skin), talk or sing to her, and maintain eye contact. Encourage your partner to do the same.

Warming the formula
To heat a bottle of formula, stand it in a bowl of warm water. Don't use a microwave oven as it can cause "hot spots." When it is at the right temperature, a few drops splashed onto your wrist will feel tepid. Before feeding, unscrew the nipple ring a little so that air can get into the bottle when your baby sucks. This prevents the nipple from closing up and stopping the flow.

Preparing for a feeding
When you feed your baby, hold her at an angle with her head slightly raised so that she can swallow easily. Until she is about 10 days old, you may need to trigger her sucking reflex by gently stroking the cheek nearest you (left). When you gently insert the nipple into her mouth, be careful not to push it too far back. You can make up batches of feedings and keep them in the refrigerator until needed – but you should never keep them for more than 24 hours.

Giving the bottle
Find a quiet, comfortable place in which to sit with your baby. You will probably find it most comfortable if you sit on the floor or use a chair that is low enough to support her on your lap. Rest her head in the crook of your elbow, with her back supported along your forearm. Hold her bottom securely. Make sure she isn't lying horizontally; she should be half-sitting so that she can breathe and swallow safely and there's no risk of choking. When she begins to suck, tilt the bottle to keep the nipple full of formula or milk, and free of air.

Always hold the bottle at an angle so the nipple is full of milk or your baby will swallow air with the feeding

Releasing the nipple
Sometimes, a baby will content-
edly suck away at a bottle even
though it is empty. If you want
her to let go, gently slide your
little finger between her gums.

Falling asleep
If your baby falls asleep
during a feeding, she
may have gas that is
making her feel full. Sit
her up and burp her.

BURPING YOUR BABY

*Support your
baby's head
with your
hand so
that it
does not
flop
forward*

Burping positions
If your baby has gas, one
of the best ways to burp
her is to put her against
your shoulder and
gently rub her back
(above). Make sure your
clothing is protected by
a clean towel because she
might bring up a little milk
(spitting up).

Another effective way to help
her to burp is to lean her
forward on your lap (right),
without bending her over
at the waist.

GAS AND BURPING

*The point of burping is to bring
up any air swallowed during
feeding or crying prior to feeding
to prevent it from causing your
baby discomfort. However,
babies vary a great deal in their
reaction to gas and, in my
experience, the majority aren't
noticeably more contented for
having been burped.*

*Babies differ greatly in the amount
of air that they swallow during
feeding. Some swallow very little,
including the vast majority of
breastfed babies. Once a baby is
clamped onto the breast, it is
virtually an airtight seal, so it's
almost impossible for a baby to
swallow air while on the breast.*

*Swallowing air is much more
common in bottlefed babies, but
even then it doesn't really seem to
be a problem.*

*The one point in favor of burping
is that it makes you relax, take
things slowly, hold your baby
gently, and stroke her in a firm
and reassuring way. This is good
for both of you. My attitude
toward burping, therefore,
is that by all means do it,
but don't become fanatical.*

*Don't rub or pat her too
hard as you may jerk her
and she'll bring up some of
the feeding. A gently up-
ward, stroking movement is
preferable to firm pats.
There isn't any need to stop
feeding halfway through to
burp your baby; wait until
she pauses naturally in the
feeding, and then put her on
your shoulder.*

MAKING CHANGING FUN

Diaper changing needn't be a boring routine. You can both have lots of pleasure by providing your baby with amusing distractions, and seeing it as a moment of togetherness.

• *Kiss and tickle his tummy, sides, and neck by making blowing noises with your mouth*

• *Chat or sing to him – babies respond best to high-pitched human sounds*

• *Keep your face close, making exaggerated, animated expressions*

• *Have a molded rubber toy handy for him to grasp*

• *Hang a bright musical mobile, plastic-coated color photographs, or a baby mirror above the changing pad, low enough for him to see*

• *While airing his bottom, bend and straighten his knees gently, so he will quickly adopt positions other than fetal ones*

You can both have fun playing when changing his diaper

CHOOSING DIAPERS

Your newborn baby will need to wear diapers day and night, and for the next two to three years, until he is toilet trained, he will continue using them. It is important to choose the type of diaper that will best suit your lifestyle and budget.

TYPES OF DIAPERS

There are a variety of sizes and shapes, but the basic choice is between disposable and cloth diapers. Think which type will be comfortable for your baby, cost-effective and manageable for you.

Disposable diapers   These are convenient but can be expensive in the long run. They are easy to use as the design is straightforward and you don't need pins or plastic pants. The standard types have a plastic outer covering and absorbent inner layer, and are secured with adjustable adhesive tabs. Disposable diapers have elasticated legs to prevent leakage, come in boy and girl styles, and in sizes that range from newborn to toddler. Children seldom notice pretty patterns and colorful characters before toddlerhood, so don't pay a premium for them.

Cloth diapers   Fabric diapers may initially work out to be more expensive since you should buy at least 24 of good quality, to allow for the number of changes you will have to make, plus pins or clips, and wraps or plastic pants. However, in the long run, they may work out to be cheaper. There's more work involved with these because they need to be washed and dried after every use, and they tend not to be as absorbent as disposables. Diaper services increase the convenience, but they also increase the cost. Pre-folded diapers have an absorbent central panel and are easy to put on. Diaper services often provide a newborn size and an older-baby size. If you are washing the diapers yourself, you will have to fold the larger size around your infant. Bird's-eye diapers are ideal for newborns; they are soft against the skin, and they fold to a small size. But, they are not very absorbent, so they do need changing frequently. If you can find them, the old-fashioned British "nappies," made from terry

EQUIPMENT AVAILABLE

Diaper liners

Terry

T-shaped

Bird's eye

Disposable

Plastic pants

DISPOSABLES

Advantages No washing, drying, pins, or plastic pants. No risk of hurting baby with a pin. More practical when traveling as need fewer accessories and less room.

Disadvantages Can only be used once. More expensive in the long run. Create garbage – never flush them down the toilet.

CLOTH DIAPERS

Advantages Only require one set so don't need to keep buying a constant supply. Work out slightly cheaper over the years. Can be used for another child.

Disadvantages Need adequate washing and drying facilities or diaper service. Need accessories. May prick baby with pin.

YOUR BABY'S EXCRETIONS

As long as your baby's healthy you need pay little attention to the contents of his diaper.

*Bowel movements vary, but there are a few signs you ought to be aware of (see **Newborn health**, p.316). For example, streaks of blood in stools aren't normal. Tell your pediatrician right away.*

Immediately after birth, your baby's urine contains urates that may stain her diaper a dark pink or red, but this is normal, so don't be alarmed. She'll urinate frequently, maybe as often as every half hour, because her bladder can't hold urine for even a few minutes. You shouldn't worry unless she ceases to urinate for several hours – then consult your doctor in case there is an abnormality in her urinary tract or she is dehydrated.

After every feeding you will probably need to change your baby's diaper

cloth, are the most absorbent. However, they must be folded and can be bulky on a newborn baby. T-shaped terry diapers are very practical. Diaper liners are useful with any type of cloth diapers. These are absorbent papers that can be put inside the diaper.

DIAPER CONTENTS

In the few weeks after your baby is born you'll notice a change in the color and consistency of his stools. During the first couple of days your baby will pass meconium, a sticky, greenish black substance. After he starts feeding, the stools will change to a greenish brown, looser consistency, and then to a yellowish brown. Breastfed babies' stools are looser and bright yellow. Bottlefed babies pass a firmer, pale brown stool, with a more pungent smell. The number of bowel movements will also fluctuate. Some babies fill their diapers after every meal, while others are less frequent.

WASHING DIAPERS

Remove all traces of urine and feces from cloth diapers or your baby's skin will become sore.

Each morning, fill a diaper pail with water and disinfectant. Urine-soaked diapers can go straight in; dump excess feces down the toilet. Next day, wash diapers in hot water with soap powder and bleach. Putting the diapers through an extra cycle with hot water only will help remove any remaining soap. You may want to experiment with detergent – it will get the diapers cleaner, but it can irritate the baby's skin, so proceed with caution.

CHANGING A DIAPER

You'll need to change your baby's diaper whenever it is wet or soiled, and this will be several times a day with a newborn. To prevent discomfort and rashes, change her diaper when she wakes up in the morning, goes to sleep at night, and after every feeding. Make sure you have a safe changing area with everything close at hand, including a covered trash can for dirty disposable diapers.

CLEANING YOUR BABY

Wipe her leg creases
Remove any feces with a tissue. Lift up her legs and fold the diaper underneath. Using one area of the cloth at a time, moistened with water or lotion, clean inside all the creases at the tops of her legs, wiping downward and away from her body.

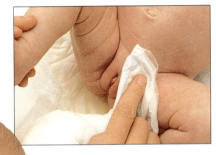

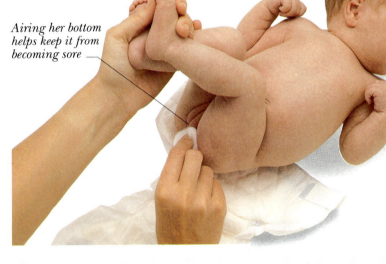

Airing her bottom helps keep it from becoming sore

Clean her diaper area
Holding both her ankles in one hand with your finger between her heels, clean her genital area. Wipe from the vagina back toward the rectum to prevent soiling the vulva. Never pull back the labia to clean inside. Wipe her thighs and buttocks in toward the rectum. Remove the dirty diaper.

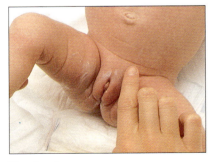

Dry her bottom
If you've used water, dry the area with a tissue, then let her kick her legs for a while, so that air reaches her bottom. Apply ointment gently around her genitals, and on her bottom to prevent diaper rash.

CLEANING A BOY
With baby lotion on a cotton ball, clean gently under his testicles, holding them out of the way. Wipe all over his testicles and under his penis, away from his body. Don't pull the foreskin back. Clean his bottom by holding both his ankles with one hand as in the picture on the right, but don't apply diaper-rash ointment to his penis – use petroleum jelly instead.

PUTTING ON A CLOTH DIAPER

Fold and fit the diaper
Fold the diaper into a triangle by lifting the bottom right-hand corner to the top left, and then the bottom left to the top right. Raise your baby's legs, and slide the diaper under, aligning the top edge with her waist.

Secure the diaper
Bring the diaper up between her legs (tuck down a boy's penis). Holding it in place, fold one side over the central panel and pull slightly to keep it firm. Then fold up the other side. For a small baby, secure the diaper with a pin in the middle; later, use a pin on both sides.

DIAPER RASH

Bacteria on the skin break down urine to form ammonia, which is toxic and burns. The baby's skin then becomes sore, and this ranges from a mild redness to inflamed, broken, and ulcerated skin.

To reduce the risk, always change the diaper as soon as it's wet or soiled. Clean the skin creases thoroughly, and expose her bottom to the air whenever possible.

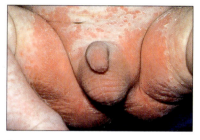

Sore bottom
Diaper rash commonly occurs. If it develops, don't wash her skin with soap and water: use baby lotion. Avoid plastic pants. You can also treat it using Desitin or a similar product. If the rash doesn't clear up within a couple of days, consult your doctor.

PUTTING ON A DISPOSABLE DIAPER

Open out the diaper with the adhesive tabs at the top. Then, lift her legs, slide the diaper underneath, and align the top with her waist. Bring the front panel up between her legs, smoothing the sides around her tummy so they tuck neatly underneath. If the top of the diaper isn't elasticated, tuck the thinner edge in over the top padding across her tummy. Unpeel the tabs. Pull one side over and across to the front flap and stick down the tab. Repeat with the other side, keeping the diaper taut at all times.

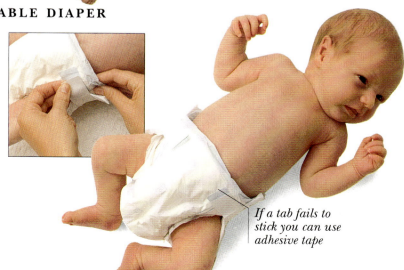

If a tab fails to stick you can use adhesive tape

Many parents feel nervous when they first bathe their babies. Once you establish a routine, both of you can relax and enjoy the time of extra closeness.

• *Warm the room to at least 68°F, and keep the time he's undressed to a minimum*

• *Make sure the bath is a comfortable height for you. Wear a waterproof apron with a towel tied around your waist so you can dry your baby on your lap*

• *Make sure everything you need for washing, drying, and dressing is within reach*

• *Always test the water first and don't add hot water while the baby is in the bath. Add baby bath liquid to the water; this is easier to use than soap*

• *Chat and smile to him constantly, and make as much body contact as possible. Most babies soon enjoy splashing around*

BATHING BABY

Your newborn baby will need bathing about two or three times a week, although obviously you can bathe him more often if you both enjoy it. You can bathe him in any room in your home provided it's warm enough, and always remember to test the water first to make sure it's not too hot by dipping in your elbow, or the inside of your wrist.

TOPPING AND TAILING

This is an abbreviated method of cleaning his face, neck, hands, and bottom without using a bath or removing all his clothes. Instead of a washcloth, use pieces of cotton dipped in cooled, boiled water and squeezed dry. Using a new cotton ball each time, wipe from the inside of his eyes outward. Clean behind his ears, over his face and chin, and around his neck. Dry him off with a soft towel.

Clean his face and neck
Wipe his face and chin and the creases in his neck with moist cotton balls to remove any traces of milk or spittle.

Wipe inside skin creases downward and away from his body

Clean his bottom
Undo any lower garments and remove the diaper. With a new piece of soft cloth, wipe around the genital area (see p.314). If he's soiled, moisten the cloth with baby lotion.

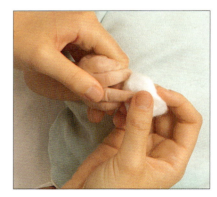

Clean his hands
Gently uncurl his fingers. Using a moistened cotton ball, or a baby washcloth, wipe over the fronts and backs of his hands, and in-between his fingers. With a new piece of cotton, wipe over his arms. Dry with a soft towel.

BATHING

Before you put him in the bath, undress him down to his T-shirt and diaper. Wipe his eyes and face with moistened cotton balls. Then, undress him completely and wrap him in a soft, clean towel.

Fan out your fingers to cradle his head

Wash his head
Hold him just above the bath so that he lies along your arm and his head is supported by your hand. Fan out your fingers to cradle his head. Use your other hand to wash his hair carefully with the bath water. Then gently dry his hair with a soft towel.

Put him into bath
Support his shoulders and neck on your forearm, hooking your hand around his far shoulder. Cradle his bottom with your other hand.

Wash him all over
Keep him semi-upright and slowly splash water over his body with your free hand. Talk and smile to him all the time. When you are finished, lift him out with your free hand held firmly under his bottom, and wrap him gently in the towel.

Always hold him securely

CLEANING HIS CORD STUMP

Your baby's umbilical cord stump dries and drops off within a week of birth. Clean this area daily to avoid infection.

Gently wipe the skin creases around the stump with a surgical baby wipe, which contains pure alcohol. Ask your doctor for a supply of these. Continue cleaning in the same way after the stump has separated so the area heals quickly. If you notice any redness or other signs of infection, ask your pediatrician for advice.

Avoid infection
Dry the area carefully after every bath, and expose to the air as often as possible.

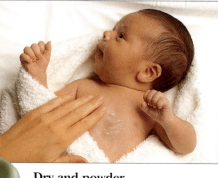

Dry and powder
Pat him dry, paying particular attention to his skin creases. If you like, apply powder, but not in his diaper area as powder cakes when wet.

317

WHEN YOU NEED THE DOCTOR

As your baby gets older, you will learn how to identify and cope with common minor ailments, but there are times when you must call the doctor.

Sometimes when your baby is ill you may find yourself torn between not wanting to bother the doctor unnecessarily and being increasingly worried about your baby's well-being. If this happens, you must not take chances with your baby's health – call the doctor promptly, especially if your baby is showing one or more of the symptoms listed below. Do it sooner rather than later.

- *He is having convulsions*
- *He is hard to awaken*
- *He is having trouble breathing, is wheezing, and has a continuous loud, dry cough*
- *He has a very high temperature, or an abnormally low one*
- *His stools are frequent, loose, green, and watery*
- *He is vomiting a significant amount (not just the usual after-meal spitting up)*
- *He has refused several of his feedings in a row*
- *He is showing the symptoms of dehydration (see main text)*
- *He is listless and crying for no apparent reason*
- *He seems to be bothered by his ears, head, or neck*
- *He has an unusual rash*
- *You have any other reason to worry about his health*

NEWBORN HEALTH

Newborn babies, especially those who are breastfed, are generally healthy during their first weeks of life but, because their immune systems and internal organs are not fully developed, there are a number of ailments that can affect them.

JAUNDICE OF THE NEWBORN

It is not unusual for babies to suffer jaundice – a yellowish discoloration of the skin and whites of the eyes that is a result of an excess of bilirubin in their blood. Bilirubin is a yellow pigment that is a by-product of the destruction of primitive red blood cells, which commonly occurs after birth.

Infant jaundice usually becomes apparent by the second or third day after birth, and lasts for about seven to ten days, by which time the surplus red blood cells have died off and the baby's liver has matured enough to mop up the excess bilirubin. The jaundice usually clears up without treatment, but if the bilirubin levels are particularly high, the baby may be given phototherapy. This involves exposing him to carefully controlled amounts of ultraviolet light, which breaks down the bilirubin pigment in his skin.

Hemolytic disease of the newborn This more serious condition is a result of an excessive amount of bile being present in the baby's blood. It can be caused by the breakdown of large numbers of red blood cells due to the action of antibodies from a Rhesus incompatible mother (see p.184). The chief symptoms are jaundice, pallor, enlargement of the liver and spleen, and abnormalities of the blood. It is usually treated by blood transfusion.

DIARRHEA AND VOMITING

Mild cases of upset stomach or diarrhea will soon pass, but a young baby's digestive system is very vulnerable. Breastfed babies are less prone to these gastrointestinal infections than are bottlefed babies, because of protective antibodies present in breast milk, but all babies may suffer from them from time to time.

If your baby vomits up all his feedings over a six-hour period or is passing frequent, loose, green, watery stools, you should contact your doctor immediately.

Dehydration The major danger to babies suffering from vomiting and diarrhea is dehydration because of the loss of fluids it causes. Its symptoms include a dry mouth, sunken eyes, abnormal depression of the fontanelle, irritability, lethargy, and refusal to eat. Never ignore these symptoms: seek medical advice at once.

CONSTIPATION

Breastfed babies do not usually get constipated, because the composition and digestibility of breast milk keeps everything moving. Bottlefed babies can, however, become constipated, usually because of a lack of fluid. If you are bottlefeeding your baby and he passes no stools for a day or two, then produces a hard one, give him drinks of water between bottles to increase his fluid intake. If this does not make his stools softer and more frequent, give him a little drink of diluted fruit juice twice a day, which will probably help to loosen the stools. If that fails, consult your pediatrician.

Urinary problems Constipation is easily treated and is usually nothing to worry about, but if your baby starts to urinate infrequently it might be a sign of a fever, or of a blockage or infection in his urinary system. If he goes for a couple of hours without wetting his diaper, give him plenty of water to drink. If his diaper is still dry two hours after that, contact your doctor.

If your baby's urine becomes strong and deepens in color, it is probable that he is not getting enough fluids. This makes the urine more concentrated, and the remedy is to increase his liquid intake by giving him several drinks of water between feedings. Should this fail to make any difference, it may be that he has a urinary infection and will need medical treatment, so contact your doctor.

FEVERS

When your baby has a fever, it is a sign that his body is fighting an infection – the rise in body temperature acts to increase the activity of the defense system. If you suspect that your baby has a fever, take his temperature, then check it again in 20 minutes to see if it has varied, noting down each reading. If your baby's temperature rises slightly but he seems his usual self and shows no other symptoms of illness, the infection is probably minor and will usually pass within a day or two. You should, however, consult your doctor. Do so without delay if your baby's temperature rises by a degree or more, or if he gets very hot and distressed or shows other signs of illness, such as lethargy, vomiting, or diarrhea.

EAR INFECTIONS

Babies often get colds, and these can lead to an ear infection called otitis media. This happens when the bacteria travel along one, or both, of the Eustachian tubes (which link the middle ear to the back of the throat and which are necessary to equalize pressure in the ears) into the middle ear. Babies spend most of their time lying down, which can facilitate the passage of bacteria. Inflammation of the mucous membrane of the Eustachian tube traps the bacteria in the middle ear, where they multiply. The symptoms include high temperature, diarrhea, crying for no apparent reason, or any kind of discharge from the ear. Call your doctor right away. He or she will examine your baby to confirm the diagnosis and to rule out meningitis, a potentially more serious condition with similar symptoms. Ear infections are easily cured by antibiotics.

COLICKY BABY

Colic affects male babies more often, and the exact causes of this exasperating blend of indigestion and inconsolable crying are not yet known.

Investigations into the cause of colic have led many researchers to suspect that it may be due to the immaturity of the baby's digestive system. Other research suggests that babies who have been subjected to maternal anxiety in the uterus are more prone to being colicky (see p.175).

In a typical colicky baby, the problem begins at about 2 weeks of age and disappears at about 3 months. The colic attacks usually happen in the evening. The baby will draw up his legs to his stomach or stick them out straight in an attempt to relieve the stomach cramps and gas, and cry loudly from distress and pain.

There is not much you can do about it except wait for him to grow out of it, but stomach massage will often ease the discomfort, as will lying him face-down across your lap with a warm towel, or a hot water bottle half-filled with warm water, placed under his belly. Other measures that may work include taking the baby for a ride in a car, putting him face-down across your knees and stroking his back, and giving him a pacifier to suck on.

Colic is no threat to your baby's health (although it can be very frustrating for you), but when it first begins you should consult your doctor to make sure that it is nothing more serious.

HOW YOU CAN HELP YOUR BABY

In addition to all the care and attention your baby will receive from specialist staff, there are things you and your partner can do to help him thrive.

- *Try to spend as much time with him as possible; he needs the same amount of love and attention as a full-term baby*

- *Touch and fondle your baby, both in and out of the incubator, whenever and as soon as you can. Cuddling, stroking, and gentle caressing have positive benefits in helping him to grow and thrive*

- *Express your breast milk at regular feeding times to give to your baby. Not only will you be providing him with the best possible food, but you will be establishing your milk supply for when he is able to suck on his own*

- *Get involved with your baby's care. Ask the nurses to show you how to help with feeding, washing, and changing him. This will both help you bond with him and give you confidence in caring for him*

- *Don't struggle with feelings of anxiety, ignorance, or worry. Seek information from the medical staff and support from your partner*

SPECIAL-CARE BABY

About one in ten of all newborn babies need to spend some time, even if only a very short time, in a special-care baby unit. Most have been born too soon or have not grown as much as they should have before birth, though a small number will be ill at birth. The aim of the special-care baby unit is to protect the baby from risks to his health and to nurture him until he has outgrown them.

LOW-BIRTHWEIGHT BABIES

In general, any baby weighing less than $5\frac{1}{2}$ pounds at birth is probably smaller than he should be and may need special care. Between 6–8 percent of all babies have low birthweights and, of these, two-thirds are premature and one-third small-for-dates.

Premature babies The pace of an unborn baby's development is geared to his being born at full term (forty weeks from your LMP) so if, for any reason, he is born a few weeks or more before full term, he may not yet be ready for life in the outside world. A baby born before week 37 is said to be preterm or premature, and he will need the help of a special-care baby unit to sustain and protect him while he catches up on his growing.

Small-for-dates babies These are babies who weigh less than expected for the number of weeks that have passed since they were conceived. A small-for-dates baby may be a full-term baby who is very small at birth, or a premature baby who is smaller than he should be for the time he has spent in his mother's uterus.

Health risks The low-birthweight baby, especially if premature as well, must contend with a number of health risks that seldom affect a full-term infant, as well as the more usual ones such as jaundice. For example, if his internal organs are underdeveloped, he will probably have difficulty breathing, regulating his body temperature, and feeding; he will also be very susceptible to infection. He may also have a low blood sugar level (hypoglycemia), which can cause brain damage if untreated, and he may need iron or calcium supplements to remedy a lack of these essential minerals.

CARING FOR BABIES WITH SPECIAL NEEDS

Today, a premature or small-for-dates baby, or one with an illness or disability, has a far better prospect of survival than he would have had 20 or even ten years ago. This is because of a tremendous growth in the knowledge of how to care for newborn babies and the application of that knowledge in special-care baby units.

A special-care baby unit is dedicated to looking after babies who need specialized pediatric attention. They are designed to be welcoming, friendly places for the parents, as well as centers of care for the babies. Most units encourage the parents to play an active part in the care of their baby by, for example, helping with feeding, washing, and diaper-changing. Many provide rooming-in facilities so parents can stay at the hospital with their babies as much as possible. Parents are encouraged to cuddle their babies skin-to-skin, as this helps babies develop more quickly (see also p.322).

Incubators   When a baby is taken into the special-care unit, he is placed in an incubator, an enclosed cabinet in which he can be kept warm and supplied with warmed, humidified air (or oxygen, if he needs it). Circular doors like portholes in the plastic top allow the nurses and parents to reach in to attend to him and attach any monitor leads, feeding tubes, or intravenous drips he might need.

A unit built into the base of the incubator provides storage for the personal items he will need during his stay there, such as diapers, clothes, bed linen, and washing bowls. When the baby is strong enough and can maintain his own body temperature, he is usually moved from the incubator and into a heated crib.

Feeding   Initially, a special-care baby will be given frequent small feedings, starting with one an hour and gradually progressing to one every three hours. If the baby is sick or very premature he will be fed a mixture of sugar and water because he will be unable to digest milk. When he is able to take milk he will be given a special infant formula or milk expressed from his mother's breasts – the ideal food for a special-care baby, as for any other baby.

Research has shown that the milk of a mother whose child is born premature contains more of certain nutrients than those of mothers whose children are born at full term. This makes up for the premature baby's lack of those nutrients that he would have received in the uterus had he not been born early, and a premature baby fed on his mother's breast milk grows and develops at almost exactly the same rate as he would if he were still in her uterus.

YOUR BABY'S NEEDS

A special-care baby's needs require specialized medical attention, but he still needs his mother and father.

While he is in the special-care unit, your baby is cared for 24 hours a day by staff members who have a wide range of technology to help him. Monitors linked to his skin by wires and stick-on contacts constantly check on his breathing, heart rate, and temperature without disturbing him and, until he is strong enough to breastfeed or bottlefeed, he is fed and given drugs via tiny tubes inserted into convenient veins or through a nostril and into his stomach.

But in addition to this care and attention, he needs to feel his parents' love. Physical contact with you and your partner will reassure and comfort your baby and will help you to develop a warm, close, and loving relationship with him.

He needs to hear both your voices, so talk and sing to him all the time; learning to recognize your smells is also important, so hold him close whenever you can.

A special-care baby
Most special-care babies, like this one, born prematurely, spend some time in an incubator. This keeps their temperature steady and monitors their breathing.

NAME *Carol Scott*

AGE *24 years*

PAST MEDICAL HISTORY *Nothing abnormal*

OBSTETRIC HISTORY *This is Carol's first pregnancy*

At 30 weeks of pregnancy, Carol noticed that her hands and feet were swollen, and that she couldn't remove her wedding ring. At her next prenatal visit she was found to have elevated blood pressure, so she was prescribed bed rest and asked to return a week later. At that visit, her blood pressure was even higher and albumin was present in her urine. A diagnosis of preeclampsia was made, and she was hospitalized immediately.

PREMATURE BABY

Premature babies have a difficult start, but the majority do well and grow up to be healthy, normal children, thanks to the dedicated staff and advanced technology of special-care units.

BABY AT RISK

Although Carol was sedated and had complete bed rest, her blood pressure didn't return to normal and albumin continued to appear in her urine. At the beginning of the 35th week there were signs of fetal distress, and it was noticed that Carol had stopped gaining weight. Her obstetrician decided that labor would have to be induced, which it was and, after a straightforward labor, Carol delivered her baby, Alice, who weighed in at four pounds.

Carol's obstetrician thought that the placenta had begun to fail at the beginning of the third trimester and therefore the baby's nutrition had been inadequate. When this happens late in pregnancy, the head is disproportionally large because of the relatively normal growth of the brain at the expense of the rest of the body. He explained that these types of low-birthweight premature babies are born with insufficient energy stores and do not have enough fat to maintain their body temperature. They are therefore more susceptible to hypothermia; hypoxia (lack of oxygen to the tissues); and hypoglycemia (abnormally low blood sugar) so it's crucial that they be kept warm. Alice was put directly into an incubator and her immature lungs were helped by a respirator. Carol was given a room next door so she could be with Alice as much as possible.

POSTPARTUM REACTIONS

Carol and Mark were quite taken aback by the first sight of Alice (see column, right), even though they had had time to adjust to the idea that she would be premature. Throughout her pregnancy, Carol had dreamed of a curly-haired cherub. Instead, Alice was red and wrinkled, and her head looked enormous in proportion to the rest of her body, which was very thin. Inside the incubator, attached to a respirator and taped with wires and tubes for monitoring and feeding, Alice seemed very far away and isolated. Carol found herself bursting into tears at the sight of her tiny daughter, so alone and shut away from her parents.

At the same time, she realized she was having difficulty relating to the baby in the incubator, even though she knew it was her longed-for baby. Mark encouraged Carol to explain her difficulties to the hospital psychiatrist who reassured Carol that her feelings were common and normal. The staff of the special-care unit were most understanding; they encouraged Carol and Mark to make contact with Alice by stroking her through the portholes of the incubator. Recent studies show that this helps a premature baby establish breathing more readily. The staff explained to Carol that her love was more important for the baby's survival than all the technology they could offer. I encouraged Carol and Mark to express all their feelings and to forget their perfect dream baby. It was important for them to be honest about their feelings and to know that many parents of premature babies feel the same.

GETTING INVOLVED

As Carol became involved in caring for Alice, she realized that she loved her and desperately wanted her to survive. The nurses showed her how to express her colostrum (see p.305) so that it could be fed to Alice via the tube. The colostrum of the mothers of premature babies is extra rich in trace minerals – those minerals the baby would be getting if she were still in the uterus – and their milk contains extra protein to help their babies grow. Meanwhile, Mark became very interested in the machines in the special-care unit. He wanted to know what each one was doing for his daughter. Busy though they were, the staff found time to answer his questions.

Skin-to-skin contact Once Alice had gained weight and her breathing had improved, she was taken off the respirator and feeding tube. The staff of the postpartum unit then encouraged Carol to tuck Alice under her blouse and hold her in an upright position between her breasts. Alice was naked except for a diaper and this meant that mother and baby were in skin-to-skin contact for long periods of time. Premature babies thrive on this treatment. A mother's body is better than an incubator for keeping a baby warm because her temperature rises automatically if her baby is cold, then falls again once the baby has warmed up. The nurses called it kangaroo care, because it is similar to the way in which kangaroos keep their infants in a warm, protective pouch. This skin-to-skin contact also strengthens the mother-and-baby bond that is so important for survival. Alice began to suckle spontaneously. The unit staff were delighted with her progress and Carol and Mark were now eager to take Alice home. The obstetrician explained that it wasn't a question of Alice reaching any target weight; each baby was considered as an individual case and allowed home when her weight and general health were satisfactory, although babies were usually kept in the hospital until they reached about five pounds.

BACK AT HOME

Once Carol and Mark were able to take Alice home, they found themselves confronting a new set of problems. Most baby clothes were too big for Alice. Their relatives set about knitting and sewing minute garments, while Mark investigated firms specializing in tiny clothes. Ordinary diapers came almost to Alice's armpits, so Carol made smaller ones by cutting disposable diapers down to fit Alice and fastening them with tape. Alice thrived at home and soon began to catch up with full-term babies of the same age.

CAROL'S BABY

Born 5 weeks early, Alice had none of the fat that a baby normally accumulates in the last few weeks, so she looked much too small for her skin, which was wrinkled and red. She made a pathetic picture.

- *Her head looked very large in comparison to her body, which was thin and tiny*

- *Her skin was loose-fitting and rather dry*

- *She had lanugo (fine hair) on her back and the sides of her face*

- *Her chest looked small, with prominent ribs*

- *As she breathed her chest rose and fell dramatically*

- *Her bottom looked bony and pointed due to lack of fat*

- *Her immature nervous system made her movements jerky*

- *She seemed to have to make a huge effort to take every breath. Sometimes her breathing would stop for a few seconds, but this is not abnormal in a premature baby*

15

Adjusting to
PARENTHOOD

The responsibilities of parenthood may weigh heavily upon you, particularly if they mean dramatic changes in your lifestyles. Watching your baby grow and develop will bring you great joy as you start to experience the closeness that only a family can bring.

YOUR TIME TOGETHER

THE FIRST WEEKS

Plan to take some time out immediately following the birth of your baby. Don't feel you have to get back to normal right away – if you try, you'll become overtired and miss out on enjoying your new baby.

Traditionally, women were not expected to reappear in society until some time after their babies' births. They spent this time regaining their strength. Nowadays we see a period of peace and relaxation in the days immediately following the birth of a baby as vital. It gives both partners a chance to celebrate the birth, welcome and bond with the new baby, and adjust to their new roles as parents.

Provisions Make sure you are well stocked up before the birth with everything you will need – favorite nutritious foods, drinks (you'll need a lot of fluid if you're breastfeeding), clothes, sanitary pads, soft washcloths, diapers.

Nurturing You and your partner will nurture your newborn baby and your partner will nurture you. Spoil yourselves!

Bonding Give yourselves both time and space to get to know and bond with your baby.

Nesting Make your bed the center of the household – talk, entertain, cuddle, and picnic there.

Visitors Restrict visiting hours. Don't feel obliged to play hostess, and do put a card on the front door saying you are resting if you don't feel like seeing anyone just then – they can always come back another time.

Callers If you have an answering machine you could alter the message to include your baby's birth announcement, and perhaps explain that you are resting at present, but that you would love to talk to them in a few days.

BECOMING PARENTS

New parents need some time to adjust to becoming parents. Many report a degree of panic at the overwhelming responsibility they suddenly have to take on for this tiny, dependent human being. As with all major changes, it can take time for you to accept and feel comfortable in your new roles and in the beginning, you may catch yourself hoping that someone else is going to come and take over.

The answer is to give yourselves time and space to get to know and feel comfortable with your baby. The initial few weeks are important too in establishing breastfeeding. Successful breastfeeding requires that you be as rested and relaxed as possible, and that you continue to eat well.

Welcoming your baby Every mother daydreams about her unborn child. Fitting the image of this "dream child" to the reality of the newborn baby in your arms may be difficult – especially if your baby is the opposite sex to the one you wanted, or isn't quite "perfect," or is simply different from what you expected.

It takes time to fall in love with your baby and to learn how to be a mother – or a father. Time spent together will give you the space you need to become adjusted, and to enable you both to make a smooth transition into parenthood.

You may find it preferable to keep your baby with you in your bedroom just at first, even if you have already prepared a room for her. Feeding will be easier and you may have more restful nights.

RESTING AND RELAXING

The first few weeks can seem like a never-ending round of feeding and changing, with snatches of catching up or resting for you when your baby is asleep. If you are exhausted all the time this can take most of the pleasure out of looking after your baby and end up making you feel resentful and irritable.

Earmarking the time immediately after your baby's birth for you and your immediate family to be together, nurturing each other, marveling at the new life with which you have been entrusted, and nesting and picnicking in your bed, will ease you into parenthood and help you regain your strength before you get back to your more normal way of living.

Friends and family A close friend or relative could make this an extra-special period for you by taking on the household chores, food preparation, etc. You may also find this person an invaluable source of support, particularly if he or she is knowledgeable about aspects of baby care and behavior. On the other hand, you may find that as new parents you are offered advice that may be confusing or contrary to your own ideas. In such cases, do not hesitate to discuss things with your midwife or pediatrician, who will be able to clear up any confusion.

You are bound to receive a lot of friendly inquiries, either personally or by phone. Discuss this with your partner and decide together how you will deal with it. Don't feel that you have to entertain. You need to conserve your strength, and being a good hostess every afternoon for the first week or so really will wear you out, so please don't feel guilty about restricting visiting hours. Put a note on the front door saying "Mother and baby resting. Please do not disturb," if you want to rest. You could also add an announcement such as "Matthew Joseph born at 11.35 p.m. on July 20th, weighing 7lb 2oz. Both mother and baby are doing very well," or put a message on the answering machine (see column, left).

OTHER CHILDREN

If you already have a child or children, then this period can be structured to include them. If you've had the baby in the hospital and have been away from home, your other children will want their share of attention. They will enjoy cuddling up with you, talking or reading to the baby, and playing on the bed, and it will help offset any feelings of jealousy. However, they probably won't want to sit still for long and you may be grateful for someone they like and trust to give them some extra individual attention.

YOUR BABY'S EXPERIENCE

He has arrived in a brand new world and in a warm, intimate, and loving environment.

Daily routine *At first he won't have a recognizable baseline of behavior. It will be 3–6 weeks before he will begin to settle down into an established routine of feeding and sleeping.*

Sensations *He will prefer looking at your face than at unfamiliar people and things; he will be reassured by the smell of your skin and his father's; he will look toward new sounds, and he will be startled if they are loud or unexpected; he will enjoy the taste of your milk; he will love being cuddled, touched, and massaged.*

Communicating *His main means of communicating is crying. He will cry if he is hungry, tired, upset, or bored or feeling lonely. He will also cry if he senses that you or his father are tense or tired.*

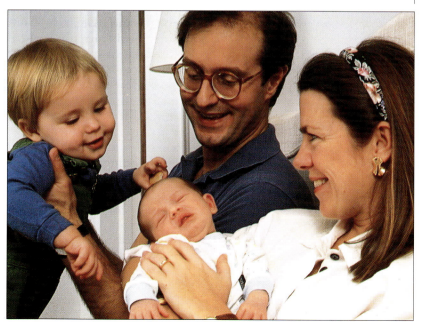

Family togetherness
Time spent cuddling, talking, and just being together without everyday demands will give you all a chance to adjust to the changes within your family.

POSTPARTUM CHANGES

YOUR CHANGING EMOTIONS

The sudden change in hormone levels following childbirth is thought to be a principal cause of the baby blues and post-partum depression.

Very soon after you conceive, the levels of certain hormones in your body, especially progesterone and estrogen, rise steeply and stay high throughout the months of preg-nancy. Then, during the first 72 hours after giving birth, the levels of these hormones crash.

The amount of progesterone in your blood falls from about 150 nanograms (thousand millionths of a gram) per milliliter to less than 7 ng/ml, and the amount of estrogen falls from around 2,000 ng/ml to 20 ng/ml. After that, the amount of progesterone dwindles to zero, and the estrogen level settles down at about 10 ng/ml.

When the levels of estrogen and progeserone drop, your body finds it very difficult to adjust. This can have a marked effect on your emotions and mental processes and, along with other factors such as personal problems, may lead to the baby blues or even postpartum depression.

Severe exhaustion, another possible postpartum problem, may be made worse by a lack of potassium in your body. Low potassium levels are easily corrected by eating plenty of potassium-rich foods, such as bananas and tomatoes.

During the days and weeks following the birth, you will be in an emotionally vulnerable state because of the abrupt decrease of your pregnancy hormones (see column, left). And, because it is such a major event in your life, giving birth is liable to accentuate any underlying personal or emotional problems you may have, and to resurrect any unresolved issues. It is, however, difficult to predict just how you will react to the birth of your baby – sometimes an elated, problem-free pregnancy can be followed by a troubled postpartum period.

If there are postpartum emotional problems, their nature, sever-ity, and duration can vary greatly from one woman to another, and from one pregnancy to another. A woman can have a trouble-free postpartum period after the birth of one child, then have a rough time following the birth of a subsequent one.

THE "BABY BLUES"

Because the most important single cause of postpartum emotional problems is the abrupt and unavoidable drop in hormone levels, you should not be surprised if, like most women after giving birth, you suffer from the baby blues to some extent. As many as 80 percent of mothers do, so it really is the norm rather than the exception, and women who escape it entirely are in a fortunate minority. For the nine months of pregnancy, you have been experiencing very high levels of hormones, and suddenly they are plunged back to the comparatively low levels of day-to-day life. This drastic but normal swing renders the majority of women weepy, prone to sudden mood swings, irritable, indecisive, and anxious.

The baby blues usually set in about three to five days after the birth and last for about a week to ten days. The onset often coin-cides with the beginning of your milk production (which itself is governed by your changing hormones) and for this reason the baby blues were known, in the nineteenth century, as "milk fever."

Becoming a mother If you get the baby blues, you usually find that the reality of being a mother seems quite difficult to cope with once the initial euphoria of having your new baby in your arms wears off. In addition to the symptoms mentioned above, you might find yourself confused, anxious about your ability to look after your baby, and frustrated because it seems to be taking you so long to learn to be a good mother. Be easy on yourself; no woman has the expertise for instant motherhood – this is something that can be acquired only through learning, which takes time.

You might also find that you are beginning to feel differently about your partner. This does not mean that you are feeling less for him, you are just feeling different, and it is not a sign that your relationship is deteriorating. It is more likely that eventually it will mature and become richer. Talking things through openly with your partner is important, because this is one of the best ways to keep the stresses and strains of motherhood in perspective and prevent them from escalating into a serious emotional disturbance.

It is also important not to overdo things. Tiredness is inevitable in the early days, but it should never be ignored. If you feel tired, stop whatever you are doing if it's not essential, and lie down with your feet raised slightly above your head. You don't have to go to sleep to conserve your strength; a good rest may be all you need.

POSTPARTUM DEPRESSION

About 10 percent of all mothers develop postpartum depression. This is, in many respects, quite different and separate from the baby blues. Postpartum depression is longer-lasting, more serious, and demands rapid medical attention. It is a psychiatric disorder that can get out of hand if left untreated, and it is absolutely essential that you get medical help early. With treatment, your depression will normally be resolved in a few weeks; the longer postpartum depression is left untreated, the longer it will take to resolve.

Symptoms There are many symptoms associated with postpartum depression, and these are experienced by different women in different combinations. In addition to depressive symptoms – hopelessness and despondency – sufferers can experience lethargy, anxiety, tension, panic, sleep difficulties, loss of interest in sex, obsessional thoughts, and lack of self-esteem and concentration.

Treatment Drugs will help your condition, but support from family and friends is vital. There are also some things you can do for yourself (see column, right). Your doctor will normally prescribe antidepressant drugs. Over a period of time, these will bring about a gentle and gradual improvement, so it's important to keep taking your medication even after you start feeling better. Some drugs may involve side effects such as a dry mouth, drowsiness, and confused thoughts. If these side effects interfere with your daily life, consult your doctor about changing your medication, but do not cut down on your dose. If feelings of depression worsen premenstrually, tell your doctor. He or she may be able to prescribe further medication to prevent this severe form of premenstrual tension. Your doctor may recommend that you see a psychologist.

PUERPERAL PSYCHOSIS

In this rare psychotic form of postpartum depression, affecting about one in 1,000 mothers, the sufferer loses contact with reality, may have delusions or hallucinations, and will have to be hospitalized. Intensive treatment with drugs, psychotherapy, and/or electroconvulsive therapy will be offered.

SELF-HELP FOR DEPRESSION

If you are feeling low, there are a number of things you can do to help yourself. The most important thing is to convince yourself that you will get better, no matter how much time that takes.

Rest as much as possible Tiredness definitely makes depression worse and harder to cope with. Nap during the day and, if possible, get someone to help with night feedings.

Maintain a healthful diet Eat plenty of fruit and raw vegetables – don't binge on chocolates, candies, and cookies. Eat little and often. Do not go on a strict diet.

Take gentle exercise Give yourself a rest from being indoors or taking care of the baby. Walking in the fresh air can help lift your spirits.

Avoid major upheavals Don't relocate or redecorate.

Try not to worry unduly Aches and pains are common after childbirth and more so if you are depressed. Try to take them in stride; they will fade away as soon as you can relax.

Be kind to yourself Don't force yourself to do things you don't want to do or that might upset you. Don't worry about not keeping the house spotless or letting household tasks lapse. Rather, concern yourself with smaller, undemanding tasks and reward yourself when you finish them.

Talk about your feelings Don't bottle up your concerns; this can make matters worse. Talk to others, particularly your partner.

NAME *Christine Rance*

AGE *33*

PAST MEDICAL HISTORY *Nothing abnormal*

OBSTETRIC HISTORY *3 children: a boy aged 4, a girl aged 2½, and a baby boy born 4 months ago. All pregnancies normal, with normal deliveries*

Christine sailed through all her pregnancies, although afterward she came down with a bump. After the birth of her first baby, Thomas, Christine went through a short spell of "baby blues," although she was over this in a few days. After Laura, her second baby, was born, she felt tired and dejected for about 2 weeks. She also put on quite a bit of weight and never regained her youthful slenderness. 3 days after the birth of Oliver, her third baby, tearfulness and lethargy set in again. The situation worsened until, at 3 weeks after delivery, she was diagnosed as postnatally depressed.

DEPRESSED MOTHER

While mild feelings of depression are not uncommon for a few days after the birth of a baby, depressive feelings that deepen and last longer than about two weeks may signal a serious condition that requires medical treatment. In such cases, post-natally depressed women become more and more debilitated and withdrawn, and are unable to keep in touch with their babies.

SOME PREDISPOSING FACTORS

Christine has never been very good at handling change within her life; she prefers a stable permanent situation. She has always felt a little inferior and unsure of herself, doesn't have a particularly clear sense of her own identity, and is rather lacking in self-respect. Obesity has become a problem, particularly as she overeats when she is depressed. She has gained weight with each pregnancy, which she has found increasingly difficult to lose. After her first pregnancy, she was 15 pounds overweight and it took a year to lose it. She then became pregnant with her second child, Laura, and the weight piled on again. After Laura's birth, she found it impossible to lose weight and in fact gained more in the first months of Laura's life than she had when she was pregnant.

Christine's husband, Stephen, often complains that she no longer looks like the woman that he married, and Christine has been on countless diets in order to try to get herself into shape, without success. She feels extremely self-conscious about her size, and tends to wear shapeless clothes in order to disguise it. Sometimes she thinks that she hasn't been too good a mother and often feels inadequate about her maternal instincts.

A SELF-FULFILLING PROPHECY?

Christine is used to the feeling of baby blues and was expecting to be sad after her third child. When depression set in it was almost a self-fulfilling prophecy. By the third day postpartum she was extremely weepy – the smallest obstacle seemed insurmountable and molehills became mountains. She started behaving in a help-less way, and refused to get out of bed.

Stephen's mother came to live at the family home in order to take care of Thomas and Laura and to help with running the house. Even though she tried to be helpful, Christine repaid her with criticism. The atmosphere became extremely tense and her mother-in-law tended to leave her alone rather than risk upsetting her.

Christine and Stephen then began to have arguments. Christine felt that he didn't really understand her situation. She wanted him to take time off work in order to support and comfort her. Stephen, not understanding completely what was going on, started to become depressed himself, and his work began to suffer.

Christine was so drowned in her own misery – at feeling so exhausted, hopeless, and guilty, at having three children to look after (especially as the two eldest had started to be difficult and misbehave), having to coordinate the household, and the tense relationships between herself and Stephen, and herself and her mother-in-law – that she could think of nothing else. She stopped communicating with her family and only talked to the baby.

Then, after a week of this, she found herself unable to relate to the baby, who seemed to have became a stranger. She felt acutely aware of her lack of maternal instincts and this made her feel more inadequate than ever. She started thinking of the awful things she could do to her baby in order to stop his crying. She didn't care about feeding him. She left him to scream until his grandmother came to comfort him.

HELP IS OFFERED

After about two weeks of this behavior, during which her midwife had reassured her that everything would get better soon and that she had to be patient, she was visited by her social worker, who realized that Christine's reaction to her baby and the state of her emotions were far from normal. She informed Christine's doctor, who visited her three weeks after delivery. He diagnosed early postpartum depression and called in a psychologist. The psychologist came to see Christine in her own home.

About two weeks after the psychologist's visit, Christine started to improve, mainly as a result of the advice that he had given her. First he advised her to forget what was happening in the rest of the house. She should think only about the baby and herself and let everything else go. Second, he advised her that sleep was essential. She must get someone else to see to the baby overnight so she could get a full night's sleep. Third, he advised Christine to attend a local mothers' discussion group twice a week where she could simply sit and talk to women in similar situations.

In addition to the above advice, Christine's doctor prescribed a mild antidepressant and mild sleeping pills to tide her over the first difficult few weeks only. He said that he would continue the antidepressant, explaining that he would reduce its dosage gradually once Christine was taking charge of herself and her life.

THINGS BEGIN TO LOOK UP

After six weeks, Christine was sleeping so much better that she asked to stop the sleeping pills, which she did quite easily. She is now continuing on the antidepressant medication, and she is determined to halve the dose during the next four weeks and be free of it in another six. Stephen feels much happier now that she is almost back to normal, and the children, too, are more relaxed.

CHRISTINE'S CHILDREN

No permanent harm will have been done to Christine's ability to bond with her new baby and, once she started to feel better, she was able to rebuild her relationship with her older children.

However, while she was feeling depressed and unable to give them much attention, her children became very anxious, difficult, and naughty. They rebeled against their grandmother's care and demanded more of their parents' attention and affection.

*In such cases of postpartum depression, children also need support, either before or after their mother has improved. Various groups exist (see **Addresses**) to help with the effects of postpartum illness on family members.*

LOCHIA

While your uterus contracts and returns to its normal size and condition after delivery, you will have a vaginal discharge known as lochia.

Lochia is the normal vaginal discharge from a healing uterus. The duration of lochia loss varies widely from woman to woman, its average length being about 21 days, although it may be as short as 14 days or continue for up to 6 weeks. Breastfeeding helps to reduce the duration of lochia production, because the oxytocin that triggers the let-down reflex (see p.304) also causes uterine contractions, and these help the uterus to shrink back to its normal size, cutting down on bleeding.

However long it continues, lochia secretion goes through 3 distinct stages as the placental site heals. For the first 3 or 4 days, the lochia is bright red then it gradually reduces in quantity and changes to pink or brown as the uterine lining is shed, and by about the tenth day it becomes yellowish white or colorless.

Lochia should have a fresh, blood-like odor; if it becomes at all foul-smelling you should tell your doctor immediately because such a change indicates an infection. You should also tell your doctor if the flow suddenly becomes bright red again. This usually means that the placental site is not getting a chance to heal properly, perhaps because you are over-exerting yourself. Your doctor will probably recommend that you rest for a couple of days and generally take things easier.

Because there is a risk of infection, you should not use tampons until about 6 weeks after delivery, so you will need to use sanitary pads until the lochia flow ceases.

POSTPARTUM HEALTH

After your baby has been born, your body begins to reverse the changes it underwent during pregnancy and labor. The withdrawal of the huge amounts of pregnancy hormones is like the withdrawal of a life force, and the period immediately following labor and delivery – known as the postpartum or postnatal period – can be a very tiring one for you. Try to get as much rest and relaxation as you can, and also make sure that your diet is healthy and includes an adequate amount of fluids (at least a pint of milk a day and four pints of other liquids such as water or fruit juice). If you are breastfeeding, you will need to take good care of your breasts and nipples.

PELVIC AREA

After delivery, your uterus, cervix, vagina, and abdomen begin to shrink back to approximately their pre-pregnant and pre-labor sizes. The shrinkage of your uterus is accompanied by a vaginal discharge known as lochia (see column, left) and by contractions or spasms called afterpains or afterbirth cramps.

Afterpains All women feel uterine contractions throughout their fertile lives. During menstruation they are known as menstrual cramps, during pregnancy as Braxton Hicks contractions, and following delivery as afterpains. After delivery, uterine contractions are stronger and more painful than usual because they are the means by which the uterus contracts down to its former non-pregnant size; the faster and harder it contracts down, the less likelihood there is of any postpartum bleeding. Afterpains are usually more noticeable if you have had a child before, because the muscles of your uterus will have been stretched by your previous pregnancy and so will have to work harder to help get your uterus down to its non-pregnant size. You may also feel these muscular spasms when you breastfeed, because the hormone oxytocin involved in the milk let-down reflex (see p.304) also causes uterine contractions. They usually disappear after three or four days.

Bowels and bladder You should get out of bed to use the toilet as soon as you possibly can after delivery. However, the bowels have often been cleared out prior to delivery so you may not want to move them for 24 hours or more, and this is quite normal. When you move your bowels you may feel the urge to bear down. Any pressure in the perineal region will stretch your tissues and cause pain if you have an episiotomy wound (see column, right). To prevent stretching, hold a clean pad firmly against the stitches and press upward while you bear down. Do everything you can to prevent constipation and the need to strain. Eat lots of roughage, vegetables, and fruit, especially prunes and figs, and drink lots of water (see column, p.335).

Drinking plenty of water, as well as getting up and walking, will help to get both your bowels and your bladder working normally. There may be some hesitancy before the urine starts to flow for the first time. This is nothing to worry about and is usually the result of swelling of the perineum and tissues that surround the bladder and urethral opening. A good way to start to pass urine is to sit in some water (a sitz bath is fine if your doctor advises against tub baths) and try out the pelvic floor, or Kegel, exercises (see p.130), passing urine into the water. This is not as unhygienic as you may think, if you wash yourself down afterward, because urine is sterile. Urine flow is often triggered by the sound of running water.

Cervix and vagina These will have been stretched considerably during labor and will be soft and slack for a while. It takes about a week for your cervix to narrow and firm up again, which it will do unaided, but you can help the recovery of your vagina by contracting and relaxing its muscles (pelvic floor exercises). You should begin these exercises within about 24 hours of giving birth, beginning with five contractions three times a day and gradually working up to five contractions ten times a day. You can also use exercises to tone up your abdominal muscles (see p.336), but do not begin these until the flow of lochia has stopped.

Caesarean wound If you have had a Caesarean section, you should avoid abdominal exercises until the wound has completely healed. Avoid lifting heavy weights; try not to climb stairs more than once a day; be careful how you move when getting up from a lying or sitting position; and generally try not to put too much strain on your abdominal muscles.

Hemorrhoids (piles) These are quite common after childbirth; they are caused by the great strain imposed on the veins in the pelvic floor during labor and delivery. They appear as lumpy swellings just inside your anus, and with proper care (consult your doctor or midwife) they will eventually shrink away.

MENSTRUATION AND OVULATION

The dramatic fall in the high levels of pregnancy hormones following delivery brings the eventual resumption of menstruation and ovulation, as well as sometimes causing cold and hot flushes (sometimes both at once, which can be disconcerting). Menstruation usually restarts some time between eight and sixteen weeks after delivery, but both it and ovulation may be significantly delayed if you are breastfeeding. However, if you want to resume making love (see p.338) before your periods have started, you must use birth control because ovulation will precede menstruation.

EPISIOTOMY WOUND

The pain from an episiotomy wound gets worse before it gets better. The wound is positioned where fluid can accumulate in the cut edges. The skin then swells, with the result that the stitches become tighter and tighter and bite into the tender skin surrounding the wound.

If you are bruised or if the stitches are really painful, it will help to sit on an inflatable rubber ring, so try to keep one with you at all times. Good hygiene is vitally important while the wound is healing, so make sure that it is kept clean. Most stitches will dissolve after 5 or 6 days.

Warm sitz baths and showers, and special perineal pads that fit between your sanitary pad and the wound, are soothing and encourage the healing process, as do pelvic floor exercises. You may also find that ice packs or local anesthetic creams are helpful. Your doctor or midwife will advise you on their use.

Don't use antiseptics as they can cause irritation. After showering, dry the area thoroughly with a hair dryer instead of using a towel, which will cause pain.

If you sit down when you use the toilet, urine, which is strongly acid, will run over the episiotomy wound and make the raw skin sting. Standing up will probably help. You could also try pouring warm water over yourself as you're passing urine, in order to dilute the acid and reduce the sting.

FATIGUE

Getting enough rest and sleep is essential if you are to combat the inevitable fatigue of the first weeks of caring for your newborn baby.

Try to rest whenever you can, especially during the first week or so when you will still be recovering from the exhaustion of labor. Avoid climbing stairs and heavy lifting as much as possible, and get your partner or someone else to help you with the baby and the housework. Take advantage of your baby's daytime naps – rest or nap yourself then, and try not to waste these valuable opportunities for rest by using them to catch up on the housework.

Ensure that you get enough sleep. At night, go to bed half an hour or so before you plan on going to sleep, and unwind by sipping a warm, milky drink and listening to the radio, watching television, or doing a little light reading to relax you physically and mentally before you sleep. If you are breastfeeding, express milk into bottles (see p.306) so that your partner can share the night-time feeding duties just as he should if you are bottlefeeding.

A healthy diet is an essential part of combating fatigue, but don't eat too much late at night because digesting it might interfere with your sleep pattern.

BREASTS AND NIPPLES

Because of the increased size and weight of your breasts, a good-quality, well-fitting cotton maternity bra will be both convenient and comfortable. Change to a clean one every day and, if you are using breast pads to prevent leaking milk from staining your clothes, avoid those that are lined or backed with plastic. Change pads after each feeding and whenever they become wet.

Cleaning and washing Clean your breasts and nipples daily with cotton balls and baby lotion or water, but avoid using soap because it strips away the natural oils that protect the skin from drying and cracking, and it can aggravate a sore or cracked nipple. Always treat your breasts with care – don't rub them dry for example, very gently pat them dry instead.

There is no need to wash your nipples before or after each feeding but, before you fasten or put on your bra after feeding, let your nipples dry in the air, and always wash your hands before handling your breasts to prevent infection.

Engorgement About three or four days after you have given birth, your breasts will fill with milk. They will become larger and heavier, and feel tender and warm when you touch them. If they overfill, it is known as engorgement. Engorgement usually only lasts a day or two, but it can be uncomfortable and may recur.

To ease engorged breasts, take off milk either by manual expression or by feeding your baby (although you may have to express a small amount of milk so that he can latch on, see also pp.304 & 306). In addition, you may also find that it helps to bathe them with warm water or cover them with warm towels, or to stroke them gently but firmly toward the nipple.

Engorgement can recur at any time during the period of breastfeeding, particularly if your breasts are never properly emptied or if your baby misses a feeding.

Blocked ducts A blocked milk duct may occur in the early weeks of breastfeeding. It may result from engorgement, from a bra that is too tight, or from dried secretions on the nipple tip blocking a nipple opening. If you get a blockage, your breast will feel tender and lumpy and there may be a reddening of the skin.

To clear a blocked duct, start feedings with the affected breast and gently massage it just above the sore area while feeding to ease the milk gently toward the nipple. If the blockage will not clear, don't offer the breast to your baby and consult your doctor immediately as it could become infected and result in a breast abscess, which is painful, although not a catastrophe.

Sore nipples When you begin breastfeeding, your nipples may feel slightly tender for the first minute or so of suckling. This tenderness is quite normal, and it usually disappears after a few days. Sore nipples, however, are a common problem in the early weeks and can turn what should be a pleasure into something of an ordeal. Incorrect latching on and carelessness when taking your baby off your breast (see p.304) are the principal causes of sore and cracked nipples, but taking care to start and finish feeding properly can prevent these problems arising, and is essential if they are to heal after they have become sore or cracked.

Sore nipples heal quickly when they are exposed to the air so, if possible, go topless or bra-less occasionally, especially when resting, in order to let air circulate over them.

Cracked nipples If a sore nipple becomes cracked, you may need to keep the baby off that breast for up to 72 hours and express milk from the breast to avoid engorgement. Cracked nipples can be very painful, and they can lead to breast infection. To help avoid cracked nipples, apply a drop of baby lotion to your breast pad.

Mastitis The first signs of mastitis (breast infection) are swelling, tenderness, and reddening of the affected area, accompanied by flu-like symptoms, which can include high fever, chills, aches, headaches, and perhaps nausea and vomiting. If you think you have developed an infection, contact your doctor; if treated promptly with antibiotics, mastitis usually subsides within a day or so. You cannot pass the infection on to your baby, because it only affects the breast tissue and doesn't affect the milk.

PROTECTING SORE NIPPLES

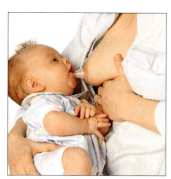

Using a breast shield
If your nipples get sore, use breast shields to protect them during feeding. The shield fits over the nipple, and the baby then sucks through it. To ease your nipple into the shield, slip your hand between breast and rib cage and push gently upward; this is also useful without a shield, as it helps your baby get the nipple fully into his mouth – and that can help prevent sore nipples in the first place.

Your baby will adjust quickly to the feel and taste of the shield

CONSTIPATION

Many women suffer from constipation after giving birth. If you find you are affected, exercise, a sensible diet, and lots to drink will help you deal with this problem.

After delivery, the passage of feces through your bowels tends to slow down, and this can lead to constipation. The slowing down occurs mainly because your abdominal muscles are relaxed and stretched and so the pressure within your abdomen is lower than normal. Relaxation of the bowel muscles themselves, because of the high levels of progesterone during pregnancy, may also slow down bowel movements. If you have had an episiotomy you might, consciously or unconsciously, hold back from passing stools for fear of causing pain.

Medication, such as laxatives, stool softeners, or suppositories, can help to get things moving again, but if you are breastfeeding it is best to avoid taking anything by mouth because it can be passed on to your baby via your milk, and can cause stomach cramps and watery stools for you.

The best remedy for constipation (and a good way to prevent it) is to eat dried prunes or figs. It helps to drink plenty of fluids; eat plenty of fiber-rich foods; avoid inactivity by getting out of bed and walking around; and, after the lochia discharge has ceased, exercise your abdominal muscles to restore their proper tone (see p.336). Practicing your Kegel exercises will return tone to your anal muscle and the anal sphincter.

FIRST DAYS

You can do a few gentle exercises just days after giving birth. Whether lying in bed, or sitting in a chair, try to get into the habit of doing something to tone your muscles.

Remember the importance of your pelvic floor muscles (see p.130). Strengthening these will help to prevent incontinence.

Tone up your stomach muscles by pulling them in as you breathe out, then holding for a few seconds. Relax, and then repeat as often as possible.

You can prevent, or reduce, swollen ankles and feet simply by moving your feet up and down as though you were pedaling.

TAKE CARE

If you've had a Caesarean, wait until 4–6 weeks before starting to exercise, and check with your doctor first. If you have had a tear or an episiotomy, don't practice stretching exercises until it has healed.

POSTPARTUM EXERCISES

A few weeks after giving birth, try to establish a daily exercise routine. This may not seem like a top priority when you're faced with the new demands of being a mother. However, exercising will tone muscles that were stretched during pregnancy and delivery, and increase your energy supply. Exercise twice or several times a day rather than for one long period. It's also good for morale.

You should feel the pull along your side

Side bends
Stand with your feet about 3 feet apart. With your left hand on your thigh, slowly bend over to the left. Run your left hand down your leg as far as you can without straining, raise your right hand over your head, and breathe deeply. Hold your breath for a short time, then straighten up as you breathe out. Repeat the exercise, bending over to the right.

Gently slide your hand down your thigh so that you can feel when it's time to stop

Try to keep your pelvis level; this will improve the stretch

Make sure that your buttocks are tightly clenched to make the most of this exercise

Pelvic tuck-in
You may have practiced this exercise before giving birth as it helps to correct the tilt of your pelvis. Kneel down on all fours with your knees about one foot apart, then tighten your buttock muscles, tucking in your pelvis and arching your back upward into a hump. Hold for a few seconds, then release. Don't let your back sink downward. Repeat several times.

Stretch your neck and push your chin forward

Cat arching
Kneel on all fours with your back straight. Breathing in, bend a leg up and lower your forehead toward your knee. Hold for a second. Breathing out, stretch, raising the leg behind you and lifting up your head. Hold for a few seconds, then change legs.

Your thigh muscles contract and stretch in a steady rhythm

Keep knees bent and feet flat on the floor

Abdominal toner
Lie on your back on the floor with your knees bent and your arms by your sides. Breathe deeply. As you breathe out, raise your head and arms, palms upward. Hold for a couple of seconds, then relax. Repeat 10 times. You'll be able to lift your head higher with regular practice.

Breathe out as you tense your stomach muscles

Raise your arms only if it is comfortable

Concentrate on keeping your back straight; this will make the exercise far more effective

Forward bend
Place your feet about 1 foot apart, keeping them parallel, and loosely clasp your hands behind your back. Keeping your back straight, bend slowly forward from your hips. Then raise your hands until they are as far above your head as you can possibly reach. Breathe deeply for a few breaths, then rise slowly and repeat.

BIRTH CONTROL

You need to consider some form of contraception when you resume intercourse after birth because ovulation could occur at any time.

If you start having intercourse before your periods have come back, don't assume that the absence of menstruation means that you won't get pregnant. You will ovulate 2 weeks before your first period, so if you have put off using contraception until after that, you may have waited too long. Even when you are breast-feeding your baby, and your periods are absent until you wean her, ovulation may still occur – so intercourse without contraception can result in pregnancy.

Contraception *Pills containing estrogen are not prescribed for women who are breastfeeding, because estrogen reduces milk production. Progestogen-only "mini-pills" may be prescribed instead; these do not inhibit milk production, but their long-term effects on babies are not yet known. They are also making worse any postpartum depression by inhibiting the natural production of progesterone.*

Because of this, if you are breast-feeding you might prefer to use a different method of contraception, such as condoms in conjunction with a contraceptive gel or cream. If you want to use a diaphragm or an IUD, you will have to wait until your first checkup before you can get one; if you previously used a diaphragm, you will need to be fitted for a new one because your cervix will have enlarged and your old diaphragm may no longer fit. Until you get your new diaphragm or IUD, use condoms and spermicidal cream.

RESUMING SEX

You probably won't be in the mood for making love in the first days, or even weeks, after giving birth, because the sheer physical exhaustion of labor and the drastic changes in your hormone levels after delivery combine to inhibit sexual desire. An initial lack of interest in sex is both natural and desirable, because your body needs time to recover from the changes and stresses of pregnancy and childbirth, and you need time to adjust to your new baby. Talk to your partner – he will probably be totally sympathetic and understanding.

YOUR PARTNER

The arrival of the baby can also have a dampening effect on your partner's libido; it is not uncommon for a father to feel a lack of desire and even to lose his ability to maintain an erection, and he might find it difficult to adjust to his and your dual, sometimes contradictory, roles as parents and lovers.

Both of you must be prepared for such problems and should not take them personally. If you are philosophical and open about your problems, and discuss them lovingly and sympathetically, you will prevent them developing into long-term difficulties.

WHEN TO RESUME

The point at which sexual desire returns varies greatly from one couple to another, and even from one pregnancy to another. For instance, a woman might have desired sex three weeks after one pregnancy, but have had no interest in it for three months or more after the next one.

There is also the question of just when it is physically safe for intercourse to take place; couples were once advised to give up sex six weeks before the expected date of delivery and to abstain from it for six weeks afterward (until after the first checkup). This well-meaning advice is now thought to be unnecessarily cautious, and the general opinion today is that penetrative sex can continue as late in pregnancy as you wish – provided there are no medical reasons to avoid it (see p.214) – and that it can begin again as soon as you like. You can also restart non-penetrative sex as soon as you like after giving birth. If you or your partner are unsure about whether it is safe to make love again, discuss it with your doctor.

If both of you are feeling happy about it, and there is no medical objection to it, you can resume sexual activity as soon as you feel the desire to do so. In addition, making love can have a beneficial effect for a number of reasons. For example, it reaffirms your affection and desire for each other, and the hormones released during sexual activity cause contractions of your uterus, which will help it return to its pre-pregnant state.

LACK OF DESIRE

Don't worry about loss of libido – it's natural. There are, however, many factors that can conspire against your desire for and enjoyment of postpartum sex. Apart from any lingering discomfort you might feel, it is quite common for women to see themselves as unattractive at first, and this can make them shy away from sex or think negatively. Your still-bulging tummy may make you feel unsexy, so starting exercises to get back into shape (see p.336) is important for your self-esteem, and pelvic floor, or Kegel, exercises will help reduce the slackness of your vagina.

Anxieties and distractions may also diminish your sexual desire or enjoyment. Fear of getting pregnant again may bother you, and resuming birth control can be worrisome or annoying. Even your baby can have a considerable influence on your enjoyment of lovemaking, because it is often hard to adjust to this new presence in the house. You may not feel as free as before or as able to abandon yourself, and you may not be able to relax and enjoy lovemaking because you half expect your baby to cry for attention at any time.

It is also possible for you to get so absorbed with your baby that you find you have little need for other emotional ties or physical contact, to the exclusion of your partner. Even your sexual responses may become focused on your baby. This is because oxytocin, the hormone that is produced during breastfeeding, is sexually stimulating, and sometimes a woman can be stimulated up to and even including orgasm.

MAKING INTERCOURSE MORE ENJOYABLE

You might find that it takes a long time for you both to regain your previous level of sexual interest. You may both need extra fondling, kissing, and other foreplay before you become sexually aroused. For the first few times you make love, you should avoid penile penetration and stick to gentle oral or manual sex. And because an episiotomy site can be surprisingly painful during intercourse and may take months to become totally pain-free, please be honest with your partner and tell him if sex causes you discomfort or pain. Getting him to feel your scar will help him to be sympathetic, and a warm bath before lovemaking plus using a water-soluble vaginal lubricant or saliva, can be a great help.

Whether or not you have had an episiotomy, extra lubrication is usually necessary because, until your hormone levels are back to normal, your vagina will not lubricate itself as quickly as in pre-birth days, no matter how much foreplay you have. Avoid non-water-soluble lubricants such as petroleum jelly because they can prevent air from reaching the lining of your vagina and this can encourage the growth of harmful bacteria.

After you have resumed intercourse, you may well find that man-on-top positions are uncomfortable. Experiment with other positions (see p.214) – side-by-side positions are especially good ones to try if you are suffering from a sore episiotomy site. Whichever positions you use, be patient, do not do too much at first, and build up your sexual activity levels gradually.

POSTPARTUM CHECKUPS

Your last visit to your obstetrician will be at about 4–6 weeks after delivery, when you will be thoroughly checked.

Your checkup At your visit, you will be weighed, your blood pressure will be checked, and your breasts examined for lumps (although this is not always done if you are breastfeeding, because lumps are not easy to distinguish from milk glands). You will have a pelvic examination to check that, among other things, your episiotomy has healed well, your cervix is closed, and your uterus is back to normal. The doctor will usually ask you how you are feeling emotionally and how you are coping. She or he will also discuss your future method of contraception with you, although you may have already decided this during your prenatal care.

Your baby's first checkup The pediatrician will check his ears, eyes, limbs, and muscle tone, listen to his heartbeat, check his control over his head movements, measure the circumference of his head, check for hip displacements, and weigh him. His weight will be recorded on his personal weight chart every time he is subsequently seen by his doctor, and the chart will be an important record of your baby's progress.

CHANGES IN YOUR LIFE

TIME FOR YOURSELVES

Find time in your daily routine when you and your partner can be alone together. This is an important part of keeping your relationship alive and well.

At home *Continue small rituals as part of your daily life together. If you always had a sundown drink together at the end of the working day, shared a bath in the evenings, did the crossword together, or read your own books and papers while chatting or reading aloud to each other, continue to do so. Not only is it precious time together, it will also help you maintain normality in your everyday lives.*

Going out *Your new baby will be surprisingly portable in the first few months of her life, but you will also need to go out together alone. Turn to someone you trust for a baby-sitter. If you are breast-feeding, express your milk so that your baby can be fed with it while you're out. It may be difficult or seem like too much hassle but persevere. It is important for you and your partner to have time together away from your baby.*

As a couple *If you want to learn a new sport or skill, or resume an old one, why not plan to do it together now? Putting aside 2 or 3 hours every week when you are booked to do something as a couple will ensure that you have time together as individuals rather than just as parents.*

Many people underestimate just what is involved in caring for a new baby. It is a demanding and exhausting job that can turn your lives upside-down. You may find yourself wondering whether you and your partner will ever be able to spend time together. Fitting in all the demands on your time and energy can be difficult, but if you approach the situation sensibly and discuss it together before the birth, you should be able to minimize the disruption and manage to spend some time alone. It does require planning, but it is possible.

STAYING ON TOP OF IT ALL

Taking care of your newborn baby will probably be much harder than you expected. In the first place, labor and birth are physically and emotionally draining; in the second you'll find that during the day, one job or activity succeeds another almost without respite.

Getting enough rest is most important – it is rare for a new baby to allow you more than four hours' sleep at a time during the night, so learn to catnap. Your diet is also very important, especially if you are breastfeeding. Continue to eat as well as you did throughout your pregnancy, and drink plenty of fluids.

Taking shortcuts, such as occasionally buying prepared meals, at least for the first few months, will help you cope, as will getting your priorities right – ensuring enough rest, for example, is far more important than cleaning the house, and your partner can always dust and vacuum when he gets home, or perhaps you could do it together at weekends.

Avoid guilt Feeling guilty seems to be a burden carried by most new mothers and quite a few well-established mothers. Remember that you can only do your best, and that it is important that you put yourself and your health high on your list of priorities. Bear in mind too that it takes about a year for your body to regain its pre-pregnancy state, so make sure that your family does not demand too much of you at first – and that you do not demand too much of yourself, because just after delivery you will find that you have very little stamina and will become easily exhausted.

Find a routine This does not mean training your baby to eat, sleep, and play according to your timetable but rather following his lead and fitting the rest of your life around his individual daily routine. It won't necessarily mean that you have to rearrange your entire lives to accommodate him; a great deal of your routine and life will continue as before.

APPRECIATE YOUR NEW ROLES

At first, it may be difficult to embrace your new roles as parents. You may resent the loss of your own income and the satisfaction of doing a demanding job well, and you may envy your partner his relatively free and independent life.

Your partner, on the other hand, may find it difficult to cope with the stress and demands of being the only wage earner, and may feel shut out from your intimate relationship with your baby. He may also feel envious of your home-based life, especially if he doesn't appreciate how demanding a baby can be.

These different experiences can result in your wondering where the closeness and intimacy of pregnancy went, and also whether you will ever get back to the easy understanding you had before you became pregnant. You will, but you need to keep talking to each other, explaining your thoughts and feelings, and trying not to let misunderstandings alienate you from each other.

MAKING TIME FOR YOURSELVES

One of the most difficult changes to manage is lack of time. Most of your waking and sleeping hours must be devoted to the care of your new baby; this can be frustrating and might make you feel resentful. Maintaining outside contacts, continuing with your usual lifestyle, and keeping the lines of communication open between you and your partner will go a long way to helping you cope with the various conflicting demands on your time and energy.

Sharing Doing things together is especially important once you have a baby. Young babies are very portable, so don't hesitate to include yours in your plans. He can come with you when you visit friends, and you may be surprised at how little effect he has on your social life in the first few months of his life.

However, you also need time together alone and, although it may seem odd having to make a formal appointment to spend time with your partner, it really can help you to maintain your relationship. One of the problems you will find following the birth of your first child is that the spontaneity you had as a free and easy couple does tend to get rather lost, so planning to spend time together becomes vitally important. It needn't be elaborate – it could be something as minor as always having a ritual drink together at the end of the day, or it could be planning to go swimming together for two hours every Sunday while a friend looks after your baby.

Time alone We all need time and space to recharge our batteries. When you have a baby it is very easy to get so caught up in the never-ending round of baby care that you lose sight of this need.

It is very important that you arrange to have at least a few hours every week when you can just please yourself, whether that be planning a special outing, seeing a friend, or following a particular interest. Make an arrangement with someone you trust to baby-sit for you – your partner, a close friend, or relative. Not only will you benefit, your baby will also benefit from the social contact.

SHARING YOUR BABY'S CARE

You'll get many offers from friends and relatives to baby-sit. Take advantage of other people who are willing to share the care of your baby.

Father *As far as your baby is concerned, her father is the second most important person in her life, after you. Daddy can do anything that Mommy can – he can even give breast milk in a bottle, so encourage your partner to take equal responsibility for the care of your baby.*

Grandparents *Perhaps itching to help and thoroughly experienced in childrearing, her grandparents can be the ideal people to help with baby-sitting and general baby care. She and they will relish the contact, and this will help them to form strong bonds of affection from the very beginning.*

Relatives and friends *Your family will probably enjoy helping you look after the new addition to the family. Friends may also be enthusiastic about baby care – and the ones who have already had children can be invaluable. Always make sure that childless or young assistants know how to handle a baby properly, but try not to watch so closely or anxiously that you make them feel uncomfortable – young babies are more resilient than they look.*

NAMES *John and Sue Benton*

AGES *25 and 24, respectively*

PAST MEDICAL HISTORY *Nothing abnormal*

OBSTETRIC HISTORY *Sue recently gave birth to a baby girl weighing 7lb 5oz*

John works in the marketing department of an engineering firm; Sue is a secretary in a large pharmaceutical company. John and Sue had been waiting for the right time to have a baby – until they realized that there was probably no such thing as a right time. Following their recent move into a larger house, Sue researched maternity benefits at her company and discovered that it is especially flexible and farsighted. Sue then gave up smoking and drinking alcohol and came off the pill. She became pregnant a few months later.

NEW PARENTS

During Sue's pregnancy, John and Sue had been determined to find out everything they could about pregnancy, childbirth, and becoming parents. They read books, attended prenatal classes, got some hands-on experience with their friends' children, and made lots of plans. However, they soon realized that nothing can totally prepare you for parenthood, and that you always have to be prepared to adapt and be flexible.

MAKING PLANS

John and Sue agreed from the start that parenthood should be a shared responsibility. Sue was determined not to stay at home playing the role of a traditional mother and, as her company operates flexi-time, she planned to go back to work three months after the baby had been born.

John was concerned about how much their life would have to change, but Sue assured him that newborn babies are very portable, so wherever they went the baby could go, too. Having discussed the different issues and thought about how they would manage, they felt reassured about being able to cope with parenthood.

THE BIRTH EXPERIENCE

I had advised Sue and John to acquire some basic facts about childbirth and the types of birth that were available in their area so that they could make a birth plan and argue effectively in favor of their choices. They visited their local hospital, talked to the staff, read books, and made a birth plan for a hospital birth with a request for no drugs and no episiotomy if at all possible.

When Sue went into labor, however, she found that she was finding it increasingly difficult to cope with the intensity of the labor pains. John found it hard to see her in such pain, although he managed to remain calm, supportive, and encouraging. Toward the end of the first stage, when her contractions were coming very close together, Sue was becoming tense and distressed, and eventually she asked for pain relief. John encouraged and praised her, and helped her to change position. However, she still found the contractions difficult to cope with, so the midwife gave her a small dose of pain medication, which took effect quite quickly. This helped Sue to relax and stay calm.

About an hour later, Sue was found to be fully dilated and she started to push. The baby's head didn't take long to crown. At this point the midwife urged Sue to stop pushing so that the perineum had time to stretch fully. Sue allowed her contractions to push her baby out, and moments later Emma was born.

Postpartum feelings   Sue and John fell in love with Emma as soon as she was born. John just couldn't get over how tiny and perfect she was, while Sue's maternal feelings were very strong from the beginning. However, Sue also felt a touch guilty that she hadn't managed to have Emma without painkillers, although she was sensible and tried not to let this detract from the pleasure and pride that she took in Emma's birth. I told Sue that it's impossible to know your own pain threshold in advance, and that she shouldn't feel guilty about requesting pain relief that was essential. Sue and John have a normal, healthy baby girl and Sue has every reason to be proud of herself and all that she has achieved.

BECOMING NEW PARENTS

When Sue and John had to deal with the day-to-day care of their newborn baby, they were quite shocked at just how much was demanded of them. For the first ten days John was at home, but even with two of them the round of feeding and changing, with short periods of sleep in-between, seemed endless.

Sue wondered how she would ever be able to manage on her own and wished that she was going back to work while John stayed at home to look after the baby. She told me that on her first day alone she had felt isolated, like a new kid on the block. However, she coped – despite feeling that she had never been so exhausted in her life – and, as Emma started to respond to her and then to smile properly, she confessed that she was rather surprised to find that she really enjoyed being with her and looking after her. She also made friends with other new mothers in her area, which gave her an opportunity to compare notes with friends who understood exactly how she felt and what she was experiencing.

Sue and John managed to socialize with their friends more than they'd ever thought they would be able to because, just as Sue had said, Emma proved to be very portable. They even managed to take Emma away on a short holiday.

Work felt as if it was in the very distant past for Sue and she found she wasn't looking forward to going back as much as she had expected. John enjoyed being back at work, despite finding the disturbed nights a bit of a strain. He found himself really looking forward to coming home in the evening, seeing and cuddling Emma, and chatting with Sue about what had happened during her day. He was pleased that Sue was enjoying being at home, but he soon realized that they couldn't afford to keep up with their mortgage payments unless Sue returned to her job.

Consequently, Sue returned to work as she had arranged with her employers and Emma was cared for during the day by Sue's mother until Sue came to pick her up at 4.30p.m.

Although things were exactly as Sue had planned them before Emma was born, she no longer had quite the same feelings about motherhood being restrictive as she had earlier. She confessed that if John had been earning enough for them to manage, she would have changed her mind about returning to work so quickly and become a full-time mother, at least until Emma went to preschool.

USEFUL ADDRESSES

American Academy of Husband-Coached Childbirth (Bradley)
P.O. Box 5224
Sherman Oaks, CA 91413
(800) 422-4784

Information on coached childbirth for parents

American College of Nurse-Midwives
1522 K Street N.W.
Suite 1000
Washington, DC 20005
(202) 289-0171

Membership organization for nurse-midwives. Directory of practices available

American College of Obstetricians and Gynecologists (ACOG)
409 12th Street S.W.
Washington, DC 20004-2188
(202) 638-5575

Membership organization for obstetricians and gynecologists. Also has informational pamphlets for the general public

American Diabetes Association
12660 Duke Street
Alexandria, VA 22 314
(703) 549-1500

Advice for pregnant women with diabetes. Provides information and support for diabetics through publications and on an information hot-line

American Fertility Society (AFS)
2140 11th Avenue S., Suite 200
Birmingham, AL 35205
(205) 978-5000

Conducts research into various aspects of infertility. Informational booklets available

American Foundation for Maternal and Child Health
439 E. 51st Street
New York, NY 10022
(212) 759-5510

American Society for Psychoprophylaxis in Obstetrics (ASPO/Lamaze)
1101 Connecticut Ave N.W.
Suite 700
Washington, DC 20036
(800) 368-4404

Organization for parents and doctors who are interested in learning about and using the Lamaze method of childbirth

Association for Childbirth at Home International (ACHI)
P.O. Box 430
Glendale, CA 91206
(213) 667-0839

Advice to pregnant women wishing to give birth at home

Birth and Life Bookstore
P.O. Box 70625
Seattle, WA 98107-0625
(206) 789-4444

Specializes in birth and pregnancy books

Cascade Birthing Catalog
P.O. Box 12203
Salem, OR 97309
(503) 378-7545

Provides catalogs on birthing supplies, baby products, baby clothes, and more

Cesareans/Support Education and Concern (C/SEC)
22 Forest Road
Framingham, MA 01701
(508) 877-8266

Information and pamphlets on Caesarean section births

Depression After Delivery
P.O. Box 1282
Morrisville, PA 19067
(215) 295-3994

Information and support to women suffering from postpartum depression

Informed Homebirth and Parenting
P.O. Box 3675
Ann Arbor, MI 48106
(313) 662-6857

Information on alternative birth sources. Also trains childbirth educators and assistants

Intensive Caring Unlimited (ICU)
910 Bent Lane
Philadelphia, PA 19118
(215) 233-4723
Parent support group providing one-to-one support and a bi-monthly newsletter

International Caesarean Awareness Network
P.O. Box 152
University Station
Syracuse, NY 13202
(315) 424-1942

Educates women about Caesarean section – working to lower the number of repeat Caesarean sections and unnecessary Caesarean sections

International Childbirth Education Association (ICEA)
P.O. Box 20048
Minneapolis, MN 55420
(612) 854-8660

Trains childbirth educators. Provides pamphlets, books, and other material on childbirth and maternity care

La Leche League International Inc.
Box 1209
9616 Minneapolis Ave
Franklin Park, IL 60131
(708) 455-7730

Helps inform women about how to breastfeed their babies

March of Dimes Birth Defects Foundation
1275 Mamaroneck Avenue
White Plains, NY 10605
(914) 428-7100

Nonprofit organization fighting birth defects

Maternity Center Association
48 E. 92nd Street
New York, NY 10128
(212) 369-7300

Birthing center

Moonflower Birthing Supply
2810 Wilderness Place
Suite D
Boulder, CO 80301
(303) 665-2120

Sells home birthing supplies

National Association for Parents and Professionals for Safe Alternatives in Childbirth (NAPSAC)
Route 1
Box 646
Marble Hill, MO 63764
(314) 238-2010

Provides information on childbirth alternatives

National Association of Childbearing Centers
3123 Gottschall Road
Perkiomenville, PA 18074
(215) 234-8068

Pamphlets available to parents provide information on birthing centers in their area, and how to select one

National Down's Syndrome Association
141 5th Avenue
New York, NY 10018
(212) 460-9330

National organization that promotes research into and public awareness of, Down's syndrome. Provides free printed information packs, video cassette, and a directory of any early intervention and parent support groups

National Perinatal Information Center
1 State Street Suite 102
Providence, RI 02908
(401) 274-0650

Provides perinatal information

National Women's Health Network
1325 G Street N.W.
Lower Level
Washington, DC 20005
(202) 347-1140

Advocacy group for women's health issues. Educates people about women's health rights

Parent Care Inc.
101 1/2 South Union Street
Alexandria, VA 22314 3323

National organization for the parents of premature babies, which puts parents in touch with their local support groups. Provides information, resources, and support

Pregnancy and Infant Loss Center
1421 E. Wayzata Blvd
Suite 30
Wayzata, MN 55391
(612) 473-9372

Offers support, resources, and education to parents and families who have experienced pregnancy and infant loss

Sibling Information Network
1776 Ellington Road
South Windsor, CT 06074
(203) 648-1205

Sudden Infant Death Syndrome (SIDS) Alliance
10500 Little Patuxent Parkway,
Suite 420
Columbia, MD 21044
(800) 638-SIDS

Research group provides support services and in-house counseling. Pamphlets also available

INDEX

P

Pain
abdominal 205
labor 95, 254–5, 264
in pregnancy 74
Pain relief
cognitive control in 109
comfort aids 244
Hawthorne rehearsal 109
in labor 244, 262–3, 264–7
prenatal classes 109
relaxation and 109
systematic desensitization 109
Palate, cleft 179
Parenthood
adjustment to 326–7, 340–3
classes 108
preparation for 16–17
Parents
new 342–3
of premature babies 322–3
see also **Fathers/Mothers**
Partogram 257
Patau's syndrome 180
Paternity leave 54
Pelvic floor
exercises 130, 333, 336
muscles 130
Pelvis
internal examination 160, 161
size 158, 170, 258
Penis, abnormalities 181
Periods *see* **Menstruation**
missed periods *see* **Amenorrhea**
Peritoneal ovum and sperm transfer (POST) 47
Pessaries
induction of labor 252
Pethidine 264, 266
Pets 150, 151
Phenylketonuria (PKU) 300
Photographing birth 278
Pigmentation 140–1, 143
Piles *see* **Hemorrhoids**
Pill, contraceptive
stopping 17
use after childbirth 338
Placenta 64, 68, 70, 78, 80, 170, 288
delivery of 288–9
previa 202
separation from uterus (abruptio placentae) 201–2
Placental insufficiency 33, 170, 203
Polychlorinated biphenyls (PCBs) and infertility 36
Port wine stains 297
Positions in labor 89, 93
on back 90
backache labor 256
for delivery 90, 275, 278–9
first stage 270–1
Post-coital test 38–9
Postpartum period
care in 300–1
checkups 339
contraception in 338

depression 329, 330–1
emotions 328–31
exercises 333, 336–7
health in 332–5
lovemaking in 338–9
Posture in pregnancy 80, 142
Potassium, lack of 328
Preeclampsia 204
Pregnancy
confirmation 51–2
diary of 138
earliest signs 50–1
ectopic 204, 205
emotions 136–9, 192–3, 250
feelings about 62, 68, 137
hazards 123, 147, 150–3
home testing 52
length of 52–3
multiple 31, 82–3
physical changes 58, 59, 60, 62, 64
preparation for 16
self-care in 59, 61, 63
tests for 51–2
see also **Prenatal care**
Premature babies 259, 320, 322–3
care of 320–1, 323
Prenatal care 59, 61, 63, 156–71
classes 108–9
clinics 156–7
diabetic mother 168–9
multiple pregnancy 82–3
older mothers 32–3, 165
Rhesus-negative mother 184–5
routine tests 158–61
special tests 164–7
ultrasound/sonograms 162–3
Progesterone 26, 27, 210
blood test 42
injections of 329
postpartum levels 328
Progestogen 17, 338
Prolactin reflex *see* **"let-down reflex"**
Proteins, dietary 116
sources of 116, 118
for vegetarians 115
Puerperal psychosis 329
Pushing in labor 274, 276
Pyloric stenosis 181

Q

Quickening 70, 176

R

Radiation hazards 147, 152
Rashes
diaper rash 315
in pregnancy 143
Reflexes of newborn 298–9
Registration of birth 301
Relaxation
massage for 134–5
postpartum 326–7
techniques 133, 238–9

Reproductive tract
female 26
male 29
Respiratory distress syndrome 180
Resting
after childbirth 326–7
in pregnancy 63, 80
Rhesus blood groups 159
incompatibility 166, 182, 184
Rh-negative mothers 184–5
Rhogam injections 184, 185
Rib pain 74, 78, 194–5
Rubella (German measles) 19, 152

S

Safety precautions 223, 225
Salmonella infection 123
Saunas 151
Semen (seminal fluid) 28, 29, 38
for artificial insemination 45
Sex, of baby 29, 31
Sexual intercourse
after childbirth 338–9
see also **Lovemaking**
Sexuality in pregnancy 210–11
Sexually transmitted disease 19
Shaving of pubic hair 90
Shivering after delivery 289
Shoes 144–5
Show 251
Siblings *see* **Children**
Sickle cell anemia 21, 24
Sickness, morning 51, 66, 192–3
Singing *see* **Music**
Single mothers 104–5
Sit-ups 127
Skin
care 140, 143
newborn baby 296–7
in pregnancy 66, 72, 140–1, 143
Sleep in pregnancy 50, 76, 80, 192–3
late stages 238
Smell, sense of 51
Smoking
effects 16–17
and infertility 36
Sneezing, newborn baby 299
Sonicaid 161
Sonograms 162–3
Down's syndrome diagnosis 166
embryo/fetus 61, 67, 71, 75, 77, 79, 163
infertility investigation 42
twins 82
Spastic babies (Cerebral palsy) 180
Special-care baby units 320–1

Sperm 28–9
chromosomes 23
count 38
donation 44–5
fertilization 30, 39
genes 22
infertility and 36–9
production 28
and sex of baby 29
tests 39
Spider veins 141
Spina bifida 179, 180
Spitting up 311
Sports 126–7
Squatting 133
**Sterilization of bottlefeeding
equipment** 308–9
Stillbirth 292–3
Stork bites 297
Stress and infertility 34, 36
Stretch marks 141
Stretching 128–9
Strollers 224, 225
Superstitions 138
Surrogate mothers 46
Swimming 127

T

Tailor sitting 132
Talipes (Clubfoot) 181
Taste, sense of 50–1
Tay-Sachs disease 21, 24
Tearing, avoidance of 275
Teeth 141
Telemetry 263
Television, radiation from 151
Temperature, body
babies 319
and ovulation 42
**TENS (Trans-cutaneous electrical nerve
stimulation)** 267
Testes 28, 37
disorders, and infertility 36, 37
Testosterone 28
Thalassemia 21
Tiredness
postpartum 328, 329, 334
in pregnancy 50, 66
Toxoplasmosis 123, 151
Toys 223
Travel
with babies 224–5
in pregnancy 153
to hospital 243
Trial of labor 284
Trimesters 58–63
first 58–9, 64–9
second 60–1, 70–7
third 62–3, 78–81
Trisomies 21, 180
see also **Down's syndrome**
**Tubal embryo stage transfer
(TEST)** 47
Turner's syndrome 21

Twins
conception 31
labor and delivery 83, 280
loss of a twin 293
naming 232
pregnancy 82–3
sonograms 82
types 83

U

Ultrasound *see* **Sonograms**
Umbilical cord 68, 78, 297
cleaning stump 317
cutting of 290–1
prolapsed 282, 286
sudden delivery 283
Umbilical hernia 178, 297
Umbilical vein sampling 165–6
Urination
newborn babies 313, 319
postpartum 333
in pregnancy 50, 76
Urine
estriol tests 171
newborn babies 313, 319
pregnancy tests 51
prenatal tests 159
Uterus 26
bicornuate (horn-shaped) 201
changes in pregnancy 58, 64
contraction ring 258
damage/abnormalities 41
fundus, height of 68
lining *see* **Endometrium**
postpartum 332
subseptate 201
X–rays 43

V

Vaccination *see* **Immunization**
Vacuum extraction (ventouse)
280, 281
Vagina
bleeding from 200
postpartum 333
in pregnancy 66
Varicose veins 194–5
Variocele 37
Vas deferens, blockage 37
Veganism 121
Vegetarianism 115, 120–1
Vernix caseosa 72, 73, 78, 80, 296
Visualizing during labor 267
Vitamin B$_{12}$ 121
Vitamin C 118, 119
Vitamin D 117
Vitamins 116
sources of 116–17, 119
Vomiting, babies 318

W

Walking 127
Water birth 88
Water retention 194–5
Weight in pregnancy 58, 60, 62,
74, 112–13, 158
Whirlpools 151
Womb *see* **Uterus**
Working women
diet in pregnancy 114
informing employer of pregnancy
51, 55
maternity clothes 144
and pregnancy 146–7
return after childbirth 147, 148
rights and benefits 54, 146
single mothers 104–5
work hazards 147, 151–2
working mothers 148–9
Word processors, radiation from 147,
152

Y

Yeast infections 194–5
Yoga 109, 127
Yolk sac 64, 68

Z

Zinc 117
sources of 119
Zygote 30
**Zygote intrafallopian transfer
(ZIFT)** 47

ACKNOWLEDGMENTS

Carroll and Brown Limited would like to thank:

Photography:
Ranald Mackechnie

Illustration:
Annabel Milne: 23, 26, 27, 29, 31, 37, 41, 43, 83, 91, 164, 185, 201–204, 215, 251, 253, 255, 256, 263, 265, 306
Howard Pemberton: 43, 48, 65, 67, 69, 71, 73, 75, 77, 79, 81, 158–162, 167, 214, 215, 276, 277, 285

Medical consultants:
Gwen Atwood; Leonora Branski; Dr. Nigel Brown; Dr. Felicity Challoner; Prof. Geoffrey Chamberlain; The Hallam Medical Centre; Dr. Kypros Nicolaides; Prof. Cheryl Tickle; Dr. Robert Whittle

Special thanks to US medical advisor James H. Weir, MD

Film outputting:
Disc To Print (UK) Ltd

Typesetting:
Roweena Feeney;
Deborah Rhodes

Additional editorial assistance:
Julee Binder; Laaren Brown; Lorna Damms; Jemima Dunne; Claire Hooper; Susan Palmer-Jones; Jennifer Rylaarsdam; Lara Tankel; Madeline Weston; Saba Zafar

Additional design assistance:
Lyndel Donaldson; Gail Jones; Alan Watt

Models:
Deanne Barnes, Joe and Jack; Sharon Caines; Nagihan Tunali Caykara, and Nyazi; Charlotte Chance; Lyndel Donaldson; Hilary and David Goodman, and Alexander; Jashu Halat; Amy Lewis; Susan Lipman, and Stephanie; David Todd

Equipment:
Mothercare UK Ltd – maternity and baby clothes; equipment; and toys

Additional photography:
Dave King; David Murray; Ray Moller; Stephen Oliver; Susanna Price; Jules Selmes

Index:
Anne McCarthy

Picture Credits:
Collections/Anthea Sieveking: 109, 265, 281; Lupe Cunha: 263; Neil Bromhall/Genesis: 57 right, 73, 75 left, 173; Sally and Richard Greenhill: 84, 85, 88, 97, 99, 103, 272, 273, 274, 276, 277, 288, 297; Howard Sochurek/Hillelson: 57 center, 67 top, 69 bottom, 75 right, 77 bottom, 79, 81 left, 155 left, 163; Nancy Durrell McKenna/Hutchison: 291, 296, 297 bottom, left, and right; National Medical Slide Bank 48; "Nurture" – University of Nottingham: 38; Science Photo Library: 37, 43 top/Biophoto Associates, 284, 285 right/CNRI, 15 left, right, 23, 28 top left, 71 top, 77 top, 81 right/Stevie Grand, 321/Manfred Kage, 41 top right/David Leah, 285 left/Moredun Animal Health Limited, 111 right, 123/Hank Morgan, 48 bottom, 49 inset, 325, 327/Petit Format/CSI, 15 center, 30 top left, center left, bottom left, 49 bottom/Petit Format/Nestlé, 27, 31 top, 41 bottom right, 43 bottom, 56, 57 left, 65 top, bottom, 67 bottom, 69 top, 71 bottom, 111 left, 120, 155 right, 166, 175, 181/Secchi, Lecque, Roussel, UCLAF, CNRI, 28 bottom right/James Stevenson 315/Andy Walker/Midland Fertility Services 30 top right, center right, bottom right/Hattie Young 20; Tony Stone World-wide: half title, title, 31 bottom, 49 top, 234, 235, 290; Dr I.D. Sullivan: 178; Dr. John Yovich/Parthenon Publishing Group: 39; Zefa/Howard Sochurek: 82

Picture Researcher:
Sandra Schneider